The Elements of Influence

Introducing The Playmaker's Standard

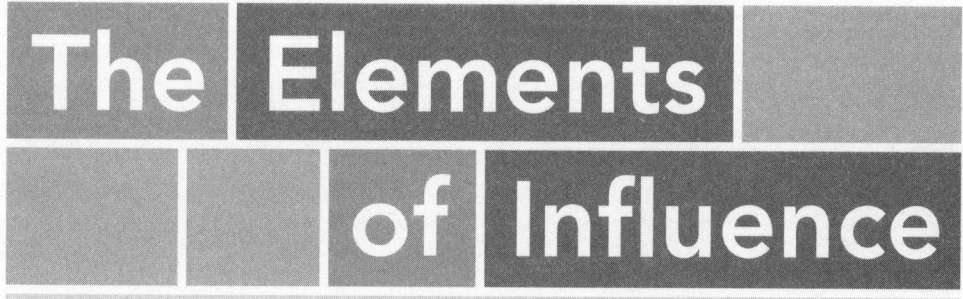

The Elements of Influence

THE NEW ESSENTIAL SYSTEM FOR MANAGING
COMPETITION, REPUTATION, BRAND, AND BUZZ

Alan Kelly

DUTTON

DUTTON
Published by Penguin Group (USA) Inc.
375 Hudson Street, New York, New York 10014, U.S.A.
Penguin Group (Canada), 90 Eglinton Avenue East, Suite 700, Toronto, Ontario M4P 2Y3, Canada
(a division of Pearson Penguin Canada Inc.); Penguin Books Ltd, 80 Strand, London WC2R 0RL, England;
Penguin Ireland, 25 St Stephen's Green, Dublin 2, Ireland (a division of Penguin Books Ltd); Penguin Group (Australia),
250 Camberwell Road, Camberwell, Victoria 3124, Australia (a division of Pearson
Australia Group Pty Ltd); Penguin Books India Pvt Ltd, 11 Community Centre, Panchsheel Park,
New Delhi – 110 017, India; Penguin Group (NZ), cnr Airborne and Rosedale Roads, Albany, Auckland 1310, New Zealand
(a division of Pearson New Zealand Ltd); Penguin Books (South Africa) (Pty) Ltd,
24 Sturdee Avenue, Rosebank, Johannesburg 2196, South Africa

Penguin Books Ltd, Registered Offices: 80 Strand, London WC2R 0RL, England

Published by Dutton, a member of Penguin Group (USA) Inc.

First printing, October 2006
10 9 8 7 6 5 4 3 2 1

LIBRARY OF CONGRESS CATALOGING-IN-PUBLICATION DATA

Kelly, Alan, 1957–
   The elements of influence : the new essential system for managing competition, reputation, brand,
and buzz / Alan Kelly.
      p. cm.
   At head of title; Introducing The Playmaker's Standard
   ISBN 0-525-94984-4 (hardcover)
   1. Strategic planning.   2. Competition.   I. Title.
   HD30.28.K453 2006
   658.4'012—dc22   2006024463

Printed in the United States of America
Set in Avenir
Designed by Daniel Lagin

For Katie and Leo.

Daddy, is your book done!?

You betcha.

Contents

Classes, Subclasses, Plays, and Surrogates

Preface

The *Elements of Influence* will change the way you look at the world and the work you do in it. It introduces The Playmaker's Standard, the first classification system of moves and countermoves that people and organizations employ in business, politics, and popular culture. Unprecedented in scope and scale, it lays bare the *plays* you run on your friends and rivals—and the plays they run on you—to drive a decision or gain the upper hand in today's busy and numbingly noisy and crowded world.

Plays are everywhere. From an audacious Super Bowl TV ad to an outrageous blog posting, from a coworker's power play to a competitor's end run, plays are the strategies we employ to get us where we need to go, whether as a by-product of our ambitions, our sense of duty, or our sense of survival. They are the strategies we use to influence the opinions, perceptions, behaviors, and decisions of our always unique and ever-competitive marketplaces.

Like the airwaves that brim with electronic voice and data traffic, plays are something we are bathed in but not something we yet understand in any tangible way. The Playmaker's Standard is a lens through which we *can* see this inundation of ploys and postures, a compass that helps us navigate the networked economy and its attendant media sphere, and a lexicon that draws together a huge community of strategists in what I call the *Influence Industries*.

> If you're in management, strategy, marketing, sales, public affairs, advertising, public relations, media, and even law, then you are a practitioner in a discipline called *Playmaking*.

If you're in management, strategy, marketing, sales, public affairs, advertising, public relations, media, and even law, then you are a practitioner in a discipline called *playmaking*. And if your interests are in research and planning, rhetoric, debate, negotiation, game theory, or even maneuver warfare, you have a stake in it too. In the same way that public officials are policymakers, legislators are lawmakers, and diplomats and negotiators are peacemakers, *you are a playmaker.* In reading this book and applying its contents, you're an early adopter of a new lexicon of marketplace management that spans strategic planning, coalition building, brand building, reputation management, and communications management, to name a few. And you are the user of a new tool that helps you better understand and master the deeds, discussions, and sentiments of your marketplace.

There is nothing like The Playmaker's Standard. It is the first system to capture and organize the fundamental strategies and methods that practitioners of influence employ to assert and defend their positions in a marketplace.* It's for executives managing a corporate merger, marketers going to market, salespeople countering a competitive bid, advertising executives building a brand, public relations managers protecting a reputation, lobbyists and politicians building a grassroots movement, lawyers preparing a cross-examination, and activists planning a protest. It is the indispensable tool of the playmaker, the professional whose job it is to develop a position or advance an agenda in a competitive marketplace.

The Barnstormers

This is a book I felt had to be written. Without it I wouldn't know how to proceed in my own professional life. The pursuits of strategy, positioning, influence, and advocacy have virtually no standard or reliable reference for plotting and planning the movements and motives of players in their marketplaces, whether of allies and rivals alike. It's not that what we do today is broken. It's just that it's archaic. The state of *our* science rests on superficially described terms of art whose documentation is inconsistent and whose application is instinctive. It's a condition that can be corrected and whose correction is long overdue.

---

* Though the word *market* is fashionable, I prefer *marketplace* in almost all cases relating to plays and playmakers. A *market* defines particular segments and subsegments of goods and services or the targeted consumers who purchase them. But a *marketplace* speaks to the broader playing field; it's where playmakers thrive in their continual effort to position and de-position, collaborate and compete, gain and regain, in their competitive places of business. And it encompasses all types of business— from the public to the private sector, from governments and institutions to venture start-ups, from not-for-profits to profiteers.

True, there is a wealth of data and metrics that beautifully reveal the activities and behaviors of a marketplace, from analytic engines and business intelligence tools to market research, opposition research, and media metrics. But these largely fail to tell users what the findings *mean* and *what* to do because they can't identify the techniques of positioning and de-positioning that underlie the data. As a result, we are like early-era chemists, applying only the compounds or molecules we know and can touch, forced to practice a kind of influence alchemy—a secret brew of the shaman—that lacks basis and measure.

The sheer size of the influence industries and their obvious acceptance into business, politics, and public life demand better analysis and understanding of how this all works, how brands are pumped up and deflated, how reputations are won and lost, how credibility is given and taken away, and how trust is earned and abused. It's time, in other words, for our own periodic table of elements, a system that properly identifies, categorizes, and organizes the plays that form and inform the way these intangible assets are managed and influenced. *Without it,* our advancement in infinitely complex marketplaces will be plodding and superficial. *With it,* our developing mastery of such things will be more fully realized.

There are rich precedents for such a system as The Playmaker's Standard. Nearly every evolving endeavor, from accounting to biology to music, to name a few, has forged one or more frameworks through trial, error, and accident. Take, for example, what is now the science of man-made flight. In the early 1900s, when the business of flying was a mere commercial fledgling, there existed a collegial but sometimes chafing relationship between the technical innovators of aviation, the engineers, and the first generation of airplane pilots.

My grandfather, an early champion of aviation safety and avionics, was a frequent collaborator with such progressive pioneers as the World War II hero General Jimmy Doolittle and famed air racer Benny Howard. Having lived 102 lucky years, he recalled for me the day he met Orville Wright in a Dayton, Ohio, instrument shop. *"I didn't care for him much,"* he later confided of the immortal Wright brother. He talked about his efforts to introduce "stick-and-rudder" types to instrument flight and the various gadgets that would lead them more safely through storm systems and across empty oceans.

From time to time, he and his fellow designers would excitedly deliver new prototype instruments to wary test pilots. *Would you like to give this a try?* they'd ask, holding, perhaps, an early altimeter. *It's very accurate and you'll know exactly how high you're flying. . . .* A cocksure pilot would cock his head, eyeing the contraption, and say with a chuckle, *Now, why would I need that? I already know I'm up in the air . . . ?!*

From where I sit, as a kind of engineer in the influence industries, playmakers are the barnstormers of the Internet age. They're up in the air, flying fast, thrilling the crowds, and enjoying a great deal of celebrity. But as gurus of positioning, brands, reputations, buzz, spin, and other maddeningly intangible skills, they have only the most informal means of understanding, teaching, and advancing their crucial craft. They have no reliable or consistent reference for calling and running their proprietary moves or for decoding and countering the moves that are made against them.

This book is *not* an attempt to unseat the seat-of-the-pants playmakers. There is enormous value in these instincts and experiences. It is not to outdate a deft political strategist, well-heeled salesperson, discerning advertising or public relations executive, or savvy litigator. In fact, its purpose is to help give structure to what *is* understood—however rationally or intuitively—and to propel both veteran and fledgling strategists toward a more efficiently deployed and insightfully applied form of marketplace management.

The Collaborators

In my own professional circles there is a considerable degree of anxiety over the ways in which the tools of business, particularly in sales, lobbying, advertising, and PR, are applied. De-positioning is a common MO in sales. Going negative is standard fare for politicians. Hyperbole is the norm in advertising. Stonewalling is a first option in a PR crisis. And so on. There is little hesitation to embellish, bend, and even misrepresent both the factual and subjective.

Many academics and professionals, particularly those in the field of communication, foresee the emergence of a two-way dialog, between management and employee, politician and voter, salesperson and prospect, supplier and customer, and spokesperson and journalist, as examples. They envision an era where organizations talk *with* rather than talk *at* the all-important stakeholder, an age of equalized communication, so-called symmetric dialog, where the dominant players (the CEOs, senators, account reps, advertisers, and spokespeople) seek agreement and give equal time to their constituents (the employees, voters, buyers, consumers, reporters, and bloggers). It's a panacea in a free market world, of course, but their concerns are worth noting for the implicit warning they contain: *Influence is a tool for understanding, not a weapon for overwhelming; use it wisely.*

In this context, playmaking might seem sorely out of step with the champions of collaboration. After all, a healthy number of the play types that populate The Playmaker's Standard are by no means two-way, much less symmetric. They exist, in fact, to embellish, bend, spin, and even misrepresent both the factual and subjective.

So why write about them? Why make matters worse in what some see as a worsening world of full-throttle hype and flexible ethics? Because they *do* exist, and this book's first purpose is to describe what is there, not judge it. Plays like the Jam, Label, and Bait—detailed in subsequent chapters—are used in every marketplace for self-serving purposes, and indeed they are not exactly the tools of collaborators. But they exist, like it or not, and they are practiced with both justifiable cause and diabolical precision. To some, they look like the work of Machiavelli, to others the work of Mother Teresa. It is, as these things go, a matter of perspective, so I won't attempt to take sides so much as to explain what one side was hoping or wanting to do to another, and why. No craft can be fully understood until its component parts are fully described. As powerful as the influence industries may be, we cannot and should not sweep under the rug the reality of what the influence industries do. To use the analogy of a classroom, we can't teach reproduction without also describing intercourse. And like a church, we can't preach morality without also acknowledging sin.

The propensity to target and influence employees, voters, buyers, consumers, reporters, and others has developed into an automatic and presumed response in nearly every corner of every marketplace. It's what my colleagues fear and would like not to dignify. In reality, I am just as concerned as they are because the professions of influence appear to be benefiting more than the societies they serve. Whether in the courtroom or the court of public opinion, we are expert at minimizing evidence and maximizing speculation. We are expert at suppressing logic and maximizing emotional appeal. And we are expert at elevating positive associations and severing weak ones.

However or wherever you come down in this dilemma, the tendencies to posture, influence, and advocate *do* exist, and so it is better to face and describe them than prejudge and demonize them. Better to know precisely how high we're flying than to just be up in the air, buzzing the crowd. As much as we are in a golden age of such things as strategy, positioning, media, message, word-of-mouth, viral marketing, influence marketing, stealth marketing, and other intellectual inventions, we still have only the most impressionistic sense of the work we do, how we do it, the payoffs our efforts derive, and the broader implications thereof. Fuller knowledge means fuller understanding, and that is why I have written this book.

Introduction

Economists have game theory. Biologists have the phylogenetic tree. Chemists have the periodic table of elements. Software developers have object-oriented programming. But for those whose work centers on strategy, positioning, or some form of marketplace spin there is nothing. There is nothing for those whose jobs involve the pursuit of influence and, accordingly, the management of opinions, perceptions, behaviors, and decisions. There is no table of elements, per se, for this emerging class of free-form yet indispensable professionals I call *playmakers*. There are myriad principles, best practices, laws, rules, and admonitions in what amounts to vast collections of terms of art. But there is no science and no transforming framework to give these pursuits measure and meaning.

The subject of this book, The Playmaker's Standard, is the result of a painstaking effort to illustrate, describe, sort, classify, and name the first generic set of unique moves that are made by playmakers everywhere—the *elements*, if you will, of strategy and the influence industries. Based on more than a decade of field trials and observation in the high technology industry, two years of literature review, and pilot programs with Fortune 500 companies, it gives a fresh foundation and lexicon for the emerging discipline I call *playmaking*. It is the first structured system for managing competitors, developing relationships, and creating and mobilizing coalitions. It is the first practical tool for understanding and executing strategy and positioning in the marketplace. It is a basis for the game plans and playbooks that organizations employ to defend their ground and advance their position.

> This new system takes the mystery out of the cultish fascinations for word-of-mouth, buzz, and spin and the guesswork out of the more formalized but still murky best practices for building brands and managing reputations.

The Playmaker's Standard is more a discovery of something that has always been than an invention of something that should be.

But it *is* both because to give it meaning and measure I have, by necessity, enhanced what I have discovered. It takes the mystery out of the cultish fascinations for word-of-mouth, buzz, and spin and the guesswork out of the more formalized but still murky best practices for building brands and managing reputations. It helps managers of all stripes understand and influence the intangibles of their marketplaces. Whether for a chief executive or an executive chef, it is a tool that helps leaders and their teams take charge of marketplace discussions rather than observe from the sidelines or be used as pawns by rivals. It allows participants to collaborate with open arms or compete with bare knuckles as their tastes and circumstances dictate.

The Playmaker's Standard

The Standard comprises three reference systems, (1) The Playmaker's Table, a taxonomy of carefully classified and unique strategies, (2) The Playmaker's Process, a methodology for running and calling plays for improved competitive advantage, and (3) Factors at Play, a source list of variables that influence playmakers and the play action* of their marketplaces. While there is much that can be written about the factors or variables that impact playmaking, and equally as much about the method or process by which plays are best run, this book focuses on the first of these three subsystems, The Playmaker's Table.

THE PLAYMAKER'S TABLE†

This first system is a breakthrough taxonomy of influence strategy, an easily interpreted and richly detailed classification of "play types" and their respective definitions, best uses, and countermeasures.

Unlike any previous attempts to describe and organize strategy, including Michael Porter's seminal work *Competitive Strategy*, Sun Tzu's *Art of War*, or the ancient *36 Strategies*, The Playmaker's Table is the first framework to reveal how stratagems—*plays*—interact in multiple dimensions. From left to right, it explains the relationships of each play to the others and how each operates, from a subtle form of playmaking

---

* I use the term *play action* in reference to the presence and movement of plays as they are called and run (i.e., identified and applied) by players in a bounded marketplace.

† This table, and all other images in this section, may be viewed at www.plays2run.com.

called *Detach* to an outright brawl called *Attack*. From top to bottom, it orders play types by the degree of complexity. The higher in the stack, the easier they are to execute. These classifications and their play types are exhaustively described in subsequent chapters through supporting illustrations, tables and tips, and case-based essays.

THE PLAYMAKER'S PROCESS

This second subsystem is a five-step methodology that helps playmakers sequence and pattern their play action moves (see graphic below). It guides playmakers as they parley and propel their agenda—from the glimmer of an idea to the glamour of a marketplace phenomenon, from a competitor's attack to a competitor's defeat. The Playmaker's Process takes the practitioner from the conception of a differentiated idea to the identification of a play sequence to the commencement of play action to countermeasures and back. By necessity, The Playmaker's Process encourages users to check their positions in a continuous circle of steps because a marketplace can change on a playmaker . . . and playmaking can change a marketplace. (For more detail, see The Playmaker's Process, p. 275.)

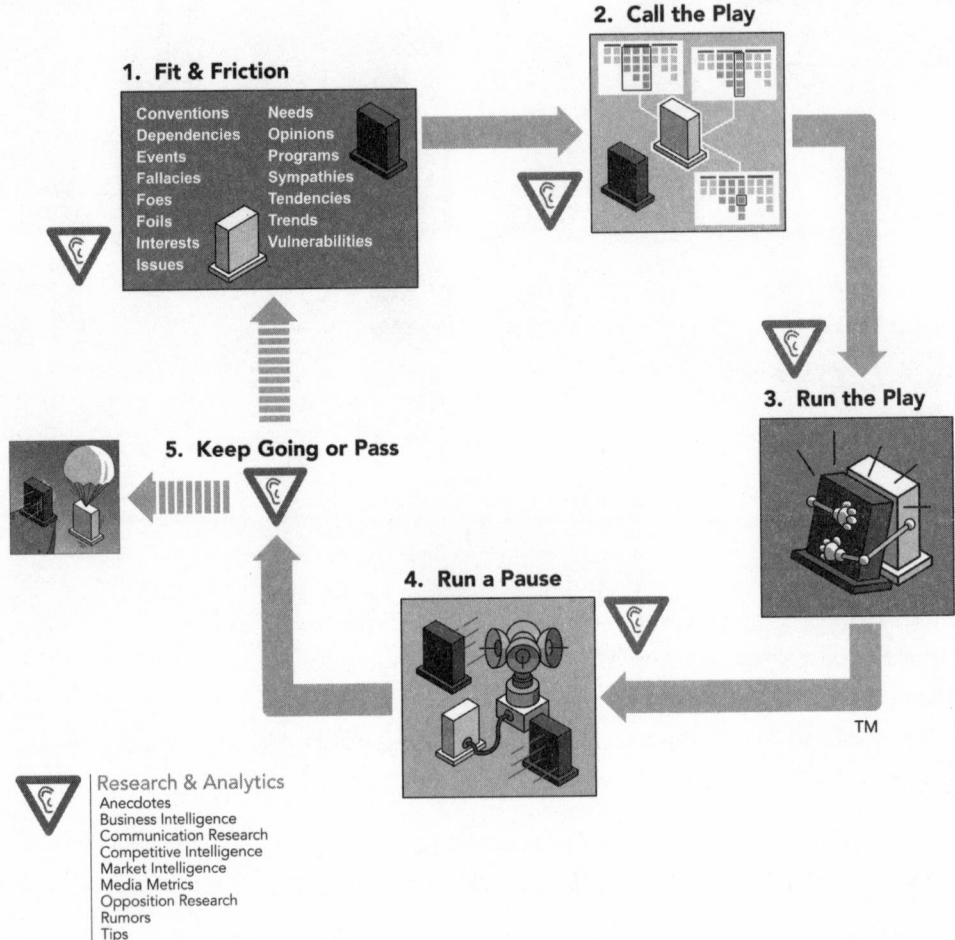

1. Fit & Friction

Conventions	Needs
Dependencies	Opinions
Events	Programs
Fallacies	Sympathies
Foes	Tendencies
Foils	Trends
Interests	Vulnerabilities
Issues	

2. Call the Play

3. Run the Play

4. Run a Pause

5. Keep Going or Pass

TM

Research & Analytics
Anecdotes
Business Intelligence
Communication Research
Competitive Intelligence
Market Intelligence
Media Metrics
Opposition Research
Rumors
Tips

FACTORS AT PLAY

This third and final piece of The Playmaker's Standard is a quick-reference resource that lists many, though not all, of the fundamental variables that influence a marketplace and help playmakers fine-tune their diagnoses and battle plans (see graphic below). It is a kind of fan to the fog that typically enshrouds strategy and influence, and when flipped on, it clarifies a playmaker's marketplace. (For more information on Factors at Play, see the expanded section on page 294.)

Tangibles	Intangibles	Communication
These are known or knowable, easily measured or counted.	These are known but hard to pin down, not easily measured or benchmarked.	These are the adjustments to your communicated ideas, decisions, suggestions, and reactions.
• Capital assets • Financial assets • Intellectual property • Patents • Products • Services	• Brand • Relationships • Credibility • Reputation • Culture • Satisfaction • Goodwill • Skills • Knowledge • Time • Loyalty • Trust	• Balance • Frequency • Breadth • Speed • Clarity • Tone • Consistency • Volume • Depth

Policies	Stakeholders	X-Factors
These influence how you make judgments and decisions and take action.	These are the constituencies of your organization, your marketplace, and ecosystem.	These are things you anticipate but that will always surprise you.
• Access • Guidelines • Attribution • Laws • Ethics • Regulations	• Community • Investors • Competitors • Legislators • Customers • Managers • Distributors • Media • Employees • Partners • Executives • Regulators	• An accident • A gift • A death • Good luck • A deceit • Bad luck

PLAY ACTION MAPS™

To help a player see the bigger picture, plays can be plotted along a timeline (see graphic below) or superimposed onto The Playmaker's Table to illuminate the patterns, sequences, trends, and tendencies of marketplace play action—of both the moves that have *been* made and those that might *be* made. This alerts executives, marketers, salespeople, lobbyists, and advertising and PR managers, among others, to the plays that might be coming and those that should perhaps be run to stay on-strategy and in control of marketplace discussions and movements. (To get other detailed Play Action Maps, see the Appendix, p. 309.)

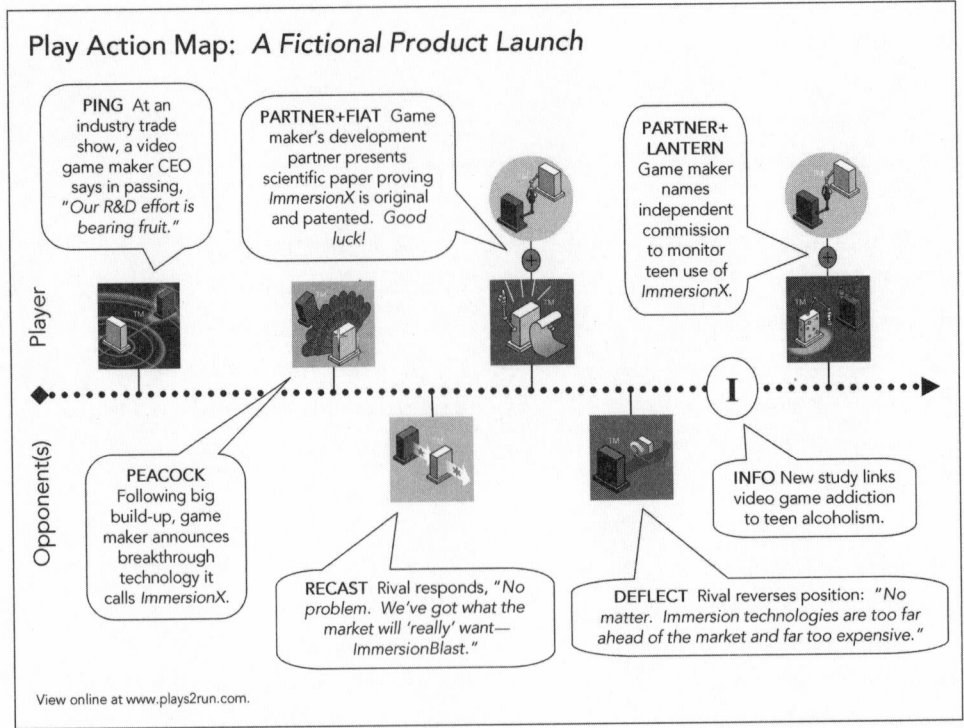

Play Action Map: *A Fictional Product Launch*

Player

PING At an industry trade show, a video game maker CEO says in passing, *"Our R&D effort is bearing fruit."*

PARTNER+FIAT Game maker's development partner presents scientific paper proving *ImmersionX* is original and patented. *Good luck!*

PARTNER+ LANTERN Game maker names independent commission to monitor teen use of *ImmersionX*.

Opponent(s)

PEACOCK Following big build-up, game maker announces breakthrough technology it calls *ImmersionX*.

INFO New study links video game addiction to teen alcoholism.

RECAST Rival responds, *"No problem. We've got what the market will 'really' want—ImmersionBlast."*

DEFLECT Rival reverses position: *"No matter. Immersion technologies are too far ahead of the market and far too expensive."*

View online at www.plays2run.com.

The Case for Playmaking

Today, the keenest challenge facing most organizations is not the management of tangibles, like production, finance, inventory, and shipping, but the mastery of *intangibles*, like brand, reputation, credibility, and trust. These are the pivot points on which an organization's success or failure turns but of which they have the least insight and poorest control.

Every organization competes in a marketplace—from nations to community centers, from Fortune 500 companies to small businesses, from governments to nongovernmental organizations, from publicly traded companies to not-for-profits, from your team to your whole industry. All of them. Some compete as collaborators, some as smash-mouth competitors. Most operate between the extremes. But every organization, without exception, strives to carve out its niche, each playing a continuous cat-and-mouse game to position itself and its allies and de-position its opponents for competitive advantage. It is a necessary skill and mind-set for playing in an ever-changing and ever-challenging marketplace.

Particularly now.

With the new requirements for financial transparency, the wide availability of information over the Net, the speed of communications through e-mail and blogs, the increased efficiency of supply chains, the empowerment of the single consumer, and the enabling of citizen journalists, the game has shifted from the physical and knowable (like manufacturing) to the amorphous and enigmatic (like service).

How does an organization survive in such a full-throttle, wide-open environment? How does an organization master it? How do leaders, managers, and workers thrive in this world of increased efficiencies, empowered individuals, and seemingly infinite nuance?

One thing's for sure: Some get it. And some don't.

Apple Computer gets it. For years, its cool brand has enjoyed unwavering loyalty. Republicans get it too. Over two decades, GOP candidates have garnered support from traditionally Democratic working class voters. But not General Motors. For all its trying, GM hasn't retained the loyalty of its base, like Apple, and it hasn't expanded it, like the GOP. Will these things change? Sure. But looking at the preceding eras, there's little doubt as to who has been the hunter and who has been hunted.

There are general ideas of why these things are and some guidelines to suggest the answers. But what playmakers lack are the systems of the established disciplines, fields, and sciences, and the insights they provide. The following table lists just a few.

SYSTEMS OF SCIENCE, INDUSTRY, AND THE ARTS
Game theorists have payoffs and decision trees, from the Prisoners' Dilemma to the Nash Equilibrium.
Biologists have 1.4+ million documented species of plants, animals, and microorganisms, from the ancient sequoia tree to the extinct woolly mammoth to the *E. coli* bacterium.
Chemists have 117 discrete elements—and counting—from the inert to the radioactive, from the natural to the man-made.
Programmers have code generators and languages, from C++ to JavaScript to Visual Basic and more.
Accountants have GAAPs (Generally Accepted Accounting Principles) to properly track and classify the movements, debts, and accruals of cash, securities, and other financial instruments.
Linguists have transformational grammar to pull apart and categorize words and their various constructions.
Musicians and composers have the music notation system and melodic scale to transcribe nearly any kind of sound, in any key, at any pitch and tempo.

Still, the discipline I presume to call playmaking has, so far, defied organizational gravity. Is it because playmaking is fundamentally more art than science? I think not. There's too much evidence to suggest that discrete strategies of influence exist and that they can be organized. Playmaking exists. One just has to know where to look to reveal its substance. So where *does* one look? In politics, it's what White House strategist Karl Rove has done so consistently to advance an agenda and win elections. In business, it's what Pepsi did to thwart Coke, and vice versa. In pop culture, it's what Oprah Winfrey has done to build her brand and audience.

Playmaking is the new and necessary skill for anyone who advocates for an idea, touches an organization's brand, influences its reputation, or is in any way involved in the development of policy, message, communication to stakeholders, or the management of media.

As it stands today, we have only a general picture of how the strategies of play-

makers wax and wane and of the tangle of plots and subplots that increase their momentum or unravel their success. John Kerry's 2004 presidential bid failed against
good odds. Wal-Mart's goodwill missions to recover its diminishing luster have been
a bust. Jet Blue is a hot young airline in an otherwise distressed air travel industry. But
why? There is virtually no reliable system to help dissect these sentiments and sensibilities or to make sense of how they are managed (or mismanaged) with repeatable,
measurable, and sustainable success (or failure). There is neither a system that is suffi-
ciently detailed nor a vocabulary that reasonably describes the processes by which
the chatter of a marketplace, the morale of an employee base, or the whims of a customer are influenced.

Of course there is no lack of trying to wrestle down these dense subjects. Economics was once just as slippery. So were biology, chemistry, software programming,
and accounting. And this is the point. Fields of interest and relevance, when studied
well enough and long enough, can reveal their inner workings. When they do, systems can then be developed that map their component parts and tendencies and elevate that field onto a higher plane of practice. It has happened in every major field
of study and even in areas of fanciful interest—from physics, geology, and meteorology to manufacturing, operations, and finance to warfare, games, music, color, food,
and wine. At some earlier stage, each of these areas defied analysis but over time
succumbed to new frameworks that triggered new understanding and the revelation
of underlying structures.

Playmaking as a discipline can be next, and if we can better explain it and teach
it, we can advance it.

Is this a good thing, to advance the skills of brand managers, reputation specialists, political campaigners, bloggers, and various other unlicensed spin doctors? Do
we need more of this? I believe the answer is emphatically yes. We might not need
more brands and more campaigns, but we surely need them to be more smartly and
appropriately applied.

To date, I have identified twenty-five differentiated play types in eight higher-
order subclasses and three overarching classes that describe a universe of strategic
moves and countermoves. This process is not born from the physical sciences, so
overlaps exist that, by default, reflect the gray lines of the social sciences. So like any
such system, it is a work in process: New plays may emerge, some may be spun off,
others may be absorbed. In any case, I hope it spurs interest and even provokes debate across industries and academia to solidify the elements of the discipline I call
playmaking and the virgin framework I call The Playmaker's Standard.

The Case for a Standard

Players of any well-developed marketplace understand intuitively the value of intangible assets—from an executive who is fighting off reckless activists to a teenager whose choice of wireless devices may determine her acceptance into a peer group. But we have only begun to understand how these assets can be strategically managed in the media swirl of a marketplace. When a brand is thought to be far more important than a company's tangible assets (as it is in the cases of eBay and Coca-Cola), the defense and development of that brand must be managed with precision and certain knowledge, not by intuition.

Today, however, intangible assets are managed largely on instinct and with erratic success, typically by professionals in management, strategy, marketing, sales, public affairs, advertising, and public relations. Contrasted to their counterparts in finance, engineering, or manufacturing, as examples, these marketplace persuaders have only a loose foundation for interpreting and practicing their crafts. And yet it is the marketers, salespeople, development officers, lobbyists, advertising and public relations executives whom most leaders entrust with such delicate and strategic assets as brand, reputation, credibility, and trust.

Playmaking in general and The Playmaker's Standard in particular give these practitioners the resources they need to establish and uphold that trust and to more effectively craft their programs and carry out their duties.

The building blocks of The Playmaker's Standard are twenty-five unique play types. They are named for their function and, in some cases adopted from arenas where they are traditionally rooted. The play type *Red Herring*, for example, owes its name to an early hunting term, where salted and smoked kippers (herrings) were once used in the training of hunting dogs. Fragrant reddish-brown fish were dragged across a hound's path in a deliberate effort to throw it off its intended tracking scent. Rival hunters also employed this tactic to gain advantage over a competitor. The metaphor grew from there and lives today as a lively rhetorical strategy. More self-explanatory plays, like the *Bait* or *Filter*, are nominated from everyday meanings. Some plays are inherently flirtatious and exploratory while others are more committed and engaging.

This work is the product of a thirteen-year development process, tested and practiced with managers and executives of both start-up and blue-chip high-technology companies and presented for the critical review of academics and experts in biology, communication, forensic debate, game theory, management, marketing, political science, psychiatry, rhetoric, and strategy. In its earliest form, when my public relations and research firm Applied Communications was representing technology companies, the competitive philosophy inherent in playmaking helped software giant Oracle Corp. build competitive advantage against one of history's most dominating players, Microsoft. For newcomer Informatica, an early entrant in the superheated decision support software category, it created a winnable debate using smart, simple data marts to topple unwieldy data warehouses. It helped shield BEA, a leader in the application server space, against the thunderous marketing attacks of IBM. And for HP, it helped win the divisive proxy war to buy Compaq.

Where Playmaking Got Its Start

The inspiration for The Playmaker's Standard came in the early 1990s in the form of what resembled for me an apprenticeship to a gifted strategist, Joseph Jennings. A disciple of the tech marketing guru Regis McKenna and a student himself of political campaigning, Jennings blended his marketing and communication acumen to run brilliant and pointedly powerful "plays" for his clients in the unsuspecting technology-first-marketing-second segments of semiconductors and information technology. Jennings's own style was purely competitive and left little room for collaborative strategies; nevertheless, this approach in an environment of self-absorbed geeks and vapid press agentry, though at first alarming, proved ultimately refreshing and infectious. For me, it stuck, and later became the adopted charter for my own firm.

To most of Applied's early clients, the notion of positioning *and* de-positioning, as Jennings would call it, was provocative and not easily infused in engineering-minded Silicon Valley executives. That changed, however, with Oracle, the offensive-minded maker of database and business software. From 1994 to 2002, my firm's philosophy of competitive communications found power users in the talented executives of Oracle and its billionaire CEO Larry Ellison. It was then that the hunch of a standard set of plays was formed and it was precisely on the morning of September 4, 1995, that it crystallized—when Ellison bluntly proclaimed at a Paris technology conference, *"The PC is a ridiculous device!"* It was vintage Larry, as they say, provoking and maneuvering to position Microsoft-based personal computers as overpriced, overengineered paperweights. *"The [PC] is so complicated and expensive,"* he continued to mock. *"What the world really wants is to plug into a wall to get electronic power and [also] plug in to get data."*

In fact, Ellison could afford to do no less. His database software was predicted to lose market share to low-end PC-based solutions, to Microsoft's SQL Server software in particular, so unless he poked holes in his rival's approach, his big-business customers would likely move en masse to Bill Gates & Company.

My team had not advised Ellison to say this. Few consultants in the tech business successfully advised Ellison to say or do anything. This embarrassing fact not withstanding, we ran to our war room, a whiteboard-covered back corner of our Burlingame, California, offices, and we started plotting. We knew that the flamboyant CEO had baited an entire industry and was challenging its highest leader, Bill Gates, to a duel. We all struggled to describe what had happened in any precise way, and that seemed odd because Ellison's move seemed so pure, like a chess master castling his king or a poker shark moving *all in*. But we could offer only rough impressions of the provocative taunt and its implications. So I asked over and over, *"What did Larry Ellison just do? He just called the world's richest man and his computers 'ridiculous'! What was that? What exactly do you call that?"*

Thus began for my team and Oracle a two-year campaign to establish a new class of computing, *Network Computing,* and its offspring, network computers or "NCs." Through a sequence of effective but still amorphous maneuvers, nicknamed plays in Joe Jennings's honor, Oracle exposed the shortcomings of Windows PCs and proved that even Microsoft is mortal. Just as important, it climbed into the ring and held its own against a company of superior brand, reputation, and overall marketplace power.

Following Ellison's lead, the Oracle marketing machine quietly fanned the fire of Ellison's insult, using third parties to draw out Microsoft loyalists, better known to Oracle as "PC bigots." Once aroused, the Windows apologists took to the news media, declaring Ellison a fool and Oracle a has-been. To its credit and at our urging, Oracle waited and watched, letting the upset over Ellison's quip swell. Traditional approaches would have sought immediately to tamp down or cut off the criticisms. But we wanted *more* tension and ridicule, not *less* of it. We wanted a debate because we believed that the argument implicit in Ellison's Paris bow shot was winnable. And if by chance it wasn't, we knew that Oracle could build a huge new base of supporters and customers where none had previously existed. The NC versus PC campaign, in other words, amounted to the calling of a technology industry election that invited voters to look at the issue and, ultimately, forced them to cast their vote for the future of computing.

As we hoped, the *bigots* went too far in their defense of Microsoft because, by any measure, PCs of that day were in fact too expensive and complicated. They forgot that Ellison's argument made sense. As much as Ellison had offended Microsoft and its millions of users, the blind defense of the so-called Wintel monopoly grated others. So with our manufactured witch hunt under way, it required little effort by Oracle to draw out more rational calls for sanity. Some argued hard in Oracle's defense, *Well, of course PCs are ridiculous. . . .* Others took lighter swings, sheepishly writing, *Maybe Larry is right. . . .* Either way, this moment was the digital-age equivalent of the lone boy observing that the emperor—Bill Gates in this case—had no clothes.

As many remember, the debate grew furious and quickly escalated from an industry skirmish to a big-business referendum. And as we expected, it *did* increase the ire of many toward Oracle. But, in the end, it created an expansive stage on which Ellison could credibly challenge Gates's Windows-based PCs and a backdrop against which Oracle could be showcased as a player with enormous strategic sway.

As playmaking is intended to do, the Oracle campaign simultaneously slowed its opponent and advanced its own position, helping shift thought leadership from Redmond to Redwood Shores and, most important, to a vision of computing that centered not on operating systems and software applications but on the power and potential of the Internet. The result was a steady showering of major national media coverage, all focused on new provocative debates—Fat Servers versus Thin Clients, Larry versus Bill, Network Computers versus Personal Computers—that put Oracle in the driver's seat and Microsoft scrambling for a new ride. The campaign was a catalyst to Oracle's new position of leadership in the information technology market, a tripling of its stock price, and a decisive edge for Oracle over Microsoft in the white-hot enterprise software market.

The popular counter that Ellison never sold an NC is largely true. He hardly made good on his promise of a five-hundred-dollar Oracle NC, so it's reasonable to conclude that the CEO's ploy was an off-strategy blunder. Right?

Not right. While the Oracle NC was in many respects a dying quail, it was also, in the parlance of playmaking, a *Call Out*, an attacking play that sparked a winnable debate: that PCs had lost their way and that network-based computing could do better. No premise was more important to Oracle, because its database software was the reigning standard for big-business computing. To get his industry to understand this, Ellison didn't mind picking a fight or even looking a little foolish, so for his efforts and determination he was, in this round of high-tech history, the victor in the argument and the prevailing playmaker.

Oracle's NC campaign was conspicuously different from typical marketing and PR programs. It generated more than mere buzz and the requisite publicity. Instead, it controlled the attention and conversation of an entire marketplace, relying on *friction*, not *fit*, to drive that dialog. Its central strategy was to first *invite* disagreement and, second, to use the resulting dissension to fuel a winnable debate. It bore an authentic quality, drawing interest for its salience, not its stunts, and so it presented itself as a more natural competition rather than an overmanaged event.

This experience, in particular, fueled my suspicion that strategy and positioning are more than a mishmash of principles, best practices, laws, and rules. The work had relied somehow on recurring and recognizable rules, not loose terms of art. Ellison and his team had teased, waited, sandbagged, and then pounced, only to do it again in a sophisticated circular cycle of catch-and-release hunting. But as clever as Ellison and his executives were, these moves didn't seem unique or special. Ironically, they looked more like standard off-the-shelf marketing techniques that had been expertly refined to suit instinct, context, and setting.

Without the benefit of The Playmaker's Standard, without the benefit of knowing a class from a subclass, of understanding the relationship of play types to factors, of knowing a freezing play from an attacking play, Oracle fomented and dominated one of tech history's most important debates. Our first attempts to describe these marketplace moves were anemic compared to the beefed-up plays in this book. But they were nonetheless the earliest deliberate efforts to explore the uncharted territory of playmaking and diagram the elusive play types that comprise it.

Like so many Silicon Valley start-up stories, the Oracle NC campaign is where The Playmaker's Standard got its start. Of course, the moment and the setting don't mark the birth of professional strategy or positioning. These are ageless and time-honored, naturally. But it might mark the beginning of the slow ground-up effort to systematically clarify the discipline of playmaking.

Section I.
The Basics of Playmaking

What's a Play?

Plays are everywhere. You run plays. Plays are run on you. Every organization and every person runs plays to increase their relative competitive advantage in busy marketplaces. Some do it well. Some try to avoid it. Some do it directly. Some use surrogates. Some run one play at a time. Some run many simultaneously. Almost all do so on instinct and fewer yet with the support of stated objectives, policies, and augmenting research.

Whether as soaring rhetoric, like Martin Luther King Jr.'s "I have a dream" speech, or nervy deeds, like the lone Chinese dissident daring the tanks of Tiananmen Square, plays are the bridges that take us from what we *wish* would happen to what we *do* to get it. Every advertisement is represented and explained

> Every advertisement is represented and explained by plays. So is every grassroots campaign, special promotion, mass mailing, press release, position paper, speech, protest, and legal brief.

by plays. So is every grassroots campaign, special promotion, mass mailing, press release, position paper, speech, protest, and legal brief. Every effort whose core motivation is to prod, position, or persuade, even subtly, is based on and executed through plays.

So what's a play?

As Bill Clinton might say, it depends upon how the meaning of the word *play* is *played*. Here's how I define it:

> def. **Play:** *A stratagem, one of a finite set of discrete strategic maneuvers a person or organization employs to improve its relative competitive advantage in a marketplace.*

Strategy as Plays

Are plays strategy? Are plays strategic? Can plays be strategically implemented? Are plays tactics? Are plays tactical? Can plays be strategically implemented tactics?

Through the bulk of my career, perhaps through the bulk of yours, too, I have been a dutiful student of strategy, its scholars and gurus. But this has not been a clarifying process. Over time, I've developed a healthy degree of awe for the potential of strategy but also a healthy degree of skepticism toward its application. Like you, I'm betting, I have counseled on strategic matters. I have conceived strategies. I have carried them out. I have strategically implemented strategy. I have been strategic in my strategic execution of strategy. I have carefully mapped strategies to strategic goals. And I have strategically supported my clients' objectives with strategically supported plans. I've committed all such tortured acts of what we loosely understand to be strategy. But to what end?

When it comes to strategy, it has become less and less clear to me when precisely I have engaged in it. And I doubt I'm alone.

What I *have* done, however, is to call upon my collective intelligence, the best available data, and the sum of my current experience to conceive smart approaches and solutions to fast-moving opportunities and prickly problems. And as you might guess, I've employed plays with a good deal of success to carry out a given approach. This, to my way of thinking, is about as close as I've come to touching the Holy Grail of strategy, whatever and wherever it may be.

Are plays a basis for the lost art of execution? Perhaps, but you'll first have to unwind the thorny possibility that *execution* is a euphemism for "implementation," which in turn may possibly be a euphemism for "tactics." In any case, I don't believe that plays are tactics or execution because a play doesn't *describe* the precise way an approach should be carried out. It *prescribes* it. And that is the central purpose of a strategy. It is a bridge that connects plans with actions.

So why the confusion? Because strategy is often hijacked to describe in more compelling terms the important but chronically effete functions of objective setting and planning. The bridge, as it were, is frequently yanked to one side of the objective/tactics crevasse, leaving room for terms like *execution* and *implementation* to assume the position of what is still, and nonetheless, strategy. How so? Strategies, to be strategies, must suggest some method by which competitive advantage should be gained. They're otherwise an objective, goal, guideline, or policy that someone needs to go out and comply with or succeed at. By the same token, any strategy that describes the *precise* way in which something should be carried out is probably not a strategy. It is a tactic. Again . . . a play doesn't *describe* the precise way an approach should be carried out. It *prescribes* it.

Consider, for example, the Red Herring, whose genesis I describe in Chapter 7. It can be run in various tactical forms. It was deployed by Microsoft to get off the antitrust ropes and onto the Internet bandwagon and it took on the form of a comprehensive but initially vacuous (and vaporous) initiative called *.NET*. It was how the famed British filmmaker Sir Alfred Hitchcock created suspense through a distracting plot device he called a *McGuffin*. And it was central to George W. Bush's early argument to invade Iraq, pushing weapons of mass destruction to divert citizens and policymakers from their interests in diplomacy to their interests in personal safety. .NET took the tactical form of a product launch. Hitchcock's McGuffins took the form of dead-end subplots. And the FUD (Fear, Uncertainty, and Doubt) of Bush's WMDs were planted in everything from speeches to press conferences to talking points. Gates, Hitchcock, and Bush, all masters of their own games, ran Red Herrings. They employed the same play, but honed and applied it with entirely different tactical expertise.

So plays are not tactics; this is clear. But could plays be objectives? Could they be those so-called big hairy audacious goals? *Let's win the Malcolm Baldridge quality award in ten years!* Or could they be simpler objectives? *Reduce factory floor accidents by 5 percent.* Probably not. Plays are the strategy shorthand that help an organization achieve its objectives; they are neither objectives nor tactics.

Consider examples of two key players in business and politics, McDonald's Corporation and Hillary Clinton, respectively. McDonald's, bitten and partly blamed for the obesity crisis, has an ambitious plan to reposition its brand and customer experience from junk food to good food, from a bad choice to a healthy choice. This won't get done on the back of one strategy. It will take many. McDonald's will likely use the Bear Hug, a deliberate move of unexpected agreement, to co-opt activists like Morgan Spurlock and incendiary commentaries like his hit documentary *Super Size Me.* They'll run a Screen, a ploy that attaches an organization to positive references and symbols to slim down their fatted brand and coax customers to *think-salad-then-order,* rather than *eat-burger-then-think.* And they'll run Fiats, straight-faced communiqués of well-placed facts and information, to prove that they're changing.

Hillary Clinton, ensnared by her husband's ethical misdeeds and de-positioned by Republicans as a self-interested liberal, has an equally ambitious objective to reposition herself as a centrist with presidential potential. She won't fire one magic strategy bullet to make her way into the Oval Office. She'll surely fire many. She'll perhaps run a Pause on the question of Iraq, staying above the fray and letting fellow Democrats decry the war on terrorism. Like McDonald's, she'll also run Bear Hugs, perhaps to confirm her opposition to violent and sexually graphic video games, and thus to acquire the patina of a family values champion. And maybe she'll run Pings, surreptitious hints of her overarching strategy, to make sure we know she's running . . . even when she says she's not. Whether as a slinger of burgers or a slinger of rhetoric, the objectives of both McDonald's and Mrs. Clinton will be supported by multiple strategies—plays, that is.

If you accept the notion that a play is a strategy, something that conceptually sits between an objective and its execution (i.e., objectives/*strategy*/execution), then there's an argument to be made for modifying this sacred triumvirate with a simple substitution of the word *plays* for the word *strategy* (i.e., objectives/*plays*/execution). This isn't a distinction I require to advance the term *play* or the book's thesis of playmaking, but it would make our frenetic marketplaces easier to understand and manage if we did. At the end of the day, plays are what we know. It's in our bones to call and run them, to play the game. But it's not in *anyone's* bones to implement a strategically aligned strategy with tactically strategic objectives . . . if you get my drift.

Compound Strategies

In many organizations, large or small, you might often hear highbrow phrases like *fan the fire*, *smoke out a competitor*, *drive a wedge*, *flood a market*, *corner a market*, *create a market*, *rebrand a product*, or *enhance an offering*. These are common phrases in the lexicon of strategists, from marketing to business development to public affairs. And they are indeed strategies because they suggest how a player might best achieve its objectives. But they are not plays, because they embody a *multiplicity* of strategic principles. As such, I call them *Compound Strategies*.

Plays, after all, are the most fundamental of strategies, and as such they embody only a *single* strategic principle.

Consider the colloquial notion of a Smoke Out strategy. Competitors can be smoked out, like an animal from its den. They can be drawn from a stubbornly held position by way of at least two plays, a Challenge or a Jam. In 1997, when Ted Turner donated $1 billion to the United Nations, he chided fellow billionaires to chip in, to stop sitting on their money. His play was a Challenge; his tactic was the donation. In 1989, when U.S. troops in Panama City aimed round-the-clock, head-splitting hard rock hits at the Vatican embassy, the unconventional ploy is said to have hastened the surrender of its entrenched fugitive General Manuel Noriega. The play was a Jam; the tactic was the sound system and its sanctuary target.

Take, as another example, the strategy to *Enhance an Offering*. A product or service can be improved or augmented by way of many substrategies, the Screen or Recast. Running a Screen, playmakers can associate an offering, like a car, with entirely positive benefits, like safety. Hence, *Volvos are safe*. And by running a Recast, playmakers can shift the values that are attached to an offering. Hence, *Safety is your first concern*.

This isn't to say that a strategy to enhance something is any better or more useful than a strategy to run a Screen or Recast. But it is to say that strategies are layered, one upon the other. Some rise quite high in the conceputal strata between objectives and execution. Others not so much. But they are strategies nonetheless because they prescribe some general action or direction that a player should take to achieve its goals.

The Purpose of Plays

In most any dictionary there are a dizzying number of entries for the word *play*. They range from the requisite sports plays to theatrical plays to the wiggling free-play in the average steering wheel. There's also the simple and pristine notion of just playing games, a definition that is fortuitously rooted in the concepts of planning, execution, and competition, well-adapted to the tenets of playmaking.

As strategies for playing games, plays are applied with a diverse set of skills and

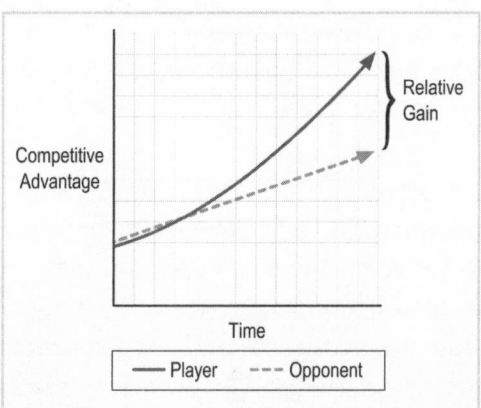

1. Elevate or accelerate the position or agenda of the player.

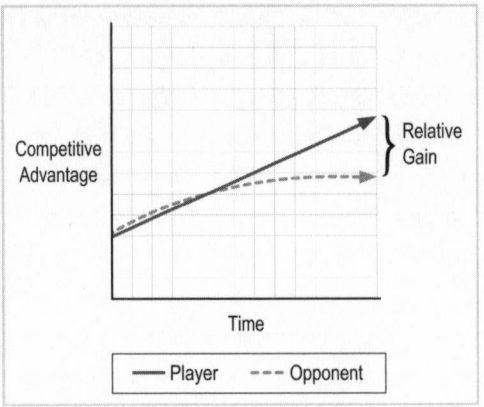

2. Slow or stop the position or agenda of an opponent.

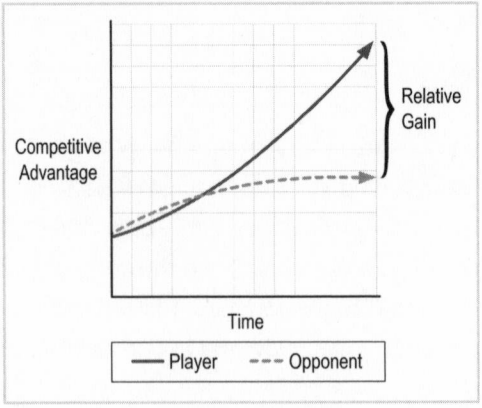

3. Or both.

philosophies—with a light hand, a velvet hammer, or a jackhammer of sorts. But however they're used, their core purpose is to achieve one or more of the following objectives:

Plays can and should move a player forward, hold another in check, or both. It's ideal, of course, to propel an entity up and away from the other guy, particularly if the plays you're running are at allies, like employees and customers. But it's okay, too, if progress is made by stopping or slowing the competition. And if both occur, so much the better, because a play's central purpose is to create *relative* competitive advantage. Since its first articulation in 1864 by Russian chemist Dmitri Mendeleev, the periodic table of chemical elements has swollen to nearly 120 unique types of distinct atomic specs, but the rate of discovery has slowed as the physical sciences have matured. Likewise, I expect that this book's proposed table of 25 plays will also grow, though only incrementally, as the criteria for plays and the variables that influence them are better understood and subjected to empirical testing.

Some attempts to create new plays have already failed, however. Take, for example, the recently euthanized play the Flood. Incubated over two years, this play embodied a strategy for overwhelming competitors with information or action, a prime example being the Friday-night White House practice of "dumping" news on weary reporters. I figured early that a Flood was a strategy to disguise a weakness, not by hiding it specifically but by surrounding it generally. But I realized over time that what made this play unique had more to do with the *way* in which it was run, not the mere fact that it *was*. The Flood, in other words, was all about repetition or volume and these, I realized, were variables of a marketplace, not the plans or ploys of a player. Any play, like a Red Herring or Lantern in the case of a news dump, could be run repeatedly and with bravado—so, with that, the Flood was absorbed into a simpler but equally important table of variables called "Factors at Play," detailed on p. 294. Four other plays—Bridge, Fan, Flop, and Smoke Out—were similarly assimilated in the process of collapsing and refining the play-type gene pool.

Will there be more or perhaps fewer than these initial twenty-five strategies? Time will tell. But in all likelihood there will be a growing recognition among marketplace strategists that the moves and countermoves we employ to advance a position or agenda can be drawn from and fully explained by a set of irreducibly simplified functions, what some in the community of artificial intelligence call primitives, what advanced mathematicians and advancing kids call games, what field generals call stratagems, and what I call plays.

Naming the Plays

To most of us, snow might just be snow. But work your way north and the icy flakes take on new meanings and measure. To Eskimos, well adjusted to arctic living, there's a clear need to differentiate one type of snow from another, what it's good for and how to put it to work. Accordingly, the natives of the north have a well-developed lexicon for subfreezing precipitation, from a few dozen to a few hundred, depending on whom you talk to.

Plays are like snow. With time and experience, they can be studied, broken down, and intelligently differentiated in their surrounding conditions. And once that's done, they can be named. These are the criteria I've used to do just that:

- First, I borrowed terms from named maneuvers in various walks of life, particularly where strategy is well practiced, such as in debate, politics, games, sports, and warfare. Why refute the experts, I thought, and why not honor their traditions and terms? This thinking is what produced the plays Crazy Ivan, Disco, Draft, Jam, Lantern, Leak, Ping, Red Herring, and Trial Balloon. The story behind each is contained in the chapter of each play.

- Second, when a play could not be matched with some established term, I defaulted to standard words of the English language, choosing those that most accurately described the base function of the strategy. Why make up something if an existing word already described the play? The by-products of this process were the Bait, Challenge, Crowd, Deflect, Filter, Label, Mirror, Pass, Pause, and Preempt.

- Third, when tradition or popular language failed me, and as a last resort, I exercised my prerogative, using various other words, actions, or symbols to derive the unnamed remaining plays. Thus, Bear Hug, Call Out, Fiat, Peacock, Recast, and Screen were christened.

From where I sit, sketch pad in hand as it were, watching marketplace jungles and their creatures at work, plays are the essential and mutually exclusive strategies that people and organizations employ to position or persuade in the free enterprise system. Plays are useful and individually different, and taken together, they tell a bigger story of the ways in which people and organizations employ them according to circumstance and resources. Finally, when combined with a set of factors to adjust for nuance and a methodology to implement them, they form a system that brings strategy to life and practitioners of influence out of the cubicle and onto the playing field. The following pages will tell you who they are and how they play the game.

What's a Playmaker?

Who calls plays? Who runs them? And are there boundaries or credentials that define the people who do? For starters, I don't distinguish between people who call the plays and those who run them, at least not by name. By their nature, plays require constant adjustment to the marketplace and involvement at every level to refine the strategy and its execution, so anyone who calls *or* runs a play might simply be called a *playmaker*. Here is a definition:

> *def.* **Playmaker:** *A strategist whose stock in trade is to call, run, decode, and counter competitive moves in a marketplace. Playmakers have influence over a player's policy, position, and agenda and are stewards of its intangible assets.*

This broad definition suggests that many different kinds of people run plays. And that's not necessarily a good thing. The late Edward L. Bernays, often remembered as the father of public relations, once repeated to me a favorite aphorism that echoed his lifelong campaign to license his unregulated craft. *"Any nut, weirdo, kook, or dope can call themselves a public relations practitioner,"* Bernays famously groused.

The same might be said of plays and playmakers. Anyone can say they're a playmaker by virtue of the fact that they run plays. Baseball catchers, coaches, quarterbacks, and point guards are playmakers, of course. So are poker players and chess grandmasters. Even spouses, partners, parents, siblings, relatives, preachers, and teachers run plays. We all do.

Remember the surly waitress who wouldn't serve you last week? She was perhaps running a Pause, a strategic suspension of activity. Remember when your minister asked each family of the congregation to give a little more? It was a Challenge, albeit a most polite one, to cross a line from a position of comfort.

Each of these, be they rude or endearing examples, are playmakers to one degree or another. You might think of them as the casual practitioners of plays, the pedestrian playmakers. But there is another class of strategist that takes the mastery of plays to an altogether higher level of scale, impact, consistency, and distinction. You might call them the professional playmakers. They are people like the notoriously clever Republican strategist Karl Rove, the driven and facile media mogul Oprah Winfrey, or the impetuous and instinctive tech entrepreneur Steve Jobs. When they run a play it's something to behold.

When President Bush talks about *keeping America safe* or that *terrorists are evil* he's running a Preempt—one might assume on the advice of Karl Rove. Though the president has of course been vulnerable on issues of safety and terrorism, his ploy is to buff up what his rivals would predictably try to scuff up. In maneuver warfare, it's called a spoiling attack, a preemptive strike that takes away an enemy's means or motivation for commencing an attack. Democrats of course have been ready to tell you that America might *not* be so safe and that terrorists might have *reason* to be evil. But their plans get spoiled because Bush, by way of Rove, is quite good at turning a liability into an asset.

When Oprah Winfrey gives away one new car to every member of her studio audience she's running a Peacock, a play that moves a marketplace through the raw power of showmanship. Unlike most other plays, the Peacock doesn't bother much to leverage the marketplace. It manhandles it. It *is* the news and when well run, it elevates mere stuntery to a decisively competitive advantage. For Oprah, the Peacock creates incredible residual goodwill that accrues to her brand and various ventures.

When Steve Jobs hunts down a new idea, he doesn't so much invent it as he borrows it and makes it radically better. He revolutionized personal computers via the Apple II and Macintosh. He changed the game in full-length animated films through Pixar. And he improved the way we possess and obsess over our music with iTunes and the iPod. His play is the Draft, a maneuver that uses the groundbreaking energy of an unwitting first-mover to soften the marketplace. It allows patient playmakers to follow closely, then shoot ahead with what Jobs might call *insanely great* improvements to merely great innovations.

Professional Playmakers

Somewhere between the ornery waitress and these celebrated black belts there are the professional playmakers—well-heeled strategists, all calling and running plays with significant expertise and serious results, indispensable practitioners and advisors to their management, employers, and clients. Below, in alphabetical order, are just a few of the many forms they come in. In all likelihood, you're one of them:

> *Account reps, activists, ad executives, agents, attorneys, authors, bloggers, board directors, brand managers, business strategists, CEOs, chief communications officers, chief marketing officers, chief negotiators, chief strategy officers, coalition builders, columnists, commentators, copywriters, creative directors, crisis consultants, dealmakers, debaters, detectives, elected officials, evangelists (of markets and religions), executive directors, field generals, filmmakers, functional managers, fund raisers, graphic designers, issues managers, journalists, litigators, lobbyists, management coaches, management consultants, marcom managers, media consultants, national account reps, opposition researchers, policemen, political campaigners, political pundits, politicians, pollsters, positioning gurus, press secretaries, product managers, PR consultants, public information officers, publicists, reputation managers, sales managers, special events coordinators, spies, spin doctors, spokespeople, union reps, warfare strategists, and Webmasters.*

I'm sure I missed somebody in this list of nearly seventy playmaker breeds, but you get the idea. Playmakers, particularly those in management, strategy, marketing, sales, public affairs, advertising, public relations, media, and even law, have full access and privileges to plays because, as the definition attests, they are stewards of their organizations' intangible assets and they influence policy, position, and agenda to manage their marketplace. Consider a few simple examples of common professional playmakers and plays they might typically run, listed by play in alphabetical order:

- A CFO runs a Deflect: *That's a complex question. I'll have to get back to you on that.* He's buying time to find the answer or figure out a way to avoid it.

- A crisis consultant runs a Disco: *I know it's a matter of principle and that they're holding a gun to your head, but you won't move ahead until you acknowledge your role in this thing.* He's advising his embattled client to take one step back in order to take two steps forward.

■ A product manager runs a Fiat: *Crest is the number one toothpaste preferred by dentists.* It's a simple communication of a product's benefit and position, not much more, but it's a play.

■ A military spokesperson runs a Filter: *These reconnaissance photos show coalition tanks approaching Baghdad's west side.* What she's not showing, however, are pictures of a much larger tank column advancing on Baghdad's south side.

■ An activist runs a Jam: *Okay . . . we'll film from one boat and run the other between the whales and the harpoon gun.* It's a made-for-media protest, designed to shame and shut down a rival's activities, this one being a commercial whaling operation.

■ A trial attorney runs a Mirror: *Then how do you explain the fact that these three people saw you pull a gun?* He's asking a defense witness to explain alibi-busting evidence.

■ A publicist runs a Peacock: *See Richard Branson's Full Monty in Times Square.* It's an attention-grabbing stunt to launch a new product or service.

■ A union boss runs a Ping: *We sure wouldn't want to have to call a strike.* It's a tacit signal that the union rep is already thinking about it.

■ A car salesman runs a Recast: *What you might lose in horsepower you make up at the gas pump.* It's a simple way of flipping a negative (a small engine) into a positive (a high-mileage car).

■ An HR manager runs a Trial Balloon: *Thanks for coming in, everybody. I wanted to get the group's reaction to some new benefits we're considering.* If they don't like the plans, they can be retracted. If they do, they can be implemented. And if they get implemented anyway, the HR manager will know the nature of their support or objections.

What's a Player?

Throughout this book, I refer many times to playmakers and players. There is an important distinction. A player represents a single interest in a marketplace and is typically made up of a collection of playmakers (e.g., a CEO, marketing VP, brand manager, advertising director, spokesperson), bound together to coordinate the player's policy, position, or agenda on a designated deal, program, campaign, issue, etc. A player *can* be an individual, like the president, Oprah, or Steve Jobs, but generally it embodies a single franchised interest, be it a committee, company, coalition, association, institution, charity, or government. There are three different kinds of players:

- **An Opponent** A foe, any player that needs to be slowed, stopped, co-opted, or somehow written out of the scene. Opponents come in the form of your keenest rival, perhaps making a claim that's false or defamatory, a skeptical regulatory body whose own sense of time is causing you to run out of it, or an uninspired employee who'd just as soon file a complaint as punch the clock.

- **An Ally** A friend, a person or organization who is supportive of you and your player's mission or marketplace activities. An ally can be a business partner with whom you want to strengthen ties, an existing customer who's ready to be upsold, an employee group that's stepping up to a challenge, or a like-minded politician or luminary who's willing to endorse your good ideas and good deeds.

- **An Independent** A neutral party or bystander. It might be a player whose interests have nothing to do with yours, whose position guarantees it some degree of autonomy, or whose function is to facilitate, regulate, or interpret activities related to you and your marketplace. It might be another company in your industry, though not a player that competes for your slice of it (e.g., Banana Republic and Ann Taylor are mostly competitively indifferent to one another). It might be a judge ruling on a case that involves you, or an accreditation body looking for chinks in your compliance program. And it might be a journalist or blogger, pledged to report the facts as they appear, however balanced or biased she may be. Independents, despite their agnostic stance, are crucial players to manage because their interpretations of your position or agenda—*they're good guys/they're bad guys, they're guilty/they're not-guilty, they're cooperative/they're secretive*—influence your marketplace and all within it.

These are the categories that players generally fall into. But like a frog in a pond, they can jump quickly from one lily pad to another. Take these three simple cases:

- A company with whom you traditionally compete realizes it needs to cooperate. This happened to Lufthansa and United Airlines. Both wanted what the other had—routes into important markets—so they went from competitive opponents to "coopetive" allies.

- A well-behaved customer whose behavior is questioned becomes a ferocious rival. This happened at a Silver Spring, Maryland, Starbucks when a breast-feeding mother was asked to cover herself. In one nursing, the coffee-sipping mother shifted from ally to activist.

■ A docile regulator becomes a huge impediment. This happened when FedEx and UPS petitioned the U.S. Department of Transportation to review the ownership percentages of its overseas competitor DHL. A typically benign bureaucracy got very involved, making life very hard for one foreign air courier.

The Discipline of Playmaking

I f I've persuaded you to this point of the existence of plays, good. And if I've convinced you that playmakers transcend the public and private sectors and various subindustries, even better. But to build a full story around these two things, I have one more mind-expanding feat to attempt: Playmakers are more than a loose-knit population of clever and directed strategists. They are also charter members of a new discipline.

Just as public officials engage in policymaking, legislators in lawmaking, and diplomats and negotiators in peacemaking, playmakers are engaged in what might logically be called *playmaking.*

Webster's New Universal Unabridged Dictionary defines a discipline in a variety of ways, but in terms of the learning and application of knowledge the dictionary offers two useful definitions: (1) *a set or system of rules and regulations,* and (2) *a branch of instruction or learning.* If there's a better term for playmaking, I'll leave it to practitioners, scholars, and other voices to hammer one out. But whatever it may be called—playmaking, war gaming, strategy mapping, or something else—there's enough evidence (in this book alone, I hope) to suggest that plays are the supporting components of a fast-ripening practice and, further, that playmakers are its modern pioneers. These are the characteristics of a discipline, and here is how I would presume to define one in the context of playmaking:

> *def.* **Playmaking:** *A discipline for deploying and systematically managing plays—in combinations, sequences, and patterns—to continually influence, control, and sustain the sentiments, discussions, and decisions of a marketplace.*

This cuts close to a variety of honed and even ancient pursuits, like rhetoric and debate in particular, first articulated by the great Greek philosophers and still a rich tradition in our culture of influence and argumentation, from the cubicle to the board-room, from the town hall to legislative chambers, from college campuses to the blogosphere, and so on. For better or worse, it's also not far from the troubled pas-time of propaganda, where it's sometimes not quite clear whether the doctrine a player is advancing is being driven by the rules of white, gray, or even black propa-ganda. Darker yet, it echoes the strategies of psychological operations—known to experts as *psyops*—where words and symbols become weapons in military opera-tions, both overt and covert. A bit more happily, however, this definition of playmak-ing smacks of the heady and quantitative field of game theory, where, as examples, Baits are run in a dueling game of chicken, Deflects are run by captive players in a sell-out-or-stick-together game of Prisoners' Dilemma, and Challenges are run in a zero-sum game of winner-takes-all.

But where playmaking is most relevant—and where it could have the biggest impact—is on marketing, sales, public affairs, advertising, public relations, the newer offshoots of buzz and word-of-mouth, and even legal affairs—all good forums for watching rhetoric, debate, propaganda, and game theory at work. Disciplines in their own right, they are counted on by organizations to manage the discussions, disagree-ments, and negotiations of a marketplace, influence the thinking of stakeholders, and project decisions and payoffs. Indeed, they're regarded today as mission-critical func-tions to most any brand-conscious, media-savvy organization.

But they all have their jobs to do. Although these functions involve the calling and running of plays, playmaking is not their reason for being. In the court of public opinion, for example, marketing exists to condition and engage stakeholders toward a way of thinking or preference. It warms the waters. The sales function, by contrast, facilitates buying decisions and fulfills transactions. It makes the sale. Public Affairs brings public policy in line with corporate strategy, and vice versa. It sets the playing conditions. Advertising does all these things, too, largely through a paid-influence model. It buys the media. PR operates largely through an earned-influence model. It influences the media. Word-of-Mouth and buzz are designed to seed discussions and spur actions, organically, from the grassroots up. And last but not least, legal affairs exists to maximize a player's position on matters of law and in the courts of law.

Each of these disciplines relies heavily on plays and playmakers to propel their crafts, and at the end of the day the marketers and sales staff, ad and PR people, buzz and worth-of-mouth generators, lawyers and lobbyists, are the power users of playmaking—innovating and moving marketplaces, for sure, but not focused specifically on their own core competencies for deploying and systematically managing plays in combinations, sequences, and patterns.

In other words, the practice of playmaking is still merely informal and so, too, is its position in business, politics, and society in general.

A Little Like Math

Would anything change if playmaking were studied and systematically taught, perhaps as a recognized discipline? I think so.

Playmaking has the potential to focus and accelerate the influence industries just as mathematics has accelerated the practices and purposes of accounting and finance, engineering and architecture, and physics and computer science. It distills a universe of applicable strategies into meaningful and potentially measurable concepts that can be used in turn to design more efficient and effective branding strategies, one-to-one customer outreach, sales promotions, ballot initiatives, ad campaigns, PR blitzes, and groundswell movements. Likewise, it serves as a paradigm for dissecting these efforts and better understanding the reasons for their success and failure.

I'm not suggesting that the influence industries don't already have their math. In fact, they're glutted with methodologies and metrics that give structure to their work. What I *do* mean to suggest is that these tools (linear planning models, field polls and focus groups, media measurement tools, dashboards, contextual search engines, etc.) are underevolved because these don't define the units on which campaigns are built and competitive thrusts are measured and analyzed. For all their wealth of experience and dedication to measurement, the practitioners of influence have neither a standard definition for their most basic foundational materials—strategies—nor a reliable framework that is easily understood or applied. As playmakers, we need a new math. And we need a discipline to nurture it.

Section II.
The Playmaker's Table

Playmakers are, naturally, more human than machine. They form up their impressions of what's happening and they call and run plays, often on-the-fly, in what can seem like a real-time rhetorical war game. So it goes that strategy in the influence industries has a visceral and less structured feel, not only because it lacks a formal discipline or a kind of periodic table of influence, but because it deals with intangible properties, fluid targets and environments, and compressed timelines.

Imagine, for example, that a company is suddenly the target of an attacking play: It's been posing too long in its marketplace, claiming perhaps that its flagship is the industry standard. It's been talking a line that's wearing thin with competitors, and now it's being exposed. The attacking Player A, tired of playing second fiddle, might say something like *These guys have no business taking this position. They're deceiving the market and now they're undermining us. It's time to call them on it!* Under siege, Player B might likely say, *We need to buy time. Let's respond that 'this is just another attempt to displace the leader.' Make 'em work through that while we think.*

With The Playmaker's Table and its supporting strategies, the two players described above might shorten their scripts to simply, *Run a Call Out* and *Run a Deflect!* Player A would know it's operating on the far right side of The Table, engaging the rival by way of an attacking and provocative Call Out play. Player B would know that it's playing more to the left, attempting to condition the marketplace by way of a diverting and time-buying Deflect play. Perhaps more importantly, each player would know if the selected play had been appropriately applied and how to decode or counter whatever came next. Through The Playmaker's Table, they'd know more surely the answers to four crucial and constantly recurring questions:

Q: *What are we doing?*

Q: *How are we doing it?*

Q: *What is our competition doing?*

Q: *How should we react to it?*

The Playmaker's Table (see below) is a carefully organized framework of 25 classi-fied play types, the playmaker's most basic tools and the building blocks of the disci-pline of playmaking. Each play type bears distinct differences from the others, but unlike the nearly 120 chemical elements of the periodic table, which are physically and precisely unique, play types are more akin to colors on the spectrum of light, vi-sually distinct but ultimately connected to one another. As products of the soft-edged social sciences, the play types of playmaking are a continuum of related concepts, not a collection of unique compounds.

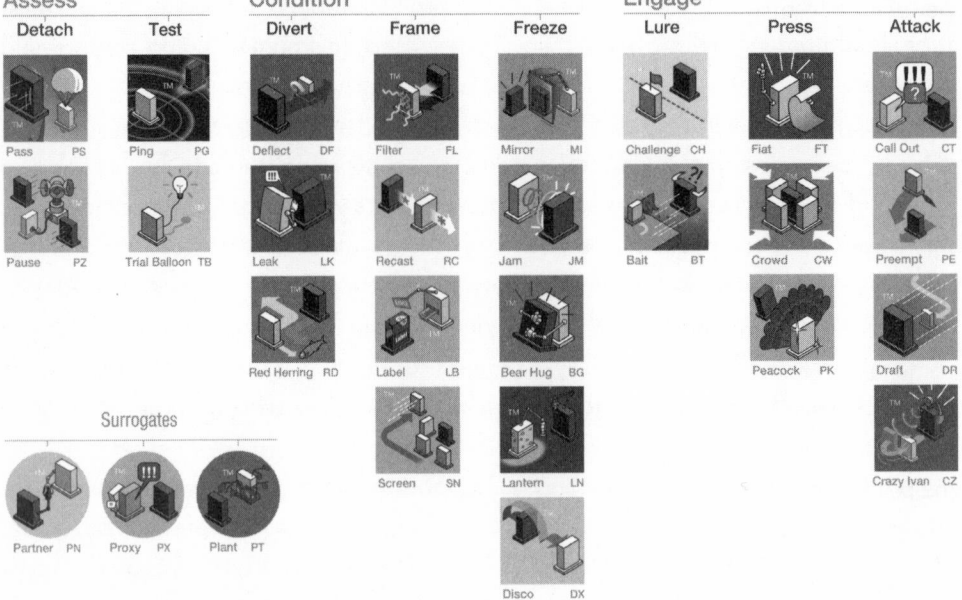

The Table is the product of field observation, working experience, literature re-view, previews, and pilot testing. (For more information on the research and develop-ment process, see The Making of The Playmaker's Standard, p. 299.) Each play type is placed on The Table according to its primary strategic function, assigned to one of three overarching classes (shown along The Table's top row) and then to one of the eight underlying subclasses (shown in The Table's second row). And each is represented by a distinctive square-shaped icon.

Classes represent the first raw cuts in the classification process, a gathering of all eight subclasses and twenty-five plays into three broad categories called *Assess, Condition,* and *Engage.* These constitute a playmaker's full and entire spectrum of activities and considerations. If a marketplace is worth a player's time and attention, there is always some mixture of assessment, conditioning, or engagement to be planned and carried out, and because there is no such thing as a noncompetitive marketplace, the game is played around the clock, in real time and without breaks—always assessing, conditioning, or engaging. In other words, a playmaker's work is never done. Of course, a player could exit a marketplace by running a Pass, but that would presumably be to focus its playmaking efforts in other more productive areas.

You might be inclined to think of the left-sided plays of the Assess class as lower risk and, correspondingly, the right-sided activities in the Engage class as chancy. Experience tells me otherwise. There can be perilous consequences to the player who runs left-sided plays, like the seemingly innocuous Pause. This play was deliberately run by the leadership of the Soviet Union in April 1986 when a reactor at the Chernobyl nuclear power plant overheated, exploded, and spewed its deadly waste. The Soviets, who refused any public comment on the spreading disaster for two critical days, might have thought this was the lowest-risk approach. But for all the fallout that the government and its people suffered—both radioactive and political—you have to think that there was a wiser approach.

Likewise, there can sometimes be little downside to running a Crazy Ivan, what some playmakers will consider the nuclear option of strategic moves (no relation to Chernobyl) and a play that lives on the supposedly more adventurous right edge of the playmaking world. Think of the innovative software companies Intuit, maker of the popular accounting package Quicken, and RealNetworks, maker of the RealAudio media streaming software program, which in the 1990s were predicted to get toppled as the feared Microsoft entered their spaces. What did they do? They fought back with strategies based largely on the Crazy Ivan, confronting their attacker with combinations of marketing, legal, and technology punches that tripped up the giant and preserved their lead. Initially, such an approach might have seemed a little crazy, but to have done anything else was sure death. The Crazy Ivan, in this case, was the lowest risk move of all.

As shown in the figure below, The Playmaker's Table is organized along two dimensions, (x) degree of confrontation and (y) ease of execution. Plays that are positioned farther to the right generally display higher levels of confrontation or friction between players. And plays that are more easily run are positioned higher in a subclass's stack. This is to mean that a play in the upper left corner of The Table is both easier to run and can be done so with a minimum of competitive interaction. Correspondingly, a play in the lower right corner is relatively more difficult to deploy and far more capable of stirring the marketplace pot.

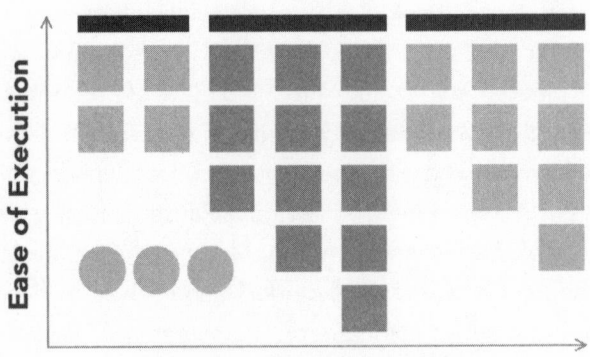

Degree of Confrontation

Key Features

The following pages, which detail The Playmaker's Table's structure and its supporting information, are written for three kinds of playmakers: (1) students of playmaking who are hungry for details, nuance, and case histories, (2) the quick-study reader or the visual learner who "gets it" and wants a quick take, and (3) the playmaker in the field, who's running and calling plays on-the-fly, looking for fast answers and great ideas. *These guys are running a play on us! Quick . . . what is it?*

To aid the fast-referring playmaker, essays and information on each play type—from the Pass (Chapter 1) on the upper left to Crazy Ivan (Chapter 25) on the lower right—are supported by the following illustrations and lists of useful and easily recalled information:

Play Symbols

Just as U.S. states, commercial airports, and chemical elements have abbreviations (e.g., *FL* for Florida, *LAX* for Los Angeles International Airport, and *Si* for Silicon), each play type has been assigned a unique two-letter symbol (e.g., *PZ* for Pause, *DX* for Disco, *MI* for Mirror, *CH* for Challenge). Like the play type icons and their definitions, these are intended to enliven the playmaker's lexicon with compact codes to use, for instance, in an e-mail or online posting—*We think these guys will run a PZ/DX combination. If they do, let's run the MI and hit 'em with a CH.* Perhaps, too, symbols might be used to jot play sequences onto a napkin or whiteboard, like a simple software script—*If TB+CH, then MI+CH.*

Play Locators

Throughout this section and elsewhere in the book, silhouette legends or "locators" of The Playmaker's Table help playmakers quickly find a class, subclass, play, or surrogate, and judge its relative degree of confrontation and ease of execution. Shown here is the Play Locator for the play type Screen, a move that's made with only moderate levels of confrontation but which is more difficult to implement than the three other plays above it (in ascending order, the Label, Recast, and Filter).

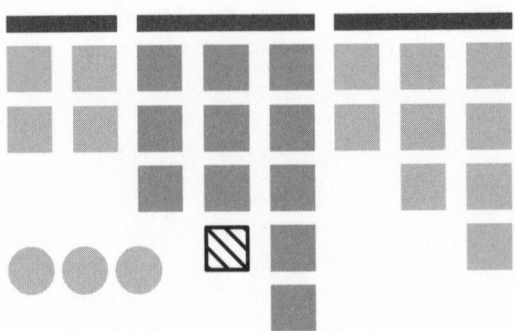

Risk/Reward Ratings

Like a financial investment, the running of any particular play suggests some level of assumed risk and anticipated reward. To help playmakers calibrate their play selections, a three-by-three matrix plots the estimated risk and reward of each play type in one of nine square-shaped cells. These ratings are based on the five-part research-and-development process described on p. 299. Over time, these ratings may have a quantitative basis, but at present, these are qualitative estimates and they should be taken as guidelines, not gospel.

Play Icons

Specially drawn icons illustrate the basic behaviors of play types, all of them rendered as comical and colorful ideograms to give levity to the otherwise serious business of playmaking. In most cases, a play's central strategy is conveyed through the actions (or antics) of two semihuman game-piece-shaped players. The fact that only two players are often featured is potentially misleading because playmaking is typically not a *Me versus You* duopoly. It's more often *Me, Jill, and Bob versus You, Jane, and Jack* and, when circumstances change, *Me, Bob, and Jane versus You, Jack, and Jill.* Players, in other words, tend to work in coalitions, and often they tend to switch teams. But to drive home the point that a play is a competitive strategy, where one organized player (or coalition thereof) works with or against a variety of alternating players (and coalitions thereof), I have used for simplicity's sake the two-player construct.

Some play type icons, like the Fiat or Trial Balloon, feature only a single player to tell the story. It's not that other players aren't involved in these cases but that the counterparts are too amorphous to show as one or a couple of distinct game pieces. Other play icons, like Pause, Screen, and Crowd, employ multiple game pieces to suggest the reality of a crowded marketplace.

Play Definitions

Though many plays bear the names of intuitively obvious words—Bait, Challenge, Crowd, Deflect, Label, Leak, Filter, Mirror, and Preempt—all twenty-five feature carefully crafted definitions to convey their precise strategic function. Some are influenced by the dictionary, of course, and some by folklore and popular slang, but each is entirely original and suited to the discipline of playmaking. (For more information see Naming the Plays, see p. 30).

Related Plays

Each play type is accompanied by a list of related play types, however similar or far-flung, to help playmakers better recognize each play's capability, when one is best applied, where another takes up, and where another leaves off. Some plays are obviously and closely related, like the Ping and Trial Balloon. As members of the Test subclass, they are best at taking measure of players in a marketplace. Some are not so obviously connected, at least to look at the Table, yet they share a kind of common ancestry. The Draft and Screen, as examples, seem almost like the proverbial twins separated at birth. Both operate in different classes at different ends of the playmaking spectrum, but both have the common inclination to borrow the resources they need to be successful. It's a kind of instinctive thievery that binds them together.

Related Terms

Included in each play chapter is a list of words and phrases—both formal and slang—that are reasonably synonymous with each of the twenty-five named plays. If I've left off a related term, I hope to know about it, and if I've imprudently chosen my own favorite over yours or someone else's, I hope you'll let me know through The Playmaker's Forum blog (http://blog.plays2run.com). This is one part of the system that is being invented, not discovered, so subjective decisions like this should reflect the will of the playmakers. Here, by example, are some well-known terms that didn't make it as play names but which appear on lists of correspondingly related terms. *Bridging*, well known to pirouetting politicians, is a form of a Recast. *Inoculation*, a technique of persuasion that insulates a playmaker from rhetorical attacks, is a form of a Lantern. *Jumping on the Bandwagon*, a popular phrase for joining in, is a form of a Crowd. *McGuffin*, a term popularized by the late Alfred Hitchcock and used widely in film and literature, is a form of a Red Herring. *Playing Possum*, the hillbilly term for fake-sleeping, is a form of a Pause. *Spoiling Attack*, a military maneuver, is a form of a Preempt. And *Trojan Horse*, named for the fabled Greek ploy that fooled ancient Troy, is also a form of a Red Herring.

Classes, Subclasses, Plays, and Surrogates

The following pages unfold the classes, subclasses, plays, and surrogates of The Playmaker's Table, beginning at the left of The Table in the Assess class and finishing at the right in the Engage class. The first plays to be detailed are the Pass and Pause in the Detach subclass. The last are the Call Out, Preempt, Draft, and Crazy Ivan of the Attack subclass. This is not to suggest that any playmaker would necessarily proceed along these lines (i.e., beginning on the left and moving toward the right). Playmaking, after all, can start and stop with any play at any location on The Playmaker's Table.

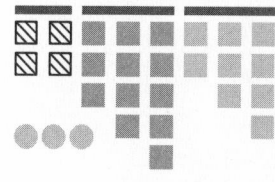

The Assess Class

Players may be inclined to tiptoe into a marketplace, possibly concealed from view or preferring a backseat to play action on the front lines. Such moves fall within the most tentative or subtle class, Assess, which houses just two subclasses and four play types.

def. **Assess:** *Subtle, typically passive, monitoring and profiling of players and marketplaces.*

To assess is to proceed with caution and care, not necessarily slowly, but with exaggerated restraint and muted intentions, all with deliberate purpose and underlying strategy, of course. Within this class there are two differentiated subclasses, Detach and Test.

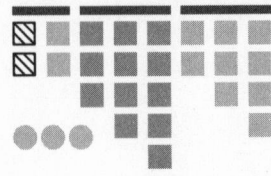

The Detach Subclass

At the extreme left of The Playmaker's Table, atop the play types Pass and Pause, Detach is rooted in the concept of strategic withdrawal. It's about getting out of the way or simply getting out of a marketplace.

> def. **Detach:** *Play action where a player exits a marketplace, briefly or even permanently.*

There are times when a player doesn't belong in a marketplace, perhaps because it's being beaten, the marketplace has been saturated, or it's underperforming. There's also the possibility that the player has done enough and needs to see how things run on their own, or that the player's resources can be better used elsewhere. In any case, players sometimes just need to step off the field, if even for a moment.

Detaching plays are not, however, a player's permission slip to duck play action, something that in my experience is quite common: It may be overworked, underskilled, or both. Its board or managers might not be giving it the resources or air cover it needs. It might not have the right team. Its lawyers might have tied its hands. It might think it's just done enough and deserves to sit this one out. But running a Pass or Pause is not for the stressed or lazy. In fact, it's for the most cunning. Players who run a Pass for the right reasons have other plans and other plays in mind in better marketplaces. And the players who run a good Pause are among the most disciplined and steely-eyed. They know how to vary their plays, when to step out, and when and for how long to let a situation play out.

These first two chapters tell you what you need to know about the Pass and Pause.

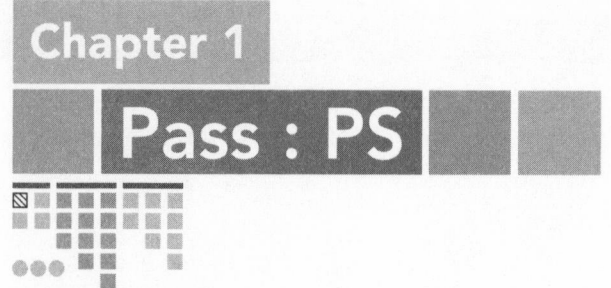

Chapter 1

Pass : PS

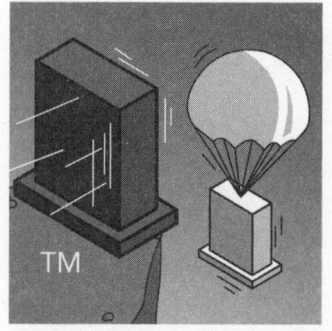

Each of the twenty-five plays of The Playmaker's Standard is designed to strategically advance a player's position or agenda in a competitive marketplace. But one play, called the Pass, is designed to improve a player's relative competitive advantage by way of *exiting*, not remaining in, a marketplace.

The Pass is not a playmaker's license to run screaming, white flag waving, from a tough situation . . . *I give up, you win!* And it's not an excuse to duck an opportunity to try to look smart for doing it—*Um, uh, Jimmy, let's . . . Oh, I know, let's run one of those Pass plays. Yeah, that's it.*

Far from it.

What we have in the Pass is a play that embodies the principle of strategic withdrawal. It's a move that helps players make smart decisions about staying with or getting out of a marketplace. When the decision is to stay, there are of course twenty-four other plays to run, in patterns and sequences to suit the playmaker's skills and circumstance. But when the decision is to get out, the well-run Pass helps players pull back rationally and to consolidate and refocus resources intelligently, rather than just surrender them.

TABLE A. BASICS OF A PASS

Class	Assess
Subclass	Detach
Type	**Pass**
Definition	The strategic withdrawal from a marketplace or play action. Typically a player will exit or "bail out" of a marketplace to preserve its resources and/or focus them elsewhere for competitive advantage.
Upsides	■ Conserves resources to create new competitive options. ■ Conditions the player to choose its shots, not to try to win every battle. ■ Cuts your losses.
Downsides	■ Proves and improves a rival's superiority. ■ Can unduly discredit the player. ■ Reduces or eliminates a player's competitive reputation. ■ Invites gloating and de-positioning by opponents. ■ Can make a player look weak or confused. Encourages rivals to come after the player in markets where it *still* plays.
Related Terms	■ Aborting ■ Bailing ■ Cutting your losses ■ Ejecting ■ Exiting ■ Retreating ■ Surrendering
Related Play Types	■ Deflect ■ Pause

Big Bail

IBM demonstrated its mastery of the Pass when in late 2004 it exited the personal computer business, selling its $9 billion-a-year PC division to China's largest PC maker, the up-and-coming Lenovo. For IBM to leave the PC business was in some measure like amputating a treasured limb of the behemoth's well-crafted brand: PCs, after all, are a staple in the information technology game and, to most, a hallmark of IBM's computing heritage. But for Big Blue, the idea of staying in the commoditizing, margin-slimming, and strategy-sapping PC sector was a move that represented unacceptably large and looming sacrifices down the road.

So it bailed on the PC business, but not under the cover of darkness, not, for instance, with a Friday-evening press dump to bury the news . . . *Oh, by the way, we sold the PC business to China. Have a nice weekend.* Instead, IBM ran a deliberate Pass, supported by at least two other soundly run plays. The Pass was IBM's overarching strategy, its *alpha* play. But to pull it off, it enlisted the assistance of two other maneuvers as *beta* plays, the Lantern, which voluntarily illuminates a flaw, and Recast, a play that reinterprets a story to a player's advantage. (For more information, see "Alpha and Beta Plays," p. 291.)

Hand-in-hand with Lenovo, Big Blue rolled out the proactive news. IBM ran the Lantern, acknowledging that PCs were a drag on its bottom-line results and its top-line aspirations. Then, it ran a Recast, touting its new headache-free 19-percent equity stake in Lenovo and the windfall of a new avenue into the high-growth Chinese IT market, a sure boon for its signature consulting services and software. Lenovo had its own good spin to add too: a mammoth new base of notebook and desktop PC customers, IBM's backing of the venture, and, for a time, the rights to sell its PCs with the prized IBM ThinkCentre and ThinkPad logos. For the competitors of each company, the deal also had an intended de-positioning effect. It brought Lenovo, already a volume-savvy manufacturer, face-to-face with rivals Dell and HP, and it allowed Lenovo to outclass its top regional competitor, Great Wall Technology, with the thud factor of the IBM PC customer base and Big Blue's brand and backing.

Rather than be eroded by the off-strategy PC business, IBM used the Pass to burnish its position in its core businesses of enterprise computing, software, and services—a powerful message to all of its stakeholders, from employees to investors.

TABLE B. EXAMPLES OF A PASS

Passes to remember . . .	
	■ ***IBM PCs*** In December 2004, IBM sold its once-vaunted PC business to China-based Lenovo Group, Ltd., giving Big Blue room to focus its resources on higher-margin businesses with greater strategic value.
	■ ***Cuban Withdrawal*** October 28, 1962: Soviet radio reads USSR premier Nikita Khrushchev's letter to U.S. president John F. Kennedy, announcing the immediate dismantling and withdrawal of missiles from Cuba.
	■ ***Dave Chappelle*** In May 2005, comedian Dave Chappelle, host of Comedy Central's highly rated Chappelle's Show, walked away in the show's third season, leaving stunned fans and a $50 million contract hanging. Months later, he cited stress and subpar quality of work as the reason for his exit.

Big Gamble

In *The Art of War,* the legendary military strategist Sun Tzu has a great deal to say about preserving resources, keeping the powder dry, if you will. So do the ancient writings of the Asian classic *36 Strategies.* Withdrawal, in fact, is elemental in the mind of any good player because games of strategy—from maneuver warfare to playmaking—represent a constant series of advances and retreats that, taken together, improve the player's relative position, on a battlefield or in a marketplace. Suffice it to say, going in reverse can be as constructive and helpful to a player as going forward, and under the right conditions, a well-timed Pass can even lay the groundwork for getting back what you might have had to give up. From the perspective of the service industry, I have personal and direct experiences in such things and, particularly, in running a Pass to save my company's hide and reset the playing field. Here's my story of bailing out . . . and climbing back in.

Clients, of course, have sacred importance to a professional services firm, and to my consultancy, this was never an exception. But in the rough-and-tumble high technology industry, where we prospered for more than a dozen years, the expectations and treatment by the well-caffeinated, well-financed, and hyperambitious professionals of Silicon Valley created more than the usual share of challenges to firms like mine. By and large, we rolled with the punches and were thankful to be involved in work that often had historic implications for doing business and living life. A key to this existence was in navigating the many management changes that regularly befell our technology clients, whether established Goliaths or start-ups. Turnover for any position was roughly eighteen to twenty-four months, so change was a constant in the extreme.

Consequently, when the executives who commissioned us were moved up or out, their chairs were filled with new faces, usually with their own ideas of what to do, where to go, what plays to run, and who to have on their team. This was all quite reasonable, except for the last part—*whom* to have on the team—because new blood often meant new consultants, too, irrespective of the accomplishments and trustworthiness of those they sought to replace. Such is life.

Often, we saw these changes coming, and in one ominous case, it was obvious that a new team would soon be marched in. From the executive assistants to the retained consultancies (mine being one), a new approach and new leadership was in the air. Senior executives with whom we still had close ties told us as much: There would be a full and thorough housecleaning. *Watch out.*

For my group, this was mind-boggling news. Our results, aided by the playmaking philosophy, were by any measure exceedingly strong. You'd think we'd earned our keep. But two engulfing political waves were still coming our way: First, we'd been told that a large share of the account would immediately be put up for bid, offered to us officially and, to our chagrin, our archrivals. Second, with our client's new organization presumably set and gathering momentum, we could also see that over the coming months, the rest of the business would be put on the block. However well we had performed, our days were numbered. The choice, given to us by our shifting client, was to compete for the business—what we believed was a disingenuous courtesy—and to take our chances from there.

It's perhaps indelicate to suggest that we ever ran a play on our client. But a lesson in this book and a reality of playmaking is that players run plays on opponents, allies, and independents alike. There are no exceptions that I am aware of. They have to, by necessity, to move their position or agenda forward in a marketplace because no player, however friendly, shares the same objectives or values of another.

Could we have taken our lumps and run a Bear Hug to preserve our good reputation? Yes, but the new client-side team wasn't planning to just let us go. By all appearances, their plans for us looked more like indentured servitude than a fair business deal: *Milk them. Pick off their stars. Dump them.* This friend had turned into a foe, so the complexion of our relationship with the turning client had to change too. Usually, our playmaking skills were reserved for our client's competitors, but this was a fate we didn't deserve and our sources were assuring us that the new management team would quickly implode. It would amount to a mere management spasm, they said. Soon, all would return to normal. *For you, maybe,* we thought. *But what about us?* From this perspective, it was clear that I could either help my new enemy get off the ground or help it self-destruct. All told, we had no choice but to run plays on our dear client, to force its hand, and maybe, just maybe, get the business back.

Our decision, after a good deal of consultation with insiders, advisors, and my own exhausted and disheartened staff, was not to fight the change but, in fact, to accelerate it. Our overarching alpha play was a Preempt, a stratagem dedicated to beating a rival to the punch, and our underpinning beta play was a Pass, in this case a swift and categorical exit from the relationship.

TABLE C. CALLING AND RUNNING A PASS	
Call and run this play because . . .	■ Your strategy or the marketplace has changed. You need to refocus. ■ You may have no choice. You may be beaten or about to get trounced. ■ It stops the bleeding. You need those resources elsewhere. ■ You've reached your mileposts but not your goals. Time to pull the plug. ■ Your program or position is off-strategy, even if you're perceived to be winning or in control. ■ Your exit can be bartered for favors or other strategic assets. ■ You can position the Pass as a strategic or graceful exit, not a desperate surrender. ■ You're beaten and your team needs to recharge. ■ It saves face and saves options. You can get out without anyone noticing.

Of course, our client's new A-Team expected us to compete for the business. *They'll be desperate for it. They'd have to be.* But we knew too much. The likelihood that we'd quickly lose it all to another consultancy was high, and surely our time was better spent looking for good new accounts rather than to try to continue working with a bad one. We needed a strategy that allowed us to take matters into our own hands because self-determination seemed the best means by which we might recover, rally, and prosper.

With the buy-in of my staff and unbeknownst to our waning client and chafing competitors, I presented to the client a letter that invoked the termination clause of our contract. I hadn't resigned the part of the business we thought we'd lose. In fact, I'd resigned it *all,* and by my own doing I'd started the clock that would tick down to our last required day and a cold-turkey departure.

Instead of preparing a certain and futile pitch during the termination period, we went about the business of transitioning the client's various projects and assignments, and most important, we stepped up our outreach to replace the lost business. It was a thrilling, though dangerous, decision but our destiny was at last in the hands of a player we trusted—ourselves.

The Pass that we ran—the wholesale resignation—triggered an entertaining series of movements by the client and our now wide-eyed competitors. It forced the new management team to accelerate its plans to switch consultancies. It also caused the bidding firms to ratchet up their own pitching engines and, perhaps, to get a little too excited. *Did you hear? The whole account's up for bid! Call New York and tell 'em we need resources.*

To do such things to a client seems somehow professionally sinful. But the client—or this iteration of it—was playing with its own rulebook, and we knew it. We had no choice but to make decisions that were not in our mutual interest. On their terms, we were being pushed off a cliff, so we placed the bet and proceeded on ours. To our relief and surprise, we soon replaced most of the lost business and we watched, wide-eyed and with secret hope, as our now former client's new organization began to unravel.

Leading up to our departure, they'd raised expectations to an impressive height, but now they'd been pressed into duty too fast. Their solutions to fill the void were suddenly overpromised and already being underachieved. And, sure enough, just as our insiders predicted, the team never got off the ground, in part because we refused to stay and help them.

Months after resigning the business, we got a call from our old client. New management was in place. The new players wanted to get back on the offense and they wanted *us*—no others—to help them do it. In a few weeks, we had in our hands a new contract that awarded us a bigger budget, a better partnership, and a fresh start. We were back in, and just as important, our rivals were out—hunting again for the business they thought they'd landed. Playmaking is, let's remember, a game of relative competitive advantage, so it was doubly useful (if not sweet) to have back what our competitors had hoped to steal.

In most cases, the Pass is designed to move a player along, to reallocate resources from one competitive setting to another. In this case, it was done with sufficient speed and determination that it also created a safe and improved avenue for returning to the marketplace we'd been forced to abandon. Our master strategy, to

Preempt our unexpected adversary's plan, had worked, perhaps to our surprise. And the Pass had exceeded our wildest dreams.

There are times to fight in a marketplace. There are times to move along. But that doesn't mean that in leaving one shouldn't also run plays. Running a smart Pass can preserve a player's resources and reputation and, sometimes, even get back for the player what it had to give up. I should know.

TABLE D. DECODING AND COUNTERING A PASS	
How do I decode this play? *(i.e., How do I know it's being run against me?)*	■ You might be approached by your rival, seeking concessions for their possible exit. ■ You'll know. You'll read it in the papers, see it in blogs, or get it by word-of-mouth. ■ Or you won't know. Your opponent disappears from view. It can't be engaged, by you or other competitors or players. It's AWOL.
How do I counter this play?	■ Run a Pause. Consider the possibilities and advantages of your rival's withdrawal from the field of play. Amass information and intelligence to determine if the Pass is instead a Red Herring, intended to draw you into a vacuum or a trap. ■ Run a Bait. Invite weaker competitors into the abandoned space to preserve counterpoint and choice. Every market needs jousting partners. ■ Run a Recast. Congratulate the exiting competitor for its efforts to focus marketplace discussion on what *you're* doing right, less on what *they* did wrong. ■ Attack the exiting player with a Call Out to ensure they don't come back and to showcase your competitive wherewithal. ■ Run a Peacock. Sound the trumpet—you just drove out the competition.

RISK

REWARD

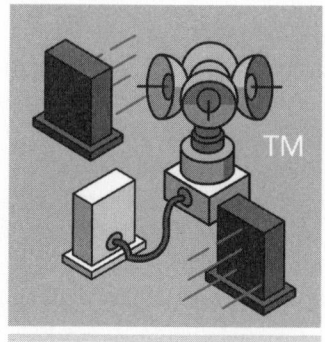

For all the emphasis I put on running plays, positioning and de-positioning, controlling discussions, moving a marketplace, etc., you'd have to think that playmaking is about *doing* things. Even without the go-get-'em verbiage, the mere existence of twenty-five core play types—none of them looking exactly shy—might suggest to practitioners of advocacy, influence, or compromise that playmaking requires a kind of professional kinetic energy to get things done—in New York, Washington, Hollywood, Silicon Valley, Tokyo, Beijing, Mumbai, Paris, London, or wherever you may be.

Maybe.

But inasmuch as playmaking's purpose is to influence and control the sentiments and discussions of a marketplace, its function is not necessarily to go out and, like a cowboy, just start shooting. Successful playmaking is more clever and usually more subtle. In so many words, it can often have more to do with *doing less*. And this is where the Pause figures so prominently in the playmaking mix.

The Pause is the play that serves to hide a player from view and to allow that player to listen to and study the marketplace without the noise of its own footsteps. It also allows a player to modulate its possibly predictable tendencies, to give an opponent a false sense of security for having briefly withdrawn, and, sometimes, to fool an opponent into thinking that it's run a Pass by seeming to have left the marketplace altogether. The Pause, like any play, changes the game but it does so through *omission,* by doing less, not more.

Think of the Pause in playmaking as rests in music. The notes are beautiful, of course, but some believe as I do that it's the silence between the notes that makes the song. To break it up, to vary the delivery, to make the listener guess a little, is very much what makes music such a powerful merging of intelligence and action. Without the silence we'd never hear a thing.

TABLE A. BASICS OF A PAUSE	
Class	Assess
Subclass	Detach
Type	**Pause**
Definition	The strategic suspension of activity by a player, intended to allow the player to assess the opposition and marketplace and let playing conditions ripen.
Upsides	■ Allows a player's strategy to develop and show its full effects. ■ Conditions a player to listen, sense, research, and evaluate. ■ Creates marketplace silence to help a player assess a rival's movements, like a hunter stopping to hear its prey. ■ Improves a player's perspective by stepping back from the playing field. ■ Briefly confuses an opponent. For a moment, there's no one to fight in the ring. ■ Creates a false sense of security in a rival. Makes 'em think they've feasted and you've fled. ■ Conserves a player's resources by eliminating or minimizing marketplace moves.
Downsides	■ Can be used as an excuse by the player to duck an issue, to do nothing. ■ Pause too much and the market may forget you. ■ Can be mistaken by enemies (or even friends) for a Pass, an exit, or retreat by the player. ■ Can cause a player to miss a playmaking opportunity, whether to defend against an opponent's move or exploit a new opening. ■ Can allow others to set the agenda by briefly ceding thought leadership.

Related Terms	■ Listening
	■ Playing dead
	■ Playing possum
	■ Sensing
	■ Stalling
	■ A strategic silence
	■ Suspending
	■ Running silent
Related Play Types	■ Deflect
	■ Pass

Strategic Silence

Sir Winston Churchill, the bellicose leader of the United Kingdom through World War II, famously employed the Pause in a historic May 9, 1940, meeting that resulted in his invitation from England's king George VI to form a national government, fight the Nazi threat, and serve as Britain's new prime minister. The meeting, which included Churchill's political counterpart, Lord Halifax, was called by the sitting prime minister, Neville Chamberlain, whose policies of appeasement toward Germany's Adolf Hitler had backfired. Chamberlain, wanting national unity and having lost his party's support, talked about which of the two—Halifax or Churchill—he should recommend to the king to replace him.

It was no secret that Halifax was Chamberlain's preference. For Churchill, who for years had invited political disfavor for his raw wit and dark warnings of Nazi intentions, the temptation to lobby his own cause was nearly irresistible. Chamberlain and Halifax surely expected as much. But Churchill, at that time first lord of the Admiralty, uncharacteristically said nothing. The consummate orator, the man whose words would later rally his country against German invasion, closed his mouth. He paused, watching to see where his opponents would go. Someone had to talk and it wasn't going to be him.

Silence overtook the room, and finally, Halifax began. At length, he talked about the great difficulties of the coveted post, the anticipated inconveniences and suffering he and the country would face. Churchill still said nothing, and soon, for lack of counterpoint, it became clear that Halifax would be hard-pressed to face the challenge. He talked himself out of a job.

The next day, when the Nazis invaded Holland, Belgium, and Luxembourg, Chamberlain sought to hold on to his post, but it was too late. Political momentum gained the upper hand, and finally, the king called for Churchill to lead the charge.

For all the speeches and writings that distinguish this gifted communicator, Churchill got the nod by *not* speaking, by running a Pause and withdrawing briefly from a critical game and letting his rivals roam, aimlessly in this case, but that was his strategy. He calculated correctly that his stance and his presumed value to the British Crown were well enough understood that levers of the parliamentary marketplace would swing in his direction, with or without a fight from Chamberlain or Halifax. He would not give his opponents anything to disagree with, so for once the British lion did not roar.

TABLE B. EXAMPLES OF A PAUSE	
Pauses to remember . . .	▪ **Chernobyl** On April 26, 1986, in the southwest regions of the former Soviet Union, the fourth reactor of the Chernobyl nuclear power plant caught fire, exploded, and spewed radioactive waste across an entire civilized hemisphere. Millions were caught in the dispersing radioactive cloud and hundreds died while Soviet officials scampered to suppress panic and save face. Two interminable days later, a stone-faced Soviet broadcaster read a forty-three-word statement confirming the devastation. ▪ **Euronext** In 2001, when rumors surfaced that the London-based exchange LIFFE was on the block, it took only a few news cycles for British tabloids to warn that the trading network must be kept for the sake of national prestige. But one bidder, and LIFFE's ultimate acquirer, Euronext, didn't bite. It bypassed the handwringers and worked its case with decision makers directly. ▪ **Winston Churchill** In a crucial meeting with the sitting prime minister, Neville Chamberlain, Winston Churchill uncharacteristically held his tongue as his rival, Lord Halifax, prattled too long and too much about the difficulties of the prime minister's post. The position—and the weight of history—went to Churchill.

Selective Silence

This same instinct was aptly demonstrated more than sixty years later, on the other side of the English Channel and on the business side of public life—by Euronext, the cross-border exchange for the trading of stocks, derivatives, commodities, and currencies. Formed in 2000 as the result of an ambitious merger of the Amsterdam, Brussels, and Paris exchanges, Euronext quickly emerged as a force in the European trading community and a keen rival to notable and powerful counterparts, particularly the German exchange Deutsche Börse Group AG (DBAG) and venerable London Stock Exchange plc (LSE).

Just as Churchill was quintessentially British, the CEO of Euronext, Jean-François Théodore, was quintessentially French and Euronext as a company and culture was purely Continental. This fact represented Euronext's central benefit and, possibly, its Achilles' heel. On one hand, the Euronext exchange spanned major financial centers in the expanding European Union (EU). On the other, it stopped short of the British Isles and the enormously strategic financial center in Britain, the City of London. Jumping the Channel, so to speak, was a crucial next step to Théodore and Euronext. So in the fall of 2001, when a British exchange called LIFFE Holdings plc (London International Financial Futures and Options Exchange) was rumored to be on the selling block, a quick solution to the Euronext gap materialized.

LIFFE was compatible with Euronext and coveted by it for a variety of reasons, not the least of which was its presence and influence in the City. It boasted a complementary mix of products and an elegant online trading system that embodied Euronext's vision for an integrated Pan-European trading platform. It was a perfect fit, except for the fact that Théodore and the whole of his management team were anything but British. When the whispers grew too loud that LIFFE was on the block, it took only a few news cycles for British journalists to set the tone and criteria of the anticipated deal. London's financers, the columnists cooed, would be well-advised to keep LIFFE in the UK family to reinforce London's strategic position in the trading game and preserve British prestige.

This may well have been the handiwork of LSE strategists who were equally motivated to acquire their local counterpart, LIFFE. If the editorializing was not the result of a deft Leak, what is at least clear is that LSE never appeared to refute the conjecture. The LSE's one unique advantage in acquiring LIFFE, after all, was its physical proximity to LIFFE and the common culture, business practices, and traditions of a London institution.

Through subtle playmaking or by willing association of an aroused national pride, the LSE essentially ran a Screen. It used the media as a surrogate to play the London Card and tilt LIFFE toward the LSE and away from Euronext and its German rival,

DBAG. The attempt was to bait the Europeans into an unwinnable public debate. But the LSE would find out later—and too late—that the public didn't have a vote.

Shortly, DBAG confirmed its interest in LIFFE, and immediately, the false threat of Continental encroachment was given a face and a name. Though damned by its obvious association with the EU, Euronext did nothing. Although its interest in LIFFE was widely rumored, it made no initial public disclosures, preferring instead a series of private face-to-face exchanges with LIFFE executives and directors. It sat to the side and watched the public hand-wringing, like Churchill listening to the prattling Lord Halifax. It ran a Pause.

In the end, the LSE lost the competition and a good bit of power, looking more like an acquiree than an acquirer. LIFFE sold to Euronext for an all-cash offer and smoother integration plan of people and technology. DBAG dropped out early. Its ploy, it was speculated, had only been to drive up the price and gain access to valuable information—a Red Herring, if you're taking notes. In this regard, the German exchange successfully penalized its competitors, forcing the winner to pay more, but for Euronext it also served as a stalking horse—a Screen—that drew a good share of attention onto the Germans, thus allowing Euronext to duck the clubby innuendo of prideful British media.

As with Churchill, it isn't so much what Euronext *did* to prevail. It's what it *didn't* do. As much as the LSE favored the Screen—promoting through benign associations the Euro plot—Euronext didn't play ball. It could easily have tried by way of a Recast, saying in effect, *We're not French?! We're European.* It could have run a Call Out, something like *You're not British. You're afraid!* It could have run a Deflect, claiming, *Our culture and our headquarters are irrelevant.* But it didn't. It ran no detectable play except to walk quietly behind the Germans' false overture.

All of this describes a Pause: *The strategic suspension of activity by a player, intended to allow the player to assess the opposition and marketplace and let playing conditions ripen.*

Euronext's best move was just that—strategic silence that allowed it to avoid play action skirmishes and to quietly pursue its agenda. As I wrote earlier, playmaking is not just about shooting your guns. Sometimes it's about holstering them.

TABLE C. CALLING AND RUNNING A PAUSE	
Call and run this play because . . .	■ It's a good time to listen, let things play out, gauge reactions to a play, research a question, set a new plan, etc. ■ You're tired or confused. You need time to think before you act. ■ You need to gather resources and prepare for a new offensive. ■ The marketplace or a competitor is doing what you want it to do—step back and let it roll. ■ A rival is egging you on—running, perhaps, a Bait or issuing a Challenge. It might be a good time to disengage and gather your wits. ■ You're unsure what the competition or the market is doing. You're short on information. ■ You need time to plan. It is often wiser to wait and make the right move than to pounce and waste an opportunity.

Stony Silence

To carry the gunslinger analogy a step further, you could say that the Pause is used to aim rather than fire. An important warning, however, is that the Pause should be used neither too often nor too long. The hard lesson of Aesop's fable "The Boy Who Cried Wolf" should leap to mind, because an overused or abused behavior can increase a player's predictability and decrease the patience and forgiveness of the player's marketplace. Too many cries can mean too few sheep.

This is to say that the Pause, for all its seeming meekness, for as far left on The Playmaker's Table as it is, can sometimes go very wrong if misused or misapplied. To that end, there is hardly a better example of a Pause's misapplication than the nuclear disaster of Chernobyl.

On Saturday morning, April 26, 1986, in the fertile southwest regions of the former Soviet Union, eighty miles north of the Ukrainian city of Kiev, one of the massive four-reactor Chernobyl nuclear power plants malfunctioned during a test, caught fire, exploded, and erupted with a massive, continuous plume of radioactivity. The toxic superheated steam reached a mile into the sky as northwesterly winds spread deadly debris and particles onto the neighboring Belarus breadbasket, over the Baltic Sea, into Sweden and parts of Scandinavia, and onward toward Europe, the UK, and the eastern United States.

By all accounts, the scene at ground zero was pure chaos. There were multiple explosions. The fire, twice the temperature of a steel-mill blast furnace, could hardly be reached, much less slowed, and so it burned for days from a lethal pool of uranium. As events unfolded, entire cities were evacuated in or near Chernobyl and millions were caught in the dispersing radioactive cloud.

You'd think that news like this would make the papers. But the first sign that anything was awry came a full two days later and almost seven hundred miles away, when panicked engineers at a Swedish nuclear power plant detected the first whiffs of the catastrophe. Only then did the global community start asking questions.

Finally, that evening, a stone-faced Soviet broadcaster read this brief statement, a Filter, to be sure: *"An accident has taken place at the Chernobyl power station, and one of the reactors was damaged. Measures are being taken to eliminate the consequences of the accident. Those affected by it are being given assistance. A government commission has been set up."*

That was it. Thousands, perhaps millions, more were in jeopardy. A rich countryside was being poisoned. A massive humanitarian, agricultural, ecological, and economic tar pit was forming.* And for that, the world received forty-three words from an unfazed talking head—two days late.

It's still a shock that such a disaster, with such obvious and deadly potential, could have been so systematically ignored and understated. One wonders if even forty-three words would have been offered had not the Swedes sounded the Free World's alarm. Game theorists, who classify the Chernobyl disaster as a *Duel*, might say no. In a duel, two players—each with one shot—maneuver for the best shot . . . and the first shot. It is a game of timing, and the challenge is to take as much of it as a player dares.

It's obvious now that the Kremlin missjudged the game, in large measure because of its loyalty to the Pause. Ignoring the awful reality of a fast-spreading irradiated cloud, the Soviets hungered for time—to understand the crisis and formulate a strategy for either hiding it or minimizing its impact. But they shot too late and lost.

When finally forced to go public, they attempted the anemic forty-three-word Filter, offering only the barest subset of the available facts and information. A week later, their choice was to run a Call Out, launching attacks on what they characterized as hyperbolic accounts of the western media. Eighteen days after the explosions,

---

* While estimates of the Chernobyl death toll still fluctuate, hundreds are presumed to have perished on or shortly after the explosions and thousands are thought to have died or are predicted to die over coming generations.

Soviet president Mikhail Gorbachev talked publicly for the first time on national television, acknowledging the disaster (a Bear Hug), restating casualty figures (a Recast), admonishing western politicians and their media (a Call Out), and intoning the dangers of the nuclear age (a Screen) in what amounted to an attempt to recalibrate and downgrade the gravity of the crisis. While delivered with a good deal more empathy it was, still, another bad call in a series of playmaking mistakes.

What should the Soviets have done? Through the rearview mirror of history, Chernobyl is not too much different from any other crisis—whether an accident, oversight, or crime. The better plays to have run fall solidly in the Freezing subclass. The Lantern, where a player takes the initiative and tells the bad news first, or the Disco, where the player makes full and unmistakable apologies, would have held more promise for tamping down the tragedy or even turning it to the advantage of the budding era of glasnost. Anything else, at least in the case of Chernobyl, would have been a dodge.

Churchill, Euronext, and the last Soviet leaders share the common distinction of having met marketplace noise with silence, of having done *nothing* really to advance their strategic positions. You'd almost wonder if this qualifies as a play at all except that the results—famous and infamous as they may be—were unmistakably due to a conscious decision to button the lips. Churchill's silence was strategic. Euronext's was selective. Chernobyl's was disastrous. And for that, histories were written and fates were cast.

TABLE D. DECODING AND COUNTERING A PAUSE	
How do I decode this play? (i.e., How do I know it's being run against me?)	■ When your competitor won't respond, but you know it's still there. ■ When your opponent's normal pattern of activity ceases. When it gets too quiet.
How do I counter this play?	■ You may not want to. Your opponent may have surrendered or moved on. Run your own Pause to see if it's true. ■ But if you want your competition back in the game . . . run a Bait. ■ Now is your time to attack; the marketplace is yours. Run a Peacock to boldly claim your position. ■ You have the stage. You can calmly run a Fiat to state your position. ■ Recast your rival's Pause as a victory for you or a failure for them.

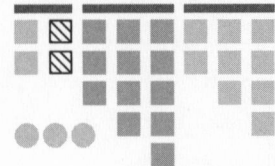

The Test Subclass

If a player is not ready to bail from a marketplace or to briefly watch it from the wings, as happens in the preceding Detach subclass, there are fully seven other ways in which to get onstage, again depending on where among the subclasses you land. This next subclass, Test, gives a player the best opportunity to edge its way into a marketplace, to feel it out, and vice versa.

> def. **Test:** *Play action that sizes up the issues, ideas, events, or developments of a marketplace and forecasts a player's needs or wishes.*

This subclass, which encompasses two of the most nuanced plays—Ping and Trial Balloon—serves a twofold purpose: to understand a marketplace and its component parts and to drop hints of what a player wants or hopes to do. It allows players to gauge reactions but also to experiment.

You should not mistake the Test subclass as the place in The Playmaker's Table where playmakers do their research. As I explain in "The Playmaker's Process," p. 275, research is one of three critical success factors to playmaking, but it's not a class, subclass, or play type in the taxonomy of playmaking. Research in playmaking happens at *every* stage of the playmaking process and it feeds off all forms of data collection—from primary to secondary, deductive to inductive, business intelligence to market intelligence, communication research to opposition research, anecdotes to rumors. The Ping and Trial Balloon do allow players to gather primary or original information, but their techniques are so self-serving that the findings they glean should be carefully scrutinized and probably supplemented with more uninfluenced data collection techniques.

In any case, the moves and countermoves of a testing player are part and parcel to checking signal strength, confirming authority, and understanding better how ideas will go down or be taken down. Here, now, are the full stories of the Ping and Pause.

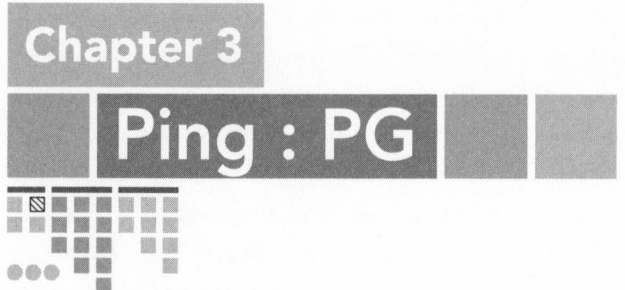

Chapter 3

Ping : PG

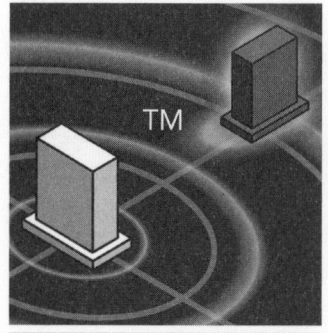

Leonardo da Vinci, the great Italian inventor, artist, and engineer of the fifteenth century, was a very curious fellow. One day, leaning over the side of a boat, he dipped one end of a hollow tube half into the drink and listened, an ear pressed into the tube's other end. Almost two thousand years earlier, Aristotle had postulated that sound could be transmitted through water, so perhaps he was following up.

What da Vinci observed was that by this strange technique the sounds of distant oceangoing vessels could be heard. In A.D. 1490, that discovery must have amounted to an act of pure magic, but it served to spur interest in underwater sound and five hundred years later gave rise to the sophisticated technique of sound navigation and ranging, dubbed *sonar*. This, of course, is a sophisticated technique for navigating and detecting subsurface objects and features. And this is where the Ping comes in.

Ping is the word given to the sound of a pulse of audible energy as it travels through water (many times faster than it does in air, it turns out). Emitted as a single round or unleashed in a stream of popping acoustic bullets, it's used by military patrols, ocean liners, and fishing boats alike to detect everything from enemy vessels to looming icebergs to schooling tuna. Also known as *active sonar*, a Ping is the man-made version of the mechanism by which bats echolocate yummy airborne bugs, how dolphins communicate with each other, and how deep-diving whales steer clear of deep-drilling oil rigs.

Water is where Ping got its start, but it found a new home as the Internet took hold. In 1983, a young computer engineer named Michael Muuss developed a compact script of programming code to help connected computers make contact with other computers—network speak for *Are you there?* Inspired by sonar, Muuss called his short script simply and appropriately *Ping.** The program was immediately adopted as a standard for checking the online status of Web sites, servers, and networked devices everywhere, and today it's what your IT guy means when he says, *I pinged Yahoo. . . . You're up.*

Influenced and informed by technology as we are, it's no surprise that Ping has been absorbed into our urban lexicon, from bankers to teenagers. Now, instead of the usual business-card swap, we sometimes suggest a digital exchange of details by e-mail. *Ping me your info and I'll ping you back.* Among the text messaging set, it's akin to a digital nod or nudge, to let a friend know you're online, to see if they've checked in or, maybe, checked out. *Have you seen Jennifer? I pinged her this morning. Maybe she's grounded.* Finally, among online gamers, its part of the lingo for the rapid-fire moves of cyber play. *Low ping bastard!*[†]

From da Vinci's imagination to the invention of sonar and, finally, to the net culture, Ping has come a long way. But there's one more step to take. Because it so closely describes a discrete activity of playmaking, it deserves yet another adaptation.

TABLE A. BASICS OF A PING

Class	Assess
Subclass	Test
Type	**Ping**
Definition	An oblique reference or suggestion, enabled either by a player's mere presence in a marketplace or its implied interest in topics, ideas, events, and developments.

---

* One of Muuss's collaborators is said to have reduced Ping to PING, for *Packet InterNet Grouper*. But to Muuss, Ping was an analogy to sonar and never intended as an acronym.

† Pinging has other meanings, both popular and obscure. It's that chattering sound in your car engine, sometimes the result of cheap, low-octane gas. It was also once a peculiar requirement of West Point military plebes, forced to walk through academy hallways, deliberate and erect, with one shoulder always touching the nearest wall.

Upsides	■ Allows a player to work from the sidelines—to size up its competition without engaging it directly. ■ Brings a player in close but just beyond the reach of an opponent, giving the player more direct experience and understanding of the rival, its makeup and tendencies. ■ Can be used to jostle an opponent, to raise its suspicions, without alerting it to the player's specific moves or motives. ■ Adds to research techniques and helps verify findings (e.g., competitive analysis, opposition research). ■ A subtle Ping gives the player plausible deniability. ■ If an opponent doesn't see you, if they don't perceive you to be behind the play, they'll show themselves.
Downsides	■ A Ping is so subtle that its intended target may miss the point. ■ If your opponent is ultrasensitive, it can draw a reaction more pronounced than your simple Ping. ■ A botched Ping can blow your cover. Worse, it can give the rival an unintended advantage. ■ Pings can take time to process. If you need fast results, you might consider a more overt play.
Related Terms	■ Dropping hints ■ Pulsing ■ Rattling a cage ■ Soft-sounding ■ A tap on the shoulder
Related Play Types	■ Fiat ■ Screen ■ Trial Balloon

Hint Rate

If you've ever made a probing phone call to an associate, a friend, or even your mom, hoping that the mere act of dialing them up would send a signal, you might have run a Ping. The same might be true if you've ever dropped a hint for a gift or a favor, whispered a concern, or nodded knowingly in someone's direction.

A Ping is an oblique reference or suggestion, enabled by a player's mere presence in a marketplace or by its implied interest in topics, ideas, events, and develop-ments. Think of the pinging boss who enters a prolonged brainstorming session, doing nothing but raising an eyebrow—all to say, *Nothing yet, hmmm?* Recall the HBO television series character Livia Soprano, who coolly suggests to her brother-in-law, Uncle Jun, that her own son, Tony Soprano, should get whacked. *Tony's running the show behind your back, and did I mention he's in therapy? God knows what he's telling that shrink.* This is all to say, *Assert yourself now, you wimp, or Tony will take you down.*

This nearly describes the Ping's close cousin, the Trial Balloon. Both sit far to the left in The Playmaker's Table, where the element of confrontation is only barely evi-dent and where both are often run with limited degrees of accountability. But differ-ent from the Ping, the Trial Balloon is used to ask questions against *unknown* factors and to measure reaction. The Ping's purpose is to make suggestions against a *de-cided* agenda and to monitor reaction.

TABLE B. EXAMPLES OF A PING	
Pings to remember . . .	■ *Gambling* Poker tables are often punctuated with Pings, the side comments of trash-talking card sharks. Players lightly rib their opponents to watch for their reactions. ■ *Greenspan* In a meandering 1996 awards lecture before Washington policymakers, Fed chief Alan Greenspan buried a two-word but incendiary phrase in his plodding forty-three-hundred-word talk—*irrational exuberance.* It chilled the market and planted a seed of caution. ■ *The Sopranos* Livia Soprano coolly suggests to her brother-in-law, Uncle Jun, that her own son, Tony Soprano, should get whacked. *"Tony's running the show behind your back, and did I mention he's in therapy? God knows what he's telling that shrink."* This is all to say, *Assert yourself now, you wimp, or Tony will take you down.*

Citing the practitioners of the Ping is a little like sighting Elvis. Why? Because the Ping is extraordinarily subtle. As such, the question of who runs Pings is more a mat-ter of inference than implication—it might be a Ping; it might be your imagination. Take, for instance, the capable playmaker, the retired chairman of the Federal Re-serve, Alan Greenspan.

From 1987 to 2006, world markets hung on the central bank boss's every word, wondering if, when, and to what degree the economist might raise or lower the discount rate for borrowing money and whether his many public utterances hinted at or hid his plans. Greenspan knew this, of course, but because Congress condones hinting and not lecturing by the head of the Fed, he was careful in his selection of plays. Baits would seem capricious, for instance. Challenges would cross the line too. So Greenspan ran Pings, plays that frequently reminded the marketplace of his position but were hardly enough to tell it precisely in what direction or at what speed he wanted it to move. Like a submarine sending the proverbial *one ping only,* he gave his constituents enough information to know what he'd *prefer* to see them do without having to *tell* them or, if necessary, *do* it for them. He hinted and suggested more than he demanded or challenged.

To ensure that no one mistook his subtle Pings for more overt and over-the-line plays, Greenspan from time to time attempted to dissuade market makers that his words were as bankable as his deeds. To do this, he didn't run Pings. He ran Red Herrings. Here are two famously elliptical quotes that helped to keep Fed watchers off balance:

- ■ *"I know you believe you understand what you think I say, but I am not sure you realize that what you heard is not what I meant."*

- ■ *"I guess I should warn you that if I seem unduly clear to you, you've probably misunderstood what I've said."*

Statements like this gave Greenspan the air cover he needed to drop his bombshell hints with relative impunity and expand his fiduciary prerogative from congressional testimonies and presidential consultations to the global mainstream media. Take for example a meandering 1996 awards lecture that Greenspan delivered to Washington policy makers. In a forty-three-hundred-word talk, he asked a wonky but rational question about something he so famously called irrational.

"How do we know when irrational exuberance has unduly escalated asset values, which then become the subject of unexpected and prolonged contractions as they have in Japan over the past decade?"

It wasn't so much a comment on Japan as it was a rather pregnant observation—that the economic run-up of the 1990s wasn't really as *exuberant* as it was just plain *crazy.* It gave away—or seemed to give away—the chairman's wariness of a happily bullish market and it left many observers to wonder if he was right and if he'd do something about it . . . like raise interest rates. Either way, the two electric words of his plodding speech—*irrational exuberance*—were picked up, and sure enough, they shocked and briefly sheared the expanding global financial markets, particularly un-witting Japanese investors. The message had been sent.

If you were a Fed follower, you had to ask yourself, *Did he do that on purpose? Or was he just talking?*

You'd be right to argue that his play was more of a Recast than a Ping. Perhaps a Mirror, too, or even a Trial Balloon. True, he might have been rebranding the bullish market as bearish (a Recast). But his speech was so interwoven and even cryptic that you'd have to wonder if the Fed chairman was more intent on alerting the market-place to an approaching bear than shooing the bull away. He might have been trying to blow the whistle on a marketplace gone bad (a Mirror). But his style was not sensa-tional or alarmist. He might have been floating the idea of a tighter-fisted monetary policy (a Trial Balloon). But he wasn't *really* asking a question the way trial ballooners do. He knew the answer already; he wanted to subtly suggest it and then test the marketplace's reaction to it.

Greenspan knew that rhetoric was a privilege of his job, not a right, so for the fac-ile Fed chief, the Ping was the perfect medium to push and prod global economies. It was his patented way of saying, *You, there . . . the ones having so much fun in the bull market . . . I'm watching you.* Even more, it was his way to see if investors could or would take a hint.

While Greenspan can be painted as a cagey sea captain, pinging the shoals for enemy inflation, his reputation for playing the game sometimes put Fed gawkers in overdrive. One TV news network picked up Pings where there were probably none—in the peculiar form of the chairman's briefcase. On the mornings when Greenspan would meet with the Federal Open Market Committee (FOMC), his last necessary step to setting a new interest rate, the Fed chief was followed by a veritable press scrum, all snapping shots of Greenspan and the modest leather pouch he regularly heaved under his arm. A bulging case, some smartly speculated, meant a certain hike or a cut. If Greenspan was planning one, he'd no doubt be loaded for bear. He'd have prepared more, read more, and taken more to drive his agenda through the committee.

If Greenspan was having fun with us, perhaps stuffing his briefcase with bagels instead of statistics, he deserves scorn and mention in some playmaker's Hall of Infamy. These wouldn't have just been deft Pings; they'd have been outrageous Red Herrings. But given his duties and the careful way in which he wove his words, it's unlikely that Greenspan was trying to throw anyone offtrack. That he continued to carry his briefcase up the steps to FOMC meetings, in fact, suggests all the more that he soon improvised against the briefcase hysteria and ran yet another series of reinforcing Pings. It was part of his act. Or was it?

TABLE C. CALLING AND RUNNING A PING	
Call and run this play because . . .	▪ It's a low-impact way to get close to your competitors, to pulse or profile them, to see how they measure up. ▪ It allows you to determine location or disposition of a rival, to lock on and track it. ▪ You want your competitor to know you're there, perhaps as a prelude to a Bait, but not to react—not yet. ▪ You want to test the marketplace for follow-on play action. ▪ You want to drop the hint and see what they'll do with it. You can't come right out and say it, but you can subtly suggest it. ▪ You need more insight into your rival than what passive or noninvasive techniques (i.e., focus groups and opposition research) can give you. ▪ Your research or your gut says you need to know more. ▪ You're commencing a "slow burn" initiative, best perhaps to start with a Ping. ▪ You want your opponent to think it was their idea.

The Ping is not reserved for privileged playmakers, like Alan Greenspan, nor is it as tricky to run as this analysis might suggest. In fact, it's probably among the most common play types because it's based on a person's natural, habitual, and very human tendency to send hints and obliquely, but affirmatively, express his view or suggest an outcome.

It's what salespeople do when they sigh suggestively and ask their competitor's customer, *So what'd you think of that awful new ad campaign?* The competitor's ad campaign, that is. It's what politicians do when they jauntily spring from their plane with the peppy family dog—or trudge away with brooding advisors. It's what probing press agents do while talking to the media—*What's your take on that story this morning?* It's what CEOs do when they visit a factory floor during union negotiations, or a customer at the quarter's close. By their words or actions they all send signals, all in various attempts to set the context for what's important and to take measure of their hinted intentions.

This verges, of course, on play types that reside under the Condition class of playmaking and the Divert, Frame, and Freeze subclasses, where strategy and execution conspire to actively *bend* the direction of marketplace sentiments and situations. But, for the most part, the Ping is for testing and assessing a marketplace. It's run for the purpose of conveying a point or supporting a point of view and, in so doing, understanding if and to what degree a marketplace and its players, friend or foe, might react as a consequence.

A good Ping is like a fly that buzzes by. A player swats at it. It flies away unharmed, noted and mostly forgotten. But the player has been profiled by the pinging fly. A bad Ping is more like a bee, swarming or even stinging. It alerts a player to trouble and forces an unintended reaction. If Alan Greenspan adds a few reports to his briefcase, it raises eyebrows and invites speculation. If he adds a few *more* reports and the briefcase buckle breaks, it raises eyebrows and invites panic. And so it goes with the Ping, a fine-tuned play that makes us scratch our heads and worry that maybe we should be paying better attention, that somebody's got a better idea.

TABLE D. DECODING AND COUNTERING A PING	
How do I decode this play? (i.e., How do I know it's being run against me?)	▪ You won't if it's done well. A good Ping is like a fly that buzzes by. You swat at it; it flies away unharmed. It's all but forgotten. ▪ A bad Ping is more like a bee, swarming or even stinging. It alerts you to trouble and usually forces you to retreat or attack. ▪ You have a brainstorm. Did someone put the idea in your head?
How do I counter this play?	▪ Run a Pause. Limit your reactions because these are what a Ping is trying to gauge.. ▪ Run a Red Herring or Bait. React in a way that is out-of-character so as to give the pinger bad intelligence. ▪ Run a Mirror. Expose the shy pinger as a deliberate manipulator. ▪ Run a Preempt. Claim credit for the pinger's brilliant idea.

A day after the September 11, 2001, attacks on New York and Washington, D.C., a human rights activist and tenured professor of ethnic studies at the University of Colorado in Boulder penned his own analysis of the terror plots and their aftermath. In an essay entitled "Some People Push Back: On the Justice of Roosting Chickens," Ward Churchill took the very unfashionable stance that, well, maybe Americans deserved it.

He brazenly compared fated white collar workers in the fallen World Trade Center towers to Hitler's dutiful deporter of Jews to concentration camps, *little [Adolf] Eichmanns,* he called them, and he suggested that the politicians who called the attacks cowardly were no less zealous than erstwhile Nazis. His broader point: Americans are hypocrites for the terrorism they've committed themselves and no one should be too surprised.

It was fully three and a half years later, when Ward Churchill was slated to speak at a small upstate New York college, that his heat-seeking essay came to light. Tipped off by a Googling professor, the student newspaper of Hamilton College ran a story about the provocateur who would be coming to town, a seemingly sympathetic voice to the Twin Tower terrorists. This was all too much for grieving New Yorkers to endure and all too luscious a news nugget for New York–based big media to ignore.

A media circus ensued, but it wasn't fueled just by the caustic writings or Churchill's combative personal style. It was also that his thesis transgressed so many hallowed territories and assumptions, from foreign policy to world wars, genocide, homeland security, and terrorism to academic freedom and freedom of speech. The story could be covered and played in so many ways and for so many news cycles.

Initial reaction and coverage amounted to a wholesale denunciation of the little-known scholar, happily teed up by conservative bloggers and driven hard by the mainstream media. CNN's Paula Zahn conducted an early interview with the unrepentant professor, a just interrogation or an inquisition, depending on your politics. Bill O'Reilly jumped in, too, declaring it his personal mission to block and belittle the heretic. Out west and back home, a Denver radio talk show raised the specter of treason and hinted at a just punishment for Churchill—execution. The Colorado governor labeled him anti-American and called for his firing. And, finally, the university's board of regents, already embattled by a football recruiting scandal, apologized publicly on Churchill's behalf and initiated a broad investigation. They wanted him out, and to get him out they would focus not only on his academic life but on his work as an activist and his works as an artist. Reports of plagiarism and the possibility that Churchill overstated his military credentials and Native American ancestry would be flushed out, too, they promised.

But Churchill wouldn't budge and he quickly inherited a loose coalition of supporters to back him and broadcast his threatened rights. It was a standoff, and from the point of view of state and university officials, it was a crisis that was costing Colorado dearly in political capital and academic credibility.

The pressure, then, to remove Churchill was enormous. But so were the legal and social complexities of doing so. A legal case based largely on freedom of speech would surely amplify Churchill's voice, and besides, the university could lose. As well, any public efforts to pressure or further ostracize the professor could only enrage his allies, mostly defenders of human and academic rights, and all quite vocal. Then, as could happen only in America, scent of a compromise soon filled the air. A financial buyout was rumored, and it was carried out in the form of a tried-and-true play, well used by cautious playmakers, the Trial Balloon.

On Sunday, February 27, 2005, *The Denver Post* quoted officials, two people familiar with internal university discussions, that the regents were considering a six- to seven-figure settlement to make the rogue professor—and a bad public headache—go away.

TABLE A. BASICS OF A TRIAL BALLOON

Class	Assess
Subclass	Test
Type	**Trial Balloon**
Definition	The preview and testing of preliminary ideas or tentative plans. To reduce a player's exposure, Trial Balloons are often run without attribution to the player or positioned as temporary.
Upsides	■ Sets a tone: Conditions an organization or even an entire marketplace to begin thinking or moving in a given direction. ■ Breaks the ice: Smooths a player's transition from one position to another: ■ Provides the player real feedback from the player's marketplace. ■ Tests reactions to ideas whose consequences are not fully understood. ■ Allows the player to fine-tune an offering or agenda. ■ Leaves room for a player to quickly endorse a position (with a Bear Hug, Peacock, Fiat, or Preempt) or safely abandon it (with a Pass). ■ Conditions the marketplace for change by setting expectations and defining the terms for discussion or debate. ■ Serves to hedge the costs of launches and new initiatives. ■ Gives the player plausible deniability in case the balloon gets popped.
Downsides	■ Can waste precious time. If the idea is that good, go with it and grab mind-share or market share while you can. ■ Can telegraph a player's intentions, allowing a rival to Preempt an avenue of opportunity. ■ Used too often, the Trial Balloon may be taken as a decision. ■ If detected by competitors, a Trial Balloon can position a player as wishy-washy, cowardly, or even manipulative.
Related Terms	■ Floating an idea ■ A straw man
Related Play Type	■ Ping

Testing Interests

Just as in meteorology, a balloon had been launched, though not this time by weathermen and not to test and transmit air quality data. This one was sent high into the media sphere by university surrogates (most likely Plants) who fed big news to a big paper (most likely a Leak) to test public sentiment and see if the embattled professor had a price. Perhaps the research had been done, focus groups or overnight opinion polls, as examples, but it's unlikely that anyone was really very sure of how the community, a nation, or rabid media would react to such a cold and material tactic for resolving such an intimate and social controversy. *This professor's exploiting his freedoms! This university is stealing his freedoms!* So the balloon was launched, lofted for three very important purposes:

- Send a clear but revocable signal to Churchill (one that could later be hedged or plausibly denied) that the University of Colorado was ready to deal.

- Smoke out Churchill, to calibrate his posture and potential. The regents simply needed to know if Churchill would take the money and take off.

- Stimulate reaction by Churchill, his champions, and the university's supporters too.

This all might seem a little overcautious. But to have approached Churchill directly would have weakened the university's negotiating stance, and certainly, it would have given Churchill more cause to crow. With a Trial Balloon, however, the regents could more safely navigate the prickly landscape and if all hell broke loose, if for example the reporting was botched or Churchill publicly mocked the overture, the regents could back out by running another play, a Deflect. They could claim that the *Post*'s sources were bad or that their queries were taken out of context.

As is the reward of well-run plays, the regents got plenty for their playmaking efforts. The rumored sum and the very idea of compromise brought both sides of the public debate off the bench and, again, spurred another round of national acrimony. But Churchill, the primary target of the Trial Balloon, was more restrained. Instead of another venomous Call Out, something like *You can't buy me!*, the balloon elicited a more encouraging response and yielded the following insights:

- It was Churchill's attorney who fielded the reporter's call, a sure sign that the professor was also on a legal footing but also an indicator that the university could work the problem through more rational and less public legal channels.

■ Churchill, said the lawyer, had not been contacted about a buyout. This may or might not have been true—people fib, especially to reporters—but to say this on the record was a skilled attempt to position Churchill as a party to an offer, not a party to a negotiation. The attorney dutifully reminded the *Post* of his first concern—protecting Churchill's constitutional freedoms, a notable bow shot to the regents. *We know our rights. We can play this rough if you want.*

■ But, most important, Churchill's attorney said he'd listen. *"If they offer ten million dollars, I would think about it. If they offer him ten dollars, I wouldn't,"* the lawyer was quoted as saying. Bingo.

Did this save the university face or merely prolong its agony? It's a matter of speculation. Negotiations did ensue briefly but then broke off, and to muddy the waters further, two members of the university's investigation soon resigned. It's safe to assume, however, that the Trial Balloon saved the university some increment of further embarrassment by sharpening its understanding of the public reaction to a buyout and, through the olive branch of a rumored negotiation, padding down and blurring the sharp lines of disagreement that feed scandal-hungry media and bloggers.

As it stands, Ward Churchill remains in his protected post, a rock star activist to some, a seditious fraud to others, but surely the target of a well-run Trial Balloon.

TABLE B. EXAMPLES OF A TRIAL BALLOON

Trial Balloons to remember . . .	■ **Disney** In 2005, Disney teamed with Apple to test the burgeoning marketplace for portable iPod video. With its cache of popular mainstream movies, animations, and TV shows, Disney saw that the time to jump in was sooner, not later.
	■ **Professor Activist** In February 2005, hoping to remove the rogue professor and so-called terrorist sympathizer Ward Churchill from his post at the University of Colorado, university regents leaked word of a six- to seven-figure package.
	■ **Comic Books** The Maryland Department of Education in 2005 used the rebirth in comic books to create a reading on-ramp for slow-to-read students.

Testing Markets

Trial Balloons aren't only a tool for navigating threats. In fact, they're quite commonly employed to explore for and measure opportunities. In the auto industry, you can see them in the form of futuristic concept cars, not quite ready for prime time but enough to make your eyes pop out and to give carmakers a pulse on the bells and whistles that rev your engine: *I'd buy it for thirty K. No way for forty K.* In the fashion industry, they can be found on the catwalks of New York and Paris, startling new lines that turn heads and turn the tables on what'll be in and what'll be out: *Pink is the new black.* In sports, they can come in the form of clubhouse chatter, quips perhaps from a manager contemplating his lineup: *Maybe we'll just play Jeter in center field . . .* In Hollywood, they can be run as advance showings of new films, strategically screened to handpicked audiences, gossip rags, and Web sites—all to calculate acceptance and commensurate investment in the flick: *Leonardo DiCaprio tries fatherhood in this rollicking family comedy.* And in politics, where the Trial Balloon is used and perhaps abused, you'll see them in the form of posturing politicians, testing for voter reaction to oblique statements: *I'd like to think that in America, marriage is possible for all, not impossible for a few.*

In the mainstream of commerce the Trial Balloon is the equivalent of the test market. It's what good marketers do to see what'll sell, how it should be positioned, where it should be priced, in what geography and demographic it should be sold and through what channel. It can be modestly implemented, like a hand delivery of a new faster-rising dough to New York pastry chefs. It can be a moderately scaled, tightly controlled pilot like the deployment of kid-finder transmitters in a hundred teen mobile phones. And it can be applied in a broadly controlled distribution like the offer of business class sleepers from L.A. to London.

TABLE C. CALLING AND RUNNING A TRIAL BALLOON

Call and run this play because . . .	<ul><li>You don't know if the dog can hunt. You don't know if a new idea or some modification to your position in the marketplace will be cheered or chided.</li><li>You need real data on a little-understood or controversial idea.</li><li>You want to get the ball rolling. You want to send a message that the future lies in new ideas, not in the present course.</li><li>You can gracefully withdraw if the Trial Balloon's a bust.</li><li>Your approach represents a large shift from tradition or convention.</li><li>Your own confidence is low and scrutiny is high.</li><li>You're coming off a mistake. Better to be cautious with your next step.</li></ul>

Take, for example, the fast work of the Walt Disney Company and the Trial Balloon it launched in 2005 to calibrate and navigate the burgeoning marketplace for portable video. With its cache of popular mainstream movies, animations, and TV shows, Disney saw that the time to jump in was sooner, not later. Who would download *Finding Nemo*, how often, and at what price was guesswork, so for Disney it made sense to figure out the answers only from the inside looking out, not vice versa, and to use its first-mover advantage to help build and thus influence the nascent market. So it cut an early deal with Apple to become the first content provider for the new video-enabled iPod, making several of its hit ABC shows, such as *Lost* and *Desperate Housewives*, available to iTunes downloaders—all for tidy sum of $1.99 an episode.*

Disney's Trial Balloon is big-league hardball, but the play's application has marketplace range. It might seem pedestrian by comparison, but a Trial Balloon was run in 2004 by the state of Maryland's Department of Education in connection with a creative reading program. Noting the rebirth of kids' comic books, administrators designed a pilot program that put the likes of Donald Duck and Batman into its students' hands, from kindergarten to high school. The Trial Balloon wasn't to see if students would pick them up. They did, happily. The play was to see if the genre would create an on-ramp to serious literature and if educators and parents would trade a little goofy humor or a little superhero violence for a little love of reading.

Unless you've opted to run a Pass (to move on and not play) or a Pause (to let your rival play through), the Trial Balloon is about as cautious an approach to play-making as any playmaker can take. But a well-run Trial Balloon can yield a bounty of feedback and hence a windfall of precious, direct insight for new play action and improved competitive advantage. It helped a major university silence a dissident professor and to recover its academic luster. And it helped to pop Disney on your play list and create yet another path from the Magic Kingdom into your home. In either case, it's a useful play to run, whether you're trying to slow a marketplace freight train or speed one up.

---

* Disney's experiment with Apple wasn't just a test to see if it could sell portable video, it was a test of Disney employees by its new CEO, Robert Iger, to see if the troops would respond as innovators or spectators.

TABLE D. DECODING AND COUNTERING A TRIAL BALLOON

How do I decode this play? *(i.e., How do I know it's being run against me?)*	■ Pay attention to the throwaway line, the kind of thing that's said or done as someone walks out the door . . . an "Oh-by-the-way . . ." remark. These are often the launch pads for clever Trial Balloons. ■ Know what issues your competitor is fighting for and map these against their words and deeds, however subtle or casual. ■ Monitor a rival's Proxies—likely suspects for floating an idea. ■ You hear rumors that a rival's test-marketing a new product or has something in the works. ■ Your opponent keeps talking about new things that can't be done, so maybe it's discovered a way to do them.
How do I counter this play?	■ Run a Label or Bear Hug to tie your opponent to its own balloon. ■ Run a Recast/Challenge combination to rework the Trial Balloon into a yes-or-no question (e.g., "So do you or don't you think an alternative minimum tax is a good idea!?") ■ Run a Mirror by rerunning, retelling, or republishing a rival's casual remark . . . over and over and over. ■ Recruit surrogates to flatter or fault the Trial Balloon depending upon what's best for your position. ■ If you can deliver the idea rather than talk about it, run a Preempt.

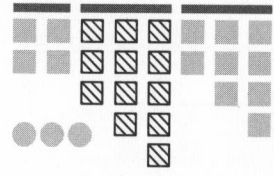

The Condition Class

Between the extremes of the playmaking spectrum are plays that have the means to shift a marketplace and its players—whether a foe, friend or bystander—but which generally shun a confrontation, shy away from direct attention or, for whatever reason, prefer collaboration over division. Here, there are three subclasses and 12 play types, the lion's share of playmaking options in a class called Condition.

> def. **Condition:** *Moderate, often indirect, encouragement or suppression of actions to influence or reform the sentiments of players and marketplaces.*

Players operating in this class are the shapers, groomers, water-warmers, ground-softeners, and otherwise Socratic dialoguers who prepare markets for new ideas, tamp down harmful trends, and accentuate good ones.

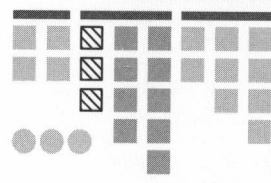

The Divert Subclass

Within the Condition class there are many approaches to greasing the skids of a marketplace but, among these, the Divert subclass is perhaps the most difficult to describe in any delicate way. This is because it serves largely as a mechanism for clearing out or clearing away opposing positions and agendas that might otherwise impact or harm a player.

> def. **Divert:** *Play action that distracts a player or re-routes its intended course of action.*

Diverting plays—the Deflect, Leak and Red Herring—are capable of keeping a player on-strategy and rivals off its back. Deflects help players buy time. Leaks help keep players on course. And Red Herrings help players send opponents off course. They all serve the purpose of keeping uncooperative elements of a marketplace in safer places, perhaps to be cultivated and brought into the tent, or perhaps to be shut out of it.

This kind of playmaking might be chilling to some because it offends their sense of fair play. Others might see it as necessary and just part of the game. In either case, these are not necessarily plays that I condone or mean to promote; they are merely plays that I know to exist and to be commonly employed by players of all kinds. The next three chapters on the Deflect, Leak, and Red Herring tell the whole story.

Chapter 5

Deflect : DF

RISK → REWARD →

Right now Mercury is in a corner perfectly aligned with my star. Mercury is no good, so if it's not good, I am going to request not to speak.

—Thailand's Prime Minister Thaksin Shinawatra, explaining to reporters in late 2004 why he wouldn't be answering questions until 2005

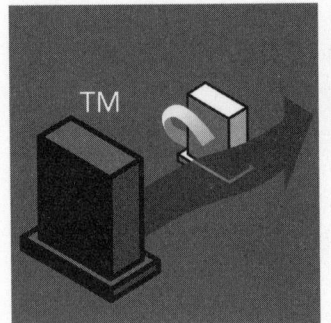

Being cornered is sometimes inevitable in the playmaking game. As much as you might try to stay on the offense, as much as the marketplace might follow your lead, things don't always go as planned and not every circumstance can be foreseen. And so, from time to time, players get pinned.

Think of the retired home-run hitter Mark McGwire when, in 2005, he and four other major leaguers were summoned before the House Government Reform Committee to testify under oath what they knew about the use of steroids in Major League Baseball. They had no choice but to face frothing lawmakers, all determined to make a show and clean up America's favorite pastime. Here's how each superstar handled the high-profile inquisition.

Baseball's bad boy and kiss-and-tell author Jose Canseco ran a Peacock. Basking in the camera lights, the former Oakland A's star boasted that steroids in baseball were *"as acceptable in the eighties and mid-to-late nineties as a cup of coffee."* Baltimore Oriole Sammy Sosa was more taciturn, running a Filter with the demeanor of an earnest schoolboy. *"Everything I have heard about steroids and human growth hormones is that they are very bad for you."* He didn't say he did, and he didn't say he didn't. His teammate, first baseman Rafael Palmeiro, who weeks later would test positive for steroids, ran a resolute Fiat, a deadpanned denial: *"I have never used steroids. Period. I do not know how to say it any more clearly than that."* And the celebrated Red Sox pitcher Curt Schilling, thought to be the lone empaneled Boy Scout, shunned Canseco and ran a Bear Hug: *"I think the fear of public embarrassment and humiliation upon being caught is going to be greater than any player ever imagined."*

McGwire's situation was different, however, and so were expectations of his testimony. He had already admitted to using steroids during his playing days. Though the substances he'd ingested were legal at the time and weaker by current standards, Big Mac had copped to pumping performance-enhancing drugs and so he was naturally expected to lay it all out. It would be a great day for the man who in 1998 broke Roger Maris's hallowed single-season home run record and helped rekindle the nation's love for baseball. Perhaps, like Schilling, he'd run a Bear Hug, or maybe a made-for-media Disco, a very big apology by the humbled hero and a very big request for the public's forgiveness. But he didn't. He ran a Deflect.

"My lawyers have advised me that I cannot answer these questions without jeopardizing my friends, my family, and myself," McGwire stuttered. To an incredulous congressman, who asked if he was invoking the Fifth Amendment, his right not to incriminate himself, McGwire said incongruously, *"I'm not here to talk about the past. I'm here to be positive about this subject."*

McGwire had essentially said *No comment* to befuddled lawmakers, a sure sign of a Deflect. He hadn't paraded about like Canseco, shaded like Sosa, or bold-faced lied like Palmeiro, and he hadn't saluted like Schilling. He'd simply dodged the bullet, or tried to. He'd done nothing fancier than try to get out of the way, to avoid the fast verbal pitches or just be grazed by them.

Of course, McGwire's Deflect was a dud. It served to further damn him in the eyes of the public because, like Sosa under oath, he wouldn't say he had and he wouldn't say he hadn't taken steroids. Anyone watching or reading the next day could only conclude that he'd probably done something worse than what he'd originally confessed to doing. McGwire, you could hear the whispers, was probably juiced, and the records he'd broken were never really his to begin with.

TABLE A. BASICS OF A DEFLECT

Class	Condition
Subclass	Divert
Type	**Deflect**
Definition	An attempt by a player to divert a rival's attack, either to avoid or minimize its impact. Deflects typically bend—they do not break or significantly alter—an opponent's play action. They are usually run under duress and on the fly by a player with inferior resources against a superior threat.
Upsides	■ Creates breathing space, time to think, for the player. ■ Enables a player to mask unflattering information or conceal a vulnerable position. ■ Enables a player with weaker defenses to fend off superior strength. ■ Can also create a psychological victory for the player—"They missed us!" ■ Can position the player as "taking the high road."
Downsides	■ Can force impulsive, defensive, and off-strategy reactions. ■ Usually only buys the player a short-term reprieve. ■ Takes a player off its game, away from its plan and its own playmaking initiatives. ■ Can leave the impression that the player is cowardly, evasive, or out of options, or, worse, trying to hide something.
Related Terms	■ A diversionary proof ■ A dodge ■ Ducking the issue ■ Jujitsu or judo (as in the martial arts) ■ Parrying (as in fencing) ■ Passing the buck ■ Redirecting ■ Taking the Fifth (Amendment) ■ Turfing
Related Play Types	■ Leak ■ Pass ■ Pause ■ Red Herring

Glancing Blows

Just a few months later and a short walk from where Mark McGwire was publicly broiled, White House press secretary Scott McClellan experienced a similar fate. The basting McClellan received came in response to his statements in 2003 about the unmasking of an undercover CIA operative named Valerie Plame.

Rumors hard originally swirled that White House deputy chief of staff Karl Rove had committed the grave error, but McClellan called the suggestion of Rove's involvement ridiculous: *"I've made it very clear, [Rove] was not involved, that there's no truth to the suggestion that he was,"* he parroted to the press corps. *"If anyone in this administration was involved in it, they would no longer be in this administration."* Sure enough, when George W. Bush was asked if he'd really fire the person who outed Plame, the president said, simply, *"Yes."*

So in 2005, when the administration's top strategist, Karl Rove, did come under investigation by the Justice Department, the tone and the answers from McClellan immediately changed—presumably to circle the wagons around the prized advisor. But, just as quickly, White House reporters checked their 2003 notes and demanded to know, Will Karl Rove be fired?

McClellan held his ground and his tongue. *"This question is coming up in the context of this ongoing investigation,"* said the aide obliquely. *"Our policy continues to be that we're not going to get into commenting on an ongoing criminal investigation from this podium."*

But you've *already* commented from this podium, reporters roared. You and the president have already said that a White House leaker would be a *fired* White House leaker! They quoted the spokesman from 2003, word for word, and asked again and again, Is Karl Rove toast? But McClellan withstood the barrage. However silly or hypocritical he appeared, the deputy held to his line, *"You can keep asking, but you have my response."*

Like the embattled baseball idol, the embattled press secretary did nothing more than duck the shots. You could say he was spinning, but more accurately he was Deflecting, incurring a good bit of damage to the administration and his own credibility, but avoiding the full blast of a political bombshell.

TABLE B. EXAMPLES OF A DEFLECT

Deflects to remember . . .	
	■ ***Steroids*** In 2005, when home-run slugger Mark McGwire was summoned to Washington to reveal under oath what he knew about steroids in baseball, Big Mac said to the incredulous representatives, *"I'm not here to talk about the past. I'm here to be positive about this subject."*
	■ ***Plame and Rove*** When rumors swirled in 2003 that White House deputy chief of staff Karl Rove had outed CIA operative Valerie Plame, White House press secretary Scott McClellan called the suggestion of Rove's involvement ridiculous and promised that a White House leaker would be a *fired* White House leaker. Two year later, when Rove did come under investigation by the Justice Department, McClellan ducked a howling White House press corps, saying guiltlessly, *" . . . we're not going to [comment] on an ongoing criminal investigation from this podium."*
	■ ***New Coke*** At a 1985 unveiling of New Coke, Coke executives were chided about Pepsi's success in forcing the switch. *"To what extent are you introducing this product to meet the Pepsi Challenge?"* reporters probed. *"Oh, gosh no. The Pepsi Challenge? When did it happen?"* said the tongue-in-cheek Coke chairman Robert Goizueta.

As the accounts above illustrate, the Deflect is a staple for the player in crisis because it buys that player time to think and gives the pursuer something to think about. It's hard to know what Mark McGwire was trying to protect. It could have been a more horrible truth than what he'd already revealed or it could just have been a horrible miscarriage of playmaking strategy. In any case, the conflicted retired athlete didn't so much try to stop speculation as he tried to divert it. He wanted, of course, to talk about the future—whatever that meant—but he was also willing to keep his skeletons closeted. Similarly, Scott McClellan didn't try to refute what he said in 2003. He just shelved it, *pending the outcome of a legal investigation. . . .* Can't you just hear him say it? His ploy didn't hold any more water than McGwire's, but what distinguished the two heavy hitters was the press secretary's ability to hold his position, perhaps just barely, whereas the baseball player slid further back into a morass of damaging speculation and disgrace.

TABLE C. CALLING AND RUNNING A DEFLECT

Call and run this play because . . .	▪ An attack is unavoidable and unalterably aimed at you. ▪ You want to avoid the full force of an opponent's punch. ▪ You want to buy time. There's little time to think or react strategically. ▪ Your resources and training are only sufficient to divert—not significantly alter—your opponent's attack. ▪ You want to find the right person to answer the insinuations or allegations. ▪ The spotlight is on you, you can't just sit there. A Pause will leave you flattened. ▪ The time is not right to reveal damaging news. ▪ You need more information to make an informed play. ▪ It's not your problem; you don't want to be the face of this issue. ▪ You have something to hide.

Deflects aren't run just in Washington. They're a staple of every reeling player trying to parry, twist away, or just hold even. It's what an inquiring reporter hears when a head-in-the-sand CEO explains, *We don't talk about the competition,* and it's what an inquiring CEO hears when her below-quota sales VP explains, *Our customers can't stop talking about the competition.* It's what a defense witness does when he says to a prosecutor, *I don't recall the time,* and it's what a prosecutor does when he says to a judge, *I need more time.* The Deflect is what players do to stay in the game, or die trying.

TABLE D. DECODING AND COUNTERING A DEFLECT

How do I decode this play? *(i.e., How do I know it's being run against me?)*	■ When the full force of your planned punch doesn't land. ■ When your rival only appears to have been "winged." ■ When your opponent seems suddenly to be talking about a lot of things, none of them the most important or obvious thing at hand. ■ When attention moves off the issue but goes nowhere else in particular.
How do I counter this play?	■ Run a Bait. Force your competitor to answer the real question or address the real weakness. ■ Run a Challenge. Reduce your rival's reaction time. *Don't fire until you see the whites of their eyes.* ■ Label your opponent with a sound bite, something that brands them as evasive. ■ Focus your play to ensure its full force is felt. ■ Run a Mirror to expose your opponent's dodge. ■ Run a Peacock. Let the marketplace know how right you were. ■ You've obviously touched a nerve. Try running a Screen to attach a bigger issue to the Player's flaw. Put their Deflect into a larger perspective. ■ Do not Pause or Pass. Now is the time to expose or attack.

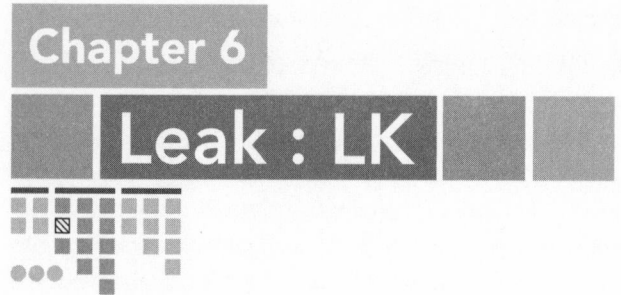

Chapter 6

Leak : LK

RISK

REWARD

TM

From 1972 to 1973, a man who became known as Deep Throat fed classified tips to a young reporter, Bob Woodward of *The Washington Post,* nudging him through a maze of secret clues that would reveal the crimes of the Watergate scandal and lead to the resignation of President Richard Nixon. Thirty years later, and nearly forgotten, the source revealed his real name and identity: W. Mark Felt, the retired associate director of the FBI, a career agent and former spy hunter. As the Bureau's number two man in the early seventies, Felt was privy to Nixon's misdeeds and believed that he should expose the scandal. But the crimes were internal and at the highest level, so he made the extremely risky decision to work the case through the media. His play of choice—a play for the ages—was the Leak, which he ran repeatedly to put Woodward and fellow reporter Carl Bernstein onto the scent and toward a blockbuster conclusion.

The Leak is one play about which all good playmakers will knowingly nod. Seldom, however, will they admit, at least with any bravado, to running one, because the Leak, at its core, is neither transparent nor even-handed and its crucial advantage is the anonymity it provides for the playmaker. To dignify such things is simply off-strategy, if not impolitic, so Leaks are something all good playmakers do . . . but don't talk about.

So let's talk about it. To be clear, the Leak is a means by which a player discloses some set of privileged facts, information, or perspectives to another player, one who might not normally get this information, before or ahead of others. Leaks come in many forms, but the most celebrated examples have been run with the happy cooperation of the news media. Here are two more of history's best:

■ **Fueling a Crisis.** Following a 1961 Vienna summit, President John Kennedy felt he'd been outfoxed by his counterpart, Soviet premier Nikita Khrushchev, particularly on the matter of nuclear superiority. To regain his prestige and position, he authorized his deputy secretary of defense, Roswell Gilpatrick, to drop classified statistics into a speech that proved, once and for all, that the U.S. had a clear nuclear advantage over the USSR. This might have been a straightforward and uniform communication, perhaps a Fiat, except that the speech was delivered to a business council meeting at a remote Virginia resort, so the distribution of information was uneven and thus extra compelling to those who got it over those who didn't. For a few months, the Leak helped Kennedy's cause, but it escalated the tit-for-tat arms race to a perilous level. In 1962, Khrushchev countered the boast by sending nuclear missiles to Cuba, a prelude to the Cuban Missile Crisis.

■ **Fueling a Movement.** In 1969, Daniel Ellsberg, a government analyst and former State Department official, secretly photocopied a damning seven-thousand-page government account of the Vietnam War that laid bare a legacy of misrepresentations and mistakes. Failing to convince members of Congress that the report should be made public, he took the monumental risk in 1971 of leaking his stolen documents, soon dubbed The Pentagon Papers, to *The New York Times.* When the Nixon administration made legal attempts to stop the *Times* from publishing the seismic revelations, Ellsberg covered his bets with a spree of new leaks to other major national papers. Were it not for the administration's general bungling, Ellsberg would have faced a life behind bars for his daring plays.*

However you might gauge these memorable cases—as clever or ill-advised, courageous or cowardly—the Leak is a high-stakes play because it operates outside the lines of a marketplace's standard operating procedures.

---

* Nixon also used illegal means to stop Ellsberg, sending henchmen into the patient records of the rogue analyst's personal psychiatrist. Their attempt to unearth embarrassing information failed, but the soon-to-be-famous crooks were nonetheless nicknamed "the Plumbers" for their attempt to fix Ellsberg's devastating Leak. Later, Nixon's men tried their hand at some other crimes, notably a botched break-in at the Democratic National Committee headquarters in Washington, D.C.'s, Watergate complex.

TABLE A. BASICS OF A LEAK

Class	Condition
Subclass	Divert
Type	**Leak**
Definition	The selective disclosure by a player of normally privileged or confidential information to a specified target (e.g., reporter, customer, prospect, colleague). A Leak is typically covert and employed to divert or accentuate a developing idea in the marketplace.
Upsides	▪ Can stop or reverse the direction of a negative idea, making it less troublesome, making it right, or even making it a problem for a rival. ▪ Passively feeds and directs developing ideas and resulting perceptions. ▪ Allows the player to retain all or some degree of anonymity. ▪ Inhibits sensational reporting, runaway word-of-mouth, and gossip. ▪ Excellent for setting up other play action. ▪ Can endear a player to a stakeholder. Leaks are often given as favors. ▪ Allows a player to carry out a campaign on two fronts—public and official versus private and informal. ▪ Strengthens the possibility that the receiving party will act on exclusive information, thus ensuring that the player (the leaker) will generate the desired actions or reactions.
Downsides	▪ Creates a habit for covert playmaking, which can enhance a player's reputation for secrecy. ▪ Conditions a player to discriminate—not a compatible trait in the new age of transparency. ▪ If discovered, can shatter relationships. It can upset those who were not taken into the player's confidence. And it can promote fear and loathing toward the one who was. ▪ Can stretch the ethical or legal obligations of a player. ▪ Places an ultimate degree of faith and power in the hands of the "leakee," the target you entrust. ▪ Leaks are seldom binding so the player has no legal recourse if the play is disclosed, stupidly or intentionally. ▪ Leaks, by their nature, exploit an imperfect channel with imperfect partners—so the risk of a different outcome is high. Your target can get it wrong.

Related Terms	■ Rumoring
	■ Seeding information
	■ A whisper campaign
Related Play Types	■ Deflect
	■ Red Herring

Some Leaks are run against the grain of discretion or propriety: Think of the downsizing HR manager who, while preparing pink slips, whispers apologetically to a friend, *I think you'd better polish up your resume.* Some run afoul of an organization's regulations or ethical codes of conduct: Think of the celebrated engineer, recruited to a rival manufacturer, who takes to his new job all his many talents but, unfortunately, a few trade secrets too. Other Leaks break laws: Think of the deep-cover spy who, through deliberate deception, learns the secrets of an archrival and carefully shuttles the intelligence into the anxious hands of her agency.

Of course, Leaks aren't always run through the news media. Leakers can just as easily tap private parties to change a marketplace and, occasionally, the course of history. Here are two to consider, representing widely varying degrees of fame and infamy:

■ **Bombshell News.** In 1942, Samuel Sydney Silverman, a member of British Parliament, received by way of the British Foreign Office secret information that revealed a shocking and credible account of Adolf Hitler's plan to annihilate the Jews of German-occupied Europe. With such incendiary intelligence, Silverman took matters into his own hands, ducking the red tape and passing the bombshell news to a prominent American Jewish leader, Stephen Wise. While diplomatically out of order, the Leak that got Silverman *in* the loop and the Leak that Silverman ran *himself* helped Wise flush the U.S. State Department from its wait-and-see perch and force the Roosevelt administration to face the horrible implications of Hitler's dreaded Final Solution.

■ **Bombshell Blues.** A similar technique was employed in 1997 by a career government worker and Defense Department employee, Linda Tripp. Having befriended a young colleague, Monica Lewinsky, a former White House intern who'd been transferred to the Pentagon, Tripp began to secretly record her telephone conversations with the chatty coworker and vivid details of her very lurid Oval Office affair with the very married President Bill Clinton. Whether it was personal politics or a sense of justice that drove Tripp, the bureaucrat ultimately traded her ill-gotten tapes with the promise of immunity to Kenneth Starr, the independent counsel investigating the Whitewater affair, Filegate, Travelgate, and other suspected scandals of the Clinton administration. What qualifies Tripp's handiwork as a Leak is not so much that she made her recordings without Lewinsky's blessing but that she delivered them solely into the hands of the probing and appreciative investigator.

TABLE B. EXAMPLES OF A LEAK	
Leaks to remember . . .	■ ***Deep Throat*** It was the FBI's number two man, Mark Felt, who leaked crucial information to *Washington Post* reporter Bob Woodward to help expose the Watergate scandal and end Richard Nixon's presidency. ■ ***JFK Leak*** In 1961 an official of the Kennedy administration leaked information that proved the U.S.'s nuclear advantage over the USSR. Khrushchev countered the play by sending nuclear missiles to Cuba, a prelude to the Cuban Missile Crisis. ■ ***Holocaust*** In 1942, Samuel Sydney Silverman, a member of British Parliament, learned of Hitler's plan to annihilate the Jews of German-occupied Europe. He bypassed channels and shot the information to the American Jewish leader Stephen Wise, who, in turn, forced Roosevelt to face the horrible truth.

Leaky Business

As much as the Leak is both celebrated and reviled in politics, it's just as commonly run in business, not only through the media but with employees, customers, clients, and prospects too.

Imagine, for example, that your top customer is wavering between your established product line, like a network printer, and the new-generation offering of an upstart competitor, a faster and more fully featured model. Imagine that *you've* also got something in the wings, an innovation that'll outdate both your own offerings and your opponent's new stuff, like a no-ink miracle option. Chances are good that you'll run a Leak, arranging a peek behind the curtain to stabilize your vacillating customer. It'll be your secret and it'll make the sale. It'll also cut out the poaching competitor and preserve your plans for a proper launch and smooth transition of your product lines.

Of course, Leaks can be just as helpful to the hunter as the hunted. Instead of your top customer, think of your top prospect, the one who's always been friendly and interested in what you're selling but *never* ready to give your products or services a try. Now, however, you've got that no-ink miracle printer option to bring him in. By hook or by crook, I'm betting you'll run a Leak, maybe by way of a side comment over lunch, maybe with the delivery of a breakthrough technical paper, maybe through a full briefing under a nondisclosure agreement (NDA). Either way, you'll be angling to get your prospect's attention and putting him finally in your win column.

In some cases, the Leak is run for the benefit of the target, given perhaps as a fa-vor by the player. *Hey, Julie, something came across my desk this morning that I thought you'd want to know about . . . but you didn't hear it from me.* In other cases, it's done purely for the benefit of the player, perhaps to backstop a slipping position. *Well . . . off the record, we're coming up short on the quarter, but it's not a demand problem. The new plant is just ramping a little slower than we'd like.* It might also be used to quell a threatening crisis. *On background, I'd encourage you to call the air-plane manufacturer. We've been complaining about the nose gear and I think other airlines have too.* And, finally, it might be used to exploit an emerging opportunity. *Hi, Ralph, I wanted you to know that we've got some major news coming up next quarter. How can you get the exclusive? Well, for starters, you'd have to guarantee page-one coverage.*

Either way, the Leak is an inevitably risky move because it doesn't play fair. With these things in mind, I should issue the following notice:

> **Warning:** *Leaks are not for rookie playmakers or the fainthearted. To succeed, the leaking player and its team require a high degree of command and control and a high degree of confidence in the one to whom the information is entrusted.*

TABLE C. CALLING AND RUNNING A LEAK

Call and run this play because . . .	■ You may need to play the game anonymously. It may be your only way to convey information without having it attributed to you directly. ■ You want to sidestep convention or (at your own risk) regulations, codes of ethics, or even laws. ■ You trust your target to hold or pass along your information in confidence. ■ A foe, friend, or bystander needs a course correction. ■ News or word of mouth is moving fast against you. There's no time to develop more sophisticated, transparent, or collaborative play action. ■ Your competitor is seeding the market with FUD (fear, uncertainty, and doubt). Your information, if properly leaked, can stop it and even flip the direction of a dangerous play. ■ You shouldn't have this information but you do, and it's relevant. Your best option is to pass it on quietly. ■ You can't come right out and just say it . . . but someone else can.

The urge to run this play is sometimes overwhelming because a private communication or secret delivery of information, however inappropriate, unfair, or ill-advised, is a deliciously quick and simple way to get a player out of trouble or back onto on the offense. Think of the prosecuting attorney who's managing a celebrity's court case and the media circus around it. Prosecutor talking to a reporter: *You can quote me as a source who's knowledgeable about the case, okay? Good. At any rate, what I can tell you is that the defense has withdrawn its motion to dismiss. Yes . . . they know it won't work, in part because we've got new evidence. What is it? Well, let's just say that the defendant's alibi is looking very shaky.*

Such a move amounts to a high-wire act, both in the court of law and the court of public opinion, particularly if a gag order's in place. If the attorney has his facts wrong or if the reporter hears something different, the resulting story might sway the jury. And if the reporter reveals his source as the prosecuting attorney, a mistrial can be declared, a criminal can go free, and a lawyer can be disbarred.

In other words, Leaks are for players who can accept high levels of risk and who have the experience and instincts to run the play well . . . maybe too well, sometimes. Take, for example, the shadowy practice of investment fund managers who target medical doctors to "consult" on their experience in drug trials of publicly traded pharmaceutical companies. The information—what can amount to insider information—often gives investors a trading edge on the drugmaker's stock. But it also puts ethical pressures on the physicians to test and sometimes break the boundaries of their NDA with the trusting drug companies. Some do it knowingly to keep the calls and checks coming in. Some do it unwittingly, determined to offer balanced perspective, but they've been known to slip at the hands of an all-too-slick analyst.

The stakes aren't always so high for Leakers. Take the very common practice of disgruntled employees who vent their frustrations online by leaking confidential memoranda and even trade secrets to company gossip sites or by seeding the blogosphere with their own angry opinions, speculation, and confidential information. The courts have still to work these things out, but Leakers on the Web and the quasi journalists they feed have enjoyed an unusually high degree of anonymity and legal protection.

If you don't run Leaks, that is your prerogative and possibly your policy. But you should at least understand how they work because, in all likelihood, they are being run on you. Leaks are a nearly universal reality of how people work with one another and, for better or worse, a permanent hazard of any marketplace. They may be employed to save someone's hide. They may be employed to save the world. But however publicly decried or privately revered its use may be, the Leak is an undoubtedly effective strategy for moving a marketplace quietly in a playmaker's preferred direction.

TABLE D. DECODING AND COUNTERING A LEAK	
How do I decode this play? (i.e., How do I know it's being run against me?)	■ When customers, clients, constituents, prospects, or media ask you about things they're not supposed to know . . . or about things that are flat wrong. ■ When marketplace information, such as a press or analyst report, avoids or only partially attributes information or statements (e.g., "an official close to City Hall today confirmed that . . .").
How do I counter this play?	■ Counter with your own Leak if you have a perspective or information that can be quickly and confidentially conveyed. ■ Expose the leaker if you can by running a Mirror with this information. Catching your opponent with its hand in the cookie jar is always useful. ■ Run a Lantern to tell the full and proper story or run a Disco to put the leaked information in its full and proper perspective. ■ Run a Bear Hug. The leaked information may be mistimed but it is on-strategy. ■ Run a Pause. See how the market responds. Do you need to react or will it just blow over? ■ Run a Red Herring. Gain sympathy by expressing shock that this information got out. Talk only about the method, not the message.

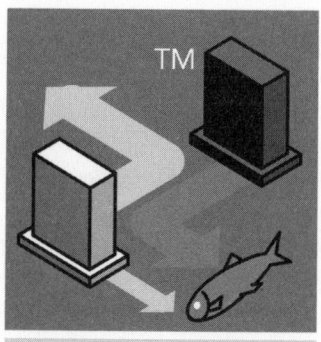

TM

If you're an adherent of Machiavelli or Sun Tzu, you'll want to take notes. If you're an acolyte of Mother Teresa you'll want to rip out this chapter, though perhaps you shouldn't. Even the virtuous are the targets of plays.

The Red Herring, for better or worse, is a fundamental strategy for diverting a rival. One cousin, the Deflect, ducks a competitor's attack, letting it whiz by a player's current position. The Red Herring, by contrast, sends a pursuing opponent onto the scents of other quarry. This naturally evokes images of the hunter and the hunted, so for this reason the play is named in honor of a technique first used in the 1800s for training hunting dogs.* The Red Herring, in fact, was coined by hound trainers who would drag rotted or smoked kippers, sardines, or herrings across an existing scent to throw the sniffers off their track. The fish were generally brown or reddish in color, hence, *red* herrings.

The practice of sending a rival off into the sticks is something we see in so many applications of strategy, from software marketers who know it as vaporware, to battlefield commanders who know it as a feint, to tournament debaters who term it a logical fallacy, to moviemakers who call it a McGuffin. Each seeks to draw the attention of a target away from whatever the targeter is doing or thinking or wherever it's going. And each faces consequences if the feint fails.

---

* Of course, Red Herrings are popularly known among investors as the SEC-required red-lettered prospectus that details a company's impending public offering. But IPOs came a bit later than hunting.

TABLE A. BASICS OF A RED HERRING

Class	Condition
Subclass	Divert
Type	**Red Herring**
Definition	The Red Herring is an action or communiqué that draws an opponent—usually a competitor—away from its preferred position or intended course of action.
Upsides	■ Creates breathing space for a player—valuable time and real estate to operate without interference. ■ Weakens a competitor by diverting its energy and/or resources into false fronts or dead ends. ■ Preserves the player's advantage by concealing its true needs or strategies. ■ A well-run Red Herring can excite a rival, causing it to quicken its pace toward the diversion and thus deepen its miscalculation. ■ De-positions your opponent as a follower—gullible and responsive to your whims.
Downsides	■ You may be fooling more than your enemies. Employees, partners, customers, etc., can be lured into the play too. ■ A poorly run Red Herring can mean lost time and money, sometimes lost friends. ■ If the play is exposed, it can tell a competitor much about a player's situation, tendencies, and fears. ■ A Red Herring can create the appearance of impropriety. You could be well within your rights to run it, but the new standards for marketplace transparency may say you're wrong to even try.
Related Terms	■ A feint ■ Logical fallacy ■ A McGuffin ■ Passing the buck ■ Playacting ■ A smokescreen ■ A Trojan Horse ■ A wild-goose chase

Related Play Types	■ Bait
	■ Deflect
	■ Leak
	■ Screen

Big Fish

Such was the case for Microsoft Corporation when, at the turn of the millennium, it was confronted by two competitive threats, each with devastating potential. On one front, Microsoft was battling charges of monopolistic business practices, spurred by angry users, rival manufacturers, and states' attorneys general, and ultimately taken up by the U.S. Department of Justice. On another front, the Internet was fast becoming an open computing and networking standard for gathering, managing, and exchanging information. Its organic popularity, fueled by early rival browsers like Netscape's ill-fated Navigator and competitive thrusts like Oracle's campaign against bloated PCs or "fat clients," threatened to dethrone Microsoft as the personal computing king. The DOJ as an organization and the Internet as a phenomenon had the competitive potential to make Microsoft irrelevant.

It's a longer story to tell of how Microsoft extricated itself from this profound pickle, but it's safe to say that playmaking was central to its efforts.

Beyond its challenges in the court of law, Microsoft had its hands full in the court of public opinion. Though Microsoft couldn't afford to be run over by the Internet, it also couldn't afford for the Internet to run away from it. It had a big problem. Microsoft, the leading maker of closed and proprietary operating systems software, had to get onto the back of the open and very public Internet and somehow lead the marketplace chatter. What did Microsoft do? It ran a Red Herring.

Tech marketers will tell you—and Microsoft might now confess—that what they served up was an unabashed version of vaporware.* It's a notorious ploy by information technology companies to tell customers about something that's coming, to buy time for developers to write and debug the design, and to beat back competitive offerings or other threats. .NET did become quite real, but in the beginning, it was more talk than walk, if you get my drift.

---

* Vaporware, to the uninitiated, is simply computer software or hardware that doesn't really exist or isn't yet for sale. Thanks to overeager marketers, word of a new technology can still be spritzed into the marketplace like a vapor cloud . . . hence the term.

On June 22, 2000, two and a half months after U.S. District Court judge Thomas Penfield Jackson ruled that Microsoft was a monopoly, the software king introduced .NET. And here's what CEO Steve Ballmer had to say about it (underlines are my emphasis):

"What is .NET? <u>.NET represents a set, an environment, a programming infrastructure</u> that supports the next generation of the Internet as a platform. It is an enabling environment for that. It is also . . . <u>a user environment, a set of fundamental user services</u> that live on the client, in the server, in the cloud, that are consistent with and build off that programming model. So, it's both a user experience and a set of developer experiences. That's the conceptual description of what is .NET."

This was leadership language from an industry leader. Ballmer declared that Microsoft would embrace the Internet, if not lead in its development as an industry standard. He said, in essence, *Forget about the lawsuits. We're in this game and you have to deal with us.* And he didn't talk price and availability.

The .NET Red Herring diverted attention from the fact that Microsoft had virtually no inherent authority or command over the direction of the Internet. It was delivered with such confidence and bravado that it conveyed a sense of stability and control over the Internet—exactly the things that the antitrust suits threatened to take away. Whether you call this vapor or vision, the strategy of distraction worked, and as we all know, neither the Internet nor the courts have done much harm to Microsoft since.

TABLE B. EXAMPLES OF A RED HERRING	
Red Herrings to remember . . .	■ **Grenada** On October 23, 1983, 241 Marines were killed when their barracks in Lebanon were bombed by the Lebanese terrorist group Hezbollah. How did the U.S. respond? Two days later, the U.S. invaded Grenada. The invasion diverted America's attention away from the tragedy in Lebanon.
	■ **Ford Explorers** In 2001, when Ford Explorers started flipping, Ford Motor sought to make it a larger problem for the auto industry, not just its popular Explorer SUV. They flooded the media with irrelevant facts and figures and pointed at the poor stability inherent in all SUVs.
	■ **Brer Rabbit** In Uncle Remus, the American folktale, Brer Fox threatens all manner of misery for Brer Rabbit. The clever rabbit feigns relief and says, *"Fine! Skin me. Snatch out my eyeballs. Tear out my ears. Cut off my legs. Anything but the BRIAR PATCH."* The too-gullible fox thus throws Brer Rabbit into the patch, a place where the hare easily makes his escape.

Soccer Bomb

The Red Herring has been decisive in other epic battles, literally on the field of battle, time and time again. Perhaps the original Red Herring was run during the Trojan War when, according to myth, Greeks tricked besieged Trojans to take in a large wooden horse filled, as it happened, with Greek soldiers who later snuck out to unlatch the city gates. While Trojans partied, Greek troops reappeared outside the city walls, crept through the now-open gates, and finally captured Troy.

Another case of Red Herrings and war—this one more recent but with increasingly mythical status—is the controversy over Iraqi weapons of mass destruction (WMDs). In 2003, as U.S. president George W. Bush advanced his case to fight terrorism and, specifically, to invade the country of Iraq, he stoked concerns for a grave threat. WMDs, he claimed to know, were in the hands of the Iraqi president Saddam Hussein, all intended for America and her allies. Whether Iraqi WMDs ever existed is a topic of considerable debate, even at this writing. What isn't in doubt, however, is that they were used by the Bush administration for playmaking advantage. If WMDs did exist but were moved or simply never found, the president was arguably running a Screen, an issue enflamed with the rhetoric Bush employed to advance his case for invasion. If the data were fabricated, it was a Red Herring, a decoy set by the president to distract his antiwar detractors.

History is a bit clearer on another wartime Red Herring. During the Second World War, allied troops got a morale boost when a single daring British pilot crossed into German territory, flying low under enemy radar. When he arrived over his target, a Nazi airfield, he dropped from his fighter a single and very unconventional package. It wasn't a bag of propaganda leaflets, though the effect was similarly corrosive. It wasn't a bomb, though the effect was psychologically explosive. It was instead a soccer ball.

To the Germans who scattered at the roar of the unannounced enemy aircraft, it was unrecognizable. The Brits had coated the ball with a thick metallic paint so it bore a sinister look. Even more, they'd pumped it full of lighter-than-air helium, which slowed its descent but, once dropped from the plane, only increased the panic of its imminent impact and presumed destruction. Germans initially shot at the alien orb but were told to cease fire, apparently for fear that this was part of a diabolical allied plot. The ball slowly descended, then bounced interminably on the tarmac before coming to rest.

It was gingerly carted away on a specially commissioned train and taken to a secret laboratory for testing. Teams of Germany's top weapons researchers were summoned to inspect and dissect the mysterious sphere, an apparent dud but a supposed intelligence windfall. Slowly, the soccer ball was dismantled, and finally, of course, the ruse was revealed. *Ach du lieber!* The Germans had played into a massive hoax. Nothing had been destroyed but egos and time and that, in fact, had been the real target of the British soccer bomb.

TABLE C. CALLING AND RUNNING A RED HERRING	
Call and run this play because . . .	▪ You need to buy time to implement your plan or decide what to do. ▪ Your opponent is getting too close to a vulnerability. You need to throw them off course. ▪ A well-run Red Herring gives opponents more to do by giving them more to pursue. ▪ You're outnumbered. You may only have your wits as weapons. Fortunately, Red Herrings rely on cunning more than cost. ▪ A rival is bent on pursuing you. ▪ You have an opportunity to give a competitor a false impression, feigning, for example, that something is too tough to fight or that you've been winged and wounded. ▪ The competition shows signs of gullibility or is hypercompetitive—a perfect target to be thrown a smelly fish. ▪ Your opponent has resources. Well-funded rivals are susceptible to Red Herrings precisely because they have the money and teams to come after you. They're prone to hunt . . . so best you give them something to chase. ▪ You can hide a morsel of bad information in a mountain of fluff.

Motel Madness

Strategy and competitive advantage are serious business to the British, but that's never to say they don't also have some fun in the running of a good play, particularly a Red Herring. This was never clearer than in the twisted and terrifying films of the knighted director Alfred Hitchcock, another inspired playmaking Englishman.

You might not think of filmmakers as playmakers, but keep in mind the definition: *Playmaking is a discipline for deploying and systematically managing plays—in combinations, sequences, and patterns—to continually influence, control, and sustain the sentiments, discussions, and decisions of a marketplace.* This is what Hitchcock did in his films, to his audience and in his marketplace. Whether it was his classic *Rear Window, North by Northwest, Vertigo,* or *The Birds,* he held his audience's attention with precision and let it wander at will.

If playmaking was Hitchcock's second discipline, his play of choice was the Red Herring. Though he called it a *McGuffin,* named after a Scottish shaggy dog story,* his underlying strategy was the same—to draw his targets off-course and buy time for the main plot's development. In the 1960 thriller *Psycho,* for example, Hitchcock set the stage with a lonely secretary, Marion Crane, played by Janet Leigh. Crane, when sent by her employer to deposit $40,000 of a client's cash, gives in to temptation and drives out of town to start a new life. The story is engaging enough, but nothing in comparison to the bad turn Marion Crane takes when she checks into the remote Bates Motel and confronts its psychotic proprietor, Norman Bates.

Whether it's vaporware, a feint, McGuffin, or Red Herring, the effort to pull players away from their original focus is often crucial to a playmaker's plans. It may be a necessary strategy for preserving a lead, as was the case for Microsoft and its .NET initiative, or it may be used to disrupt a leader, as it was by World War II psychological warfare pioneers and their ingenious helium-filled soccer ball. In either case, the Red Herring is a critical strategy to hold a player's attention but to do so with something that is in fact irrelevant or, as Alfred Hitchcock would contend, is nothing at all.

---

* In 1966 Hitchcock explained the meaning of a McGuffin to François Truffaut: *"It might be a Scottish name, taken from a story about two men in a train. One man says, 'What's that package up there in the baggage rack?' And the other answers, 'Oh, that's a McGuffin.' The first one asks, 'What's a McGuffin?' 'Well,' the other man says, 'it's an apparatus for trapping lions in the Scottish Highlands.' The first man says, 'But there are no lions in the Scottish Highlands.' And the other one answers, 'Well, then, that's no McGuffin!' So you see, a McGuffin is nothing at all."*

TABLE D. DECODING AND COUNTERING A RED HERRING

How do I decode this play? *(i.e., How do I know it's being run against me?)*	■ If an opponent's reactions are inconsistent with its agenda or MO. ■ If your competition is more fox than deer, per se, watch out. A fox is better at cunning than running. ■ If you've been running Crowds or Drafts on a rival, watch for them to counter with a Red Herring. They can't afford for you to keep sticking your nose into their business. ■ If it seems like a good idea to pursue a new course of action. Are you being set up? ■ If you're following something important, but it only just came on your radar. ■ If an overabundance of information is released: Is your opponent burying something?
How do I counter this play?	■ Go public. Run a Red Herring of your own. Feign disgust and injury that's out of proportion to your actual setback. ■ Go private. Run a Pause. If you've been fooled by the Red Herring, minimize your reaction. This will deprive your rival of knowing precisely when you stepped into its trap and how badly you were damaged or thrown off course. ■ Run a Mirror. Expose your rival's attempt to draw you off-course. ■ Bait your competitor to run more Red Herrings. They won't know you're onto them, and in the end, they'll regret it. ■ Run a Bear Hug. Sing the praises of your opponent. Force them to go down their own blind alley. ■ Send a subtle Ping toward your opponent that you're sniffing or lunging at the Red Herring they laid out. See how they react.

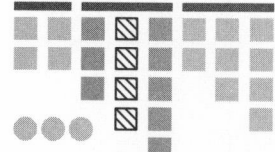

The Frame Subclass

Moving toward the center of The Playmaker's Table, now in the heart of the Condition class, we come to the fashionable subclass called Frame.

*def. **Frame:** Play action that adjusts the criteria and context of discussions and actions in a marketplace.*

The notion of framing has lately gained a good deal of popularity, particularly in politics, where the lens or frames through which constituents judge issues, activities, or initiatives have become as important as the issues, activities, or initiatives themselves. "Family values," for example, is probably a universally supportable idea, but Republicans have framed it in such as way as to suggest that the GOP is the better party for families—all by connecting the phrase to concepts like patriotism, same-sex marriage, and faith. This, of course, has put Democrats in the unenviable position of seeming to be out of touch with family values or even against families. Accordingly, the traditionally more populist party has scrambled to create its own frames, either to change the family focus altogether or to alter the associated meanings currently attached to family values.

There are many ways beyond Framing to change the rules in a marketplace, particularly with the more activist moves of the Pressing and Attacking subclasses. Unabashed plays like the Challenge, Peacock, and even the Crazy Ivan, have this ability and are none too shy in their attempts to drive new thinking and behaviors. But when a shift has to be made in more subtle ways with more subtle plays, the strategies of Framing offer a more suitable set of options.

More comfortable in the midsection of the playmaking spectrum, political party strategists typically go here in their attempts to frame and reframe their various positions and agendas: They convey only what they believe to be important through the Filter. Anything that's off-topic, they rephrase or recharacterize through the Recast. They synthesize clever sound bites that flatter themselves and demonize the opposition through the Label. And they attach their various causes to other indisputable achievements and works through the Screen. By these methods, they frame their vision and then, depending on the opposition, they defend or assert it using other elements of The Playmaker's Table.

Inside or outside politics, Framing is a crucial and central skill for bending the will of a marketplace or, at least, for setting its perspective and agenda. Here, next, are the four plays that get the job done, the Filter, Recast, Label, and Screen.

Chapter 8

Filter : FL

RISK

REWARD

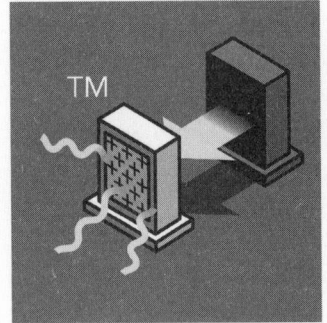

TM

Playmakers have the power of the pen. Whether they are in the public or private sector, whether they are appointed officials, self-appointed bloggers, or something in between, they have enormous influence over what goes out the door and what stays behind because, like a news editor, they have the discretionary authority to manage and move, keep or kill, the copy.

The Filter, perhaps more than any other play type in the playmaking system, reflects this prerogative power. It is, in so many words, the play that *edits*, that lets some things through and holds other things back. It is often the first among many options available to playmakers because it serves as a kind of triage technique. It determines which acts, facts, and information might be used, which might be ignored, and in some cases which might be suppressed.

This, of course, creates two considerable sources of tension. First, it challenges the playmaker to perform a balancing act between its obligation to comply legally and ethically with its duty to operate competitively. Second, it invites a clash of perspectives because what may be storytelling to one playmaker may be sanitizing or even whitewashing to another. Such was the case in the tragedy of an NFL star turned soldier.

TABLE A. BASICS OF A FILTER	
Class	Condition
Subclass	Frame
Type	*Filter*
Definition	The selective retransmission of information, where a player promotes and/or withholds information to build or defend its position. A Filter is typically employed to reshape characterizations so that their impact or relevance is minimized or, better, put to work for the player.
Upsides	▪ Gives the player the power of the pen, to disclose what is on-strategy and withhold what is not. ▪ Changes the complexion—and sometimes the entire meaning—of a player's statements and/or position. ▪ Presents a sliver of good news as the whole story.
Downsides	▪ A Filter's omissions can antagonize the competitor which, in turn, can invite unanticipated counterattacks. ▪ Shrewd opponents will expose poorly run Filters and embarrass the playmaker. Information that's filtered should appropriately and legitimately support a player's position. ▪ There may be legal, ethical, or practical implications to telling only part of the story.
Related Terms	▪ A strategic omission ▪ Telling part of the story
Related Play Types	▪ Label ▪ Recast ▪ Screen

Broken Play

Six months after the terrorist attacks on New York City and Washington, D.C., Patrick D. Tillman walked away from a multimillion-dollar contract extension as a celebrated safety for the Arizona Cardinals of the National Football League. He had bigger ideas of where he should dedicate his talents, time, and energy. To the utter astonishment of his friends, family, and particularly football fans, he enlisted in the U.S. Army and by 2002 had completed his training for the Army Rangers. But on April 22, 2004, he was gone, killed at twilight in an Afghanistan firefight near the Pakistan border.

Tillman's death hit hard at home—a poster warrior killed in action, an act of stunning patriotism. No one had ever asked Tillman to do this. He gave up a lucrative contract for a fraction of his football pay and he assiduously avoided the spotlight in his new capacity. It was not about him, he said many times, it was about his country.

A week later, on April 30, Tillman was posthumously promoted to the rank of corporal and awarded the Silver Star and Purple Heart. He was, the army said, a hero, *"killed while charging at the enemy up a hill, allowing the rest of his platoon to escape alive."* Family, friends, fans, and dignitaries marveled that this charismatic and handsome hero had paid the ultimate price for his single-minded sense of doing right. Four days later, on a nationally televised May 3 memorial attended by army officers, Tillman was eulogized as the new war's most famous volunteer.

But then a wrinkle appeared in this perfect picture of patriotism. Three weeks later, on May 29, the army released a one-page statement that repainted the final images of the hill-charging Ranger. Tillman, it said, had died *"as a probable result of friendly fire."*

Oops.

TABLE B. EXAMPLES OF A FILTER

Filters to remember . . .	
	■ **Pat Tillman** In the spring of 2004, when U.S. soldier and former NFL star Pat Tillman was killed in Afghanistan by friendly fire, the army didn't tell the full story. Later reports revealed that the army's selective or "filtered" accounts of the tragedy masked a platoon's disarray in the field and accentuated Tillman's bravery.
	■ **Enron** The fallen energy giant Enron also had a penchant for withholding information. Creative accounting (i.e., concealing debt) and selective disclosure (i.e., shredding documents) were some of its methods for keeping investors and regulators in the dark . . . at least for a while.
	■ **AMD** In September 2005, microprocessor and computer memory maker AMD trumpeted the news that it had finally outsold Intel in the microprocessor segment. While this was true, they didn't make so much of the fact that their overall revenues were a mere fraction of their giant rival's, still a semiconductor juggernaut.

The revelation that Tillman went down at the hands of fellow soldiers was as un-settling as the original report of his death. Questions were immediately raised as to what the army had really known and when it had known it.

Over the ensuing weeks, it came to light that the army had known most everything—long before it went public and even before it notified Tillman's family. By May 8, 2004, three weeks before the army's first admission of probable friendly fire, an internal report on Tillman's last battle was reportedly submitted to army brass documenting that Tillman died as a result of *"fratricide during an extremely chaotic enemy ambush."* The specialist, it said, had been caught in the spraying bullets of disoriented and confused troops from his own platoon.

It was not exactly the image of precision warfare that anyone, particularly the army, wanted to portray to a jittery public. Adding to the army's shame, senior military commanders, including General John Abizaid of the U.S. Central Command, were notified of the fratricide at least four days before Tillman's memorial service. And yet they waited to tell the truth.

However you score it, the army's Filter was, at the least, a controversial applica-tion of playmaking power. It served at first to preserve heroic and strategically valu-able images of Tillman, and it masked an embarrassing account of disarray in the field. But whatever upside it might have yielded initially, it created enormous long-term downside, heightening the public's scrutiny of the war and cratering the army's credibility and trust. It wasn't what the army *did* disclose so much as what it *didn't*. Like an editor's pen, it let some things through and held other things back, the very definition of a Filter.

As the Tillman case suggests, the Filter is not a casual play. Those who run it as-sume the tacit responsibility for playing a bit of God because they are, in effect, de-ciding what to keep and what to give away.

TABLE C. CALLING AND RUNNING A FILTER	
Call and run this play because . . .	■ You have information, some of which supports your position, some of which doesn't. ■ Your opponent's rhetoric needs to be edited and rebroadcast. They'll otherwise move into the marketplace unchallenged. ■ Your rival's communications cannot be stopped or diverted (e.g., by running a Deflect). ■ Information can or should be segregated, some to be withheld or deemphasized, some to be conveyed or underscored. ■ You have faced a mountain of bad news: You need to get some positives out there. ■ The whole story might cause an uproar.

Broken Promises

A filtering playmaker can operate across a wide continuum—from selfless to selfish. At one extreme, the Filter may be run to protect others from something that's perhaps inappropriate, personal, or even frightening. At the other, it may be employed to protect only a player's self-interest, let's say to hide some embarrassing or dangerous truth. As a consequence, it's not always clear if a player has its stakeholders' best interests in mind.

Imagine that you're sitting on an airport runway and the pilot comes over the PA. *Uhh, ladies and gentleman . . . one of our aft lavatories is acting up a bit, so we're going to turn back and give it a look.* Airlines these days don't exactly operate with a surplus of customer goodwill. The phrases *Extra leg room, It should only be a few minutes,* and *I'd be happy to check that for you* have been used a few too many times. And so you're left to wonder, is it really a leaking lavatory? Or is it a leaking *fuel tank*?!

This is to say that Filters create a moral dilemma for any filterer to consider—particularly airline personnel, in my humble opinion. Without full trust in the playmaker, they create big questions for the filteree. They certainly do for me. But despite being a serious play with serious implications, the Filter is routinely—and perhaps habitually—run in almost any marketplace, even some you might not think of as marketplaces. Here are a few simple examples:

■ It's what **a CEO** does on a quarterly call. Beyond the necessary detailed disclosures any public company must make, many chief executives or their CFOs offer additional statistics or anecdotes to paint a more optimistic picture than what the data alone might instead describe.

- It's what **a salesperson** does in a competitive pitch **or a marketer** does in a new product launch. Benefits and brand attributes are emphasized. Liabilities are rationalized or downplayed.

- It's what **a politician** does with personal information. If it's about her, she'll likely disclose everything that's flattering and little that's not. If it's about her opponent, she'll do quite the opposite.

- It's what **a spokesperson** does to portray his organization in the best possible light. Some facts are released because some stakeholders have a right to know. Some are withheld because others, especially competitors and enemies, do not.

- It's what **a film board** does when considering the rating on a film. How offensive is the language? How graphic is the violence? How explicit is the sex? How it judges the content determines who gets to see the movie.

- It's what **high-security organizations** do to limit access to proprietary information. Whether a spy agency, military command center, skunk works, or R & D lab, those who need to know will be told. Those who don't, won't.

The preceding examples are probably what you'd think of as playmakers—CEOs, salespeople, marketers, spokespeople, politicians, censors, and spies, even generals and top-secret scientists. But there are others, a bit below the normal radar, who are just as focused on running good Filters.

- It's what **law enforcement officials, health care professionals, and journalists** do to protect the privacy of a suspect, victim, patient, or source. They'll withhold names, addresses, ages, affiliations, etc., according to prescribed policies or promises.

- It's what **a school board** does when it reviews a new textbook for a curriculum. Is it accurate? Is it offensive? It is relevant? Boards will add it or ban it accordingly.

- It's what **teachers and parents** do to guide a child's development. There are books and TV shows that are in bounds. There are words and Web sites that are not.

Even if their priorities are to please rather than compete, everyone operates in a marketplace of competing attentions and loyalties—from boardrooms, newsrooms, war rooms, and courtrooms to operating rooms, classrooms, and family rooms. Everyone runs plays to protect or enhance their position, not the least of which is the Filter.

TABLE D. DECODING AND COUNTERING A FILTER

How do I decode this play? *(i.e., How do I know it's being run against me?)*	■ When your own ideas have been altered or their meanings have somehow been reversed. ■ When a clearly communicated idea is misconstrued, perhaps in the media or by a customer, client, or prospect. ■ When, suddenly, you have to restate or even defend what you thought was a good, well-communicated position. ■ When instinct, anecdote, rumor, or research tells you there's more to the story.
How do I counter this play?	■ Run a Call Out or a Bait on the filterer. Accuse the opponent of plagiarism or dare the rival to debate the issue. ■ Expose your rival with a Mirror. Make sure the marketplace knows it's telling only part of the story. ■ Run your own Filter. Restate your original point, this time more carefully. ■ Recruit Proxies to run Recasts or Fiats to get your point across. ■ Switch topics. Run a Recast to avoid a "clinch" with your rival. Don't let the filterer slow or tie up your good thinking. ■ If the filtered arguments can't be beat, run a Bear Hug/Recast combination. Tell the marketplace, *"Exactly . . . that's what I was saying."*

Chapter 9

Recast : RC

RISK

REWARD

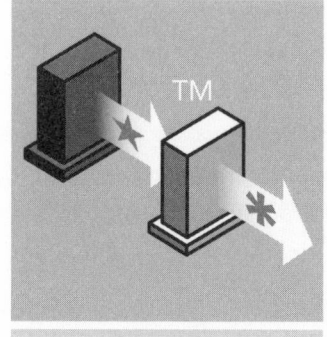

TM

With a tip of the hat to the late Theodor Geisel, better known as the children's storybook author Dr. Seuss, I want to bring to your attention the 1961 classic *The Sneetches and Other Stories.* Sneetches, you might remember, are a comically segregated species of dopey yellow, beach-walking birds. Half, it seems, have green stars inexplicably pasted onto their generous pear-shaped bellies. Half do not. And therein lies both the problem and opportunity for a clever character named Sylvester McMonkey McBean, who drove one day onto the divided scene.

To the relief of all plain-belly Sneetches, McBean rolled up with his special Star-On machine. Plain-bellied birds, the dregs of Sneetch society, had no life; they were never invited to *picnics or parties or marshmallow toasts.* And so the self-proclaimed Fix-It-Up Chappie found himself a market. That day on the beaches he sold a lot of stars to a lot of disenfranchised Sneetches.

This, of course, incensed the original star-sporting birds, so they jumped at McBean's next sham—a Star-Off machine. Another market was made and soon no Sneetch could remember, as it's written, *which one was what one . . . or what one was who.*

The story is a gentle lesson in prejudice, but for my purposes it serves to set the stage for one of playmaking's most instinctive and widely run plays—the Recast.

This play amounts to an attempt by a player to acquire or shed the certain meanings of things—illustrated by way of the class-conscious Sneetch. It is run to blur a line of distinction, enhance a player's position, or co-opt or eclipse a competitor's. This may also describe the Recast's close cousin, the Label, a handy play for pasting competitors with hard-to-remove sound bites or for plastering oneself with self-applied praise. But what I'm driving at is not so much the act of labeling as *relabeling*. The Recast is a move that doesn't just *apply* meanings and pithy sound bites to things (the next chapter describes all that). It defines a process that reforms existing facts, acts, ideas, events, and information into competitively useful playmaking currency. Recasters, like Seuss's Sneetches, are the recyclers of playmaking. They turn what is *not* useful into something that adds to their war chest (like getting a star on a belly), removes something from it (like taking a star off), or both. They turn liabilities into assets.

But enough about Sneetches. Think instead of the popular and polarized AM dial political commentators Rush Limbaugh and Al Franken. Sitting at opposite ends of the political spectrum, they are in a constant state of bending and reshaping current events to propel their positions.

Imagine, for example, a news day that produced reports of a sustained nationwide increase in abortions. Limbaugh, speaking to his conservative listeners, might refashion the statistic as another example of social self-indulgence or yet another reason to overturn *Roe v. Wade*. At the other end of the ideological spectrum, Franken, talking to his liberal adherents, might also run a Recast, but to him the worrisome factoid might be positioned as, let's say, another unfortunate consequence of a prudish right or of the debilitating restrictions on prescription birth control and classroom reproductive education. In either case, right wing or left, the political pundits will likely have morphed the nasty news to suit their agendas.

TABLE A. BASICS OF A RECAST

Class	Condition
Subclass	Frame
Type	**Recast**
Definition	The reinterpretation of an action, event, information, message, or symbol by a player so as to lend support to that player's position or agenda or to neutralize or weaken that of its rival.
Upsides	▪ Uses your opponent's words to advance your position. Repurposes (i.e., "recasts") a competitor's content so that it can be used to the player's advantage. ▪ Slows, stops, or diverts an opponent's ideas from reaching their intended target(s). ▪ Well-run Recasts allow a player to *dodge* a bullet and force a rival to *take* one. ▪ Recasts also reverse morale and momentum. They take the wind out of the sails of an attacker and build confidence in the recasting player.
Downsides	▪ Can position the player as an "angler," not a leader. ▪ Can condition the player to spin its way out of tight spots, rationalizing more than confronting. ▪ Can draw the player and opponent into a circular and often unproductive game of tit-for-tat. (Though this can sometimes be on-strategy.) ▪ When you are caught recasting, it's easy for your opponent to Label you as a spin doctor.
Related Terms	▪ Bridging ▪ Changing the subject ▪ Diversionary proof ▪ Morphing ▪ Putting words in someone's mouth ▪ Saying it in your own words
Related Play Types	▪ Filter ▪ Label ▪ Screen

Me Too Computing

Here's a real example of a workaday Recast, nothing fancy, just enough to get three companies over a hump and into a marketplace.

Through the 1990s and into the new millennium, when centrally configured workhorse computers were becoming more of a computing problem than a solution, there was a flourish of Recasts when Forrester Research, the prominent technology and market research firm, foresaw a new class of computing. Its analysts called it "Organic IT," which, in a nutshell, hailed an era of dramatically faster, more flexible, and less costly computing solutions.

The idea was fine and it was about time, everyone agreed. But *Organic IT? Eeww*, said the focus groups. *That name would never do for the mainstream IT buyer*, the marketers said. *And, gee whiz, we've been talking about that stuff for years*, technologists noticed. So Sun Microsystems, long an authority on such things and custodian of the famous tagline "The Network Is The Computer," jumped in. But not with an *organic* computer. Loath to follow Forrester's lead and bent on finding that razor's edge of distinction, Sun called its design simply and innocuously *N1*. Next came IBM, which, to its own chagrin, had already invested a good deal of time and money in similar so-called autonomic and grid computing approaches. Big Blue confidently called its entry "On-Demand Computing." Computing when you want it, as you want it. Finally, it was HP's turn, not a shabby innovator itself and a dogged veteran of the enterprise computing market. HP's vision, it insisted, was even bigger: Utility Data Center.

. . . Which, in the end, didn't seem so far from the clumsy Organic Computing. But, oh, well. The Recasts were run. An original idea was morphed and morphed again to suit the needs of a tight crowd of competitors, all vying for a modicum of originality in an otherwise predefined space.

Neither IBM, Sun, nor HP did much more than rephrase an incumbent idea, so these Recasts were ultimately just low-level marketplace pirouettes. HP's Utility Data Center, for example, only modified and never trumped IBM's On-Demand. This is not to diminish the sizable campaigns that drove the N1, On-Demand, and Utility Data Center programs and which later on amounted to Crowding plays. But at the end of the day, the differences were only incremental and largely reconstituted semiproprietary efforts to rip apart and rebuild Forrester's original thesis.

TABLE B. EXAMPLES OF RECAST

Recasts to remember . . .	
	■ *Al Gore* Plastered with the label that he's wooden, 2000 U.S. presidential candidate Al Gore barnstormed the late-night talk show circuit to satirize—and humanize—himself. He was still wooden, but funnier than most thought.
	■ *Organic Computing* With the advent of collaborative "grid" computers, major players of enterprise computing rushed to name the trend. IT analyst firm Forrester coined the phrase "Organic Computing." IBM then called it "On-Demand Computing." Sun called it "N1." And HP called it "Utility Computing." They all had it, but each had its own name for it.
	■ *Bob Dole* *"What he's saying is 'Watch your pocketbook, because here I come!'"*—Bob Dole's quip at Bill Clinton's promise for federal support of state programs in the third and final 1996 U.S. presidential debate.

Sensitive Campaigning

Move over Sun, IBM, and HP, there are better Recasters than you. Take, for example, the handiwork of Lynne Cheney, second lady of the United States and wife of two-term U.S. vice president Dick Cheney. In 2004, as she was campaigning for the Bush/Cheney ticket in Joplin, Missouri, someone asked Mrs. Cheney an oddly loaded question: *What did she think about the Democratic challenger John Kerry's comments on conducting a sensitive war?* *

Six days earlier, on Thursday, August 5, 2004, in Washington, D.C., John Kerry had delivered a 4,500-word stump speech to a conference of minority journalists. The play he intended to run was a Fiat. New to his message was this 39-word statement: *"I believe I can fight a more effective, more thoughtful, more strategic, more proactive, more sensitive war on terror that reaches out to other nations and brings them to our side and lives up to American values in history."* The passage was a biting dig at GOP policy in Iraq, but the operative phrase, *sensitive war,* was vulnerable.

---

* It is said that in politics there is no such thing as coincidence. If you agree, then it's safe to say that Mrs. Cheney's questioner served as a subtle surrogate—a *Plant,* a trusted person to the ticket who could be relied upon to get the ball rolling, to set the faulty premise and ask the loaded question. Without this, the second lady would have seemed to be overstepping her bounds had she presented her opinions as statements rather than responses. And perhaps without her rapid-fire Recast, Kerry's sensitive stumping might have sunk in.

Sitting there in the Show Me State, the second lady seemed especially well prepared to expose the flaw. *"With all due respect to the senator,"* she said, head sadly shaking, *"it just sounded so foolish. I can't imagine that al Qaeda will be impressed by sensitivity."*

Bam.

In two sentences, the savvy bench player Mrs. Cheney dismantled the first stringer John Kerry and his play. First, she positioned Kerry's pledge as patently foolish. Second, she associated sensitivity with passivity. Third, she implied that al Qaeda would exploit passivity. It was a brilliant (perhaps rehearsed) twisting of terms that emasculated Kerry's Fiat and lent new meaning and reason to the uncompromising Bush/Cheney war strategy.

That was plenty clever, but Lynne Cheney wasn't done.

As I suggested earlier, the Recast has range. It can blur distinctions, as Sun, IBM, and HP did with Organic IT. It can enhance a player's position, as Lynne Cheney did with *sensitive war.* But it can also eclipse a competitor's agenda, as the second lady did next: She finished by saying that Kerry's comment was an expression of the *"extreme left"* idea that Americans bear responsibility for the terrorism now threatening them.

Ouch.

TABLE C. CALLING AND RUNNING A RECAST	
Call and run this play because . . .	■ The marketplace has misunderstood your message or misinterpreted your actions.
	■ The issues, ideas, and activities of your competitors are largely subjective. It's your job to contextualize them, to recast what you can in a favorable light.
	■ Your rival may be saying or doing things that should or must be reinterpreted—either to mute their position or support yours.
	■ The meaning of a competitor's position can be hijacked to enhance your own agenda.
	■ A rival's position is too broad—it can be picked apart and reapplied to your own platform or agenda.
	■ You're in trouble. You need to bridge the conversation back to your agenda.
	■ Your rival has your story wrong. You need to correct it.

If you're a Sneetch on the wrong end of a star system, the game is to reshape or at least dismantle the system. If you're a computer maker, late to get the vision thing, the game is to modify the latest new-new thing. If you're a radio icon facing a troubling statistic, the game is to position and de-position that statistic or its source. And if you're a politician trying to avoid an accusing finger, the game is either to duck from the direction it's pointing or to bend it back at the finger-pointer.

These examples are not far from other plays. As I wrote earlier, the Sneetch re-starring story may also have been a good example of a Label. But this is about the blurring of labels, so it only works up to a point for the goofy yellow birds. Likewise, Sun, IBM, and HP might seem to be running a Label, but their ideas don't come out of thin air. Their takes—N1, On-Demand, and Utility Data Center—aren't anything new so much as they are, in fact, rehashings of Forrester's very sticky Label—Organic IT. The idea of Rush and Al spinning their way out of an abortion boom might have a familiar ring. It smacks of a Filter, a move where a player holds back what it wants and rebroadcasts the rest. But in this hypothetical case, there's more than an editor's pen at work. Rush and Al are editing *and* interpreting the news of the day; they're actively enhancing those facts that they choose to sanction and pass along. Finally, Lynne Cheney might have seemed to be running a Mirror or Call Out, but from her small stage in remote Joplin, Missouri, she wasn't so much reflecting the facts back onto her opponent or calling him out as a fraud as she was morphing *his* ideas to suit *her* ticket's needs.

The Recast, in so many words, is a Label that gets ripped off, remade, and reapplied. It's a Filter on the front end and a spin machine on the back end. And it's a Mirror with an opinion and a Call Out with an implied verdict. So whether you're a Sneetch or second lady, the Recast is a good bet for changing your circumstances, for moving from a defensive position to a neutral one—which, if you're curious, is where the Sneetches all wound up. And if you're really good, the Recast is for reversing the threat entirely, which is where Lynne Cheney wound up, as though you didn't know.

TABLE D. DECODING AND COUNTERING A RECAST

How do I decode this play? *(i.e., How do I know it's being run against me?)*	■ Your words are being bent, taken out of context. ■ The competition is dodging the meaning or implications of your actions or messages. ■ The competition is using your position or agenda to strengthen its own platform. ■ You feel like you're doing more to help your competition than hurt them.
How do I counter this play?	■ Modify your position, removing those elements your rival is using to run its Recast, and then run a Fiat or Filter. ■ Run a Call Out or Mirror to tell the marketplace that your rival twisted your words. ■ Issue a Challenge. Dare your opponent to stick to the subject. ■ Label your opponent a spin doctor. ■ Deflect it. Don't dignify their spin with a response. ■ Run a Bear Hug. Agree with your opponent, telling the marketplace, *"We're glad you've got it right."*

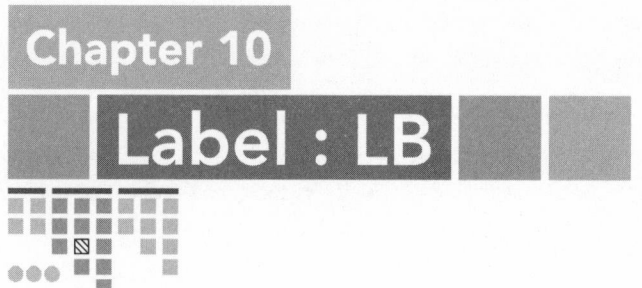

Chapter 10
Label : LB

RISK

REWARD

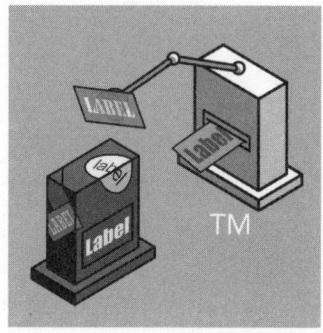

TM

Early in his watch as General Electric's CEO, Jack Welch cut a hundred thousand jobs, earning himself the unfortunate moniker "Neutron Jack," a reference to the bomb that leaves buildings standing but its inhabitants quite dead. A similar fate awaited the late hotel magnate Leona Helmsley, who, through her uncompromising and abusive management style, was tagged with the nickname "Queen of Mean." Others have inherited titles that have enhanced, not hurt, their reputations. Think of "The Big Unit," a big name for a big baseball pitcher, Randy Johnson. Think of "Big Blue," another big name, for a big computer company.

You wouldn't think something as simple as a nickname rates in the panoply of playmaking options. But these things have a crucial purpose. Whether they're used to enhance a benefit or enflame a sensitivity, they allow players to reduce the meanings and motives of both friends and foes into simple and memorable labels; hence, the play's name.

The Label reduces the complex to something that is more easily grasped. It creates an abbreviation, usually by way of a symbol or metaphor, that conveys in shorthand the attributes and circumstances of a player in its marketplace. The Label enables players to reinforce their own positions in more or less favorable terms, to self-label, if you will, and to rally their allies. Take Bill Clinton, for example, who liked to call himself "The Comeback Kid." And, as you'd expect, Labels are also run to cast rivals in disadvantageous positions, to de-position enemies and their affiliates and bind them up. Again, take Bill Clinton, whom others liked to call "Slick Willy." Labeling is a strategy we learn early and learn well. Just ask "Neutron Jack." It's an essential move for creating competitive advantage in your marketplace. Here are a variety of famous and infamous cases of the Label.

TABLE A. BASICS OF A LABEL	
Class	Condition
Subclass	Frame
Type	*Label*
Definition	A word or phrase—self-given by a player or attributed to an opponent—that reshapes or deepens the meaning of the recipient's position, brand, or reputation. A Label, typically rooted in symbols and metaphors, is characterized by simplification, alliteration, and other semantic tricks.
Upsides	■ Boils complicated issues down to easily digestible sound bites. ■ Magnifies a player's good side or, conversely, an opponent's bad side. ■ A well-run label is like the Energizer Bunny—it keeps going and going and going. ■ Produces powerful symbols or references that can be adopted by a player for flattering effect or pinned on an opponent for competitive advantage. ■ Can make an opponent the butt of marketplace jokes. Can draw even more laughs when the rival tries to remove the Label. ■ A Label can be used to set up a Bait, Challenge, or Call Out. ■ Labels are often humorous, a good way to capture the attention of the marketplace.
Downsides	■ Can breed scrutiny of the self-labeling player. The labeler can be seen as out-of-touch, shallow, or self-aggrandizing. ■ A self-applied Label might oversimplify or misrepresent your total offering. ■ Pasted on opponents, Labels are often taken as personal attacks. However necessary, appropriate, or tightly targeted, they can provoke an enemy to attack with disproportionate, even irrational, fury. ■ Can breed sympathies for the labeled opponent and/or a backlash toward the labeling player. The labeler can be seen as cruel or dishonest.
Related Terms	■ Nicknaming ■ A sound bite ■ Tarred and feathered

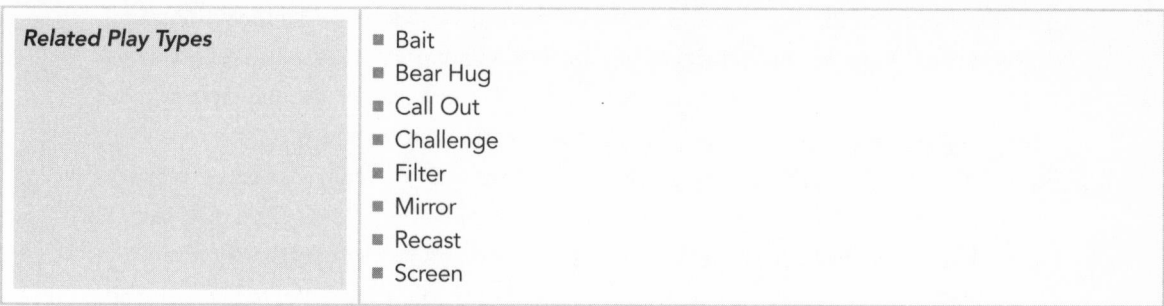

Related Play Types	■ Bait
	■ Bear Hug
	■ Call Out
	■ Challenge
	■ Filter
	■ Mirror
	■ Recast
	■ Screen

Windows Is a Hair Ball

One of the most adept labelers in business has to be Scott McNealy, the bad-boy co-founder and chairman of computer maker Sun Microsystems. His barbs have entertained the tech industry for years, not only because they're so well crafted but because they are so perfectly aimed. Like a comic, McNealy has a keen sense of what will play and when to deliver his best line. In the 1990s, when the rival operating system Windows seemed more like a kitchen sink of software than a well-designed operating system, McNealy took its maker, Microsoft, to task. Windows is a *"hair ball!"* he sniffed to the press and in speeches. It was, at the time, an audacious and gutsy thing to say, given Microsoft's rising power. But it drew laughs and it focused industry attention onto a valid issue—that the complexity of Windows was enough to make any user choke, like a cat hacking up its fur. McNealy's words and his amusing delivery resonated with Windows and Sun users alike, and it put Microsoft on the defensive.

Another patented McNealy Label, one that I confess came at the expense of a client, Hewlett Packard, was delivered during the tense drama of HP's campaign to acquire Compaq. *"It's like two garbage trucks colliding!"* McNealy heckled.*

The best Labels don't just influence history, they drive it. McNealy's Labels, for instance, are applied with such force that they have a self-fulfilling quality. After all, what would Windows have been without the hair ball tag? And what would the HP/Compaq merger have been without the garbage truck sign hanging over it? There is hardly anything so effective as a well-tuned, well-timed, and well-targeted Label. Pound for pound, it is one of the most cost-efficient and lowest-risk moves in a playmaker's arsenal.

---

* Much later, I learned from an industry insider that that HP CEO Carly Fiorina had placed a call to McNealy, begging him to stop his needling. This is a little like asking a shark to stop biting.

There is, naturally, a downside to these chiding Labels, and McNealy's habitual barbs serve as material evidence. Labels, similar to Peacocks, have a natural ability to get noticed. But they are less capable of driving relevance for the labeling player. They can materially confuse, upset, hold back, and minimize the progress of a rival (fair game in playmaking), but they don't so easily or automatically increase a player's relevance, even for the attention that is given to the labeling player. True, McNealy's peppering derision of Windows once put speed bumps in Microsoft's way and they didn't do the HP/Compaq marriage much good, either, but they never really drew the attention of the software marketplace onto an alternative, in this case Sun's own operating system, Solaris. When McNealy nicknamed Steve Ballmer and Bill Gates "Ballmer and Butthead," it hurt Microsoft's top executives; it reminded many that the duo seemed like an awkward pair. But it didn't confer a superior competence onto McNealy and *his* team. Some will argue, in fact, that McNealy's jibes did more to diminish his standing than his opponent's. To some, he is high entertainment. To others, he is horridly childish.

This is not to say that the Label should be mothballed, even for the organization that prefers to rise above, to take the high road. This is because the direction of the Label can be flipped to inspire and motivate. Even McNealy, who seems to have a preference for rhetorical street fighting, knows this. A case in point is his zealous dedication to the simple but profound tag "The Network Is The Computer." Few phrases have done a better job at explaining and challenging an industry to think. A bit more obscure, but worthy of mention, is McNealy's famous mantra *"Put all the wood behind one arrow,"* coined in 1989 to rally all of Sun's resources to a radical microprocessor design called SPARC. The Label was further reinforced when April Fool pranksters built a giant arrow—tip, feathers, and all—and mounted it through McNealy's executive office window.

TABLE B. EXAMPLES OF A LABEL	
Labels to remember . . .	■ **Scott McNealy** Sun Microsystems CEO Scott McNealy is famous for his barbs. About the 2002 HP/Compaq merger, he quipped, *"It's like two garbage trucks colliding."* About rival software from Microsoft, he proclaimed, *Windows is a "hairball."* The labels all stuck.
	■ **Johnnie Cochran** In his closing argument to jurists of the O.J. Simpson trial, defense attorney Johnnie Cochran said, over and over and over, *"If it [the glove] doesn't fit, you must acquit."* The clever verse was thought to have aided Simpson's eventual acquittal.
	■ **Political Labels** Republicans have successfully embedded the label "Liberal Democrats." Likewise, though with less success, their rivals have called themselves "Progressives" and conservatives "Radical Republicans."

Fahrvergnügen

Where Labels are consistently applied is in advertising. Subtle, suggestive, or some-times in-your-face, they are simply everywhere, usually in the form of taglines and slogans. This is not to diminish a delicate process in a vaunted craft. For all its appar-ent simplicity, the development of a two- or three-word jingle often overlies a back-bone of deep research and masterful creativity. In the end, however, the production of that perfect phrase is often a crystalline example of a Label.

These Labels below (listed alphabetically) are particularly well conceived and in many cases have enjoyed long, successful lives for various organizations, people, products, services, and causes.

- *Fahrvergnügen.* (Volkswagen)

- *Have it your way.* (Burger King)

- *I am the greatest!* (Muhammad Ali)

- *Intel inside.* (Intel)

- *Invent.* (Hewlett-Packard)

- *Just do it.* (Nike)

- *Keeps going and going and going.* (Energizer batteries)

- *Like a rock.* (Chevrolet trucks)

- *Only you can prevent forest fires.* (United States Forest Service)

- *Tastes great. Less filling.* (Miller Lite)

- *The happiest place on Earth.* (Disneyland)

- *The most trusted name in news.* (CNN)

- *The Network Is The Computer.* (Sun Microsystems)

- *The Pepsi Generation.* (Pepsi-Cola)

- *This is your brain. This is your brain on drugs. Any questions?* (The Partnership for a Drug-Free America)

- *We answer to a higher authority.* (Hebrew National hot dogs)

- *We bring good things to life.* (General Electric)

- *We make money the old-fashioned way—we earn it.* (Smith Barney)

- *When it absolutely, positively has to be there overnight.* (FedEx)

- *You're in good hands.* (Allstate Insurance)

Some of these are direct appeals, like Pepsi-Cola's *The Pepsi Generation* or HP's *Invent*. I call them self-nominating Labels because they go straight to an organization's defining core value. They tell you, straight up, who the brand is or what it's all about. Some require more effort to discern, like VW's hard-to-say *Fahrvergnügen* or Nike's easy-to-say *Just do it.* But once you're keyed into a tag's finer points, in these cases of driving comfort and athletics, the takeaway is unavoidable.

Of course, some advertising Labels make their mark with a double-edged sword. They position *and* de-position. This is the case with Intel's *Inside.* It says, in essence, We're in and you're not. Same goes for Disneyland's innocent-sounding *The happiest place on Earth*—the operative word being *happiest.* It makes the presumption that no other theme park is quite so happy a place, *on Earth* no less.

Then, of course, there are slogans that care only about the competition, not themselves. They are bent solely on de-positioning the threat. The Partnership for a Drug-Free America takes this approach to a skilled extreme: Recall in the 1987 TV commercial a raw egg hitting a hot griddle and the chilling voice-over: *"This is your brain. (Sizzle.) This is your brain on drugs. (Sizzle.) Any questions?"**

---

* In this case, the player being de-positioned is not a company, person, product, or service. It's an issue—the social ill of teen drug abuse.

TABLE C. CALLING AND RUNNING A LABEL	
Call and run this play because . . .	▪ A well-crafted sound bite cuts through the clutter of a complicated issue. ▪ It's an easy way to buy time, bind up a competitor, and draw attention to a rival's vulnerability. ▪ Applying a Label to yourself is also an easy way to give yourself credit. ▪ You have a Label that will stick . . . like in comedy, when you have a line you know will get a laugh. ▪ You want to poke, jab, or flummox your opponent. You don't want to press or attack. You just want to rib them. ▪ The marketplace doesn't understand what you're doing. Help them by attaching a pithy Label to yourself or your efforts. ▪ Your rival has something to hide that can be justifiably exposed and exploited.

I Have a Dream

All of these Labels have been run in free markets, in what many refer to as the court of public opinion. But the court of law is not exempt from the gamesmanship of play-making. Take, for example, the cunning of the late trial attorney Johnny Cochran, and his defense of the retired football star O.J. Simpson. During the famous 1995 double murder trial, his prize client had seemingly struggled to fit his large hands into gloves like those connected with the crime. Recalling the scene in his closing argument, Cochran cried with vindication, *"If it [the glove] doesn't fit, you must acquit!"* He said it again and again, despite the fact that O.J.'s hands did, however snugly, still fit inside the gloves.

No discussion of the Label is complete without a quick tour through politics. Take the 1962 address of U.S. president John F. Kennedy at Rice University in Houston, Texas, where he confidently intoned the famous line *"We choose to go to the moon."* For the record, the play most fundamental to Kennedy's famous moon speech was a Challenge; JFK used the Label to support his appeal to send men to the moon.

In the same era, Martin Luther King Jr. delivered his historic address at the March on Washington for Jobs and Freedom, a peaceful and massive demonstration for African-American civil rights. *"I have a dream!"* King thundered, nine times in his sixteen-hundred-word address.

Two decades later, in 1987, U.S. president Ronald Reagan stood before a crowd of rapt West Germans at the Berlin Wall, the symbol of communism and a foil to

Reagan's crusade against it. Framed by the Brandenburg Gate, he metered out his famous demand, *"General Secretary Gorbachev, if you seek peace, if you seek prosperity for the Soviet Union and Eastern Europe, if you seek liberalization, come here to this gate! Mr. Gorbachev, open this gate! Mr. Gorbachev, tear down this wall!"*

Each of these reflects an impressive mastery of the Label. Kennedy, King, and Reagan, each in his own way, each in support of his own agenda, reduced their positions into single, memorable phrases that held rich meaning to their constituents and the competitive potential of their ideas vis-à-vis their competitors'. Like all plays, this is what the Label is meant to do.*

But, of course, not all political playmaking is quite so distinguished. In fact, you might think of the Label as an abused substance in Washington, D.C. Self-nominating, double-edged, or threat-focused, labels abound in a lively game of playmaking tag. Democrats are painted as *Liberal Democrats* or, worse, *Massachusetts Democrats*. Republicans are painted as the *Radical Right* or, worse, the *Christian Right*. Democrats cast themselves and their ideas as *Progressive*. Republicans cast themselves and their ideas as having *Family Values*. And so it goes. Some of it self-nominating, some of it competitive, some of it defensive.

Richard Nixon suffered much at the hands of the Label. Remember *Tricky Dick*? It stuck, but nothing so well as the Label he inadvertently plastered to himself as the Watergate scandal of the early 1970s unfolded. When Labels are well conceived, when they resonate, whether appropriate or accurate, they don't easily come off. In fact, attempts to peel them away typically magnify the Label. Like a mosquito bite, I tell my kids, it's sometimes best to ignore them.

But Richard Nixon had to scratch. He didn't see himself as a criminal, the gist of how Watergate was going down. As a longtime public servant, he resented the inference. So in his third televised speech on the Watergate scandal, he read the infamous line *"I'm not a crook."* And there, he said it: *crook*. With so much suspicion left unchecked, he said what was on everyone's mind. It resonated and the sound bite played, over and over and over. Despite himself, Nixon had labeled himself.

---

* McNealy's "Hair ball," JFK's "We choose to go to the moon," MLK's "I have a dream," and Reagan's "Tear down this wall" were more than mere Labels. Each, in fact, employed the Label in support of broader strategies or *alpha plays*. "Hair ball" and "I have a dream" were Call Outs, intended to expose an obvious weakness or pretense of a rival—Microsoft and the U.S. government, respectively. "We choose to go to the moon" was a Challenge to the American people to lead in technology and science. So was "Tear down this wall" aimed at the Soviet Union and its system of communism. The Labels in these contexts operated as *beta* plays. For more information, see "Alpha and Beta Plays," p. 291.

Countering a Label is, well, tricky business. If a Label is correctly run, it really can't be removed unless or until the pasted player changes his fundamental position or platform. Nixon's solution was to run a Recast on what he felt were damaging Labels, generated by a hostile media. History confirms that he only made it worse. We know, of course, that the president would have been better served had he run a Lantern, the best play for self-disclosing, and then a Disco, the best play for salvaging a position and moving forward. Both, it should come as no surprise, are Contras—plays that are inherently counterintuitive to a playmaker's conventional interests.

When Labels don't have resonant strength, when they are not innately true and, perhaps, just amusing or needling, like "Tricky Dick," the player stands a better chance to remove them, usually by means of a Deflect or Mirror. The player can also just ignore the Label and go about his business, but savvy playmakers know this approach is problematic. If a Label carries, it creates a one-sided discussion that is never in the player's favor. It lets the labeler go on and on, as McNealy has been allowed to do. Many times, too, the Label is just run in fun so the player is best advised to laugh too. Sometimes that's all that's really required.

TABLE D. DECODING AND COUNTERING A LABEL

How do I decode this play? *(i.e., How do I know it's being run against me?)*	■ When a complex issue is boiled down to a single memorable word or phrase. ■ When your competitor gives *itself* a new nickname, and it sticks. ■ When your competitor gives *you* a new nickname, and it sticks. ■ When a joke keeps playing, the marketplace keeps laughing . . . maybe at you. ■ When you're trying to Deflect, but the Label sticks anyway. ■ When your efforts to change the Label's meaning just makes the Label stickier.
How do I counter this play?	■ If it's a Label your competition has given to itself, (1) run a counter-Label, to reduce the effects of the original Label, (2) run a Mirror to expose the rival's hypocrisy, (3) run a Bait to suggest the opponent is posing, or (4) Recast the Label as a bridge to get back to your strategy. ■ If it's a Label you want removed, (1) run a counter-Label to reduce the effects of the original Label, (2) take the high road by running a Deflect, but factor in the consequence of appearing disengaged or effete, or (3) run a Bear Hug or Disco. Sometimes it's better to laugh at yourself.

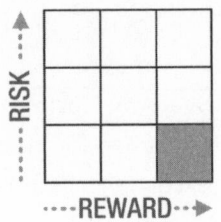

Chapter 11

Screen : SN

RISK ↑

←·····REWARD··→

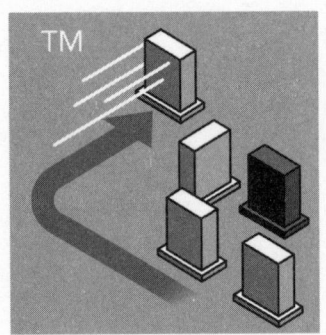

Playmaking is not a term borrowed from theater but playmakers borrow from it liberally to advance their positions or agendas—plot development, lighting design, set design, costumes, direction, casting, and acting as examples. They know to tell their story in the most interesting possible way, to build to a dramatic conclusion, to time the delivery of a line or gesture, to play off other characters, and so on. To go it alone in playmaking is otherwise dicey because one player, taken alone, conveys only a limited set of ideas in a marketplace. So playmakers—the good ones, at least—look for props to enhance their play action, and one of these is the Screen.

TABLE A. BASICS OF A SCREEN

Class	Condition
Subclass	Frame
Type	**Screen**
Definition	An attempt by a player to borrow issues, ideas, events, or other symbolic references to advance its agenda or thwart a competitor's movements.

Upsides	▪ Strengthens the impression that a player's agenda has a broader meaning or impact. ▪ Builds legitimacy for the player's position by creating new reference points *not* normally associated with the player. ▪ Elicits an emotional connection to your brand or position. ▪ Either deepens understanding and support for a player's agenda or distracts the marketplace and rivals from a player's self-interest. ▪ Allows the marketplace to better understand a player's position.
Downsides	▪ Can be seen as concocted, a thin veil to prop up a player's weak platform. ▪ Can position the player as running on fumes, not fundamentals. ▪ A player can attach itself to an issue or idea that is too grand or too great. ▪ Can leave egg on a player's face. Objects used to Screen (e.g., a celebrity, hero, or organization), may feel duped and will cast off the player, sometimes very publicly. ▪ Attach yourself to the wrong player, issue, or idea and your powerful Screen becomes a weighty anchor.
Related Terms	▪ A stalking horse ▪ A reference point
Related Play Types	▪ Bait ▪ Bear Hug ▪ Draft ▪ Filter ▪ Label ▪ Ping ▪ Recast ▪ Red Herring

Big Ideas

Take again the example of the late civil rights leader Dr. Martin Luther King Jr., an ordained Baptist minister and playmaker of unparalleled skill. He had a message that was engaging enough, no doubt, but it was his techniques for staging and contextualizing his vision that drew attention, broadened understanding for his ideas, and helped spur new laws to ensure equal rights for African Americans. His were not simple sermons delivered from simple pulpits; they were grand and sweeping and delivered against the richest metaphors. King's 1963 address to the March on Washington for Jobs and Freedom, in which he famously opined, *"I have a dream . . . ,"* was delivered to a quarter-million marchers. While this famous phrase is also evidence of a self-applied Label, as discussed in the previous chapter, it confirms his prowess as a playmaker, and particularly his use of the Screen. King's overarching strategy, his alpha strategy, was to run a Call Out. He plainly intended to expose lopsided government policies and through that process create a road down which his agenda could be driven. His supporting beta strategies for running this play were masterfully picked and planned. Chief among them was the Screen, a play type more subtle than most and whose purpose is to expand the context of a player's agenda or position in a way that both supports the player and unhinges the opposition. (For more information, see "Alpha and Beta Plays," p. 291.)

Screens, in other words, make for good theater. They are used to attach the player to ideas or issues that are larger than the player itself. Like a perfume, they are used to apply positive references onto the player and all that it has to say or do. Here's how King put this play to work:

In his sixteen-hundred-word speech, King repeatedly ran Screens to put his plight in a noble context. Laying the groundwork for his Call Out, he first invoked the image of the great emancipator, Abraham Lincoln, whose white-pillared memorial rose behind King as he commenced his address: *"Five score years ago, a great American, in whose symbolic shadow we stand today, signed the Emancipation Proclamation. . . ."* King's setup was clear—that the emancipation of slaves had perhaps been a hollow victory.

You might take this for a Draft because, indeed, King was riding the coattails of a former president and his heroic acts of conscience. But Drafts differ from Screens in that they are run against fast-moving competitors or fast-developing issues. Screens are run against slower-moving, inanimate and organic things, in this case the legacy of Abe Lincoln.

The reverend then moved to another sacred symbol of fair play, reciting a crucial line from the Declaration of Independence of 1776, reminding his audience that all men, black or white, *"would be guaranteed the 'unalienable rights' of 'life, liberty, and the pursuit of happiness.'"* Next, he borrowed from the national hymn, "America," nearly singing the lyrics, *"My country, 'tis of thee, sweet land of liberty . . . "* And, to close, he excerpted the slavery-era spiritual, roaring confidently, *"Free at last! Free at last! Thank God Almighty, we are free at last."*

Each of these passages connected King and his message to symbols that King could argue also stood for the cause of the African American. And so, by association, they served as a prop—a Screen—behind which King could move his agenda forward. Without these comparisons, his rhetoric would never have soared so high. It isn't that Martin Luther King was hiding behind anything. He was, in fact, quite clear about the comparisons he sought. But the connections he made to large and memorable symbols of freedom expanded his rhetoric and the merits of his mission. With his Screens, he made the rights of a marginalized minority a cause for an obligated majority. (For an illustrated analysis of King's "I have a dream" speech, see the Appendix, Play Action Maps, p. 312, or visit www.plays2run.com.)

TABLE B. EXAMPLES OF A SCREEN	
Screens to remember . . .	■ ***WMDs*** In the run-up to the second Iraq war, the Bush II administration fanned public worry over Iraq's reported weapons of mass destruction (WMDs). None were found and the White House suffered enormous credibility loss for having run the play.
	■ ***Reagan, the Pope, and Schiavo*** The Republican Party employs *Screens* with famous and, sometimes, infamous mastery. The GOP used the deaths of Ronald Reagan and Pope John Paul II, in 2004 and 2005 respectively, to connect its conservative agenda with the two leaders' legacies. But with less success, it exploited the media circus around the tragically brain-dead Terri Schiavo to advance its prolife position.
	■ ***MLK*** In his historic "I have a dream" speech of 1963, Martin Luther King Jr. invoked the image of the great emancipator, Abraham Lincoln, whose white-pillared memorial rose behind King as he commenced his address: *"Five score years ago, a great American, in whose symbolic shadow we stand today, signed the Emancipation Proclamation."* King's implication was clear—that the emancipation of slaves was thus far a hollow victory.

Big Winds

Other players also don't mind the masking effect of the Screen. Take, for example, Larry Ellison, the flamboyant CEO of business software powerhouse Oracle Corp., whose close shave on the high seas helped take the edge off his immodest reputation.

In December 1998, Ellison and his crew of professional sailors entered the Sydney-to-Hobart Yacht Race, a storied six-hundred-mile match held annually on the open ocean of the Tasman Sea and Bass Strait between Australia's Sydney Harbor and Tasmania's port city of Hobart. One hundred fifteen yachts had entered this rendition of the legendary race, Ellison's pristine eighty-foot *Sayonara* among them. But only forty-three completed the race as hurricane-force winds caught the fleet by surprise, swamping many, sinking others, and ultimately taking the lives of six souls. Ellison, his crew, and boat survived and, in fact, won the race, but the aftermath suggested that the billionaire software mogul could easily have been lost at sea or swallowed by it.

By his own account, Ellison gave the helm over to veteran sailors and watched in horror as his state-of-the-art sloop climbed up and careened down endless sets of forty-foot waves. This was not an image of Ellison that many might have recognized. Since founding Oracle, he had gained a well-deserved reputation for his ruthless management style. He'd also become a source of gossip for his personal exploits, as a playboy and pilot, in particular. In many respects, this served him well. It was arguably a necessary ingredient in the hectic and fast-growing software business. But what was never seen in Ellison or attributed to his popular caricature was the element of humility. He seemed to fear nothing, he seemed vulnerable to no one, and he seemed to exploit this privilege. The Sydney-to-Hobart Race changed all that because it put into the public record the undeniable fact that Ellison had contemplated a terrible death.

Back home and dried off, sitting before his peers and news media at San Francisco's St. Francis Yacht Club, Ellison recounted the details of the killer storm. It was a genuine session with a man widely perceived to be disingenuous, a legitimate Screen that sanded the sharp edges off one of history's most successful entrepreneurs. Did it change Larry Ellison? I can't say. But it made him mortal, at least for a while.

TABLE C. CALLING AND RUNNING A SCREEN

Call and run this play because . . .	■ There may be prominent players, symbols, and other developments out there whose brands, reputations, ideas, or meanings can be brought into the game.
	■ You don't need to operate on your own; you can enjoy the support or association of other ideas, events, and trends.
	■ Something in the marketplace speaks to your own ideas. Or . . . it contradicts, confuses, or de-positions your competitor's platform.
	■ You want to be associated with a newsworthy idea or some kind of innovation.
	■ Your position or agenda can be clarified by hitching it to a better-understood player, theme, or idea.
	■ Your position isn't resonating . . . and your rival's is.

Big Worries

Insurance is fundamentally a hedge against risk, and so it is a fundamental necessity of insurance carriers to communicate the value of security in order to sell policies. Homeowners are warned of the potentials for fire and theft among other accidents and incidents, car owners of collision and injury, parents and spouses of an untimely death, executives and doctors of errors and omissions. Through myriad marketing vehicles, policy holders are all conditioned to expect—and insure themselves against—the unexpected and to feel better for it. Some do this with care, promising, as Allstate does, that you're in good hands. Some do it with comedy, like the Aflac duck or the GEICO gecko. Others are more direct. Take, for example, the edgy campaigns of John Hancock or The Hartford, which have obliquely featured death, divorce, and adoption. Either way, they are running Screens. They attach themselves to large issues and they walk behind them, camouflaged by more engaging and motivating matters. Whether trusting hands, quacking ducks, or sudden death, they all serve as the Screen behind which insurance policies are sold.

Health care companies are similarly geared. Whether it's the availability of a new drug, the advancements of a new birthing center, or the speed of a new imaging technology, they are selling against the Screens of two important emotions—hope for better living and fear of disease and disability. They don't sell a new therapy for erectile dysfunction, they sell a saved relationship. They don't sell a new maternity ward, they sell a healthy baby. They don't sell a new CT scanner, they sell a clean bill of health.

Among many playmakers, the Screen is called a "Stalking Horse," a term that owes its beginnings to a long-forgotten technique of bird hunters. As they entered a field, fowlers would dismount their steeds and stalk their quarry on foot, hiding behind their mounts and nudging them forward for a better shot. In this way, the horse is quite literally a screen, a physical prop used by the player (a hunter with a gun) to advance its position against its competitor (a bird with wings).

Usually, however, the Screen is a more abstract device for complementing or cloaking a player's agenda or position. Take, for instance, the critical role it plays in business, particularly in bankruptcy proceedings. When a company is up for auction, enterprising investment bankers and nervous creditors will scour the investment community for a safe first bidder, a person or organization who's willing to make a reasonable bid and thus ensure against low-balling buyers and resulting fire sales. The bidder is called a stalking horse, though not because the bid is illegitimate. To the contrary, a stalking horse sometimes gets its wish. But the mere existence of a bona fide offer implies value and that, in turn, spurs competitive bidding from other suitors. Just like the bird hunter, the stalking horse bidder serves to conceal the player's actual position.

Similar moves are sometimes made in political campaigning where a weak candidate may be sent into the hustings to feel out the voting public. Such was thought to be the case in the 2004 U.S. presidential election when General Wesley Clark entered the fray as the tenth candidate for the Democratic presidential nomination. Pundits immediately saw the Arkansas native and former Clinton administration NATO commander as a stalking horse, trotted into the political paddock to scatter the field, rein in the left-leaning and fast-running Vermont governor Howard Dean, and set up a last-minute bid by Senator Hillary Rodham Clinton. Beltway insiders fingered former president Bill Clinton as the master playmaker, a close confidant of Clark's and a presumably loyal champion of his wife's political ambitions.

Wesley Clark was a mere statistic in the pantheon of political screens. Others have been run with more famous and infamous effect. Republicans deftly showcased their platform in the 2004 death of former president Ronald Reagan. Whether out of love for "The Great Communicator" or to spite Democrats, Reagan was memorialized by conservatives as a symbol of the Republican Revolution. GOP fingerprints were also evident in the passing of Pope John Paul II in 2005, when conservative leaders were quick to connect their party's legacy with the popular pope's fights against communism and for families. For better or worse, a former president and former pontiff were deftly enlisted as Screens to the GOP's agenda.

Screens are symbols and metaphors that players use to advance their cause. They are typically part of a marketplace's natural or ambient setting and, as such, are free for the taking. They come in the form of subjective issues, like the renewed debate over evolution and so-called intelligent design. They come in the form of trends, like the movement toward corporate transparency and social responsibility. And they come in the form of people, like the ill-fated Florida woman Terri Schiavo, whose slow death polarized the court system, legislators, and special interest groups alike.

Whether it's Martin Luther King Jr. using the Declaration of Independence to stop a conflict or George W. Bush using weapons of mass destruction to start one, the Screen is instinctive to savvy playmakers and one of the most common and powerful tools in the playmaker's arsenal. Is it a noble or ethical play? That, of course, is a matter of perspective and rich debate. What is justifiable positioning to one player is often unjustifiable de-positioning to another. In either case, the Screen is no doubt alive and well in business, politics, and popular culture and if it's not your play of choice, it at least deserves study. Screens, like all plays, are everywhere.

TABLE D. DECODING AND COUNTERING A SCREEN	
How do I decode this play? *(i.e., How do I know it's being run against me?)*	■ Take careful note of the people or things that your competitors reference. These are clues, either to the flags your rivals like to salute or the barriers they like to put in your way. ■ Screens are often run by a player when they are talking about themselves, not about you. This makes them hard to detect. ■ Poorly run Screens look like disingenuous Bear Hugs and are easy to detect. ■ Watch for spontaneous eruptions of information, often in the form of gossip or news, that grows to represent a broader issue (e.g., a baby's death is blamed on a general flu-shot shortage). ■ When your opponent references a person, organization, issue, or symbol that elicits an emotional response.
How do I counter this play?	■ Run Screens of your own to build reference points for you . . . and speed bumps for your opponent. ■ Counter with Proxies to expand your support base. ■ Run a Challenge to force "screenees" to abandon, or even publicly disavow, your rivals. ■ Run a Mirror. Expose your rival for exploiting sacred ideas or revered people. ■ Run a Call Out. Find a flaw in your opponent's understanding of the Screen they just referenced. ■ If the Screen is also good for your brand, co-opt it, run a Bear Hug.

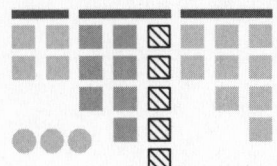

The Freeze Subclass

The final third of the Condition class, Freeze, is not as diplomatic as its counterpart, Frame, and just as capable as its sibling, Divert.

*def. **Freeze:** Play action that inhibits the movement of a competitor, confuses its motives, or prevents further erosion to a player's position and agenda.*

Where diverting plays keep rivals and competitive developments off a player's back, freezing plays help the player move forward. They help it clear a path and they do so with the assistance of no fewer than five play types—the largest set of plays in any subclass—Mirror, Jam, Bear Hug, Lantern, and Disco.

A Mirror is used to expose the weaknesses of a competitor, to force a rival to contend with the truth of its own record or past deeds. The Jam is run to stop a threat and, even literally, disable the machinery that makes a rival formidable and dangerous to a player. The Bear Hug is for co-opting a smartly positioned foe, a means of forcing it to share its idea or share the stage. The Lantern is a preemptive spotlight, cast onto the player, by the player, to proactively reveal its own flaws. And finally, the Disco, a term borrowed from the traditions of parliamentary debate, is employed to resuscitate a damaged position or platform. It is, in essence, a strategy that moves a player one step back to move two steps forward.

Freezing does as its name implies. It stops runaway rivals, whether it's a run amok competitor who needs to be taken down a notch or a mouthy competitor who needs to give up some of the stage. It stops meltdowns, too, by heading them off before they happen or salvaging them when they do. Up next are the full stories of the five Freezing plays, the Mirror, Jam, Bear Hug, Lantern, and Disco.

Chapter 12

Mirror : MI

RISK

REWARD

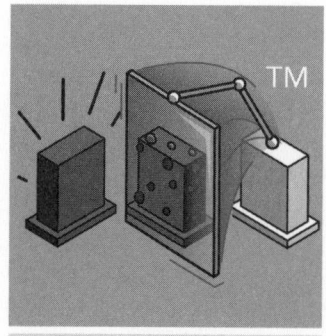

™

There's a saying, Mirrors never lie. In the Bible, in Shakespeare, and elsewhere, mirrors serve as symbols of honest reflection, of what is actual, not what is acted. So it goes that in playmaking the Mirror is the play type that sets the record straight—or tries to in the eyes of the mirroring player. Held up, metaphorically, of course, against posing players, Mirrors attempt to tell a fuller story and show the marketplace the portions of a rival's play action that are fact or fabricated.

The Mirror operates in the Condition class of plays, serving alongside the Jam, Bear Hug, Lantern, and Disco to *freeze* opposing players, to stop them in their tracks or in some way dismantle or dismast their programs. It also has a crudely effective quality insofar as it relies on the raw force of the information or facts that it reflects to slow or stop a rival. It's really not very tricky, but it is the play that says to an opponent, and to anyone who's listening: *This is who you really are. This is what you're really doing. Deal with it.*

At the risk of being too clever, I should explain that the Mirror is, well, the mirror opposite one of the freezing plays just mentioned, the Lantern. The difference is that players who run Lanterns do to *themselves* what the Mirror might threaten to do to them. It's also a close relation to the Call Out. Like twins separated at birth, the Mirror serves to expose information and, similarly, the Call Out serves to exploit it. One freezes, the other attacks.

TABLE A. BASICS OF A MIRROR

Class	Condition
Subclass	Freeze
Type	***Mirror***
Definition	A specialized form of a Call Out, a Mirror introduces new facts or information into a marketplace which contradicts a rival's position or point of view. Like forcing someone to look at her own reflection, a Mirror typically prevents a rival from credibly pursuing its agenda.
Upsides	<ul><li>Can shatter marketplace perceptions of a rival's strength.</li><li>"Freezes" or stops a competitor from taking a position, using a particular approach, or running a set of plays.</li><li>Forces public inspection of an opponent's claim or point of view.</li><li>Allows the mirroring player to resume its agenda, no longer forced to play defense.</li><li>Focuses marketplace discussion on your opponent's flaws, not your own.</li><li>Establishes a history that your opponent doesn't play fair, or is hiding something.</li><li>Levels the playing field.</li></ul>
Downsides	<ul><li>A Mirror can consume enormous energy and resources, usually in the form of research. Thus, it can reduce a player's forward momentum.</li><li>Mirrors that fail to freeze a rival are like wounding a bear—they can draw the attention, even the fury, of a larger and more dangerous player.</li><li>Used inappropriately or too often, Mirrors can backfire, triggering accusations that the mirroring player is using smear tactics and going negative.</li><li>We all have skeletons in our closets. If you expose theirs, they may expose yours.</li></ul>
Related Terms	<ul><li>Pulling back the curtain</li><li>Stating the obvious</li><li>Skeletons (as in, letting them out of the closet)</li><li>Turning evidence</li><li>Whistleblowing</li><li>White elephants (as in, noticing them in the room)</li></ul>

Related Play Types	■ Bear Hug
	■ Call Out
	■ Disco
	■ Jam
	■ Label
	■ Lantern

Plain Politics

For two memorable mirroring plays, think of the managed photo-op of Massachu-setts governor Michael Dukakis when, during the 1988 U.S. presidential campaign, the former lawyer donned an oversized helmet and earphones and boyishly jumped aboard an M1 Abrams tank. *Look at me, I'm a tank driver!* The image was such a stretch for the bushy-eyed Bostonian, so obviously absurd, that all GOP operatives had to do was to make sure every news media outlet got the photo. The quipping captions practically wrote themselves. They also used the images in their ads, casting Dukakis as anything *but* a commander-in-chief. Republican strategists did the same in the 2004 presidential race when John Kerry took to a patch of Ohio farmland for an afternoon of goose hunting with average Joes. The aristocratic senator was so clearly out of place in his hunting fatigues that his attempt to court moderate Na-tional Rifle Association voters all but backfired.

This is not to suggest that the other guys don't also know their way around a Mir-ror. In 2003, the political satirist and comedian Al Franken published a photo of the conservative network broadcaster Bill O'Reilly that required little translation (i.e., it told its own joke). Prominently planted on the cover of Franken's 2003 best-selling book, *Lies and the Lying Liars Who Tell Them,* the candid picture caught O'Reilly with a jabbing finger, a fierce scowl, and what Franken flippantly described as a "splotchy" complexion. As some Mirror objects are prone to do, the rival took the bait: Appear-ing with Franken at a book publishing conference, O'Reilly reportedly accused the comedian of doctoring the photo. Al still insists that it was unretouched, splotches and all, that it was a true image of his rage-prone counterpart. But Bill didn't like what he saw, a predictable reaction for a rage-prone opponent to a satirical reflection.

Mirrors that weren't so comical, which in fact served to expose oversight and scandal, were run by the gutsy Cynthia Cooper of WorldCom, Sherron Watkins of Enron, and Coleen Rowley of the FBI. Their Mirrors were courageous and successful attempts to alert their big employers to big improprieties. They were often called whistleblowers. What serves to distinguish Cooper, Watkins, and Rowley from typical tattletales, however, is that they ran their plays *inside* their organizations and on their *own* companies. Cooper, an internal auditor, reported her revelations of massive accounting fraud in a 2002 report to WorldCom directors. Rowley, an FBI staff attorney, wrote a letter in 2002 to her director, Robert Mueller, suggesting that the Bureau had botched or buried pre-9/11 information that could have thwarted the airline hijacker Zacarias Moussaoui. Watkins, a corporate development executive, detailed her grave worries over improper accounting methods in a 2001 e-mail to her chairman, Kenneth Lay. All three were playmakers of a different sort, working initially to advise their superiors, not *out* them. In each case, they held up their information against conventional wisdom and contrary to popular views, to set the record straight.

TABLE B. EXAMPLES OF A MIRROR	
Mirrors to remember . . .	■ ***DHL versus FedEx/UPS*** In 2002 UPS and FedEx filed separate petitions asking the U.S. Department of Transportation to review the ownership of their smaller rival DHL Airways, whom they suspected to be owned by subsidiaries of the German government. ■ ***Boeing versus Airbus*** For years, U.S. aircraft manufacturer Boeing has publicly chided its European rival, Airbus, for receiving subsidies. Recently, Airbus has put a mirror up to its enemy, suggesting that Boeing, too, is receiving tax breaks from local and state auditing boards. ■ ***Whistleblowers*** Cynthia Cooper of WorldCom, Sherron Watkins of Enron, and Coleen Rowley of the FBI ran Mirrors inside their companies to root out corruption. All three bucked conventional wisdom to set the record straight.

Plane View

Mirrors ensure balance in a marketplace and the perspective of its players. To that end, perspective has been a constant source of struggle in the big league game of the civil aircraft industry.

Chicago-based Boeing Company and Toulouse-based Airbus SAS of France, the makers of most every large operating commercial jetliner in the world today, have waged a trade war of words—and Mirrors—in their respective attempts to expose financial strategies as financial aid. What started as simple sniping in the 1970s by Boeing at its then infant rival Airbus has developed into a barely civil, though usually very public, catfight, one that motivated Boeing to terminate a 1992 trade agreement with the European Union and appeal the matter to the World Trade Organization.

The issue, originally presented by Boeing, is fairness. Airbus, it has long claimed, is having its cake and eating it, too, as a recipient of "launch aid" and other government-sponsored research programs and tax breaks from member states of the European Union. These, Boeing has argued, allow Airbus to charge less for a comparable product and win valuable contracts—a clear cheat in the spirit of fair play and of support for international trade agreements.

Airbus, which has acknowledged the existence of its financial safeguards, has run its own Mirror, countering that Boeing's accusations are hypocritical. The American system, its executives have scoffed, virtually guarantees Boeing's financial health, claiming that state subsidies provided to its Washington-based design and manufacturing operations, to say nothing of military and government contracts and federally funded research, allow Boeing to perform its high-wire manufacturing act over a very large safety net.

What's notable about the mirroring between Boeing and Airbus is that it's repetitive. Tit for tat. In speeches and interviews, with legislators and regulators, the airplane makers repeat their positions over and over, as though they've not been heard the first time, as though the position of each is patently more valid than the other's. The result is a form of playmaking gridlock: two competitors, faced off and ticked off, neither of which has seemingly anything new to say or has any better way to modulate or advance its respective business strategies. Their arguments are internally cathartic, but for others watching—especially their customers—the images are hardly inspiring.

This full-blown subsidy fracas is probably not what Boeing had in mind when it first yanked at Airbus's curtain. Boeing, the Boy Scout company that it is, ahem, just wanted to let everyone know their upstart competitor had an unfair advantage. But Airbus saw the Boeing stance differently, more as an act of protecting a double standard than promoting fair play, so they took a pull on Boeing's curtain, too, and, bang, the game was on.

TABLE C. CALLING AND RUNNING A MIRROR	
Call and run this play because . . .	■ Your competition is promoting a fallacy or flat-out lying. ■ It puts a check on your competition, making them more accountable for what they say and do. ■ You see a chink in your opponent's armor that can be pried open or exposed. ■ Your opponent's background or history suggests they are not sincere. ■ You have information on your rival that can be fairly and credibly brought to light. ■ If you don't expose your rival, who will? You have the right to fairly and aggressively compete in your marketplace.

Plain Naked

What Boeing probably had in mind was something more straightforward—a simple exposure of an embarrassing truth. Perhaps, in their early strategy sessions, someone mentioned the well-worn and earliest told tale of a well-played Mirror: the 1837 Danish children's tale by Hans Christian Andersen, "The Emperor's New Clothes."

You'll recall that this classic ends as a youth watches his king parade about in what subjects are told is the most modern of gowns. It begins, however, when the king is taken in by a pair of con men posing as expert weavers, eager to sew a suit of ultimate forward fashion for this fashion-forward king. The critical feature, the weaver's insist straight-faced, is that only his most cultivated and intelligent subjects will be able to actually *see* and admire the gown. Others will be too stupid to marvel at the finery and will see nothing at all. The king, eager to flaunt his new threads and happy to separate the cultured from the classless, gleefully accepts their pitch and sends them spindles of gold thread and bolts of silk to complete the project. The weavers, of course, stash away their booty and pantomime the rest—weaving, cutting, pinning, and sewing their hoax together.

Anxious for his new finery, the emperor brags of his commission and sends gullible advisors to check the work. Seeing nothing, of course, but believing they *should*, they report good progress to the king. And so it goes. Before long, an entire royal court and its subjects are breathless with anticipation of a royal procession of the king in his state-of-the-art threads.

When the day arrives, the king obliges his weavers to remove *all* his clothes and he steps in as the gowns are laid upon him, air upon bare. No one flinches. Everyone is tight-lipped and pleased. The king has once again set the bar for elegance in his land. And so he sets about for a stroll through the village, happy to flaunt his new duds. His subjects coo and clap, each a little perplexed but each ready to accept the possibility that they are only too thickheaded to see the unseeable elegance of the emperor's new clothes. There are holes, of course, in this sphere of influence and one young boy, looking upon the scene, innocently blurts, *"But he has nothing on at all . . . ?"* The crowd, rocked by the child's clairvoyance, begins to mumble and soon everyone has to admit that, indeed, the king is buck naked.

He wasn't so clever as Al Franken, as bold as Cynthia Cooper, Sherron Watkins, and Coleen Rowley, or as hasty as Boeing. The boy just said what he saw, with no malice intended, and in one quick flash of the Mirror, his king was told, in so many words: This is who you *really* are. This is what you're *really* doing.

The emperor was busted.

TABLE D. DECODING AND COUNTERING A MIRROR	
How do I decode this play? (*i.e., How do I know it's being run against me?*)	■ When you're confronted by your rival or others, particularly prospective customers or members of the news media, to answer questions about your past decisions, actions, or background. ■ When information surfaces that undermines your credibility or the viability of your agenda.
How do I counter this play?	■ If the Mirror is true, run a Disco to apologize for or explain your motivations. ■ If the Mirror is off-base, run a Deflect to buy time or take the high road. ■ If the Mirror is false and even slanderous, run your own Mirror to explain why it's wrong and to put the competitor on notice. ■ Label your opponent as malicious or inaccurate. ■ Run a Recast to recharacterize the accusations of the Mirror. ■ Run a Red Herring. Feign shock at your attacker's methods.

Chapter 13
Jam : JM

RISK ↑

····REWARD····▶

Plays are run with the intention of improving the relative competitive advantage of an organization. However it gets done, the critical result is that Player A should end up in a better place vis-à-vis Player B. The greater the separation, the greater the relative competitive advantage. There are three ways to get this done (as shown on pp. 27–28): (1.) Elevate or accelerate the player. (2.) Slow or stop the opponent. (3.) Or both.

The featured play of this chapter, the Jam, is suited exclusively to the second option: It serves to suppress or slow opponents.

Now, if you think of yourself as more of a competitor than collaborator, you'll happily keep the Jam in your bag of playmaking tricks. To you, it matters not if you win by raising the level of the marketplace lake, by floating everyone's boat, so to speak, or by opening the floodgates and taking everyone down a few notches. But if you're more about the win-win than the win-lose, this play is probably not a favorite. After all, it *takes away* from your rival. It stops them. It holds them back. It runs counter to how you like to do business. It's just not a very nice way to do business, gosh darn it.

The problem, of course, is that not everyone plays it so clean. When opportunities arise to cut off a rival or disorganize or disorient the enemy, many players will do so—and you may be their target. So whether you're a bounty hunter, customer hugger, or something in between, the Jam is a play that every player must at least understand, if not master.

TABLE A. BASICS OF A JAM

Class	Condition
Subclass	Freeze
Type	**Jam**
Definition	An attempt to disable or disorganize a rival's activities or communications. A Jam is typically intended to obscure, slow, or stop the delivery or acquisition of ideas or information of a rival.
Upsides	■ Slows or stops offensive play action by a rival. ■ Disables an opponent's method(s) for communicating to or working with stakeholders. ■ Forces the opposition to divert resources to build or repair channels and programs. ■ Destabilizes, usually for a short term, a rival's rapport with target audiences. ■ Jams can require very few resources. They can be used by Davids to topple Goliaths.
Downsides	■ Can be seen as tampering, aggressive, mean-spirited, or simply destructive. ■ Even if a Jam is justified, legally and ethically, this play can invite Labels you might rather not wear and consequences you might rather not endure. ■ A good Jam denies a player something it wants to have or wants to do. You may get a stronger counterreaction than you want or can handle.
Related Terms	■ Barrage jamming ■ Blocking ■ Crossing the wires ■ Scrambling ■ Short-circuiting ■ Spot jamming
Related Play Types	■ Bear Hug ■ Disco ■ Lantern ■ Mirror ■ Preempt

The Jam is the second of the five freezing play types, meaning that it's only incrementally more complex or dicey than its close companions the Mirror, Bear Hug, Lantern, and
Disco. What makes it so distinct, however, isn't its associated degree of difficulty but that
it's simply and purely focused on the rival. It does nothing directly to advance the
player's position except for the very important fact that it improves the player's *relative*
position by worsening that of its rival. It obscures a rival's vision so a player can be left
alone. It slows an opponent so a player can catch up or pull ahead. It stops a competitor so a player can stand pat without losing ground. Here are a few quick examples
you may recall:

- In 1989, U.S. troops in Panama City made life, and rational thinking, very difficult for
  the refugee general Manuel Noriega, the newly deposed Panamanian dictator who
  had received asylum in his country's Vatican embassy. American generals ordered
  the construction of a huge wall of audio speakers on the front lawn of the normally
  placid Nunciatura. Through the Christmas holidays, they blasted hard rock tracks
  into Noriega's clever sanctuary, both to prevent eavesdropping reporters from listening in and to harass and unsettle Noriega and his henchmen. Psyops (psychological operations) specialists later claimed that the maneuver unnerved Noriega
  and hastened his surrender.

- For years, activists from the animal rights group PETA (People for the Ethical Treatment of Animals) have resorted to all manner of pranks to stop the exploitation of
  animals, from their use in laboratories to their use as, shall we say, luxuries. Fashion
  magazine editor Anna Wintour of *Vogue* earned PETA's wrath when she refused
  to withdraw ads for animal fur garments. For her apparently callous disregard of
  nature's furry children, she was unceremoniously met with a tofu pie in the face, a
  raccoon carcass on her restaurant lunch plate, and a box of rotting animal intestines delivered to her office. She also became the poster child for a PETA antifur
  campaign—a contorted picture of the defiant editor with the slogan *"Fur Is Worn
  by Beautiful Animals and Ugly People."*

- U.S. president Bill Clinton lived up to his nickname "Slick Willy" during 1998
  grand jury testimony when he made a big attempt to parse a very small word—
  surely in the interest of derailing his detractors. When asked about an earlier
  pledge that no hanky-panky had occurred with intern Monica Lewinsky, his inter-
  rogator was incredulous. *"Your . . . statement was an utterly false statement. . . . Is
  that correct?"* To which the president responded intellectually, *"It depends on what
  the meaning of the word is is. If the—if he—if is means is and never has been,*

that is not—that is one thing. If it means there is none, that was a completely true statement."

And that, dear reader, is a Jam.

TABLE B. EXAMPLES OF A JAM	
Jams to remember . . .	■ **Rathergate** In 2004, *60 Minutes II* broadcast its discovery of memos from a Texas Air National Guard squadron commander that questioned the service and commitment of one Vietnam era pilot—George W. Bush. Bloggers from Free Republic, Little Green Footballs, Powerline, and other conservative sites generated a litany of howling posts that questioned the memo's authenticity and CBS's reporting techniques and, in the end, forced the resignation of veteran anchor Dan Rather.
	■ **Republican National Convention** In the heat of the summer of 2004, thousands of protesters from scores of nongovernmental organizations (NGOs) descended on Manhattan to dismantle, redirect, and generally sabotage the messaging machine of the Republican National Convention.
	■ **Manuel Noriega** In 1989, U.S. troops in Panama City blasted head-splitting hard-rock hits on the front lawn of the Vatican embassy. The effect was said to have hastened the surrender of General Manuel Noriega, a refugee inside the normally placid Nunciatura.

Blog Jams

The Jam is akin to what battlefield commanders do in conflict and war. In fact, this is where the play gets its name. From barrage jamming to spot jamming, the military is expert at electronically obscuring, slowing, or stopping an enemy from delivering or acquiring ideas or information. One form of this, called acoustic jamming by the U.S. Department of Defense, has a particularly pointed and eerie definition: *"The deliberate radiation [of] signals with the objectives of obliterating or obscuring signals that the enemy is attempting to receive and of disrupting enemy weapons systems."*

Deliberate radiation? Obliteration? Disrupting enemies? Who does anything like *that* in a marketplace? In a word . . . *bloggers.*

On the night of September 8, 2004, monitoring *60 Minutes II*, the Wednesday edition of the prime-time news show, watchdogs from conservative blogs hit the net in a spontaneous blitz of jamming plays. Their objective was to freeze what they believed to be a media-assisted attempt to rekindle suspicions of President George W. Bush's military service record. Democratic operatives, they guessed, were attempting to breathe life into old reports of a dodgy National Guard stint (a Screen) and they were doing it through sympathetic journalists (Proxies) and doctored documents (Plants).

Reporting for the CBS newsmagazine, veteran TV news anchor Dan Rather revealed what he expected to be another *60 Minutes* blockbuster exclusive: photocopies of four typewritten memoranda dated from 1972 to 1973, two of which bore the apparent signature of the commander of the Texas Air National Guard squadron to which Bush was once assigned. These memos, Rather suggested, were proof positive that the young Lieutenant Bush received preferential treatment while serving as a Guardsman and, worse, that he evaded military duty by swapping his pilot's wings for wingtips to work in a U.S. Senate campaign.

In the days when the mainstream media—and *60 Minutes* in particular—reported on stories with authority and exposed targets at will, the piece might have scored a direct hit. But now Rather and CBS had competition.

Within hours (and in one case minutes) of the aired segment, bloggers from the likes of Free Republic, Little Green Footballs, and Powerline generated a litany of howling posts that questioned the memo's authenticity as well as CBS's politics. The accuracy of their claims varied but they were taken seriously nonetheless by CBS and its more typical news rivals in print and broadcast.

The self-styled citizen journalists raised the possibility that the memos had been doctored or flat-out forged, accusing CBS not just of a case of bad reporting but of promoting a pet liberal conspiracy theory. They produced experts who claimed that typewriters in the early seventies couldn't handle proportional spaces or generate the superscripted "th" symbols (i.e., 4th, 5th, 6th, etc.) evident in some memos. They argued that the lingo of the memos was off-stride, not in keeping with how military terms and procedures were typically referenced. The word *billets* was misused, they argued. In this context, the word *positions* would have been the norm. The motives and politics of Rather himself, long ago plastered by conservatives with a liberal Label, were also questioned. So were those of Rather's producer, Mary Mapes, and her sources. Was she doing her job inside CBS? Or was she doing an inside job for the Democrats? bloggers wondered.

It's not known to what extent conservative bloggers worked in concert as they punched away at the *60 Minutes* report. But what's materially obvious is that they served notice of the playmaking prowess of citizen journalist bloggers. Collectively, they stuffed the public record with credible sound bites that overwhelmed CBS.

The resistance by liberal bloggers and CBS was hardly on a par. CBS ran only a weak series of Deflects, claiming that in the early seventies typewriters *did* exist that could bang out a superscripted "th." *And when you've run documents through photocopiers so many times,* they moaned, *who's to say what's sans and what's serif?* Ultimately, as most know, CBS ran a full and unequivocal Disco through the sacrificial early departure of Dan Rather from *The CBS Evening News* and the firing of Mapes and three others.

Inasmuch as the Jam describes the motivations of the bloggers, it doesn't account for their specific actions. So where was the Jam? As I describe in "Alpha and Beta Plays" on page 291, the bloggers' Jam was an *alpha* play. It was the strategy that generally guided or fueled the online outcry. And like any alpha play, it was punctuated by a series of supporting moves, called *beta* plays: The postings about typewriters and billets were Mirrors (if they were true) and Red Herrings (if they were not). Reminders of Rather's liberal leanings were Labels, reapplied with vigor. And accusations that Mary Mapes's sources were Democrat shills were Call Outs (if they were true) and Baits (if they were not).

This begs a question: Could the CBS critics have run a jamming beta play? The answer is yes. Beta-level Jams could have been run that directly disabled CBS or the elements of the Bush memos story. Saboteurs could have clipped the physical wires on its network antennae and crazed liberal-media-hating protestors could have chained themselves to the front doors of CBS headquarters. But these, to my knowledge, were not undertaken, so no Jams were run, at least as beta plays, to beat back CBS.

As most know, the bloggers did more than just freeze a dangerous story. They created a phenomenon in their marketplace. Through a cascade of follow-on stories their blog-induced scandal earned two spontaneous and damning labels: *Memogate* it was called hopefully by liberals, *Rathergate* by the rest. The bloggers turned a probing and possibly legitimate investigative piece into a referendum on the relevance and political bias of mainstream media. They removed further scrutiny of the president and his duties during the Vietnam era. They foiled a Democratic attempt to expose a president. And, last, they liquidated a member of the mainstream media said to be so troublesome to the conservative cause. (For an illustrated analysis of the plays of the CBS/Blogger face-off, see the Appendix, Play Action Maps, p. 313, or visit www.plays2run.com.)

TABLE C. CALLING AND RUNNING A JAM

Call and run this play because . . .	■ Sometimes it's eat or be eaten. In developed markets, where market share trumps market growth, it's as important to slow or stop your competitor as it is to advance your own position or agenda. ■ A rival's words or deeds are so overpowering or directly threatening to your platform that your own attempts to elevate your position are fruitless. ■ Your competition runs a propaganda factory. You can't move your own program forward until you do something about theirs—better, perhaps, to dismantle the rival's machinery than to be beaten by it. ■ You can't afford, for practical or even moral reasons, to let your opponent carry on.

Traffic Jam

There are more conventional ways to run a Jam, off the Net and onto the streets. In 1999, in downtown Seattle, Washington, when the World Trade Organization convened delegates from its 135 member nations, it didn't get much work done.

Its agenda, focused as always on matters of international commerce, was met by a diverse and hostile coalition of more than forty thousand party crashers—union members, environmental and consumer-protection activists, concerned religious groups and students, and self-styled anarchists who denounced cross-border trade as job-killing, poverty-creating, and nature-exploiting selfishness. To these uninvited guests, the WTO represented only the interests of powerful countries and greedy corporations, so they came to balance the agenda with their own series of makeshift and made-for-TV plays, most of them Jams, each a beta play that was designed to carry out their strategy to stun and stop the WTO proceedings.

Converging on downtown Seattle, the protesters effectively locked up the city and blocked WTO dignitaries and representatives from making their meetings. Rubber bullets, pepper spray, tear gas, and a draconian curfew by the city's mayor were no match for the glut of banners, signs, leaflets, news releases, megaphones, and other largely nonviolent acts of civil disobedience. Activists just wanted to stop what they saw as insanity, and by and large, they did. With Jams.

German Jam

In contrast to the CBS bloggers and WTO protesters, jammers can and do work alone. In 1987, a teenage West German student pilot was dubbed "The New Red Baron" when he played out an ambitious and seemingly foolhardy plan to fly his single-engine Cessna through a mesh of Soviet radar and fighter patrols and actually land on the open expanse of Moscow's famous Red Square.

Mathias Rust, like many through the years of the Cold War, was fear-struck at the possibility of nuclear war and that his neighboring homeland was a first-strike target. He wanted somehow to showcase the foreboding Soviet military threat. He wanted to slow or stop what he saw as madness.

Rust's strategy—his jamming beta play—could be taken for a Crazy Ivan, because, indeed, he felt the situation was dire. It could also be taken for a Call Out since Rust's daring flight ultimately served to expose confusion in the Soviet military command structure and certain holes in its own defenses. But a play should be evaluated against the intentions of a player—not how a rival might see it—and in Rust's case, his sole purpose was to change the tense dynamic of nuclear politics, to risk being shot down and thus to portray the Soviets as bullies or even frauds. He didn't care what might go wrong. He simply wanted to do something and to wreak a modicum of havoc on the system that scared him so.

Standing back from the resulting chaos of Rust's daring flight, the CBS bloggers, or WTO Seattle protesters, you'd have to scratch your head and wonder how anyone pulled these things off. These players were minute in size and scale in comparison to their rivals, and their logic and sensibilities were often strained. But a few haters of nuclear-armed communists, liberal-minded broadcasters, and business-friendly trade councils *did* sink some very big ships. And they did it with a Jam—a play that is centrally located on The Playmaker's Table, a play that is not merely designed to condition the marketplace but, in that capacity, to freeze it stone cold.

TABLE D. DECODING AND COUNTERING A JAM

How do I decode this play? *(i.e., How do I know it's being run against me?)*	■ When you're suddenly on the defense; you should suspect someone of short-circuiting your system. ■ It's under your nose (think protesters in front of your building). Or it's undercover (think AWACS radar jamming enemy transmissions). With Jamming, you'll know right away or you won't know at all who's crossing your wires. ■ When you wake up to rumors, erroneous accusations, broken channels of communication, and general misunderstanding (e.g., *Why are you polluting the river? Why'd your CEO get that bonus? Why are you hiding from this?*). ■ When normal modes of communication suddenly malfunction.
How do I counter this play?	■ You have a strategy for dealing with a jammer, set it up using a Luring play (i.e., a Challenge or Bait)—draw them toward you. ■ If you don't have a strategy, run a Diverting play (e.g., a Deflect or Red Herring) to draw them away from your position, or a Framing play (e.g., a Screen) to strengthen your position. ■ If they're an inferior competitor, Pause. It may be better to let little jammers have their day. Often a Jam is designed to feed off your reactions, so it's sometimes better to "cut off their air," per se; give them nothing to breathe. ■ Run a Red Herring. Feign that the Jam has done more damage than it actually has. ■ Set a trap. Bait your rival into a false debate to catch them in an act of sabotage. ■ If you have good evidence of sabotage, Leak information to key customers, media, etc., on your opponent's jamming high jinks and Label them accordingly.

Chapter 14

Bear Hug : BG

RISK

REWARD

To know your Enemy, you must become your Enemy.

—Chinese general and military strategist Sun Tzu (c. 400 B.C.)

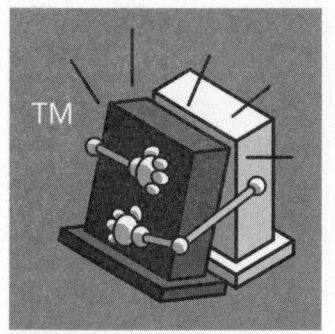

TM

magine that you're a drug company and your rival announces a breakthrough in the trials of a promising new medicine. You've been readying a similar announcement but there, on a Monday, is your opponent, basking in the limelight of its wonder product. And your announcement is scheduled for Tuesday. You've been beaten. The competition has run a Preempt.

What do you do? Do you ignore them, running Trial Balloons, Recasts, or Red Herrings to bend attention away from your competitor's quick move? Do you challenge them, forcing them to defend their new position, running Baits or Call Outs to expose weaknesses in their program? Or do you join them? If you do—and perhaps you should—you'll want to run a Bear Hug. Here are some real world examples of the most "affectionate" of play types.

TABLE A. BASICS OF A BEAR HUG

Class	Condition
Subclass	Freeze
Type	**Bear Hug**
Definition	The conspicuously public support or embrace of an opponent's position or message.
Upsides	▪ Helps a player co-opt an opponent's brand, position, or agenda. ▪ Creates the impression that a player's opposition to a potential rival does not exist and, as such, that there is no argument or difference between rivals. ▪ Like a Crowd, dilutes an opponent's attachment or thought leadership with an issue or point of view. ▪ Like a Ping, gives the player an opportunity for close inspection of a rival. ▪ Briefly disarms the opponent, forcing them to expend cycles to run their play without interference. ▪ Bear Hugs are easily run with a minimum of expense and resources.
Downsides	▪ Can cede thought leadership to the opponent. Bear Hugs are adamant statements of approval—"We agree completely with Delta Airlines—air fares have got to go down!" ▪ Might signal opponent that they are in control, thus encouraging them to make leadership moves. ▪ Can suggest to observers that the player has fewer options or is playing catch-up. ▪ Creates a disingenuous image of the player: a shameless copycat.
Related Terms	▪ Affiliating ▪ Endorsing ▪ Violent agreement
Related Play Types	▪ Crazy Ivan ▪ Crowd ▪ Disco ▪ Jam ▪ Label ▪ Lantern ▪ Mirror ▪ Screen

Big Fat Hug

Imagine how the folks at McDonald's must have felt when in the summer of 2004 the hit independent film *Super Size Me* swept through theaters, essentially conducting a perceptual lynching of the iconic hamburger franchise. The low-budget documentary followed the exploits of the film's producer and director, Morgan Spurlock, as he toured the country, eating three square meals a day for thirty days, all under the golden arches. Nothing else. Admitting his routine was extreme, Spurlock gained twenty-five pounds and risked serious damage to his health for the stunt. But he made his point, colorfully, and to the extreme chagrin of McDonald's.

What did McDonald's do? It took a few shots at the film, framing it as a *"super-sized distortion"* and suggesting (as Spurlock already had) that a thirty-day Micky D's binge was an irresponsible gimmick. Also, just weeks before the film's general release, it abandoned its upselling big-meal Supersize option—a mere coincidence, according to McDonald's executives. For the most part, however, it chose the only remaining option: It joined the pressuring parade of consumer and health advocates and cranked up its balanced-lifestyle campaign.

To be fair, the server of billions hardly needed a wake-up call. It had already been targeted in lawsuits for causing obesity, and its own programs to rebalance its high-calorie, fat-heavy menu, educate its customers, and advocate physical activity were well under way. Though the film probably didn't tell McDonald's anything it didn't already know, *Super Size Me* caused the hamburger chain's progress to look positively glacial. Like a Dickens ghost, Morgan Spurlock gave Ronald McDonald a crystal-clear view of what he had to do. The only option for McDonald's was to accelerate its plans . . . and run a Bear Hug.

The Bear Hug lives in the Condition class of play types. It exists for the purpose of molding the marketplace, not testing it, not actively engaging it. It exists to stop or freeze marketplace moves. It's also a member of two special clusters of play types—*Contras,* which are counterintuitive plays, and *Linkers,* which endeavor to attach a player to some element of the marketplace. The Bear Hug, in other words, is a very well-equipped play for steely-eyed and pragmatic playmakers. (For more information, see "Play Type Clusters," p. 268.)

As defined, a Bear Hug amounts to the conspicuously public support or embrace of an opponent or its position or message. It is the simple act of greeting and *agreeing* with your competitor, a disarming squeeze of support that lets the player get close, fulfilling Sun Tzu's advice to *"know your Enemy."*

Such an action is not exactly a natural reflex for ambitious playmakers. It doesn't advance a player's competitive position, and to some extent it flatters a rival. In fact, it has the appearance of taking a player backward. What it does do, however, is decrease a player's relative *disadvantage,* and as I'll write many times in this book, it is not *where* you are on a marketplace race track but where you are *positioned* vis-à-vis your competition.

Since we're talking about bears, I'll remind you of the story of the two guys who are running from, you guessed it, a bear: The one in back shouts to the one in front, *"Run faster! The bear's catching up!"* The one in front replies, *"I don't need to outrun the bear, I just need to outrun you!"* It isn't necessarily distance that secures a player's advantage, it's position.

The Bear Hug brings a player onto the same stage as its strutting competitor. Sure, it's a concession to a leader. But what else are you going to do? Ignore a first-mover at your peril? Nope. In McDonald's case, it would have been foolish to even try to blow off Spurlock and his following. Do you instead challenge your competitor? Of course not. Again, using the McDonald's example, such a response would have only strengthened the link between Big Macs and heart attacks.

The essence of the Bear Hug is to make a gesture of unmistakable support for the position or plank of your foe—to embrace it. When properly run, it blocks a leader from getting sole ownership of thought leadership. It reduces perceived chasms between you and your rival and gives you a crack at a new opportunity. It gives you a brief but up-close-and-personal perspective on your competitor. And, most important, it diffuses a ticking marketplace bomb.

Time will tell if McDonald's co-opts the obesity crisis and averts the calls for its corporate head. But to have hidden from or moved against the rising tide of the *Super Size Me*–induced outcry arguably would have been suicidal.

TABLE B. EXAMPLES OF A BEAR HUG	
Bear Hugs to remember . . .	■ ***Super Size Me*** In 2004, McDonald's took its licks from independent filmmaker Morgan Spurlock and his blockbuster documentary *Super Size Me*. Initially, it framed the film as a "supersized distortion" and irresponsible gimmick. But, at the same time, it abandoned its upselling big-meal Super Size option and cranked up its balanced-lifestyle campaign. ■ ***McCain Hugs Bush*** During the 2004 GOP convention, Senator John McCain all but kissed President George W. Bush in speeches and media interviews—a public Bear Hug to kill off talk of his rumored support for John Kerry. ■ ***Godfather*** In the 1974 blockbuster film *The Godfather Part II*, Al Pacino, playing mafia don Michael Corleone, recalls the words of his father: *"He taught me—keep your friends close but your enemies closer."*

Standard Hug

Arizona senator John McCain was probably thinking something along those lines (i.e., *I'll just shoot myself instead*) in the summer of 2004. The victim of George W. Bush's negative campaign tactics during his run in the 2000 presidential primaries, McCain might rather have died than to do anything nice for the incumbent president. But Bush and the GOP held the keys to McCain's future bids, so when Bush was struggling to get four more years, McCain thought it better to give his rival an uncharacteristic Bear Hug. He might have preferred a more punishing kind of embrace,* but having veered toward the political middle, in what sometimes looked like a spirited defense of Bush's rival, John Kerry, McCain knew his best bet for a 2008 shot at the top office was to cozy up to the boss.

As election day drew near, McCain was back on board the GOP bus, saying what he was supposed to say. During an August whistlestop in Florida, McCain wrapped both arms around the president and squeezed. Not to be outdone, Bush gave him a conciliatory peck on the forehead.

---

* The Bear Hug is a wrestling move where one opponent clasps arms around the other and squeezes, sometimes crushing but at least immobilizing his rival. From the legitimate Greco-Roman wrestling to Scottish "brawlin'" to the gruesome "gouging" of the American frontier to the showmanship of the World Wrestling Federation, the Bear Hug is a time-honored move of long-armed aggressors.

TABLE C. CALLING AND RUNNING A BEAR HUG	
Call and run this play because . . .	■ Your rival will steal your idea. Without throwing a Bear Hug on 'em, they'll mow through your playing field unopposed. ■ Your opponent's idea is a good one: It helps propel your agenda. ■ Your research shows that the marketplace will react positively to your competitor's idea, and you don't want to miss out. ■ A competitor has moved first to a position that's strategically important to you. ■ There's room on the stage to stand with your rival. ■ You can't run a Crowd. The price of joining the fray is merely singing the praises of the first-mover, your competitor. ■ You can't run a Call Out. The leader's position has to be honored, not hampered.

Imagine that you're a consumer electronics company, a leader and visionary in your industry. You have an idea that will catalyze a huge market for digital media. You have a way to do it, an exacting design that adheres to an exacting specification. You develop and demonstrate the technology. It works. It's elegant. You evangelize it to the marketplace. You cajole industry influences, associations, standards committees, and even other competitors to adopt your proposed brainstorm. But, as it turns out, yours isn't the only bright idea being run up the flagpole. A competitor is touting a different design with the same benefits, preaching a similar vision, and pushing its own spec in what amounts to a playmaker's Trial Balloon. Worse, its design is gaining momentum.

This scenario—a standards battle—is played out from time to time in virtually every marketplace. And as these things go, there are winners and losers. Recall, if you can, the 1970s-era "format wars" for a home videocassette tape recording standard, where Sony's Betamax was pitted against JVC's VHS. Though Betamax was initially a higher-quality technology, it ultimately lost out to a savvier VHS campaign. Think of the sweepstakes battle for control of the personal computer operating system. In the final match, it was IBM and its vaunted OS/2 versus Microsoft and Windows. As most insiders will tell you, OS/2 was also a superior feat of programming code, but it never had a chance against the marketing muscle of Microsoft and the Windows program.

These things happen at all levels of industry. Think of the garment industry, for example. At some point in time, you'd figure that the marketplace decided that the buttons on women's blouses should go on the left and that men's shirt buttons should be sewn on the right. At some point, one manufacturer had to retool and another didn't. One had to hug, the other had to *be* hugged. Sony, as much as it hurt, scrapped its Betamax and started producing VHS recorders, a lot of them. IBM did the same, becoming a market-leading maker of Windows-compatible personal computers. And outdone shirtmakers scrapped a few right-side-buttoning ladies' blouses and left-sided-buttoning gentlemen's shirts.

Bear Hugs have been run by every player in every marketplace from finance* to politics, videotape to digital tape, seat belts to taillights, runways to roadways, and electric plugs to electric cars—all in an effort to slow or stop a leading competitor and to get a bite of its bigger, juicier burger.

TABLE D. DECODING AND COUNTERING A BEAR HUG	
How do I decode this play? (i.e., How do I know it's being run against me?)	▪ When an opponent publicly adopts (or even rips off) your message or agenda. ▪ When an opponent does more than simply stand with you, as in running a Crowd. All of a sudden, you're their hero. ▪ When you're not the only one receiving credit for your idea.
How do I counter this play?	▪ Intensify or narrow your position or message to force the hugger to hold the Bear Hug or loosen its grip and Pass. ▪ Run a Call Out. If your opponent holds on, chide the rival for playing copycat. If your opponent backs off, tease it for exiting. ▪ Encourage the Bear Hug. Similar to being Drafted, it may be on-strategy to have your rival play second fiddle or to keep them on stage, at your side. ▪ Run a Bait. Ratchet up your rhetoric and see how long they'll hold the hug.

* The Bear Hug is known in the mergers and acquisitions industry as a preemptive, unsolicited offer by one company to buy another. In the parlance of finance, it's an offer a board of directors can't refuse.

Chapter 15

Lantern : LN

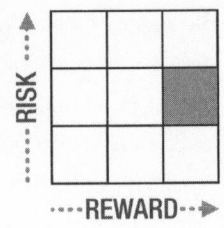

RISK

REWARD

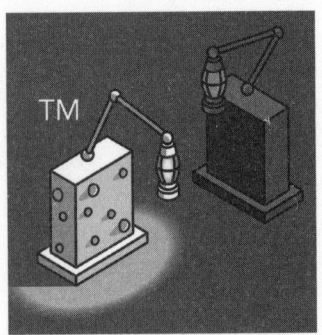

There is today a kind of inevitable tension in almost any marketplace that conveys to all of us the sense that the missteps we make, however justified or private, will ultimately be exposed. Between Sarbanes-Oxley, tabloid journalism, and runaway blogging, few things seem to go unsaid. So now, more than ever, organizations carefully weigh the consequences of what to say, how much to say, and when to say it. Corporations do this, for example, when faced with information that a defective product or service could somehow cause injury or damage to a customer. *Should we recall the product? What are the chances we'll be sued if we don't . . . or if we do? What's our ethical stance?* Homeowners, when preparing to sell their house and facing mandatory disclosure laws, do this as they consider what and what not to report as missing, broken, or bent. *What are the chances the buyer will notice? Can we live with ourselves if we hold something back?*

In this age of transparency, mistrust, and citizen journalism, the chances are now quite good that the wool can't be pulled over anyone's eyes, so it's better to confront a flaw than hide it. This is what the Lantern is born to do.

You might think of the Lantern as a combination of the Mirror and Preempt. It's the harsh reflection you'd rather not see, though this time it's *you* who are holding the mirror, not your competitor. It's a voluntary confession of sorts that keeps you out (or gets you out) of trouble and helps you stay your course. It is a good emergency exit for troubled or trouble-bound players, and it can liberate or even reverse a player's deteriorating situation if done in time and done in full. It's not a last option, by any means; the Disco and Crazy Ivan are better for that. But the Lantern does go against the grain of natural instincts because it's not the play that every red-blooded, competitive player would ever want to call. Not if it has to. Consequently, the Lantern falls into the Contra cluster, joining the Pause, Disco, Crazy Ivan, and one other contrarian play, the Bear Hug.

TABLE A. BASICS OF A LANTERN	
Class	Condition
Subclass	Freeze
Type	*Lantern*
Definition	The deliberate and preemptive disclosure by a player of its own flaw, mistake, or some source of potential embarrassment or controversy.
Upsides	■ Reports the bad news on your terms, before someone else can report it on theirs. ■ Can transform you from villain to victim, making the story more about your honesty than your infractions. ■ Shortens a player's time in perceptual jail. Works to return the player to an offensive stance. ■ Sets a tone of full disclosure, transparency, honesty, accountability. ■ Can derail a competitor's negative agenda by absorbing and rerouting marketplace gossip and speculation. ■ We're all human. We all make mistakes. A Lantern can humanize the player.
Downsides	■ A Lantern might not be necessary. It could create—rather than solve—a problem. A player considering a Lantern might overrate the potential of being exposed by a rival's Mirror, for example, thus drawing attention to a problem no one would otherwise notice. ■ A partial Lantern may intensify scrutiny and raise suspicions of motive, honesty, etc. ■ A premature Lantern might guarantee or accelerate the crisis. ■ A late Lantern may force you to run a Disco or encourage your opponent to run a Mirror or, worse, a Call Out.

Related Terms	■ Airing dirty laundry ■ Fessing up ■ Full Monty ■ Hanging a lantern (on your problem) ■ Inoculation ■ Letting a skeleton out of the closet ■ Preemptive disclosure ■ Taking the heat
Related Play Types	■ Bear Hug ■ Crazy Ivan ■ Disco ■ Jam ■ Mirror

Checkered Politician

In 1952, to keep his place as the running mate to the Republican presidential nominee and World War II hero General Dwight D. Eisenhower, a young California senator named Richard Nixon had to fend off accusations that he'd accepted illegal campaign contributions. Nixon attacked the charges in a nationally televised address, later dubbed "The Checkers speech." It might have been a diverting play (i.e., a Deflect, Leak, or Red Herring) that he intended to run, but his underlying strategy lay in the fact that he would surprise his detractors by doing the unexpected. Instead of dodging the charges, he would confront them directly. Point by point—from his real estate holdings to his wife's cloth coat to a cocker spaniel that'd been given to his daughters—he disclosed his entire financial history. All of it, Nixon said, was the result of hard work and none of it, not even the dog, now named Checkers, would be regretted or returned.

You might say that Nixon performed the political equivalent of a Full Monty, figuratively stripping himself and leaving nothing to the imagination. He gave away information that some thought he'd withhold and far more than anyone was asking. In any case, his play was a Lantern: *a deliberate and preemptive disclosure by a player of its own flaw, mistake, or some source of potential embarrassment or controversy.*

There's more to the story, of course. Having put all his financial cards on the table, the politician then harnessed his presumed newfound credibility and ran a clever second play, a Bait, daring his counterpart, the Democratic presidential nominee, Illinois governor Adlai Stevenson and his running mate, to disclose *their* family fortunes. Sometimes, a Lantern is so effective that the certain amnesty it garners for a player can be used to flip the direction of wagging fingers.

Leading up to his famous Checkers speech, Nixon was all but cooked. He could have run a Pass and simply withdrawn as so many GOP leaders were calling on him to do, but Nixon gambled and won, at least for a time.

TABLE B. EXAMPLES OF A LANTERN	
Lanterns to remember...	■ **Kerry/Edwards** Following his announcement of running mate John Edwards, U.S. presidential candidate John Kerry said to frenzied supporters, *"We've got better vision, better ideas, real plans. We've got a better sense of what's happening to America—and we've got better hair."* It was a crafted attempt to *proactively* shed light on Kerry's and Edwards's youthful mops, and to imply that the graying President Bush and balding VP Cheney were aged and out-of-touch. ■ **Honda Recall** In December 2004, Japanese carmaker Honda sent letters to more than three hundred thousand owners of its CR-V models and its dealer network, listing simple steps to avoid possible engine fires. The move was a deliberate and proactive attempt to reduce a potential danger and avoid a reputation crisis. ■ **Reagan Quip** Ronald Reagan, having suffered some senior moments in his first 1984 presidential debate with Walter Mondale, opened the second contest with this classic: *"I want you to know that also I will not make age an issue of this campaign. I am not going to exploit, for political purposes, my opponent's youth and inexperience."*

The Lantern is named for the phrase *Hang a lantern on your problem*, a maneuver begrudgingly undertaken by politicians who face the dilemma of telling their own bad news before an opponent can tell it for them.* Ronald Reagan's famous comeback line in his second 1984 U.S. presidential debate with Walter Mondale was the essence of this play. Under pressure to acknowledge embarrassing senior moments

---

* The Lantern might also have been named after Inoculation Theory, inspired by academics in the field of persuasion, which holds that a player can better defend its ideas when those ideas are first tested with a weak but threatening argument. It's an analogy to medical vaccines, used to strengthen a body's resistance by subjecting it to real but only marginally harmful doses of toxins or microbes.

in his first debate, the then seventy-three-year-old Reagan said tongue-in-cheek, *"I want you to know that also I will not make age an issue of this campaign. I am not going to exploit, for political purposes, my opponent's youth and inexperience."*

The ploy drew peals of laughter and it still registers as an epic turning of the political tables. But this example of a Lantern explains only Reagan's motivation, not his method, because the candidate never actually hung a lantern on his problem. In point of fact, he hung it on Mondale. The Lantern guided Reagan's overarching objective—to proactively shine a light on his advancing years. But the actual strategy that was employed, the specific play that Reagan undertook, was a Recast, commonly known in politics as *bridging,* where an accusation is refashioned into something more palatable and on-strategy.

Plays that define objectives are called *alpha* plays to indicate their higher-order position. Plays that carry out a strategy are called *beta* plays to indicate their supporting position. In the case of Reagan's second debate, the Lantern is the alpha play, the beta is the Recast. The overarching or alpha play of the Nixon Checkers speech was a Crazy Ivan, a last-resort play that confronts an impending attack and banks on the element of surprise to salvage a bad situation, and the beta, of course, was a Lantern. (For more information, see "Alpha and Beta Plays," p. 291.)

TABLE C. CALLING AND RUNNING A LANTERN

Call and run this play because . . .	<ul><li>A problem or negative information about you or your organization is very likely to be disclosed. Why not, at least, determine the place and time of the embarrassment? Do it yourself. Do it first.</li><li>A Lantern builds credibility by conveying humility. It earns you sympathy in the marketplace, which can soften, even neutralize, the blow of your bad news.</li><li>You have a moral or ethical obligation (e.g., a health or safety risk).</li><li>Your opponent is prone to secrecy or is seen as evasive. *Your* Lantern will contrast with your less-open rival.</li><li>You've got credit in your trust bank; you've got a Boy Scout's reputation.</li><li>You *need* credit in your trust bank; you *don't* have a Boy Scout's reputation.</li></ul>

Savvy Capitalist

The fine differences of the Lantern and the lessons of alpha and beta plays are just as evident in business. Take, for example, the case of Crosspoint Venture Partners, a storied and veteran venture capital (VC) firm of the high technology industry. At the turn of the millennium, when dot-coms were beginning to turn themselves and seemingly every related industry into dot bombs, the partners at Crosspoint faced an uncomfortable truth: Their newest venture fund, a planned pooling of $1 billion of elite investors' money, would not, could not, bring the returns typically associated with venture-based tech funds. It was a ticklish matter, not only because VC fund investors, so-called limited partners, had already been recruited, but because it could be interpreted within the notoriously tight-knit VC community that Crosspoint had lost its edge. After all, no other VC seemed to be slowing down or downplaying its funds.

Crosspoint knew better. It was not an impulsive or inexperienced firm. Far from it. It had a thirty-year track record with seven funds under management. It knew that the problem was real, not managerial, so to speak, and so it considered the obvious and distasteful option of canceling its precious new fund. But how, exactly, would this be done? Would it simply drop the bomb on its committed limited partners and let the word spread? If it did, would it have *any* influence over the gossip chain? These questions, played against a small fraternal industry, told the nervous VC that the news, however negative, had to be announced and that the process, however poorly it might play, had to be aggressively managed. This, of course, is where the Lantern came in. To tell the truth, to tell it before anyone else knew it, to tell it before it *had* to be told, was an attractive though counterintuitive option. It was Crosspoint's best bet for managing what could be a runaway train of speculation and innuendo.

As much as the partners feared the fallout, they also saw the potential for quieting the skeptics, particularly the management teams of competitive VCs. Crosspoint, in other words, knew that other funds would inevitably be curtailed or canceled by other VCs, so the advantages of exposing, not hiding, their own bad news were appealing. As well, the Lantern had the advantage of cutting cords with the now dying era of irrational exuberance and moving Crosspoint decisively toward a new landscape of smart investing.

In the context of game theory, Crosspoint was in a prisoner's dilemma, balancing the benefits of a shared penalty with the promise of an individual reward. It was a question of whether VCs would keep quiet and suffer together or if someone would talk first. Crosspoint didn't feel the secret could or should be kept.

In January 2001, the VC took the plunge with a full and thorough Lantern, shocking the tech investment community with the news that it would cancel its $1 billion fund and release tens of millions of dollars of already committed investment dollars. Industry pundits estimated that the Crosspoint partners each walked away from three to four million dollars each in management fees alone, and they gossiped and speculated as to why they would. Some saw the move as the surrender of an old guard, fattened from a good run and ready to retire. Some saw it as a bellwether, a confirmation and concession to a looming down cycle. Some saw it as savvy, an inevitable decision that put other VCs on the defensive and preserved Crosspoint's golden reputation. Some saw it as a breach of unwritten VC-industry etiquette.

To Crosspoint, the suggestion that the cancellation amounted to surrender or a sellout was stinging. But that it was also taken as a responsible warning helped to salve the wounds. That it put competitors in the awkward position of having either to confirm or deny an investment slowdown was probably bittersweet, given the close associations Crosspoint partners shared in the VC community. Nonetheless, when asked if they might also cancel prized venture funds, rival fund managers were faced with the difficult choice—a *zugzwang*, as termed by chess players—to confirm Crosspoint's wisdom and reset their own limited partners' expectations or to deny it and take their chances in a crashing economy.

All this might easily be taken for a much simpler play, a Preempt. As its name implies, the Preempt seeks to create competitive advantage by beating a rival to the punch. Which play did Crosspoint run? In point of fact, it ran both. The Preempt was its beta play, its game plan. The Lantern was its alpha play, its strategy for nipping a bad development in the bud.

You might hate to think that playmaking is what saved Richard Nixon, but it did, at least in his early years. Then again, depending on your politics, you might be pleased to know that it also saved Ronald Reagan. As much as it's a tool for the sinner, playmaking is also sometimes a tool for the sainted. In any case, its effects are powerful for lawmakers and moneymakers alike, and as these cases show, plays like the Lantern are capable of changing the course of events and even history.

TABLE D. DECODING AND COUNTERING A LANTERN

How do I decode this play? (i.e., How do I know it's being run against me?)	▪ When a competitor says, "I goofed," shows the marketplace it goofed, apologizes for goofing . . . and suffers little for it. ▪ When the marketplace and the media don't make much of your competitor's revelations. ▪ When there's pressure to follow suit, to run your own Lantern.
How do I counter this play?	▪ Play the watchdog. Make sure that the rival feels the full heat of its Lantern; make sure that all its facts are disclosed. Run a Mirror if they are not. ▪ Run a Recast to flip the focus back onto your message. ▪ Employ Proxies to Call Out the sincerity or accuracy of the disclosure. ▪ Taunt your rival. Bait them into telling more than they should. ▪ Pick at the flaw they exposed; find a Label that welds it to them.

Chapter 16

Disco : DX

RISK → REWARD →

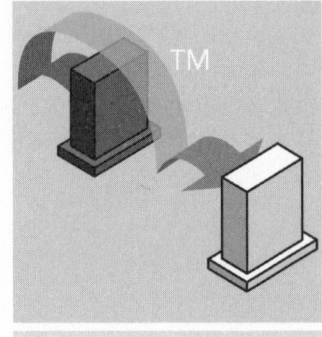

Did you ever hear the Johnny Cash classic "A Boy Named Sue"? The legendary country singer recorded it live in 1969 before raucous inmates of California's San Quentin State Prison. It was a hit across the airwaves, too, topping the charts that year in both country and pop. The lyrics, written, incongruously, by the children's poet Shel Silverstein, tracked the hardships of a neglected son, fatefully named Sue by his runaway daddy. I listen to it now and then with my own son and we laugh out loud every time—*My name is Sue. . . . How do you do!?* Well . . . the Disco is a little like that. It's an odd name attached to a good play. But it's a good play nonetheless.

So why name a play type the oddball equivalent of Sue? Because someone named it first, and the people who did know what they're doing. Disco lives and breathes in debate—or forensics, to be precise, the art or study of argumentation or formal debate. No one, in my experience, knows more about playmaking than the practitioners of this amazing, albeit obscure, pastime.

If you've ever been to a debate tournament, you'll immediately understand its relevance to playmaking. It's a rapid-fire competition of ideas, of positioning and depositioning, assertions and rebuttals, soaring rhetoric, and punctured ploys. It is the single best training ground for playmakers. The goods news is that debate is still taken quite seriously, particularly at elite high schools and colleges throughout the U.S. and UK. The bad news is that its relative popularity among extracurricular activities is extremely low. Debate doesn't exactly hold a candle to Friday-night Texas high school football. Nonetheless, debate carries forward the art and tradition of argumentation and offers a window into how playmakers operate in their respective marketplaces. Obscure or not, it's a fundamental influence on, and a supporting element of, the playmaking discipline.

So where's the Disco in debate? Listed in the National Textbook Company's authoritative *Dictionary of Debate, Disco* is defined as a technique of argumentation where competitors *"drop or agree with certain arguments in a debate in order to make a case for winning the debate."* When I first saw this I laughed, just as I laugh at "A Boy Named Sue." It's a reasonable description of a strategy I have observed time and time again in business. But I wanted, as Johnny Cash once sang, to *kill that man that [gave it] that awful name.* However, I went with it. I've seen nothing better to replace it . . . and they named it first.

TABLE A. BASICS OF A DISCO	
Class	Condition
Subclass	Freeze
Type	*Disco*
Definition	Requires a player to concede or sacrifice an element of its platform in order to preserve or advance its overall agenda or argument. The central tenet of a Disco is that forward progress cannot be achieved by the player unless or until the player first moves backward (i.e., one step back, two steps forward). Disco is a technique of argumentation, coined by debate teams in the 1980s.
Upsides	■ Keeps the centerpiece of a player's agenda or position intact despite the loss of supporting elements. ■ Turns a negative into a positive. The effect can be a complete turnaround, from scorn to praise of the player. ■ Builds credibility through an admission by the player that something was not working, something went wrong, or something was not done right or well. ■ Pacifies, even disarms, the opposition by conceding that a player's position is not wholly valid or that the opponent's point of view has merit. ■ Shows solidarity with the opponent, who is likely right. Some of their brand equity can rub off on you.

Downsides	■ Depletes the player of options and assets, thus increasing the player's vulnerability.
	■ Can convey an admission of guilt, wrongdoing, or culpability that creates competitive and sometimes legal exposures.
	■ If not well run (i.e., as a full and thorough concession), a Disco can exacerbate the player's problem.
	■ If employed too often or too predictably, Discos can erode a player's credibility.
	■ The full weight of the issue can land on your shoulders, even though it might not be entirely your fault.
	■ Egos can get in the way: It can be difficult to get your own company behind an apology or admission of wrongdoing.
Related Terms	■ Chewing off your arm (or leg)
	■ A gambit (as in chess)
	■ Losing the battle to win the war
	■ Punting
	■ Setting a back fire
	■ Sacrificing
	■ Salvaging
	■ A tactical retreat
Related Play Types	■ Bear Hug
	■ Crazy Ivan
	■ Jam
	■ Lantern
	■ Mirror

Just Own It

Discos are typically run when something goes wrong or breaks. They're run when some part of a player's position or agenda fails to materialize, or fails to operate as it should, and has to be discarded or figuratively amputated from a player's main theme or argument. Like a debater who concedes a specious supporting point to salvage his principle point, the Disco forces a player to deal with the deadwood before it moves on. Like a dance step, it's a two-part move: One step back, two steps forward. Strictly in that order.

A frequently cited case of a Disco occurred in 1982. When cyanide-laced Tylenol tablets were found to have killed seven Chicago area residents, drugmaker Johnson

& Johnson accepted responsibility for its all-too-easily-opened packages. It pulled thirty-one million bottles of the painkiller off store shelves and blazed the trail for tamperproof containers. It cost J & J dearly, millions in the short term; but it guaranteed billions of future revenue and profit over the long term and it preserved the company's good name.

Many companies would have thought to sidestep the crisis, to handle it quietly, to keep it out of the press and away from other healthy businesses. But J & J saw it differently. Its code of conduct and underlying culture made what is often a counterintuitive call a first instinct—to face the problem, make reparations and corrections, and, in so doing, to retrieve what might have been irretrievable—its credibility in the marketplace.

J & J's situation was not unlike a debate. Overall, it had the winning position. Indeed, it was well regarded for its products and industry leadership and it was difficult to challenge or unseat in its many marketplaces. But the random criminal sabotage it faced was a gangrenous event that threatened its general health and position. After all, many wondered, what was to prevent another wacko from lacing more J & J drugs? Irrespective of J & J's do-right culture, it *had* to act. In the spirit of the Disco, it had to go backward before it could move forward.

This, of course, is never a pleasant or natural thing to do. In most marketplaces it's simply contrary to prevailing wisdom, executive ego, the shareholder-value ethic, and often legal advice. To acknowledge a mistake or a vulnerability, after all, creates exposures and potential liabilities that most attorneys are loath to confront, whatever the merits.

The Disco belongs to a cluster of plays that deliberately go against the grain and in so doing can flip a marketplace dynamic to help a player regain its position of control. All of these—the Pause, Bear Hug, Lantern, Disco, and Crazy Ivan—run contrary to logic and are thus nicknamed *Contras*. (For more information, see "Play Type Clusters," p. 268.)

Johnson & Johnson is still credited with one of the fullest and most complete acts of contrition in business. It's among the deepest bows ever made by a corporation to its customers, the community, its employees, the media, and other stakeholders. But the problem, as you might detect, is that the Disco is not the norm. What J & J did is something few organizations ever do, but they should. A simple Disco might have saved many souls in the case of the Catholic Church's sexual abuse scandals. It might have salvaged the sinking fortunes of Enron and WorldCom. And it might have preserved the legacies of Martha Stewart and Bill Clinton. It is a powerful play that preserves and even strengthens a legacy, because when it's done fully and without equivocation it arrests a player's slide in the court of public opinion and arguably dwarfs its penalties in the court of law. Through the power of apology, it starts turnarounds and helps leaders rebuild their empires.

TABLE B. EXAMPLES OF A DISCO	
Discos to remember . . .	■ **Nike Sweatshops** Through most of the 1990s, sports-gear maker Nike suffered blow after blow for its use of third-world labor subcontractors. It took a full and unadorned apology from CEO Phil Knight to make amends with concerned Nike customers and frothing human rights activists and to turn a source of corporate neglect into corporate leadership.
	■ **Iran-Contra** In 1987, as the Iran-Contra controversy unfolded, President Ronald Reagan finally conceded that he'd traded arms for hostages. To put it behind him, he said, *"Now, what should happen when you make a mistake is this: You take your knocks, you learn your lessons, and then you move on."*
	■ **Tylenol Crisis** In 1982, after cyanide-laced Tylenol tablets killed seven, Johnson & Johnson accepted responsibility, pulled thirty-one million bottles off store shelves, and blazed the trail for tamperproof bottles. It cost them millions in the short term; it guaranteed billions over the long term.

Just Deflect It

Two determinants to a Disco's success are timing and intent. To be fully effective, Discos need to be run quickly, with as little time as possible separating the Disco from the matter gone wrong. When too much time passes, players are often forced to face a Mirror, thrown up by rivals or other players who have found the misstep first and are happy to force an off-strategy reaction. As well, Discos need to be run with full transparency. As a rule of thumb, players should endeavor to give more information than they might like or might think is appropriate. This is because most players who confront a recallable product, a revisable financial statement, or a regrettable slur, as examples, are probably not in the best position to know what's appropriate to those who are affected by a mistake or misdeed. It's better, then, to err on the side of overdisclosure—to show and tell everything and, even more, what you, the player, have done and what you'll do about it.

TABLE C. CALLING AND RUNNING A DISCO	
Call and run this play because . . .	■ During a crisis or emergency, when responsibility should be taken or apologies offered, you otherwise risk the loss of valuable credibility or influence. ■ Your competition or other organizations in the marketplace (like regulators or legislators) can only be mollified by a sacrifice. A well-run Disco throws them a bone. ■ You may be perceived by the opposition to be hoarding power or influence. Giving up something might be strategic. ■ Your position seems too good to be true and stakeholders won't buy it—downsize it to where your position is credible. ■ You are clearly in the wrong. Mistakes happen, so use it as an opportunity to come clean and move forward. ■ You need to stop the bleeding. The bad news will continue until you acknowledge your flaws and/or faults.

One case of a Disco, one that was perhaps danced a bit too slowly, if you will, but ultimately used to the advantage of the player, came at the hands of Nike, the phenomenally successful and dominating sports-gear maker. Through most of the 1990s, Nike faced increasing acrimony from human rights nongovernmental organizations (NGOs) over the working conditions of Nike's contract laborers in Asian manufacturing plants. Nike workers, they cried, were being paid pennies per hour. Some, they claimed, were abused by local plant managers and often exposed to dangerous equipment and chemicals. Even worse, some were underage, often as young as fourteen and sometimes twelve.

The wages of these laborers were comparatively handsome by local standards and the working conditions were set by independent contractors, not Nike. So, in theory, the problems were not the sports-gear maker's concern. But images of gaunt children sewing sneakers in equatorial sweatshops did Nike little good, and soon put the untouchable sports-gear maker in its own suffering sweatbox. Through the megaphones of the NGOs and the lens of the press, Nike looked like a colonial throwback, with slaves in the field and gentlemen on the veranda. This, juxtaposed with lucrative endorsement contracts—multimillion-dollar deals with superstars like Michael Jordan and Tiger Woods—created a firestorm of boycotts and protests that eroded Nike's dominant position and corroded its prestigious brand. Nike, the brainchild and personal passion of its founder, Phil Knight, had become a target and symbol for the evils of globalization.

From 1992 to 1998, Nike made a series of moves to address the concerns. It hired a major accounting firm to audit the targeted facilities. It helped found an industry apparel group, championed by President Bill Clinton. It established its own department for labor practices. And it hired the evenhanded civil rights advocate Andrew Young to monitor its newly minted code of conduct. (For an illustrated analysis of the plays of the Nike Sweatbox, see the Appendix, Play Action Maps, p. 449, or visit www.plays2run.com.)

To Nike these were substantial concessions, but to the NGOs these were insincere and incomplete measures. No one believed that Nike really cared or that anything had really been achieved. It may have been that Nike's competitors played it better and kept farther out of sight. (They, too, used low-wage Asian labor.) It may have been Nike's continued sponsorships of its superrich athletes. It may have been the taciturn founder whose resentment slowed Nike's responses. In any case, sales flattened and once-dominated competitors slipped free of Nike's grip and gained new ground.

Finally, in 1998, Phil Knight went on the offensive, first taking the podium at the high profile National Press Club and then granting a variety of lengthy major media interviews. Standing before the Washington press corps, Knight said grimly, *"One columnist said Nike represents not only everything that's wrong with sports but everything that's wrong with the world. So I figured that I'd just come out and let you journalists have a look at the great Satan up close and personal."*

This was probably not how Knight's strategists had intended him to begin. What they had intended as a gesture of ultimate humility came closer to a Bait or even a Crazy Ivan. But Knight settled into the role of apologist, outlining plans to protect workers against further abuses, improve their safety and factory conditions, and provide education. The next evening on PBS's *NewsHour with Jim Lehrer,* his comments included these remarks: *"We have always tried to do the right thing. . . . But it is true, I think, that the criticism probably sped up some of our efforts. . . . We really look at [offshore manufacturing] as more than just a subcontracting relationship, that it's really a partnership—not in the legal sense but in the moral sense—with the Asian factories."*

And there, he'd said it. He'd acknowledged that the controversy hinged more on morals than technicalities and, finally, had stood to face it. After six years of negotiations with third-world governments, attacks by NGOs, defections by its customers, and falling financials, Nike ran a Disco.

Could the contrarian play have been run sooner? Did it do the job? In the minds of Nike executives, it was the right move at the right time and, in fact, is seen as the beginning of the company's commitment to improved overseas working conditions, not the end. In the minds of Nike's detractors, it was the right move too late. However *you* might score it—as a successful recovery, permanent blunder, or something in between—the Disco is arguably a playmaker's best hope for correcting a mistake or an oversight and getting back into the game. Without it, many a player in many a marketplace would be doomed.

TABLE D. DECODING AND COUNTERING A DISCO

How do I decode this play? *(i.e., How do I know it's being run against me?)*	▪ When your opponent makes a statement or takes an action that says, in essence, "You are right" or "I am wrong." ▪ When your opponent changes its product mix. ▪ When your opponent gains position in the marketplace, yet they recently did something wrong.
How do I counter this play?	▪ Consider running a Recast to twist the praise your opponent may be receiving for the Disco. ▪ Be prepared to run a Mirror, a reminder to your opponent of its original mistake, if your opponent gets too cocky too soon. ▪ If the Disco is incomplete or seems insincere, run a Challenge. Demand that the rival tell all, not a little. Run a Label, suggesting the opponent has something still to hide, that it's hedging and evading the truth. ▪ Run a Preempt to dilute the positive response that the other player received. ▪ Run a Fiat to plainly state how your behavior in that same situation would be different.

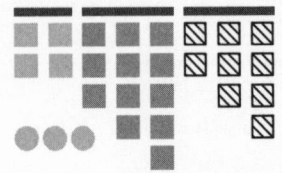

The Engage Class

In the Engage class, on the right side of the playmaking spectrum, there live the most self-determinant play types: nine plays in three subclasses. This is not to say they're not subtle, because they can be. This is not to say they're not collaborative. They can be this too. What differentiates the plays in this third playmaking class is an ability to intervene in the affairs of other players and marketplaces, not merely to stir the pot, though that is sometimes a valid motive, but to actively and overtly present a case, spur a debate, challenge an assumption, take a lead . . . or take a chance.

> def. **Engage:** *Active, usually overt, interventions that destabilize players and marketplaces, assert a player's leadership, or invite competitive responses.*

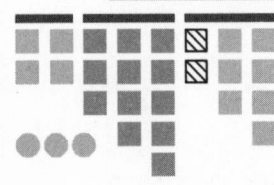

The Lure Subclass

Here is where the playmaker comes out of its shell, not content to hint or cajole, but to run plays in full view of the competition because to play with the competition it's sometimes necessary to get the competition to play with you.

> def. **Lure:** *Play action that dares a player to take action.*

Luring is not a euphemism for picking a fight. It can be, but that's not its overriding purpose, as evidenced by the JFK moon speech, discussed in the next chapter. Luring, which is achieved through two play types, Challenge and Bait, is used to draw a competitor in, perhaps to joust, yes, but just as easily to work with them. To that end, Challenge and Bait have the ability to grab a player's attention and not let go. The Challenge dares a player to cross a line from a position of comfort into a zone of unknown. Similarly, the Bait teases competitors to do the same, but usually with a higher degree of antagonism and a commensurate antagonistic response.

Whether they bring a curious or furious reaction is all a matter of strategy and subsequent moves. But in either case, the effect is to bring a player in, like dropping a lure into a fishing hole and getting the fish to hit it. These next chapters on Challenge and Bait tell you how to get it done.

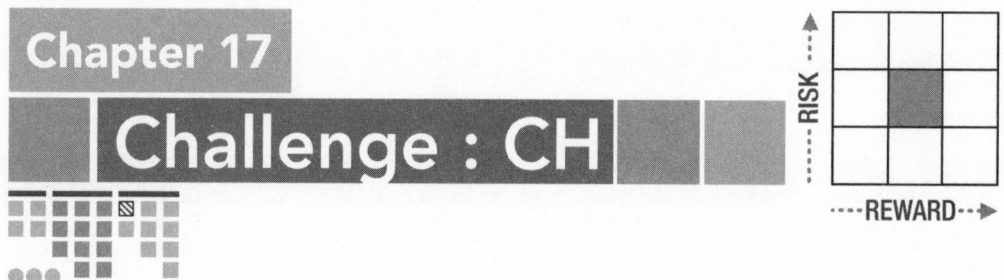

Chapter 17

Challenge : CH

RISK

REWARD

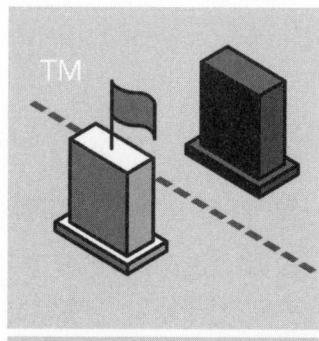

Perhaps you're expecting me to write about *the Pepsi Challenge*. I can't. As I explain in Chapter 22, p. 222, the Pepsi campaign was a Challenge in name only. It was, instead, a Call Out, conceived by Pepsi to expose a specific vulnerability in its rival megabrand Coke. It was also a Red Herring, if you want to get technical, because the name "The Pepsi Challenge" was designed to distract Coca-Cola from Pepsi's real intention—to publicly pull down Coke's pants, to show that the taste to the tongue didn't match the taste to the eye. What, then, constitutes a Challenge? Let's begin.

As you move to the right on the spectrum, from Assess to Condition to Engage, you wander closer to certain conflict. You move from a position of silence and discretion to outright advocacy—from the flicking of a feather under a drowsy competitor's nose, as you might do with a Ping, to the yanking up of its eyelids, as you might do with a Crazy Ivan.

The Challenge requires planning and a measure of courage. It is typically the opening move in what a good playmaker believes to be a winnable game. In many cases, the Challenge amounts to the proverbial poke in the chest, or maybe the eye, if the provoking player wants a guaranteed conflict.

Challenges are everywhere, in personal life, business, politics, and more, and their tone can vary. They can have a nurturing, aspiring quality: The student whose parents encourage her to get top grades, perhaps to attend college. Or the coaches and managers who set an athlete's season goals, maybe to increase his assists per game, yards per carry, runs batted in, etc. They can also have a competitive, embracing quality: a public radio station holding its annual drive, maybe an invitation for listeners to match a donor's pledge.

TABLE A. BASICS OF A CHALLENGE	
Class	Engage
Subclass	Lure
Type	**Challenge**
Definition	A public appeal, suggestion, or demand by a player, designed to mobilize and/or inspire a person, organization, or broader constituency to consent or take action. While Challenges may range from timid to caustic, they convey a benefit to the targeted player.
Upsides	■ Positions the player as a force for positive change, a thought leader in the marketplace. ■ Positions the player as a contender, as a willing combatant. ■ Helps to dictate the terms of a market discussion by engaging an opponent on a topic of the player's choosing. ■ Pressures a rival to acknowledge that a player has a point . . . and that the rival may have to act. ■ Changes the game. Creates a basis for new discussions and debates in a marketplace.
Downsides	■ Can be ignored by an opponent if the Challenge has a weak delivery or limited upside. ■ Can be positioned by the opponent as a self-serving and irrelevant ploy by the player. ■ Can weaken a Challenger's credibility, should the Challenge not be met.
Related Terms	■ A call to arms ■ Issuing a challenge
Related Play Types	■ Bait ■ Call Out ■ Crazy Ivan ■ Label

Money Mouth

In the heyday of Silicon Valley, I was witness to a variety of colorful and pugnacious Challenges. My client of eight years, Oracle Corp., was famous (perhaps infamous) for issuing Challenges to customers and competitors alike. In 1999, Oracle's CEO, Larry Ellison, promised Wall Street that by running his company on his own new integrated software products he would save a billion dollars in operating expenses. *A billion dollars.* And he did it, though any credit to Ellison, as always, was begrudging.

Liking this approach, Ellison repeated the play in 2000. This time, he issued a blanket guarantee that his databases and e-commerce software would run Web sites three times faster than similar solutions from IBM and Microsoft. *"If the performance doesn't triple, we'll give you a million bucks,"* Ellison famously crowed.

No one ever proved him wrong, so Ellison barreled along. Combining his Challenge with a Call Out, another play at which he is expert, the software magnate promised to give $10 million to anyone who could match Microsoft's database test results.

Challenges typically seem to follow the rules of physics. They often elicit an equal and opposite reaction. If Miller Brewing, for example, runs a Challenge on Anheuser-Busch through a new beer campaign, it's likely to get a reaction because Anheuser-Busch is not afraid of Miller and, in fact, likes to feed off the confrontation of its rival. It's good business.

In my experience with Oracle, however, this was seldom the case. Ellison ran his plays with such bravado and unrelenting consistency that his competitors rarely attempted any direct counteraction. This is not necessarily good. If you issue a Challenge as public and unequivocal as Ellison's you will want a response that is comparable to the size of your dare. Your brilliant play can otherwise look like an ineffectual Peacock.

This was often Oracle's problem in Ellison. He fought so hard—he erred so consistently to the assertive right of The Playmaker's Table—that his rivals preferred simply to lean on the ropes and let him punch himself out. Responding to the million-dollar challenge, for example, a midlevel Microsoft executive said, *"It's nothing more than a PR stunt. . . . It's clear they're scared that we're encroaching in their space. They basically have to scare people to not use our technology."* This was a Recast, an attempt to reshape Oracle's program as a gimmick and admission of fear. The rival executive was right on the first count, but not the second.

TABLE B. EXAMPLES OF A CHALLENGE	
Challenges to remember...	▪ *Larry Ellison* In 2000, Oracle CEO Larry Ellison issued a blanket guarantee that his database and e-commerce software would run Web sites three times faster than similar solutions from IBM and Microsoft. *"If the performance doesn't triple, we'll give you a million bucks,"* Ellison famously crowed. No one ever proved him wrong. ▪ *Ted Turner* The 1997 pledge of $1 billion by media mogul Ted Turner to the United Nations was a historic act of charity and a notable Challenge aimed directly at fellow business billionaires. ▪ *Moon Speech* In 1962, U.S. president John F. Kennedy challenged Americans to put a man on the moon by the end of the decade.

In so many respects, the Challenge resembles a Bait. Particularly with grenade throwers like Larry Ellison you get the feeling they are teasing more than tempting, though in Ellison's case it's usually more his style than his words that grate. You get the feeling they're trying to trick you, not treat you. What the Challenge and Bait have in common is that each is indeed designed to lure players, to bring them to some defined action or point on a playing field. Where they differ is that the Challenge is overt and collaborative. It seeks to have a player commit to some act of self-improvement. The Bait does not. It is covert and competitive. It seeks to have a player do something self-destructive. Nevertheless, each is an attempt to pull a rival player toward something, to make it cross a line that it's otherwise quite comfortable standing behind.

Moving competitors over the line is in many respects the goal of politics. It is a process that is riddled with dares and counterdares, so the Challenge is easy to spot: Think of Senator John McCain's 1999 challenge to fellow U.S. presidential candidates to refuse soft money. Think of independent Ross Perot's challenge to his fellow U.S. presidential candidates to step up to deficit reduction and campaign finance reform.

TABLE C. CALLING AND RUNNING A CHALLENGE

Call and run this play because . . .	■ You need to draw attention to yourself (the things you *can* do) and to your opposition (the things they *should*). ■ You need to assert your leadership. ■ You want to start a skirmish. To provoke your opponent to force a response to your claim or appeal. ■ You want to advance the common good. ■ Your leadership position is threatened or you're running a clear second. ■ Your brand or reputation is perceived to be a market follower. ■ You can do something that your opponent clearly cannot.

My favorite, far and away, is the moon speech, the famous 1962 address at Rice University in Houston, Texas, where U.S. president John F. Kennedy challenged Americans to put a man on the moon by the end of the decade. A few excerpts follow:

"We choose to go to the moon. We choose to go to the moon in this decade and do the other things, not because they are easy, but because they are hard, because that goal will serve to organize and measure the best of our energies and skills, because that challenge is one that we are willing to accept, one we are unwilling to postpone, and one which we intend to win, and the others too."

He ended with the words *"And, therefore, as we set sail we ask God's blessing on the most hazardous and dangerous and greatest adventure on which man has ever embarked."*

Now, *that's* a Challenge.

The play was a prelude to JFK's plan to land a man on the moon. It was a lure to encourage the support of Americans. And it was an invitation to cross a line into a new and mutually beneficial place. And by any measure of history, it worked. Larry Ellison, John McCain, and Ross Perot, take note.

TABLE D. DECODING AND COUNTERING A CHALLENGE

How do I decode this play? *(i.e., How do I know it's being run against me?)*	■ A Challenge is overt, a public dare. If it's done with any power, you'll know it's directed at you. ■ When media, customers, prospects, or other important stakeholders ask (or demand), "What're you going to do?"
How do I counter this play?	■ Duck it. Run a Deflect to buy time. ■ Up the ante, if you dare, with a corresponding Challenge. ■ Research flaws in the rival's Challenge. ■ Recruit Proxies to Call Out the play as ill-advised or self-serving. ■ Run a Mirror or Red Herring to dilute or distract the point of the Challenge.

Chapter 18
Bait : BT

RISK

REWARD

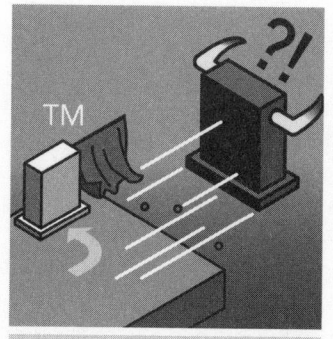

TM

I n civilized society you'd like to think we don't need plays like the Bait. It doesn't do much for the standards of ethics and etiquette to have a play that drags down the game. The Bait, after all, is a play whose sole function is to taunt or lure a player into doing something that's *not* in that player's best interest. It edges the playmaking from a fair fight to an ambush.

I'll admit here to feeling a little like a video-game manufacturer explaining away violent and sexual content. But I doubt you're a kid. I suspect you're a strategist battling in your own marketplace, and I suspect it's not always a fair fight that draws you into the fray. So here's what the Bait is all about.

When you *were* a kid, you probably watched your share of cartoons. I did, and my favorite was Bugs Bunny. One scene that is still vivid in my mind is the image of Bugs as a comic matador, taunting a seething bull. Bugs is unfazed by the brute's steaming nostrils, his chafing hoofs, and red, popping eyes. The rabbit, as usual, has a trick up his sleeve. He flicks his red cape at the bull. The beast charges full-speed at Bugs. And at the last second, of course, Bugs steps to the side, raises the cape, and exposes to the doomed bovine an iron anvil. *Clang*, goes the bull. *"What a gulli-bull,"* quips Bugs, strutting away. *"What a nin-cow-poop."*

That is a Bait. It is the intentional taunting by a player of its rival to attack, and to attack without much forethought. It's what heavyweight boxer Muhammad Ali did to tire his hulking opponent George Foreman in the legendary 1974 bout in Kinshasa, Zaire, better known as "The Rumble in the Jungle." His rope-a-dope boxing style invited Foreman to slug himself out in the African heat, battering away while Ali leaned against the ropes, conserving his energy. Finally, in the eighth round, with Foreman tiring, Ali came off the ropes and scored a stunning knockout to regain his title.

TABLE A. BASICS OF A BAIT	
Class	Engage
Subclass	Lure
Type	**Bait**
Definition	The overt provocation of an opponent through action or information, usually intended to draw an emotional, rather than rational, response. This play typically compels an opponent to move in the direction of the player—like a bull charging a cape—against its better judgment.
Upsides	■ Draws an opponent from an advantaged to a disadvantaged position, even into a trap. ■ Stalls the competition or encourages it to go in directions that are helpful to the player, disadvantageous to rival(s), or both. ■ Conditions an opponent to focus on the lure and ignore traps, thus becoming vulnerable to follow-on play action. ■ Provokes an emotional, credibility-sapping response from the rival.
Downsides	■ Can decrease the predictability of an opponent's response because the response can be emotional. ■ May prolong off-strategy exchanges with the opponent, again because of the emotional factor. ■ A failed Bait can strengthen an opponent. If the baiting player pulls out, the rival wins by default and probably gets credit for weathering the attack. ■ If the Bait is not credible, it can be positioned as trickery.
Related Terms	■ Goad ■ Making a dare ■ Mock ■ Tease ■ Throwing a barb ■ Throwing down a gauntlet

Related Play Types	■ Call Out
	■ Challenge
	■ Label
	■ Red Herring
	■ Screen

From cartoons to boxing to the movies—you might know of the famous scene from the 1983 film *Sudden Impact,* which stars Clint Eastwood as a vigilante San Francisco police detective. At his favorite diner, Eastwood's character, Harry Callahan, is immersed in his morning paper. The patrons and his waitress seem tense, but Harry's lost in his routine. His waitress loads his foam cup with an unending stream of sugar, and finally, the detective departs. Taking a sip outside, Callahan grimaces, spits out the coffee, and turns back, only to see the diner's front window sign being flipped to closed. *Odd.*

Inside, three gun-toting thugs have emerged to demand the patrons' valuables and cash, relieved the cop is gone. But Harry returns, this time through the back. Surveying the scene, he says grimly, *"Every day for the last ten years, Loretta there has been giving me a large black coffee. Today she gives me a large black coffee, only it's got sugar in it. A lot of sugar. And I just came back to complain."*

The robbers tell him to leave. Callahan replies, *"We're not going to let you walk out of here."*

Says one robber, *"Who's we?"*

Replies Callahan, *"Smith & Wesson and me."*

He pulls his gun and starts shooting, hitting all three. One of the wounded puts a gun to Loretta's head and faces Callahan. Sirens can be heard; the police are on their way. Callahan points his gun at the robber's head and a catchphrase is born, *"Go ahead. . . . Make my day."* The man puts down his gun and surrenders.

TABLE B. EXAMPLES OF A BAIT	
Baits to remember . . .	■ **Rove and Dean** In 2003, White House strategist Karl Rove stoked the fire of the Howard Dean presidential campaign. He was seen at a parade, exhorting the crowd and jeering, *"Come on, everybody! Go, Howard Dean!"* ■ **Dirty Harry** In the 1983 movie *Sudden Impact,* Clint Eastwood's Dirty Harry foils a robbery and points his Magnum at a cowering crook, sneering the famous line *"Go ahead, make my day."* ■ **Famous Duel** On the morning of July 11, 1804, former U.S. vice president Aaron Burr and his nemesis Alexander Hamilton met on the dueling grounds at Weehawken, New Jersey. They marched ten paces, turned, and fired their single shots. Burr was unscathed. Hamilton was mortally wounded and died the next day.

Moving from movies to politics, the Bait evolves as a much more nuanced move. Take, for example, the gamesmanship between the White House and early Democratic front runner, former governor of Vermont Howard Dean in the 2004 U.S. presidential race.

Fully a year before the elections and before the wheels of the Internet-driven Dean for America campaign came off, Republican strategist Karl Rove seemed to unnecessarily stoke the fire of the Dean for America movement. Attending a July Fourth parade, he chuckled to a friend as a corps of giddy Dean-bedecked campaigners marched by. *"Heh, heh, heh. Yeah, that's the one we want,"* he was heard to say, and soon enough Rove was exhorting the crowd, *"Come on, everybody! Go, Howard Dean!"*

Was he being serious or condescending? It wasn't quite clear but that was part of Rove's play, a Bait combined with a veil of bravado or sarcasm or both.

Progressive bloggers howled. *He can't be serious?! What do you mean, Dean can't beat Bush? He could slaughter him. Look at the groundswell under Dean!*

It also confounded Dean's immediate challengers, like John Kerry. *Wait a minute, we're a bigger threat than Dean!* But the Kerry camp's press machine had been brilliantly gagged by the backhanded insult.

Like a schoolyard shove, the remark maddened Bush's dark horse opponent. It was a dare to punch back and this, Rove and his operatives surely knew, was not in Dean's best interest. After all, the Dean camp was dealing with a problem of management and organization, not strategy, so to increase the hysteria for Dean was, in fact, to increase the chaos building inside the upstart's campaign. Said Dean for America campaign manager Joe Trippi later about Rove's taunt, *"Oh, yeah . . . he knew what he was doing."*

Like Bugs flicking his cape, Clint Eastwood waving his .44, or Rove pushing his sound bite, each is an invitation to a rival player to do something quick, something careless, and something that's obviously not in its best interest.

TABLE C. CALLING AND RUNNING A BAIT

Call and run this play because . . .	■ Your competitor can be jostled from their comfortable position. They'll sit tight if you don't. ■ Your opponent is oversensitive or prone to overreaction. ■ Your rival's competitive tendencies are well understood, so bait the hook. ■ Your opponent's reaction to the Bait can be reasonably predicted.

Bad Baits

These preceding cases are simple examples of players daring direct competitors—of rabbit versus bull, cop versus criminal, and strategist versus screamer. They all describe situations that pit players against opponents, good guys versus bad guys. But there is a well-entrenched form of the Bait that should be mentioned, however unbecoming it may be, that pits players not against enemies, but friends. We know it by the common name, the *bait and switch*, where a dangled item is swapped for a more expensive or more fully featured alternative.

It shows up most often in the form of low-ball advertising. You see it everywhere, vendors drawing in customers on the promise of a great deal, a savings of time, a guilty pleasure, and so on: *Drive away in a BMW for $199 a month. Relax first class in the Bahamas for as little as $99 a day. Buy two mobile phones for the price of one. Get term insurance today with no physical examination required. Order your desktop computer online for $349.*

Again, this play is not about playing fair. It seeks to fool, to draw a player in a direction that is not where that player might rationally prefer to go. So if the leased BMW turns out to be a *used* BMW, if the Bahamas vacation is spent in the luxury of a janitor's closet, if the second mobile phone requires upgrades or incurs hidden fees, if the insurance policy deductible looks more like an annual premium, and if the $349

PC has no memory or monitor, you can safely assume these *offers* are in the exclusive interest of the player and thus are full-fledged Baits.

What if the offers are honest? What if the sports car really is just $199 a month and for your vacation you get a real room with a view? Then you may consider them Challenges, Crowds, Fiats, or Peacocks, each relatively more straightforward propositioning plays. They're otherwise masked attempts to tighten the grip on customers' wallets, to sell them what they want for much more than they intended to spend.

It may be unconventional for one player to target someone or something whose intentions are not notably competitive. But playmaking is, first and foremost, a discipline for creating competitive advantage. It is, technically, indifferent to loyalties. When people or organizations in a marketplace, however close or friendly to the player, can be compelled to help improve the position of a player, it is logical in any marketplace that the player can, should, and will incorporate them into its playmaking plans. Playmakers do this, of course, with widely varying applications of motive and ethics. Think of Dr. Martin Luther King Jr., the great champion of civil rights, and Osama bin Laden, the notorious terrorist, each as a playmaker and you'll get the idea. Who they are, how and why they do it, however, does not alter the evidence that what they are doing is running plays. Any stakeholder—from a political rival to prospective customer—is a constituency that is subject to playmaking and is as vulnerable to a Bait as it is to a Bear Hug.

Would you run a play on an employee? I'm often asked. *Surely you wouldn't run plays on shareholders or regulators?* clients probe warily. The answer is emphatically yes. To do otherwise is a breach of a player's obligations to compete in a marketplace. The key, of course, is to tailor plays and play action that are appropriate to the situation and setting. A management team negotiating with an employees' union will surely apply a more collaborative form of playmaking than, say, an NGO that's gearing up for a protest. One might be subtle and more transparent. The other might be quite the opposite.

In any case, the Bait is not a play to be taken lightly. In the right hands, it creates resounding competitive advantage for a player. In the wrong hands, its effects are also pronounced, though often coming in the forms of unfair advantage and lost friends.

TABLE D. DECODING AND COUNTERING A BAIT

How do I decode this play? *(i.e., How do I know it's being run against me?)*	■ When something seems too good to be true. You could be walking into a trap. ■ When other player(s) make unusually repetitive statements or gestures. They may be trying to get your attention. ■ When new information or actions surface that mock your position or agenda. ■ When the teasing is so incessant or shrill that it can't be left alone or ignored. ■ The best indicator is your temper. Most Baits are designed to move you from a comfortable position; they seek to draw an emotional, even irrational, response. If you're about to lash out at something in the marketplace, think first. Is it your competition who's pushing your buttons?
How do I counter this play?	■ If you can't calculate the effects of the Bait, run a Pause to gauge reaction to it. Or initiate play action in another segment, like a Red Herring. ■ Run a Pause. They're just baiting you. If they really had something, they'd be running a Call Out or a Challenge. ■ If the Bait creates new strategic opportunities, run a Pause to feign disinterest. Then . . . take the Bait. ■ Run a Mirror. If your opposition research is good, expose the Bait as self-serving. ■ Deflect it. Ignore the Bait and swim on. ■ Recast it. Flip the conversation back to your strengths or your opponents' weaknesses.

The Press Subclass

Of course, when the play action can't be *brought to* the player, the player can always *go to* the play action. Sitting in the middle of the Engage class, the Pressing subclass is home to three play types—Fiat, Crowd, and Peacock—that are well suited to drive a player into a marketplace, invited or not.

> *def.* **Press:** *Play action that employs authority, ability, or audacity to establish or assert a player's position in a marketplace.*

Pressing plays are a little like party crashers. The Fiat amounts to a declaration by a player that, hopefully, has sufficient power to make a marketplace take notice. The Crowd is designed to dilute a competitor's position or agenda, whittling down the lead of another player, likely a rival, and forcing it to share what it's already won. And the Peacock is a little of both, except that it's employed with a considerable degree of showmanship. Peacocks amount to the pluming of a player's feathers, fluffed enough to draw attention and engage a marketplace.

With any of the three, the effect is to wedge or press a player into the role it seeks. Like an actor, the player might only want a line. It might only want a part. Or it might want the whole stage. But by whatever means it does get onstage, Pressing amounts to the persistent elbowing and clamoring by a player to get to the front and force a marketplace to contend with who it is, what it thinks, and what it does.

Up next are the three plays of the Pressing playmaker, the Fiat, Crowd, and Peacock.

Chapter 19

Fiat : FT

RISK ·····▶

····REWARD··▶

The Fiat, named for the notion of an edict or declaration, is the last-discovered element of The Playmaker's Table.* Despite the fact that two dozen stratagems were vetted and categorized before it, this twenty-fifth play drops into place an important piece of the playmaking puzzle. It accounts for the myriad cases of straightforward acts and simple delivery of facts that neither position nor de-position, defend nor aggress. Here are three well-known examples:

■ Google Inc. announced today that it has filed a registration statement with the Securities and Exchange Commission for a proposed initial public offering of its Class A common stock. . . .

In 2004, as Google made plans for its long-awaited IPO, the search engine company was required by the Securities Act of 1933 and SEC regulations to release this boilerplate statement of its big plans. It's just the facts, of course, so it wasn't a Peacock. It was distributed over a commercial wire service, so it certainly wasn't a Leak. And, yet, this simple release of information spoke volumes and influenced other players and a white-hot marketplace. Google's Fiat amounted to a no-nonsense notification.

---

* Sorry, the Fiat was *not* named after Italian automobiles. If you're wondering, the century-old carmaker FIAT owes its four-letter name to *Fabbrica Italiana Automobili Torino*. Some tortured owners of the sporty and temperamental cars prefer to read it as *Fix It Again, Tony.*

TABLE A. BASICS OF A FIAT

Class	Engage
Subclass	Press
Type	**Fiat**
Definition	The declaration of informaton or demonstration of capability to a marketplace. Fiats are characteristically run without fanfare and rely on the position of the player or the merits of the declaration to shift a competitve dynamic.
Upsides	■ Cost-efficient and quick. ■ Minimizes hyperbole, maximizes focus. ■ Difficult to defend or play off of.
Downsides	■ Players can overestimate the power or relevance of a Fiat, so their point can be missed. ■ Likewise, competitors can shrug off weakly run Fiats as marketplace noise. ■ Fiats can be ineffective because they don't create agreement (fit) or controversy (friction).
Related Terms	■ An announcement ■ Bully pulpit ■ A claim ■ A decree ■ Happy horseshit ■ Straight refutation ■ A submission of evidence ■ A threat
Related Play Types	■ Crowd ■ Peacock ■ Ping

■ But I want to say one thing to the American people. I want you to listen to me. I'm going to say this again. I did not have sexual relations with that woman, Miss Lewinsky. I never told anybody to lie, not a single time. Never. These allegations are false.

At a January 26, 1998, news conference President Bill Clinton clarified his testimony to special investigators about his relationship with White House intern Monica Lewinsky. It wasn't a Recast; Clinton was actually sharpening his original statements under oath, digging himself deeper, not digging his way out. It wasn't a Disco; he wasn't apologizing. It might have been a Jam to derail his pursuer, Kenneth Starr, but such an emphatic statement could only have served to bait the investigator. Was it a Bait? Surely not. Clinton didn't have the chess pieces to lure and trap the tenacious investigator. Clinton's backpedaling Fiat was what forensic debaters call a straight refutation, a denial.

■ Whether you like it our not, history is on our side. We will bury you.

During a 1959 diplomatic reception at the Kremlin, Soviet premier Nikita Khrushchev issued this infamous matter-of-fact prediction to attending Western diplomats. It wasn't a taunting Call Out or Bait; Khrushchev was posing for the cameras more than he was exposing his rival. And yet it wasn't a flaunting Peacock or a pulsing Ping; the blunt-speaking premier wasn't thought to be that clever or that subtle. Khrushchev's Fiat amounted to a threat—straight punches in what is usually a martial arts contest.

Fiats convey or demonstrate a player's stance on an issue, idea, event, or development. While not as flashy as their close relation, the Peacock, or as subtle as their more distant cousin, the Ping, they serve the important purpose of inserting competitively compelling facts, acts, or other information into a marketplace. What differentiates Fiats from the Peacock or Ping or in-your-face plays like Challenge, Bait, or Call Out, is that they don't attempt to leverage or apply any source of competitive fit or friction. Their purpose is not to play up or play against any source of agreement or controversy, at least not in any overt way. A Fiat-running player just comes to the marketplace and says or does what's on its mind, relying on two things, (1) the heft of its position or (2) the sheer gravity of its words or deeds, to impact the marketplace, to declare *by fiat,* if you will, its position in a marketplace.

TABLE B. EXAMPLES OF A FIAT	
Fiats to remember . . .	■ **SEC Filing** *Google Inc. announced today that it has filed a registration statement with the Securities and Exchange Commission for a proposed initial public offering of its Class A common stock.* The white-hot Internet company Google was required in 2004 to release this just-the-facts statement of its big plans to go public.
	■ **Hurricane Katrina** At 10:00 A.M., August 28, 2005, the mayor of New Orleans, Ray Nagin, issued this warning: *"[Hurricane Katrina] is intensifying, and is still pointed toward New Orleans. . . . I am, this morning, declaring that we will be doing a mandatory evacuation."* As most know, the mayor's warning was heard, ignored by some, and probably too late for others. It was the right play, run at the wrong time.
	■ **Osama bin Laden** *"The operations are under preparation and you will see them in your houses as soon as they are complete, God willing."* Rebroadcast in early 2006 by Al Jazeera television, these are the words from a cryptic audio clip and reportedly the voice of Osama bin Laden who coolly warned Americans of al Qaeda's preparations for new attacks on American soil.

Here are other memorable examples of Fiats, each of which banks on the law, the influence of the player, or the merit of an idea to press a point:

An Agreement *Yahoo! Inc. ("Yahoo!") welcomes you. Yahoo! provides its service to you subject to the following Terms of Service ("TOS"), which may be updated by us from time to time without notice to you.* Like most online or software companies, Yahoo requires its users to acknowledge and adhere to agreements that regulate the terms of the use of its services and products.

A Threat *"The operations are under preparation and you will see them in your houses as soon as they are complete, God willing."* Rebroadcast in early 2006 by Al Jazeera, these are the words from a cryptic audio clip and reportedly the voice of Osama bin Laden, who coldly warned Americans of al Qaeda's preparations for new attacks on U.S. soil. Clearly, the statement was designed to carry out a variety of other higher-order alpha plays, perhaps a Red Herring, thrown by bin Laden to divert pursuers, perhaps a Peacock to impress his own people. In either case, his undergirding beta play was a simple and powerful Fiat designed to press his rival and advance his agenda.

A Resolution *We hold these truths to be self-evident, that all men are created equal, that they are endowed by their Creator with certain unalienable Rights, that among these are Life, Liberty and the pursuit of Happiness.* The Declaration of Independence, signed in 1776, had enormous playmaking power because it expressed an idea that both mobilized a coalition of players (the thirteen American colonies) and dislocated a rival (England and King George III).

An Edict *Honor your father and your mother. . . . You shall not murder. . . . You shall not commit adultery. . . . You shall not steal. . . .* The Ten Commandments, said in the Old Testament and Hebrew scriptures to be God's words and a directive to the Israelites through Moses, are based on a set of principles that in 1500 B.C. helped define a player, the early Hebrews, and how they would operate in their religiously and culturally competitive marketplace.

An Idea *It is quite conceivable that a naturalist . . . might come to the conclusion that each species had not been independently created, but had descended, like varieties, from other species.* Charles Darwin penned *The Origin of Species* in 1859, not as a Recast of existing theories or a Call Out of erroneous competing works but as an original offering of new findings. Through the power of his methods and observations, his work confronted a marketplace of scientists and religious scholars with a new vision of man, nature, and their genesis.

A Yahoo online agreement, a bin Laden threat, an early-American declaration, an edict from Moses, and a treatise from Darwin . . . these are the moves of very influential players, so you'd have to say they had a head start. By virtue of who they were, what they represented, or their vested powers, they didn't need to run more extroverted plays to get their points across. This is not to say, however, that the Fiat is only for privileged and powerful people and institutions. It can work just as well when the content has its own gravity, irrespective of the player's background, position, pedigree, or regulations. Consider the following examples of Fiats that make the grade more for what they have to say or do than for who is doing the talking or taking the actions.

A Breakthrough In 1996, Scottish researchers at the Roslin Institute in Edinburgh successfully cloned a female sheep from an adult sheep cell. The ewe, known throughout the world as Dolly, represented a major step forward in the replication of mammals and stoked both hopes and fears of human cloning.

A Mission *To make, distribute & sell the finest quality all-natural ice cream & euphoric concoctions with a continued commitment to incorporating wholesome, natural ingredients and promoting business practices that respect the Earth and the Environment.* This is the product mission of the ice cream maker Ben & Jerry's, well known for its values-led approach to business, life, and good eating.

A Warning At 10:00 A.M., August 28, 2005, the mayor of New Orleans, Ray Nagin, issued this warning: *"[Hurricane Katrina] is intensifying, and is still pointed toward New Orleans. . . . I am, this morning, declaring that we will be doing a mandatory evacuation."* As most know, the mayor's warning was heard, ignored by some, and probably too late for others. It was the right play, run at the wrong time.

TABLE C. CALLING AND RUNNING A FIAT	
Call and run this play because . . .	■ You're a major player or you have a major development. It's all you need to do. ■ You're strapped for budget or resources. It's all you can do. ■ Your hammer is velvet-covered. You don't want to crush a competitor or bully your marketplace. You want to low-key it. ■ Your point is so strong that you only need to state it. No window dressing is required. ■ Your brand, message, or actions can carry the day. ■ You need to fulfill disclosure requirements. ■ You don't want to stir up the marketplace . . . but you still want to be in it.

As Ray Nagin, Bill Clinton, and Nikita Khrushchev knew, Fiats can fall quite flat. But in most cases, Fiats fail not because a player lacks judgment but because the play lacks the critical success factors, again these being the influence of the player and/or the merits of the declaration. When a player has neither the heft of position nor the leverage of good content, Fiats lose their lift. They take on the characteristics of filler and are very much the culprits of our noisy and strategy-glutted marketplaces. Like ants at a picnic, weak Fiats are everywhere. Here are just a few simple generic examples:

- **Spam** *Hot Stocks Will Make You Money.*

- **A Tombstone Ad** *A-B-C Capital Announces the Acquisition of X-Y-Z Leasing Corp. by 1-2-3 Lending Services, Inc.*

- **A Customer News Release** *On-Demand-Software Corp. today announced that On-The-Road Trucking, Inc., has adopted its suite of customer relationship management solutions.*

- **An Automated Telephone Solicitation** *"Hello . . . this week we're offering an expanded cable family package for four ninety-nine a month."*

- **Direct Mailer** *You've been preapproved for a 0% credit card through next year.*

- **A Circular** *Going Out of Business. Everything Must Go. This Saturday at Noon, Downtown.*

- **A Pop-Up** *Web Security Cams: $19.99.*

Sure, the phone solicitation is getting hits; it has a percentage chance (however low) of upgrading a customer. And, sure, the news release is adding a customer to its ranks; it's building (however hopefully) a bandwagon effect. But they're only incrementally effective. They impart information and stroke a customer's ego but they fail to generate or leverage any distinct source of interest or conflict to induce a favorable competitive shift. All of these hypothetical examples, in fact, are marginally strategic because they are only vaguely motivating or relevant to their targets. But they are Fiats nonetheless because, like skipping a stone, they do in some small measure make a ripple in their ponds.

The Fiat, it's obvious by now, covers a huge swath of the playmaking landscape. It ranges from the sweeping resolution (*We hold these truths to be self-evident*) to the breakthrough discovery (*Scottish researchers clone a sheep*) to the chilling threat (*We will attack you on your own soil*) to the ineffectual claim (*You've been preapproved*). Some Fiats are run with doltish repetition, others with devilish cunning. Some have no leverage and operate on hope; others have a surplus of power, yet don't use it. But they're everywhere, and without this twenty-fifth play we'd never see the whole picture.

TABLE D. DECODING AND COUNTERING A FIAT

How do I decode this play? *(i.e., How do I know it's being run against me?)*	■ With Fiats, you don't need a palm reader. This play is straight-ahead, overt, and declarative. ■ As such, you may feel like you've been sat on by an elephant or shoved off the end of a park bench by a gorilla. ■ Or you may simply feel blocked—the result of a well-timed statement or move that can't be refuted or ignored.
How do I counter this play?	■ Fiats are difficult to leverage because they are inherently underplayed and their underlying words or deeds are inherently relevant. You can only join 'em or bend 'em. ■ Run a Crowd or Bear Hug to dilute or thin the move. ■ Run a Recast to reframe its significance or a Filter to selectively edit its content. ■ Run a Red Herring to detour marketplace discussion. ■ Run a Bear Hug/Recast combination. Agree with the Fiat and bridge it to your agenda. ■ Run a Pass. If the marketplace is ignoring it, why shouldn't you? ■ Run a Peacock. Your opponent did a nice little dive. Why not do a cannonball and steal the show?

RISK

REWARD

TM

Most plays of the playmaking system are capable of moving the ideas and dialog of a marketplace in a preferred direction. But what if your marketplace is already moving ahead without you? If it is, you'll need plays that allow you to join the parade. This is where the Crowd comes in handy. Crowding is about moving into a space, standing shoulder-to-shoulder with another player, often a rival, and saying in essence, *Me too, I've got what you've got*. A Crowd can dilute an incumbent's position because it forces a rival to share the limelight, which in turn focuses marketplace chatter more on a category and less on the player(s) that occupy it.

In the music recording industry, for example, a good Crowd can build the buzz of a trend instead of the artist or the group. Nirvana hits and suddenly every band in Seattle has a record deal. Britney Spears makes it big and, whoosh, there's Christina Aguilera. In each case, the crowding player sacrifices talk of its brand, at least exclusively, but it also denies it to its opponent.

TABLE A. BASICS OF A CROWD

Class	Engage
Subclass	Press
Type	**Crowd**
Definition	The attempt by a player to match or adopt an opponent's position in a marketplace or to affiliate with a trend, idea, or issue.
Upsides	■ Holds a rival in check, preventing them from running away with a category. ■ Helps create a category in a marketplace. ■ Creates a new venue for expanding a player's platform or offerings. ■ Dilutes an opponent's position of exclusivity and leadership. ■ Forces an opponent to share portions of their brand. ■ Reduces a rival's ownership of a trend, idea, issue, or market space. ■ Lowers the cost of competing: It's generally cheaper to enter an already established market than to create one. ■ Increases the likelihood of success. If you can replicate your opponent's offering, you stand to profit.
Downsides	■ Limits a player's ability to drive distinction and build leadership into its brand and reputation. ■ Can draw a player into a market space that's off-strategy. Better, sometimes, to make competitors follow you. ■ Paints the player as a follower, not a leader. ■ Copycats are almost never as good as the original in terms of quality or perception. The Player's brand may suffer. ■ You will always be a second tier player in this market. (Otherwise, it's a Draft.)
Related Terms	■ A copycat ■ Diluting ■ Jumping on the bandwagon ■ Riding the coattails ■ Watering down
Related Play Types	■ Bear Hug ■ Fiat ■ Draft ■ Peacock

Big Gamble

In the summer of 2005, Crowding was easy to spot when General Motors made the bold gamble to offer its sacred employee discount program to customers. The move was a Fiat (the play, not the car), a relatively subdued announcement, but one that had sufficient power to make the new car marketplace sit up and take note. GM was desperate to increase sales volume, restore slipping market share, and unload fuel-gulping models, so it resorted to what customers perceived to be the ultimate in price cutting.

The program drew immediate interest, perhaps to GM's surprise, and punched up GM's new car sales. And as well-run plays will often do, it also put GM's rivals, notably Ford Motor Co. and DaimlerChrysler AG's Chrysler Group, at a disadvantage. It achieved relative gain in both dimensions. Employee discounts suggested to new-car buyers that in GM cars they'd get the best value and the least runaround. It had the patina of a down-to-the-bone, no-sales-job program. And it worked, putting GM simultaneously on the offense and their rivals on the defense.

What happened next was what game theorists will tell you is a game of chicken, a stare-down, a test of nerves.

Ford and DaimlerChrysler indeed had two awful choices to contemplate. They could indulge, even encourage, GM in its self-destructive binge, giving it enough leash to fatten its sales but starve its profits. Or they could match the program, take a bath on profits themselves, and hope for an industrywide return to saner discounting strategies. While they thought about it, however, they had to accept the fact that their customers were defecting to GM. There were no easy outs.

Within weeks, Ford and DaimlerChrysler caved. They each ran a Crowd, opening up their own employee discounts to customers. They said, in effect, *Hey, lookie here, we have the same program! Come on back across the street.* They literally copied their way into a marketplace hot spot and said, *Me too!* Once that happened, the novelty of employee discounts was wrenched from GM's grip and shared with Ford and DaimlerChrysler. Though the crowding diluted GM's newfound distinction, it expanded popularity of the program and created a buying surge for all three.* But it conferred an important honor upon GM that couldn't be stolen. It proved that GM still had juice, that it could still throw its weight in the marketplace.

---

* With Detroit's Big Three offering customers employee discounts, pressure mounted on foreign manufacturers to do the same. But none were drawn in, a move that was costly to foreign manufacturers in the short term but that upheld their brands' values.

Crowding often results in everyone's boat getting floated. This is good for the short term in any marketplace. But for the long term, it does nothing to drive brand distinction for players in a tight marketplace. The Crowd narrows competitive gaps for trailing players by bringing them up to the leaders. But it doesn't expand competitive advantage for the latecomers, to say nothing of the incumbents.

TABLE B. EXAMPLES OF A CROWD	
Crowds to remember . . .	▪ **Game Shows** After ABC's enormous 1999 ratings success of *Who Wants to Be a Millionaire*, rival TV networks rushed their own productions into the exploding prime-time game-show space. Copycats like *Weakest Link* aired in hopes of milking the trend established by ABC's hit show.
	▪ **Employee Discount** Through the summer of 2005, General Motors offered its sacred employee discount program to customers, sacrificing margin for market share in an attempt to dump inventory and rewin customers. Ford and DaimlerChrysler had little choice but to join in the profit-losing game of chicken.
	▪ **Linux** IBM's early support of the open operating system Linux was diluted when rival HP jumped into the fray, also in support of Linux.

Big Game

Who wants to be a millionaire? From 1999 to 2002, this question was on most every American television viewer's lips. It was, of course, kneaded into the public consciousness by ABC's TV smash hit game show of the same name. Adapted from a similar hit in Britain, and hosted by the avuncular Regis Philbin, the show made its debut in late summer of 1999 as a limited-run summer replacement show. It caught on and over time vaulted ABC from last to first in the ratings race. Not since *Happy Days, Charlie's Angels,* and *Barney Miller,* almost two decades before *Who Wants to Be a Millionaire,* had ABC done so well.

When a marketplace moves this quickly, you have three choices: Track it, change it, or lose it. The *Millionaire* movement spread so quickly and established such a formidable lead that ABC's competitors had little choice but to follow suit, to Press into it. Any attempts to change its course, by Luring or Attacking the phenomenon (the other options in playmaking's Engage class), would have taken too long and cost too much. The only reasonable response was to jump in and hold on. And so they did, each with a solid Crowd. Less than six months after *Millionaire*'s debut, the airwaves were filled with game-show copycats, including: NBC's *Weakest Link* and *Twenty One*, CBS's *Winning Lines*, and Fox's *Greed*, as examples.

These might have seemed like attempts to Draft. After all, each of the game-show rush jobs was coming up fast, tucking in behind *Millionaire* and feeding off its energy like a NASCAR tailgater. But the difference has everything to do with attitude. The Draft is about following in the shadow of a player, using its resources and planning an *overtaking* move. The Crowd is these things, too, except for the overtaking part. In contrast to the Draft, it serves as a play that tracks, not attacks.

Despite *Millionaire*'s popularity, rival networks were loath to concede the standard *Millionaire* was setting, so they never positioned their late entries as also-rans. True to the Crowd, the early copycats were all presented by their networks as equals in the prime-time TV game-show glut. As crowders, they were to *Millionaire* what Ford and DaimlerChrysler were to GM, at least in the case of employee discounting.

TABLE C. CALLING AND RUNNING A CROWD	
Call and run this play because . . .	■ Left unchecked, your competitor will gain a foothold in a new discussion or market segment. If this is a space where you should play, too, you have to make the move. ■ It's a great way to create a category. A Crowd forces influencers and customers to look more at what's happening than at who's making it happen. ■ You can take market share from your competitor. ■ Your opponent has already carved out the niche. They have saved you the time, trouble, and cost. ■ You can match a competitor's pace and resources. You don't need to or don't want to Draft. ■ You can't afford to be left out of a discussion, market, etc. ■ You need to switch horses. Your traditional markets or the issues you typically drive are slow or unproductive. ■ You're content to jump in and take your profits.

GM's employee discount program and ABC's *Who Wants to Be a Millionaire* suggest that the Crowd can be used by a player not only to elbow its way into a marketplace but to cut off its oxygen. Only four months after GM rolled out its new pricing scheme, it was pulled. Only three years after ABC blazed the trail with *Millionaire*, the genre was all but gone from prime time. What killed it? Overexposure. What caused the overexposure? You'd have to blame the crowders. They made something special so common that its significance was lost (in the case of employee discounts) or cheapened (in the case of weeknight TV game shows). GM's and ABC's opponents literally choked the life out of two powerful and dangerous threats by marginalizing one and saturating another.

For the record, ABC saw it coming. Rather than fight the game-show clones, ABC ran its own Crowd, taking *Millionaire* to no fewer than four times a week in a pragmatic attempt to wring the fad dry. NBC did it, too, airing *Twenty One* two nights per week. The self-crowding blitz may have accelerated the demise of *Millionaire* but it helped ABC get its fair share of the craze and the ratings—at least while the craze and ratings could be gotten.

However cynical this may seem, the Crowd is an excellent and demonstrably effective option for diluting and perhaps killing a rival's new idea. It gets you into the game for a share of the action and narrows the gap between you and a leader. Be advised, however, that for all the Crowd does to recoup market share, revenues, or profits, it does comparably little to build a brand or enhance a reputation. The Crowd is the move of a copycat. For some, that's fine. For others, that's never enough.

TABLE D. DECODING AND COUNTERING A CROWD

How do I decode this play? *(i.e., How do I know it's being run against me?)*	■ When your key messages are lifting but your brand ID is falling. ■ When your category is building but your position isn't. ■ When your market share is falling or leveling off. ■ When someone else is using your words. ■ When you have more competition in your space. ■ When your market matured faster than you expected.
How do I counter this play?	■ Pause. An opponent entering your space can sometimes do more to legitimize that space than minimize your first-in-the-box position. If it's a lesser rival, scoot over and offer them a seat. Give them a Bear Hug, in fact. ■ If the crowder is a greater rival, run a Bait. Taunt the opponent for having to follow rather than lead. ■ Label them a copycat and a producer of inferior products. ■ Run a Crazy Ivan: Make a fast move and try to shake them off your tail. ■ Peacock. Trumpet that your ideas are so strong, they are copied. Show the marketplace the difference between an innovator and a follower. ■ Leak information that the crowder's product is inferior.

RISK

REWARD

The Peacock is an attempt by a player to bring attention to itself, like the old joke about the guy who says, *Well, enough about me, whaddaya think about my new tie?* It's run outside a marketplace's conventional boundaries because—for whatever reason—the marketplace isn't watching or listening to the player. It's the legendary oil baron John D. Rockefeller in the 1920s, handing dimes to children. It's Lucky Strikes–smoking women marching in Manhattan, carrying what their publicist Edward L. Bernays dubbed "Torches of Freedom." It's Taco Bell jokingly buying and renaming the Liberty Bell the "Taco Liberty Bell" on April Fool's Day in 1996.

By necessity, the Peacock relies on novelty and sometimes shock value to serve a competitive purpose. It is arguably one of the least sophisticated plays to run because it isn't done in opposition to competitive forces and it isn't run in the context of the marketplace. It's basket weaving for jocks, if you will, because it doesn't require much intelligence to run one and it fills a requirement. It is, however, one of the toughest plays to run well, precisely because it operates without foils, comparisons, or contentions. Here's why:

Peacocks are generally reserved for two types of players: the desperate and the dominant. Desperate players can't pick a fight because no one will stoop to fight 'em. Their offering is so little known, unusual, or unappealing that is lacks comparisons in the marketplace. They're taken for dead. Dominant players can't pick a fight because no one will dare to fight 'em. Their offering is so entrenched or untouchable that it lacks comparisons in the marketplace. They're taken for granted.

The temptation, then, for a start-up and a market leader alike, is to *force* the marketplace to watch and listen, even if the attention comes with no guarantee of relevance or competitive advantage. Like the bird itself, this play has the curious tendency to strut about, sometimes aimlessly. Peacocks are called more out of habit, a part of the entrenched ritual in marketing and sales to trumpet a new product or service. They are usually filler, and when they are not filler they are fluff.

The primary challenge in a Peacock, as with any play, is to find themes and innovations that can be credibly championed by a company and which resonate with customers, influencers, and the broader public. The secondary challenge is to overlay those themes against the weaknesses of competitors and to create winnable discussions in a marketplace's rhetoric. The goal is to create a kind of attention that can accrue to a brand and influence decisions and behaviors—like a decision to buy something or vote for something or someone.

TABLE A. BASICS OF A PEACOCK

Class	Engage
Subclass	Press
Type	**Peacock**
Definition	The unsolicited parading by a player of a novelty to generate attention in a marketplace. Peacocks typically hinge on a novelty—an unusual action, innovation, or precedent-setting development—to spur market talk.
Upsides	■ Helps a player break through marketplace noise. ■ Gets attention for a player (i.e., its fifteen minutes of fame) on the marketplace stage. ■ Builds awareness through word-of-mouth, media coverage, buzz, etc. ■ It can dress up a bland offering. The stunt can build heat that the announcement or product could not on its own. ■ Good Peacocks have staying power: They're remembered for years.

Downsides	■ A poorly run Peacock deepens a player's reputation as irrelevant, desperate, silly, self-interested, or self-congratulatory. ■ May work as a stunt but fail as a branding device. Peacocks get mindshare but they don't always change minds or behaviors. ■ Habituates a player to marketing myths—that buzz builds brands, that any news is good news. ■ May provide only short-term exposure to targeted decision makers. ■ A Peacock can be an inside joke. It'll play in your niche but fall flat outside it.
Related Terms	■ Parading ■ Posing ■ Posturing ■ Preening ■ Trumpeting ■ A Stunt
Related Play Types	■ Crowd ■ Fiat

Runt and Stunt

Take a look at any mainstream attention-getting event: *C'mon Down to Our Labor Day Bonanza, Meet an Astronaut and Blast Off to Hawaii, Enter Today and Win a New Satellite Dish.* Ask yourself, *Is it making a show and turning me off?* Or, *Is it spot-on, creating heat, forcing me to compare, forcing me to act?* Peacocks always seem to totter between the two, on the brink of bad marketing.

I call efforts like these "runts," the kind of Peacocks that catch my eye but fail to make me care, much less reach for my wallet or make that all-important buying or voting decision. There is a second form of Peacock that tries a whole lot harder, though not necessarily with greater success, well known to all as "stunts."

I had a first-row seat to a veritable circus of stunts during my tenure in Silicon Valley, particularly through the historic dot-com run-up where the Peacock became the play of choice for buzz-obsessed Internet start-ups and their impatient investors. The rate at which VC-funded dot-coms were expected to grow and go public required a well-developed, fully differentiated brand almost overnight. Looking for quick hits, the moneyed microdots turned to the Peacock for instant publicity in ink, on air, and over the Web. There were, as most remember, the outrageously ill-advised Super

Bowl ads of 1999 and 2000: turbo-charged hamsters that blasted inexplicably through walls for the Disney-funded Go.com, and the beloved sock puppet that shilled for pets.com. Less well known, but worth noting, were the stunts of the discount start-up named Half.com that conned the small logging town of Halfway, Oregon, to change its name to Half.com, Oregon. And no one should forget my personal favorite, Got-Marketing.com, whose CEO bid up nearly a quarter million dollars of her investors' money to play an extra on what was then the very popular TV series *Ally McBeal*.

We remember these Peacocks for the infamy. They were all spectacular disasters that, indeed, drew the attention of their marketplaces but accrued almost nothing to their brands.

TABLE B. EXAMPLES OF A PEACOCK	
Peacocks to remember . . .	■ ***Car Giveaway*** For her first show of the fall 2004 season, daytime TV host Oprah Winfrey worked with General Motors to surprise every member of her 276-member audience with a new G6 car. The hysteria generated unprecedented positive press. ■ ***Branson Stunt*** In July 2002, Virgin's Richard Branson pulled off another audacious publicity stunt. With the Broadway cast of *The Full Monty,* he donned a nude suit and was hoisted by crane high above New York City's Times Square to hawk Virgin's new mobile phone service. ■ ***Dot-Com Ads*** Peacock advertising flooded Super Bowl television coverage during the dot-com boom. The most notorious were pets.com's sock puppet and E*Trade's chimpanzee.

Diva and Knight

On general inspection, the Peacock seems less capable than its play-type peers of achieving competitive advantage. When you see a Peacock, you have to wonder that it's going to work—if the player is trying all that hard (i.e., running a runt) or trying too hard (i.e., running a stunt). But there are masters of the Peacock who wield the bird more like a hammer than a headdress—one TV diva and one British knight in particular.

It's Oprah Winfrey who proves that the Peacock is a viable weapon in the playmaking arsenal. To get her 2004 fall season off to a fast start, producers of the day-time ratings leader, *The Oprah Winfrey Show,* worked secretly with the giant carmaker General Motors on a Peacock of historic proportions. On the first show of its nine-teenth season, having worked her 276-member studio audience into a frenzy of curi-osity, Winfrey put into the hands of every audience member the keys to their own spanking-new Pontiac G6 sports sedan. No questions asked. A gift with no strings at-tached. The audience went crazy, of course, and the glowing publicity came forth like an uncapped fire hydrant. A 276-car giveaway in one fell swoop.

The outcome for Oprah was undeniably good. In one orchestrated move, she re-minded her industry and her viewers of her position as the uncontested queen of daytime TV. But for GM, the payoff for its $7 million giveaway was less clear. Subse-quent sales of the new G6, through its launch and into the 2005 selling year, were un-impressive and failed to curb growing sales of the targeted competitors, Toyota's Camry and Honda's Accord.

What's notable about the Oprah/GM giveaway was the weak response of day-time TV and car company competitors. Oprah's rivals were effectively AWOL, seem-ingly cowed by her audacity and, probably, her bulletproof reputation. But so were Ford, DaimlerChrysler, and Toyota, and yet each had opportunities to clip the Pea-cock's feathers, even to reverse the gushing praise. Through surrogates or directly through their executives, they could have run a Call Out saying, *This proves that GM cars can only be given away. They're desperate.* Or a Label like *Free cars are cheap cars* or *You'll notice GM didn't give away Cadillacs.* But they didn't. Ford, in fact, fol-lowed suit with giveaways to the reality TV shows *Extreme Makeover* and *Dr. Phil.*

A few professors waded into the mix. Perhaps they were Proxies of Ford, Daim-lerChrysler, or Toyota, recruited to warn of the dangers of giveaways, but their pres-ence was so obscure and inconsistent that they were probably operating on their own. There were no other deliberate or widespread attempts to flip the positive out-pouring as gullible blather or to spark a backlash about commercial excess. Environ-mental groups could have positioned the stunt as an outlandish waste of resources. Consumer rights groups could have accused the duo of fanning the flames of run-away consumerism, saying, in effect, *This is great for Oprah, but wrong for America.* They could have poured verbal kerosene onto the fact that the "free cars" would cost every new owner as much as seven thousand dollars in taxes. But they didn't. No one did, and Oprah and GM got away with it.

TABLE C. CALLING AND RUNNING A PEACOCK	
Call and run this play because . . .	■ You have something unique and legitimate to do or say. Strut your stuff. ■ Your product or message has "show potential." You can tickle the funny bone, strum the heartstrings, or grab the eyeballs of your audience. ■ You want to break the mold. You're tired of the status quo. You want to shake it up, maybe even have some fun . . . or cause some trouble. ■ The meaning or message of your Peacock can accrue to your brand—if it changes behavior, not just minds. ■ Your competitors are hidebound, locked into tradition or conventional wisdom. ■ Your marketplace is in flux. The rules are flexible and can be challenged or safely broken. ■ Your competition won't engage with you; they won't or even be provoked. ■ You're number four in a "Big Three" marketplace.

If Oprah redeemed the Peacock, it is Sir Richard Branson, Virgin's audacious chairman, who also understands the bird's full potential. Plays must be run in context to influence marketplace discussions and activities or, better, to build competitive advantage. And often they are better matched with things that create *friction* than things which *fit*. Oprah, of course, leans toward the latter, pulling on the sympathies and needs of her audience—things that fit. Branson, however, goes the other way. Charming as he is, the ebullient entrepreneur regularly mines for sources of friction that create debate, controversy, and beg competitive responses to his grandiose Peacocks—things that create friction. Here's just one example of Branson at full strut:

In 2002, the British magnate donned a nude suit and with the Broadway cast of *The Full Monty* hoisted himself high above New York City's crowded Times Square on a refrigerator-sized model of a Kyocera mobile phone. This was done to publicize the launch of Virgin's new mobile service, a campaign dubbed "Nothing to Hide." Though he delighted in showing what few body parts he supposedly had to hide, Branson's real motive was to unmask the fine print lock-in contracts of his rivals—to offer phone customers a deal that had literally nothing to hide. In this way, Virgin's master plan, its *alpha* play, was based on the Call Out. But the strategy was carried out in the form of the *beta* play Peacock. (For more information, see "Alpha and Beta Plays," p. 291.)

The stunt was entertaining and it drew for Branson a windfall of news coverage and word-of-mouth so crucial to the yacky mobile phone market. But the brilliance of the stunt lay in the fact that Branson's frolic converted the novelty of a naked billionaire onto the promise of a brand—that Virgin users were unfettered and uncheated. It was funny and fun for the eyes, but it spoke to the pocketbook and strengthened Virgin's opening moves in a hotly contested marketplace.

There is nothing wrong with putting your best foot forward, telling a good story, and letting a customer know about something new, but to drive real competitive advantage, it's essential that the display is relevant to the business of the marketplace, that it has value, that it meets a customer's need, and that it's clearly different from or superior to another competitor's, well, tail of feathers.

TABLE D. DECODING AND COUNTERING A PEACOCK	
How do I decode this play? *(i.e., How do I know it's being run against me?)*	■ You'll know. Peacocks are never covert. ■ Your customers, clients, constituents, prospects, or media are buzzing about the Peacock . . . and are asking you what you're gonna do about it. ■ The trick worked—you can't get the jingle, sound bite, or shtick out your head.
How do I counter this play?	■ Pause and measure. Ask yourself, *Is anyone noticing? Will anything change?* ■ If the play is working—if it's moving the marketplace, not just mouths—run a Crowd or Bear Hug to pull even or just stay close while the frenzy peters out. ■ If the Peacock has crossed the line, run a Challenge or Mirror to lure or force the preening opponent to expose the indiscretion. ■ If the play is fizzling, run a Recast, perhaps with the aid of a Proxy, to position the Peacock as vapid and vain.

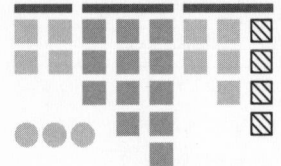

The Attack Subclass

To the relief of the kinder and gentler playmaker and to the chagrin of the anything-goes sort, only one of the eight subclasses of The Playmaker's Table is dedicated to outright aggression. Maybe this is what you thought playmaking is all about—attacking. But as you're no doubt coming to learn, the discipline is more akin to playing a game than waging a war, one that requires a diverse set of skills and tools to achieve a winning advantage. So it is, however, that there are times in the realm of running plays when players must indeed attack.

> def. **Attack:** Play action that commits a player to compete directly for its desired position.

There are four plays in this Attack subclass that take a player up close and personal to a competitor—Call Out, Preempt, Draft, and Crazy Ivan. Call Outs amount to a player's public dissing of a competitor. They shout, in so many words, *You're not up to the task!* And, of course, those are usually fighting words. Preempts don't so much go *at* the competition as they go over or around it. Through savvy words or swift deeds, they move players past a rival in one motion—again, a provocative maneuver that usually invites countermoves. Drafting is similar except it comes in two motions, not one. It follows and feeds off a competitor's position and resources and then, when the time is right, it slingshots a drafting player ahead. Finally, we come to the Crazy Ivan, a move that's, well, a little nuts because it picks the fights a player perhaps shouldn't pick. But Crazy Ivans—loosely adapted from submarine warfare strategy—gain their power through timing and surprise. A player might be outmatched, but choosing the time and circumstances of an impending altercation, turning on a rival when they're not expecting it, can sometimes even the odds and even change the game.

There are probably a few players who err toward the attacking plays because it's their nature. I've worked with a few and I'll bet you have too. But fire breathing playmakers don't own this subclass. Even the meekest player, even the most risk-averse, even the we-take-the-high-road types, all routinely face situations where an opponent has to be called on its antics, where another has to be passed, where one has to be followed and exploited, and where yet another has to be faced down. It is a necessity for maintaining relative competitive advantage, and that, of course, is elemental to the game of influence and The Playmaker's Standard.

Here are the last of the twenty-five plays that fill out The Playmaker's Table, the Call Out, Preempt, Draft, and Crazy Ivan.

Chapter 22

Call Out : CT

RISK ···▲

···· ▶ REWARD ··▶

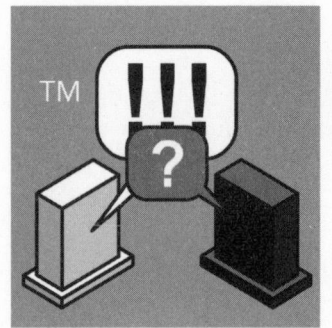

Playmaking is a response to two needs. It brings structure to the rich but amorphous pastimes of influence and advocacy. And it demystifies the tough and sometimes unpleasant sides of those inherently manipulative processes. It puts a name and face, of sorts, on what we know to be true as persuaders and what we are taught so often is taboo.

Playmaking, then, is a little like the forbidden novel you snuck away to read as a teenager (mine was *Summer of '42*). That is, it reveals things that are generally known but not discussed in professional life, much less taught. It's also a little like that frog you dissected in eighth grade. It's the product of careful dissection and, then, of organizing and classifying what's been found.

What we have in the Call Out is a piece of the playmaking puzzle that is not for the prudish or squeamish. It's what some would like *not* to know, much less ever employ in their day-to-day work. But for others, it's a permission slip to think and work freely for their causes and companies.

A Call Out is an act or expression of public doubt. Its street name is quite apt: *Calling Bullshit*. It can serve to put someone or something down. Such was the case in 1995 when Oracle CEO and software billionaire Larry Ellison crowed, *"The PC is a ridiculous device!"* Or it can serve to put someone or something in its place, as U.S. senator Lloyd Bentsen did in the 1988 U.S. vice presidential debate when he verbally cuffed his boyish opponent, Senator Dan Quayle, for obliquely comparing himself to John F. Kennedy. Ellison fired his shot in a keynote speech at a Paris technology industry conference, preceding his archrival Bill Gates of Microsoft. Bentsen did his handiwork on national TV, spiking this famous comeback: *"Senator, I served with Jack*

Kennedy. I knew Jack Kennedy. Jack Kennedy was a friend of mine. Senator, you're no Jack Kennedy."

TABLE A. BASICS OF A CALL OUT	
Class	Engage
Subclass	Attack
Type	**Call Out**
Definition	An overt public expression of doubt or concern, usually aimed at a competing person or organization, intended to call into question a flaw in the opponent's position or message set. Call Outs often have a tone of moral authority; they're judgmental and direct.
Upsides	■ Exposes a rival's shortcomings or misdeeds. ■ Keeps the competition honest. ■ Destabilizes an opponent's broader message platform. ■ Pressures a rival to reroute offensive resources to defend the Call Out. ■ Improves *relative* competitive advantage by de-positioning opponent.
Downsides	■ Can cast the attacking player as overzealous, even cruel or unethical. ■ Can unduly discredit an opponent. ■ Can bring undue public embarrassment to an opponent. ■ May draw the ire of the opponent (or the sympathies of others), putting the attacking player's credibility at risk and/or sparking a grudge war.
Related Terms	■ Begging the question ■ Calling a bluff ■ Calling bullshit ■ Dissing
Related Play Types	■ Bait ■ Challenge ■ Crazy Ivan ■ Draft ■ Label ■ Mirror ■ Preempt

However entertaining, well-run Call Outs state the obvious. They can be employed with a range of emotions and styles, from mean spirit to high moral authority, but they are Call Outs nonetheless. They are an attempt to expose what is true to one player and hidden by another and to send a pretender back to its proper position in a marketplace.

The Call Out is high risk because it has the potential to shame an opponent and spur a reaction, particularly if the blow is personal. Let this serve as a reminder that some plays, as in physics, often invite reactions of equal and opposite force. They are best used to start play action, not end it, and in fact enflame an issue or provoke an opponent. They are used by master strategists as opening gambits and preludes to a series of subsequent moves.

It took some time for Ellison's play to sink in, but Gates and Microsoft fought back hard, initially with Deflects to buy time, personal Labels to peg Ellison as a malicious bad boy, and Recasts to co-opt Ellison's spin on network computing. Many contend that Ellison lost in the end . . . badly. After all, he never shipped his vaunted NCs, or network computers. Others believe it put him on the map, chiseled Oracle's flagship products onto the short lists of every major business, and served as a competitive barrier against Microsoft's attacks in the huge enterprise software segment. Dan Quayle fought back too. Sort of. The political machinery of his running mate, George H. W. Bush, defeated Bentsen and his presidential nominee, Governor Michael Dukakis, but Quayle's reputation as a poser was forever sealed.

TABLE B. EXAMPLES OF A CALL OUT

Call Outs to remember . . .	
	■ **Larry Ellison** *"The PC is a ridiculous device."*—Oracle CEO Larry Ellison, 1995, calling out Bill Gates and the Microsoft/Intel stranglehold.
	■ **VP Debate** *"Senator, I served with Jack Kennedy. I knew Jack Kennedy. Jack Kennedy was a friend of mine. Senator, you're no Jack Kennedy."*—U.S. senator Lloyd Bentsen calling out Dan Quayle in the 1988 U.S. vice-presidential debate.
	■ **Rapper War** *"Youza poptart sweetheart, you soft in the middle."*—Gangsta rapper 50 Cent calling rival Ja Rule's street cred into question in his 2003 album *Get Rich or Die Tryin'*.

Rapper Wars

CEOs and politicians know their way around the Call Out, but there's another constituency of playmakers that take this play to an entirely new level. They are the MCs of hip-hop, the syncopating rap artists who have turned popular music on its ear.

Until the emergence of rappers like Kanye West, whose upbringing was as a privileged preppy, not an up-from-the-streets *gangsta,* the essential requirement for rap artists has been their *street cred* (i.e., street credibility). They have defined themselves—and their personal brands—for their dangerous lifestyles in tough neighborhoods, indexing their positions against their exposure to hardship. Whoever has run closer to the line of bad living and death has often sat higher in the pecking order of the rap marketplace.

Toughness is the trait rappers compete for and run plays to control. As a rule, they run Screens to underscore their hard lives, pinning their personal stories against the rich backdrops of drug dealing, gang violence, and other street crimes. But rap, despite its impressive growth, doesn't have unlimited demand and the artists themselves, as in any genre, are bound by the laws of economics and are forced to compete for space in their marketplace. By virtue of their crafted thug personas, what works best for rappers are the plays of The Table's right side, the plays of the Engage class, and, in particular, the plays of the Attacking subclass. This, then, is how rappers arrive at the Call Out. It's a learned skill of anyone who's survived the streets and it's employed by rappers with a punch-counterpunch style that mimics their gun-and-run brands.

Take, for example, the pitched rivalry between two hugely successful gangsta rappers, Ja Rule and Curtis Jackson, the latter being better known as "50 Cent" or sometimes just "Fiddy." Raised in crime-ridden sections of the New York City borough of Queens, they have waged a war of words largely through their lyrics.

Where did this feud begin? Ja Rule, who made it first into the pop charts, is said at one time to have snubbed unceremoniously the up-and-coming 50 Cent. So Fiddy, a former drug dealer who brags of being shot at nine times, made him pay with Call Outs designed both to expose and embarrass Ja Rule and position himself as the real deal. On *Get Rich or Die Tryin',* 50 Cent's first major album, he peels back Ja Rule's thin veneer in a track titled "Back Down." *Youza poptart sweetheart, you soft in the middle,* he raps, teasing Ja Rule as someone who *never sold nothing, never popped nothing.*

To get his street cred back, Ja Rule countered with his 2003 album, *Blood in My Eye*, a tribute to his hatred for 50 Cent. His track "Thing's Gon' Change" is Ja Rule's desperate attempt to recover from the attacking Call Out. *Put a vest on yourself and your chilld-ren*, he warns, over the sounds of gunshots. *You's ain't gangsta, you sweet as duck sauce.*

This surely sells music and, as in the World Wrestling Federation, you have to wonder if the moves are rehearsed between the players for that very purpose. But if you're scoring this playmaking brawl, the round goes to 50 Cent.* His lyrics all but paint Ja Rule as a fraud—*Youza poptart sweetheart, you soft in the middle*—and they back up the charge with specifics, *Never sold nothing* [drugs], *never popped* [shot at] *nothing.* By comparison, Ja Rule flails with threats, *Put a vest on yourself and your chilld-ren*, and insults, *You's ain't gangsta, you sweet as duck sauce.* It's brave patter, but the shots miss their mark. This time, 50 Cent is bulletproof.

TABLE C. CALLING AND RUNNING A CALL OUT	
Call and run this play because . . .	■ You're certain you are right and your opponent is wrong. ■ You need to put a check on your competition, to chisel off a facade or peel back the thin curtain your rival is standing behind. ■ You need to set an example or raise the standards on a particular issue or topic in your marketplace. ■ Your opponent may be advancing a message that is not only self-serving but bad for you and others. You may have no choice. ■ Your opponent's qualifications or credentials are false or used out of context. ■ A rival is championing something they have no business championing. ■ A competitor is using a double standard, saying one thing and doing another. ■ You know that your opponent is not up to the task and you are the right player to call them on it.

---

* 50 Cent also won this Call Out at the cash register at better than ten to one, selling more than ten million copies of *Get Rich or Die Tryin'* in comparison to Ja Rule's five hundred thousand copies of *Blood in My Eye.*

Cola Wars

Looking back farther into playmaking lore, another Call Out for the ages was the famed soft drink campaign "The Pepsi Challenge" of the early 1980s. You'd think that the play type that best defines it would be, well, a Challenge. But a Call Out more accurately describes Pepsi's central strategy—to document, expose, and *drive* the fact that more cola drinkers preferred Pepsi over Coke. Like Larry Ellison's barbs toward Microsoft, like Senator Bentsen's lecture to Dan Quayle, like 50 Cent's hammering of Ja Rule, Pepsi's intention was to pull back the curtain on a new, measurable truth and grind it into the consciousness of the cola drinkers' marketplace.

The approach resembles other plays in the playmaking system. It could be taken for a Bait because Pepsi's national taste-testing TV ad campaign was thought to be teasing the giant Coke brand. It obviously resembles a Challenge, as discussed in Chapter 17 (p. 185), because the campaign seemed to dare Coke to take action, to cross a line. The Mirror play type might be assigned because the taste-testing data was used to reflect information back at Coke. And it might be a Preempt because the taste-test results put Pepsi in control of its marketplace discussion, which, as I note throughout the book, is a top goal of playmaking.

These four plays, at least, can be used to describe the central strategy in what is remembered as "The Cola Wars." But there is one difference that distinguishes the Call Out from the Bait, Challenge, Mirror, and Preempt. It is that Pepsi's original and most basic intention was to create doubt about Coke's superiority. Pepsi's tasting gimmick made the Bait possible. It manifested itself in a Challenge. It allowed the number two cola company to Preempt the number one player. And it forced Coca-Cola to take a long look in the Mirror. But the original intent, the core strategy employed, was to declare the emperor cola to be naked and make everyone notice. *You soft in the middle. The PC is a ridiculous device. You are no Jack Kennedy.*

Playmaking wonks will have noticed that the Bait and Challenge make up the entire Luring subclass. Likewise, the Call Out and Preempt are half of the Attacking subclass plays. So no matter how you cut it, the Pepsi Challenge operated in two of the most provocative subclasses of playmaking—always working to pull or *lure* its competitor near and to *attack* at will.

Industrial history marks the Pepsi Challenge as a marketing hit. It improved sales of Pepsi and put a pop into the bottler's stock. It diminished Coke's cultivated brand and diminished the reputation of its maker, Coca-Cola. It positioned and de-positioned to increase Pepsi's relative competitive advantage—what Call Outs are so capable of doing.

Call Outs are overt, like Mirrors with attitude. They enable players to make unvarnished attempts to reveal a competitor's weaknesses and force a reaction. As such, playmakers should always assume that a Call Out will provoke a response. It sure did from Coke. Coca-Cola's own tests had confirmed the findings that, yep, blindfolded tasters preferred Pepsi over Coke. Their stock was sliding. Their share was shrinking. Their precious Coke, one of the world's best known and most valuable brands, was in peril. So Coke responded. They introduced with great fanfare something new, really really new, something tastier, something bold . . . *New Coke*.

Combatants often talk about winning by biting off the head of the snake. Inexplicably, Coca-Cola did it to themselves. It was only when they reintroduced Coke Classic in 1985 that they began to make their way back.

From PCs to VPs to MCs, the Call Out is a serious play for serious players. It shines a light on a vulnerable opponent and never takes it off. If properly done, it elevates the player and diminishes the rival, perhaps permanently. Just ask Dan Quayle. And if underdone, it brings a ferocious response. Just ask Larry Ellison and 50 Cent.

TABLE D. DECODING AND COUNTERING A CALL OUT	
How do I decode this play? (*i.e., How do I know it's being run against me?*)	■ Call Outs are never subtle. You'll know. ■ When a rival goes out of its way to get your attention and blasts you—attacking a specific assumption or element of your philosophy or thinking. ■ When customers, clients, constituents, prospects, or media ask you loaded questions (e.g., "Are you guys really using child labor . . . ?!") ■ When you read it in the papers or see it in the blogs.
How do I counter this play?	■ Run a Mirror. Use opposition research to confront your rival with their own soft spots. ■ If what your opponent is saying is true, consider running a Disco. A quick acknowledgment and/or apology might put it to bed. ■ Run a Pause to determine the veracity and pickup of the Call Out. It may be coming from a small player who can be ignored. It may be obscured by other market conditions, like an end-of-the-quarter sprint or a heavy news day, so best to turn the other cheek. ■ Run a Recast to bridge the opponent's argument back onto your agenda. ■ Run a Deflect. Dismiss it. Don't show your opponent that their Call Out is bothering you.

Chapter 23

Preempt : PE

RISK ▲

◄····REWARD··►

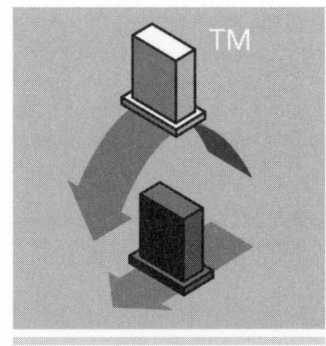

TM

As play types go, the Preempt is a right-winger. Not in political terms, of course, but in the strategic context where moves on the left side of The Playmaker's Table are generally cautious and suggestive, and moves on the right are notably more assertive and declaratory. Teamed with the Call Out, Draft, and Crazy Ivan in the Attacking subclass, the Preempt lives at the extreme right of this most animated end of the playmaking spectrum.

The Preempt is the most basic of any Attacking play because it helps a player gain the upper hand solely on the merits of its own resources. It's not a play type that banks on the clever gamesmanship or marketing physics of its close cousins. It doesn't seek to call a competitor's bluff like the Call Out, milk a leader like the Draft, or invite a fight like the Crazy Ivan. The Preempt is designed to create advantage by helping a player under its own power reverse its competitive position . . . usually by surprise.

As the name implies, the Preempt is all about beating a rival to the punch, sometimes to improve a player's position, sometimes to preserve it. Here are two cases to bring it into focus—one we've never forgotten, a story about the space race, and one we might never notice, a story about the obesity crisis.

TABLE A. BASICS OF A PREEMPT

Class	Engage
Subclass	Attack
Type	**Preempt**
Definition	Reverses competitive position, giving the player a superior advantage, limiting a rival's ability to exploit a player's weakness, or both. Preempts are usually decisive and swift so as to surprise and disable the competition.
Upsides	■ A doubly powerful play that simultaneously preserves or advances a player's agenda and robs an opponent of its competitive options. ■ Helps shift attention of the marketplace from the opponent to the player. ■ Often puts a rival in a following position, even sometimes forcing it to acknowledge the player's new lead and vision. ■ Disrupts an opponent's strategy and planning, forcing realignment and consumption of valuable resources. ■ Disables an opponent's ability to react quickly through the element of surprise.
Downsides	■ Promotes competitive lockup (e.g., pissing contests, one-upmanship, etc.). The player who's just been leapfrogged or beaten to a punch is often spurred to try the same. This can lock players onto one another, irrespective of more productive opportunities. ■ Can condition the player to outrun, rather than outperform, the competition. ■ Can force mistakes by the player in its haste to Preempt its opponent. ■ Can force a player to make a move before it's ready.
Related Terms	■ Beating to the punch ■ Leapfrogging ■ Spoiling attack
Related Play Types	■ Call Out ■ Crazy Ivan ■ Draft ■ Jam

Space Race

History has recorded well the stunning Preempt run by the Soviet Union when on October 4, 1957, it launched and successfully orbited the first space satellite. Given the cuddly name *Sputnik,* Russian for "companion," this crude two-foot-wide silvery ball with four swept-back antennas and its beep-beep-beep could be heard on living room radios and seen every ninety-six minutes, tracking through the night sky. It was jaw-dropping proof that science fiction was fast becoming nonfiction.

To many Americans, Sputnik was a terrifying sight, not for what it was—a 183-pound orb containing two radio transmitters and other monitoring equipment—but for what it could be. Known to have nuclear weapons, the communist regime of the Soviet Union now seemed only one arbitrary step away from replacing the testing instruments atop a Sputnik rocket with an atom bomb. The possibility of that terrifying image came into view each time Sputnik drifted across American night skies, an untouchable invention—and maybe an unattackable weapon.

What did come next was not a big bomb but a poor little dog named Laika, sealed into Sputnik II and left by Soviet engineers to perish for lack of a landing-and-recovery strategy. But whether it carried beeping transmitters or a barking dog, *Sputnik* kicked the Cold War into high gear and signaled the start of the great space race, a historic match of leapfrogging Preempts that spanned the first satellites to manned earth orbits to lunar landings to shuttles and space stations.

There's no doubting Sputnik was a surprise. But what did it beat? What did it preempt?

In a nutshell, Sputnik was a calculated attempt to edge out a touted Eisenhower-era program called Project Vanguard that would orbit the first space satellite and, in effect, award bragging rights to the United States in a new frontier of exploration and military defense. The Soviets, though at the time less conspicuous in international space committees and conferences, had similar ambitions, so they were loath to concede technological superiority to their American rivals, much less to give them a psychological leg up. The Sputnik program, largely dismissed by Western scientists and intelligence officers, was thus commissioned, mobilized, and accelerated to nip the first Vanguard attempt, slated to launch during the so-called International Geophysical Year, a predicted high point of solar activity that would extend from July 1, 1957, to December 31, 1958. It was the last thing anyone expected from the lumbering Russians—a savvy bit of engineering and timing—that worked well enough to win the first heat in the race to space.

The success of running and calling plays relies on a trio of capabilities: (1) Command and Control (2) Sense of Urgency, and (3) Research.

Of course, any play benefits from superior management, hustle, and great data, but the Preempt is more reliant than most on a uniform abundance of these preconditions. Sputnik, quite obviously, could never have succeeded without a high degree of political priority and logistical coordination (Command and Control). But, equally, it could never have achieved its objectives without an obsessive focus on a timeline (Sense of Urgency) or a thorough understanding of the competitive landscape (Research).

TABLE B. EXAMPLES OF A PREEMPT	
Preempts to remember . . .	■ ***Obesity Crisis*** Determined to get ahead of the looming obesity health crisis, Kraft Foods, Inc., the $30 billion maker of popular brands like Oscar Mayer bologna, Maxwell House coffee, and Jell-O, attempted in 2005 to preserve its competitive position by stopping, not starting, a race. It voluntarily eliminated targeted advertising of some of its most popular foods to kids under twelve.
	■ ***Olympics Sponsorship*** In 1984, the upstart camera film manufacturer Fuji paid $1 million for sponsorship rights of the Los Angeles Summer Olympics, a preemptive strike in the backyard of Kodak, their unwitting U.S. competitor.
	■ ***Space Race*** In 1957, the former Soviet Union launched the crude satellite Sputnik. Then, in 1961, it hastily engineered the historic orbit of Cosmonaut Yuri Gagarin. Each preempted the U.S.'s more meticulous plans and earned the USSR an early perceived lead in the space race.

Weight Race

The Preempt has the macho quality of crossing a finish line first and getting there ahead of a specific competitor. *Weeee arrrre the champ-yonnns. . . .* That's pretty much how it went with *Sputnik*. It was a daring attempt that brought honor to one player and embarrassment to another.

This next case, however, shows that the Preempt can be used less like a hammer and more like, well, a sickle. Read its definition: *An action that reverses competitive position, giving the player a superior advantage, limiting a rival's ability to exploit a player's weakness, or both. Preempts are usually decisive and swift so as to surprise and disable the competition.* What this really means is that the Preempt isn't just for beating rivals. In fact, it's just as useful for avoiding them. If a Preempt serves to propel the position of a player forward, so be it. But equally, if a Preempt reduces a competitive threat or somehow slows or pulls back a competitor, the effect and benefit are the same.

As a practical matter, then, you might say that Preempts can be used to make history as much as to avert it.

In 2005, Kraft Foods, Inc., the $30 billion maker of popular brands like Oscar Mayer bologna, Maxwell House coffee, and Jell-O, attempted to do the latter, to preserve its competitive position by stopping, not starting, a race. Rather than be surprised by an unwelcome Challenge, it took preemptive measures to soothe, not enflame, a rival and to do so in a way that limited its financial risk and the certain fame and glory (and sometimes gory reports) of having won or lost a battle.

For over a century, Kraft has enjoyed a leadership position in the packaged foods industry. But things are getting harder for Kraft and other food and beverage companies these days because kids, we've figured out, don't exercise or eat the way they used to. We're also finding out they're getting rather chubby. We *all* are, of course. From newborns to new parents, the obvious fact that we're more flabby and fat has acquired the predictable aroma of a national health problem. And when it comes to our kids, the matter is moving toward a national crisis, fueled in part by health studies that point a finger of blame at the advertisers of colas, burgers, fries, cookies, candy, crackers, and cereal that so many kids have been allowed—and perhaps conditioned— to crave.

Inasmuch as Coca-Cola, McDonald's, and other producers of happy-to-eat meals and big-gulp drinks have gotten the get-healthy-or-else message, Kraft probably has the most seasoned sense of how bad things can get. Owned largely by Altria Group, Inc., it is the sister company to Philip Morris, the tobacco products giant, which in 1998, along with its major competitors, was hit with a landmark $250 billion, twenty-five-year payout settlement for its marketing of cancer-causing cigarettes. If the Joe Camel cigarette campaign of the eighties and nineties could be put on trial, who was to say that SpongeBob SquarePants Macaroni & Cheese might not get subpoenaed?

Determined to avoid another costly legal stare-down, Kraft took matters into its own hands in early 2005, announcing that it would eliminate targeted advertising of some of its most popular foods to kids under twelve. The move was a Preempt, different from the space race and Sputnik insofar as the play was run to *prevent* a loss, not chalk up a win. But it was similiar in that, just as a simple satellite could instead take the form of a nuclear warhead, so could independent health studies trigger draconian regulations or class action lawsuits.

Time will tell if Kraft manages the crisis or gets mangled in it, but its initial moves have been welcomed by a wary Congress and questioning consumers. Its calculated risk is that the loss of millions in revenues over the short term will protect billions over the long term and another ugly loss in both the court of law and the court of public opinion.

TABLE C. CALLING AND RUNNING A PREEMPT	
Call and run this play because . . .	■ Your opponent is hobbled or moving too slowly. Seize the opportunity. ■ The competition has insufficient time to react or course-correct. ■ It's a question of "take or give." A Preempt creates competitive advantage and salvages a poor defensive position. You can sit still and take your lumps, or you can run the Preempt and give 'em. ■ Your team is ready; you have the resources in place to beat your opponent to the punch. ■ You're sure to have the element of surprise.

Contrasting the space race to the healthy food races, there's one more difference to point out. When you run a Preempt for offensive advantage, just as the Soviet Union did in 1957, you run the risk of not just passing, but passing *and* provoking your competition. Done with some element of humility, you can earn and keep the lead. Done with too much bravado, you can lose it.

Five months after Sputnik, and on its third attempt, the U.S. finally launched a mere three-pound *Vanguard* satellite. It was a flawless mission by all accounts, but Soviet premier Nikita Khrushchev, still giddy over his surprise win, chided the effort, calling it *"the satellite grapefruit."* It was an ill-advised Label that probably diminished the effects of his country's Preempt because it angered and further embarrassed the Americans. Their resolve, it's safe to say, was never to lose again. By contrast, you'd hope that Kraft will not send SpongeBob SquarePants to dance on the Capitol steps if or when Congress lets food and beverage companies off the junk food hook.

TABLE D. DECODING AND COUNTERING A PREEMPT

How do I decode this play? *(i.e., How do I know it's being run against me?)*	■ You read about it in the papers. Your plans have been derailed; your competitive advantage has been stolen. ■ Your competition is suddenly getting credit for ideas or initiatives you have traditionally owned. ■ Overnight, you're perceived to be in a following position. ■ Your industry is asking, *"What's your response? What's your next move?"*
How do I counter this play?	■ Run a Call Out. Ask the marketplace, *"Whose idea is this, anyway?"* ■ Bait the preempter. Ask them publicly, *"Where'd you get that idea?"* ■ Run a Recast. Reorganize the facts and tell the marketplace a different story. ■ Run a Pass/Fiat combination. Amass your resources, abandon the contested space, and take the market in a new direction. ■ Run a Bear Hug. Grab on to anything that's left. ■ Label your opponent a thief.

Chapter 24

Draft : DR

RISK

REWARD

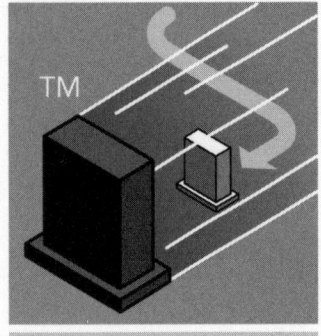

TM

Play types are a little like chickens and pigs. As you move across the spectrum of play types, from left to right, you go from the casually involved to the very committed. Play types that reside in the Framing subclass, for example, are more about positioning the competition than confronting it. They're the chickens, if you will. Quick to cluck. Happy to dispense eggs. Play types in the Attacking subclass are quite the opposite. They are more about poking a finger in a player's chest than wagging it in someone's face. They're the pigs. Ready to root, ready to get dirty.

The Draft is one of four play types that players may employ to meet the competition directly and with purpose. It is not the most straightforward. That is reserved for the Call Out. It is not the most audacious. That is where the Crazy Ivan comes in. But it is probably the most clever attacking play.*

The Draft is to playmaking what judo is to the martial arts. It uses the energy and movements of opponents to disable and overtake them. It is the essential strategy that bicycle racers, car racers, and other sports competitors employ to hunt down, tire out, and pass leaders. It's Lance Armstrong, shadowing the peloton pack, forcing

---

* The name of this play type, *Draft* or its inflected form *Drafting*, is adapted from popular uses which refer to something that is following or benefiting in the shadow or wake of a leader. Four of thirty definitions in Webster's *American College Dictionary* appear to support this popular use of draft: (a) a current of air in any enclosed space, esp. in a room or chimney, (b) a device for regulating the current of air in a fireplace, etc., (c) an act of drawing or pulling loads, and (d) something that is drawn or pulled; a haul.

leaders to lead, sapping them of their energy, and planning his attack. It's your favorite race car driver, going bumper-to-bumper, slipstreaming the leader, and waiting for an opening to slingshot ahead.*

The Draft is designed to deliberately place a player in the wake of a hardworking leader and—like a goose in formation, like a porpoise surfing a bow wake—to take advantage of that leader's energy and resources in order to conserve energy, feeding off the leader's success. Most important, however, the Draft is designed to position the player for an overtaking move. To do anything less is to execute a mere Crowd, a Pressing play designed only to hold a position or dilute a competitor's advantage.

TABLE A. BASICS OF A DRAFT	
Class	Engage
Subclass	Attack
Type	**Draft**
Definition	An attempt by a player to feed off the energy of a developing marketplace, innovation, or best practice with the intent of overtaking incumbent leaders.
Upsides	▪ Gives the marketplace a point of reference—someone else to watch and compare to the leader. ▪ Lets the leader (often a rival player) spend valuable marketing capital, say, to create a new market category or push a new product or class of service. ▪ Lets the first mover make all the mistakes. ▪ Keeps the drafting player in the game. In the vacuum of the leader, the player stays close, mimics the leader's message, and maintains relevance with far less effort and expense. ▪ Distracts the leader, can force mistakes. ▪ Buys time for the drafting player, giving it time to watch, think, and plan an overtaking move—to slingshot ahead when the front-runner tires.

---

* The 2004 Indy Racing League fan's guide offers this definition: *Drafting/Tow—As a car moves around a track at 215 mph, it literally splits the air, some of which goes over the car, and some of which goes beneath. This lack of air behind the car creates a vacuum, which a trailing car may use to be pulled or towed by the lead car.*

Downsides	■ Potentially robs the drafting player's brand or reputation of its leadership qualities. ■ For a short term, surrenders strategy to another player or a competitor (the one being drafted). When a player drafts, it follows someone else's moves, not its own. ■ Promotes marketplace blindness. The drafting player's market view and opportunities are limited to what the leader will provide or stumble across. ■ Timing is critical: pass too soon and you'll be ahead of the market. Pass too late and you'll be behind it.
Related Terms	■ Flanking ■ Following the parade
Related Play Types	■ Call Out ■ Crazy Ivan ■ Crowd ■ Preempt ■ Screen

Draft du Jour

There is hardly a better practitioner of the Draft than Steve Jobs, the legendary tech entrepreneur and CEO of Apple Computer. Since founding Apple in the mid 1970s, Jobs has risen to the upper echelon of business playmakers. He has made a career of revolutionizing large established categories with easy-to-use, compelling products. His first attempts, of course, were in personal computing, with groundbreaking upgrades to early and balky machines. In 1977, with cofounder Steve Wozniak, he introduced the Apple II, an attempt to draft the cottage industry in personal computers. The Apple product caught fire, immediately outdating popular mail order kits and converting geeks everywhere to the Apple platform. He did it again in 1984 with the launch of the Macintosh, a PC so elegant that it made fast-selling IBM-compatible PCs look like antiques.*

---

* The inspiration for the Macintosh and its less successful precursor, Lisa, came during an infamous visit to Xerox's Palo Alto Research Center. Having somehow escaped the requirement of a nondisclosure agreement, Jobs was shown the first graphical user interface (GUI) under development by excited Xerox researchers. He properly, though shamelessly, adapted the idea to the Lisa and Macintosh systems and set in motion the dominant paradigm for illustrating and managing digital information.

Despite his reputation as an innovator, Jobs has never been first to market, whether in personal computing or in his more recent forays in film animation and digital music. He enters markets that thrive on innovation and which feature incumbent leaders. He figures out where they're coming up short and then delivers products that fulfill the failed promises of the market leaders. After his first stint at Apple, he did it in the movie business through his leadership of the film animation studio Pixar, the maker of Oscar-winning flicks like *Toy Story* and *Finding Nemo*. Here, he drafted the feature-length animated film craze. Back again at Apple, he did it with the massively successful iPod portable music player and iTunes digital music software and music store—a flawless Draft of the music recording industry, not just of the giant recording houses but of the upstart alternative schemes like Napster, KaZaA, and LimeWire.

Like a porpoise surfing the wave of a freighter, Jobs is expert at pulling up and riding behind rumbling leaders, assessing their weakness and, ultimately, moving to the front with superior products and services. The result for Jobs amounts to a triple play in the game of playmaking: computers that are easier to use, movies that are more fun to watch, and music that is easier to enjoy.

TABLE B. EXAMPLES OF A DRAFT	
Drafts to remember . . .	■ ***PCs, Cartoons, and iPods*** Steve Jobs is a veteran drafter, having followed and later blown by the early leaders in personal computing, feature-length animation, and the music recording industry. ■ ***Lance Armstrong*** Champion cyclist Lance Armstrong—shadowing the peloton, forcing leaders to lead, sapping their energy, planning his attack in the mountains of the Tour de France. ■ ***NASCAR*** The late Dale Earnhardt Sr. was an expert drafter, going bumper-to-bumper, slipstreaming his NASCAR competitors.

Some might think that Steve Jobs's handiwork is child's play in comparison to the successes of his neighbor to the north, Bill Gates and Microsoft. Microsoft, too, has seldom been first to market but has come off the sidelines to dominate many segments of the technology industry. The irony, as most know, is that much of Microsoft's success came at the expense of Apple. Many of Gates's plays were taken from Jobs's playbook. The most notable among these, I believe, is the Draft that Microsoft ran on Apple in the 1980s when its customers were lusting for a Mac-like GUI so they could drag and drop their files, rather than having to type arcane DOS commands.

Microsoft introduced the Windows operating system. It sported the look and feel of the Mac, a distinction for which it earned considerable controversy and legal threats. But similarities aside, it represented a deliberate effort to copy a leader and innovate its own shortcomings. Windows was not as elegant as the Mac, that wasn't where Apple had erred. What put Microsoft back in the lead was Apple's refusal to license its Mac OS to PC manufacturers, an oversight of monumental proportions that essentially allowed Microsoft to bring a Mac-like solution to the masses . . . under its own brand.

This was by no means a seldom-run play at Microsoft. Microsoft Word drafted the massive adoptions of word processing software and the category leader, WordPerfect. Excel drafted the overnight success of electronic spreadsheets and the pioneering VisiCalc. And Internet Explorer drafted fast-rising browser technology and the early front-runner, Netscape's Navigator. Each crept up on explosive markets and their respective incumbent competitors. Each fed off their energy and resources and pounced forward for dominant market shares.

TABLE C. CALLING AND RUNNING A DRAFT	
Call and run this play because . . .	■ An opponent can be tracked but not beaten, at least not right now. ■ You don't have the resources to mount a significant initiative . . . yet. Let someone else develop the market for you. Wait until you're rich enough in funds or ideas to challenge the leader. ■ The timing isn't right. Best to tuck in behind the leader, feed off of its energy, and wait for your moment to pass. ■ It's a good way to learn about a marketplace, letting others make mistakes. Listen carefully and plan to innovate. A twist on your opponent's approach may propel you ahead. ■ You want to rattle the market leader. Jump in behind them. They'll know you're there. You may force a mistake.

Draft du Soleil

Drafting isn't just for the young or the technical. It can be spotted in much slower-moving marketplaces, even the relics. Laaaydieeees and gentlemen, I give to you . . . the Circus!

In 1984, a group of street performers from the small town of Baie-Saint-Paul near Canada's Quebec City decided to take their show upmarket. What they envisioned was a different kind of production, something that blended their artistic talents with the traditional big top. At the outset, you might not have cared. This circus had no animals. It had no stars. It had no cotton candy. It had no clarinets or calliopes. It had one ring, not three. It did not, by any traditional measure, approach the grandeur of the big acts, like that of the legendary market leader, Ringling Bros. and Barnum & Bailey.

Some essentials of the circus experience it did keep. It had a big tent, acrobats, a flying trapeze, and clowns. And some things were new. The music was mysterious and bold, with synthesized instrumentation and beguiling vocals. There were dancers, not dancing elephants. The master of ceremonies was a miming clown, not a barker. The sets were high tech, not low. And the seats were high-backed and soft, not hardwood bleachers.

This, you might have guessed, was the magic formula that vaulted Cirque du Soleil to the front of the circus pack, a death-defying Draft by observant entrepreneurs against a bloated and defocused performance model. Looking at it now, you'd think the traditional circus was begging to be drafted. It was a show that pleased the eye, but with the overhead of caged wild animals, the huge casts of characters and performers, and the necessary supporting staff and equipment, the circus was slowly dying.

Team Cirque didn't see the problems so much as it saw the audience. They stripped low-margin, high-overhead features (e.g., tigers and human cannons) and augmented high-margin, low-overhead attractions, like the Cirque's trademark musical scores and set designs. Like the Macintosh drafting the IBM PC, like *Toy Story* and *Finding Nemo* drafting *The Little Mermaid* and *Aladdin,* like iTunes drafting fifteen-dollar two-hit CDs, Cirque du Soleil followed a leader, copied what it thought worked, and innovated where it felt it was lacking. And today, as most know, the best circus in town belongs to a smart, agile troupe from Canada whose tagline is not "The Greatest Show on Earth," but "We Reinvent the Circus." And they did, largely through the strategy of drafting.

TABLE D. DECODING AND COUNTERING A DRAFT

How do I decode this play? *(i.e., How do I know it's being run against me?)*	■ When measures of your brand ID show you're leading other wannabes. ■ When lesser players parrot your key messages, adopt your position, or try to flatter you. ■ When followers start to innovate, and the marketplace reacts positively. ■ When your market share shrinks, at the hand of a formerly insignificant competitor.
How do I counter this play?	■ If a trailing opponent seems well behaved, run a Pause, and watch them carefully. Enjoy the company because their presence builds legitimacy for your efforts and leadership. ■ If your trailing opponent tries to overtake you, (a) run a Challenge on the rival's credibility, (b) Recast your message to test their ability to start a new parade, or (c) Pass on the initiative and let trailers wither. ■ Label your opponent a follower. ■ Run a Crazy Ivan. They are following you; they don't expect you to suddenly turn and attack. ■ Run a Red Herring. They may follow that too.

Chapter 25

Crazy Ivan : CZ

RISK

REWARD

There can be times in a marketplace when a player is running on fumes, when there are no remaining routes to recovery or escape. Whether due to bad luck, bad timing, poor performance, or strong competition, a player's options can sometimes run thin.

As a playmaker looks over a widening chasm, there are at least two moves that can be run before taking the exit or bowing to the ax. One is the Pass, a last option that stems a player's losses and allows a strategic withdrawal. The other is a less common and more provocative strategy—the Crazy Ivan.

This, of course, begs two basic questions: Who is Ivan? And why is he crazy?

Most plays are named for their function. The Pass, for example, is an obvious and self-evident tag. Others, like the Red Herring, aren't so intuitive. And the Disco, of course, defies any logic at all. But each has a legitimate history and application. The Red Herring is borrowed from hunting, where rotted herrings were once slathered across a field to teach hounds their tracking task. The Disco is a technique of argumentation and parliamentary debate where a player takes one concessionary step backward to take two steps forward. Finally, the Crazy Ivan is based loosely on a deliberate military strategy, first deployed by anxious and exhausted Soviet submarine captains and famously featured in the 1990 hit film *The Hunt for Red October*.

Practiced and perfected in the high-stakes crucible of the Cold War, Crazy Ivan was a nervy move honed by Soviet and American submarines, each attempting to track and foil their rival's missions in an underwater game of guts.

American subs, generally more stealthy and quick, were the better bloodhounds, often locking on to their enemies and following closely behind without detection, staying in their quarry's noisy prop wash to mask the sounds of their own whirling motors and swooshing control surfaces.

Out of frustration—and often out of paranoia—Soviet captains developed a technique to quickly check this troubling blind spot. At random, they would stop their engines and pumps, silence all work and shipboard chatter, and pivot their subs sharply, left or right. Using supersensitive acoustic equipment, they then listened all around for signs of their shadowing pursuer and, sometimes, caught them red-handed in the sounds of their headphones.

For today's submariners, the ploy is a routine precaution. But originally, dumbfounded Americans called this *crazy* because it invited an underwater collision. Like driving into a fogbank, their tailgating tactics could cause an underwater rear-ender as their Soviet quarry essentially disappeared into silence and the dark waters just ahead.* It was called *Ivan* simply for the nickname given to Russians by the American military—a gibing Label, by the way.

The disciplines of maneuver warfare and playmaking can and do intersect. They share similar predicaments and opportunities and, correspondingly, use similar strategies to gain an upper hand. But don't assume playmaking is reconstituted war gaming. Maneuver warfare is largely based on the objectives of attrition and elimination. Playmaking, indeed, shares the objective of attrition—what better way to gain control in a marketplace than for your opponent to be weakened or for its ranks to be thinned. However, playmaking is *not* about elimination. It is well and good if an opponent's capability or number is reduced, but it is not good if the opponent goes away altogether. This is even true in the unlikely event that a player has cornered a market, because monopolies need the camouflage of surrounding wannabes. They need a veneer of choice to maneuver freely and to be chosen freely. And, most important, they need a partner to make the marketplace dance. We all do to run plays.

---

* Amateur historians and bloggers have speculated, some say carelessly, that this was the cause of an August 2000 sinking of a nuclear-powered Russian cruise missile submarine, *Kursk,* said to have tangled with a U.S. sub in the Barents Sea. Another suspected but unconfirmed case of a Crazy Ivan gone bad occurred June 20, 1970, when the USS *Tautog* reportedly collided with a Soviet Echo-class submarine.

TABLE A. BASICS OF A CRAZY IVAN	
Class	Engage
Subclass	Attack
Type	**Crazy Ivan**
Definition	Alters the course or circumstances of an impending attack by inviting or initiating the attack. It is most commonly employed as a last option.
Upsides	■ Surprises your opponents. Catching them off-guard—even when you're outgunned—may be your best or only chance for victory. ■ Allows a player to get over it (the attack) and get on with it (the business of playmaking). ■ Improves a player's lousy odds by minimizing a rival's preparation time and allowing the player to dictate the time and place of a predicted attack. ■ Confuses your opponents: They might not know how to handle your irrational behavior.
Downsides	■ May hasten a player's demise. ■ May turn a nonevent into a skirmish. ■ May turn a skirmish into a battle. ■ May position you in the marketplace as irrational or desperate.
Related Terms	■ A defensive blitz ■ A preemptive strike
Related Play Types	■ Bear Hug ■ Challenge ■ Call Out ■ Draft ■ Disco ■ Lantern ■ Preempt

That said, there are times in a marketplace when a player is all but toast and has few other options but to run a smart Pass or a more adventurous Crazy Ivan. Here are a number of examples, from business to literature to sports to politics and elsewhere, of the slightly crazy play at work.

Are You Kidding?

In the year 2000, a rogue technology startup called Napster was playing out a final act in its brief but phenomenally successful rise. Fourteen months earlier, cofounder Shawn Fanning and his team had published a breakthrough file-sharing program that music enthusiasts soon figured out could be used to swap songs over the Internet . . . free, of course. Anyone with a CD player and the Napster software could transfer his favorite ripped CD tracks to anyone with an Internet connection and Napster. The practice spread and soon the people who were accustomed to making money off music—recording artists and record labels in particular—were facing a crisis of historic proportions. Instead of buying new CDs, fans were blithely downloading the contents of a single shrink-wrapped original, and at epidemic rates. A simple, free program, distributed over the Internet, was single-handedly breaking the music recording industry and breaking the copyright rules too.

This quickly materialized into what game theorists call a game of chicken. The music companies and their recording artists threatened legal action against Napster and its users for wanton piracy of legitimately copyrighted music. But Napster and its following had found such a watertight work-around that traditional legal remedies seemed weak and incapable of quashing the Net-enabled anarchy. Just as one does in a game of chicken, they postured and threatened and tried to make each other blink—one large, organized industry of music suppliers staring down one large, loosely knit coalition of unrepentant music consumers.

Within the music industry, another game-theory favorite was being played out— the Prisoner's Dilemma. Weighing its options and loyalties to its own industry, the German giant Bertelsmann broke from the pack, deciding to negotiate privately with Napster before others did.* Like any of its competitors, Bertelsmann wanted Napster

---

* In *Game Theory in the Social Sciences: Concepts and Solutions* (Cambridge, Mass.: The MIT Press, 1982), Martin Shubik cites the example of two prisoners who are suspected of having committed a crime. They are interrogated separately by the police. If both maintain silence, at most they can be booked on a minor charge. Each is encouraged to incriminate the other with a promise of leniency if he is not himself incriminated. If they double-cross each other, they are both in trouble. The prisoners in this case are Bertelsmann and its competitors. Each was believed to covet Napster but only for themselves. If they acted together, they could probably destroy Napster and get back to business. But if they acted alone, one might get Napster to save its hide and the other would be left out in the cold, facing a compounded and mounting problem.

out of the way. But it also saw it as an asset—if only it could get it for itself. At the same time, Napster was looking for a way out of its self-inflicted success and mounting legal troubles. For all its power, it was clear that the standoff would not end in victory for Napster. The Internet start-up was, in fact, nearly out of options. So before Napster ran a Pass, it ran a Crazy Ivan.

In an audacious ploy, Napster's CEO, Hank Barry, convinced Bertelsmann to cross the line and join them. *With Napster you'll see the future—and control the future of music,"* he argued to the beguiled Germans. Coyly to his poised enemy, he invited Bertelsmann to invest in the venture and underwrite a legal Napster-branded music download subscription service.

Most times, the Crazy Ivan is used to salvage a player's position, to make the best of a bad situation. Initially, for Napster, the Crazy Ivan seemed to have snatched victory from the jaws of defeat. As much as it feared the seething music producers, Napster convinced the Germans to join forces. Bertelsmann, anxious to hop on the Napster bus, invested $50 million in the upstart and, later, another $35 million plus controlling interest.

In the end, the Napster/Bertelsmann team didn't move quickly enough. They were soon marginalized by newer and more clever approaches from the likes of KaZaA and LimeWire and, ultimately, upstaged by Apple and its iTunes music downloading service. But from the perspective of the playmakers at Napster, it is the Crazy Ivan that saved their bacon, at least for a while. They took one hard run at their competition, buying time and getting cash, before their vision vanished.

TABLE B. EXAMPLES OF A CRAZY IVAN	
Crazy Ivans to remember . . .	■ *Tiananmen Square* In June 1989, following a springtime of student protests, one lone Chinese dissident faced off against a column of communist tanks in Tiananmen Square. It was a brave gamble whose simple image ensnared the government in its own conformist policies. ■ *Little Round Top* At the bloody 1863 Battle of Gettysburg, ordered to defend the Union army's flank at Little Round Top, Colonel Joshua Chamberlain was running out of ammo, men, and options. So he ordered the far left end of his Twentieth Maine Regiment to charge downhill, bayonets drawn, onto the advancing Fifteenth Alabama. Combining this with a frontal assault of his remaining soldiers, he caught the Confederates off-guard. *"We ran like a herd of wild cattle,"* they later lamented. ■ *Baseball* In the spring of 1974, Dock Ellis, the quirky and confessed LSD user, thought his division-title-winning Pirates had lost their swagger, particularly at the hands of the hated Cincinnati "Big Red Machine." Before the Pirates' first game against the Reds, Ellis announced, *"We gonna get down. We gonna do the do. I'm going to hit these motherf——."* He nailed the first three—baseball legends Pete Rose, Joe Morgan, and Dan Driessen.

Just Kidding

The Crazy Ivan isn't always so complex. It surfaces in the simplest settings. For example, the Crazy Ivan was run with outrageous flair in the spring of 1974 when Dock Ellis, the quirky professional baseball pitcher for the Pittsburgh Pirates, didn't like the way things were going. The Pirates had lost their swagger, he felt. Though his team had won three consecutive division titles from 1970 to 1972 and even the World Series in 1971, Ellis thought his Steel City teammates had all but given up at the hands of the Cincinnati Reds. In the 1972 National League Championship Series, the Reds had come from behind to snag the pennant from the Pirates and, adding insult to injury, continued through the 1973 season to manhandle Pittsburgh.

Understandably, Ellis wanted to jump-start his team. Less understandably, he did something that most observers would say was just nuts—a common prerequisite for running a Crazy Ivan, by the way.

Scheduled to start May 1 in the Pirates' first game against the Big Red Machine, Ellis announced before the game, *"We gonna get down. We gonna do the do. I'm going to hit these motherf———."* Just as he promised, Ellis opened with a first-inning barrage of misdirected pitches, drilling—and putting on base—baseball legends Pete Rose, Joe Morgan, and Dan Driessen. Somehow, he missed cleanup hitter Tony Perez, who drew a walk and forced in the first run. But Ellis didn't care. Next, he took aim at the head of the number five hitter, the great Johnny Bench. This was enough for Pirates manager Danny Murtaugh, who finally benched Dock. The playmaking was done. The drama was over.

Ellis didn't have to do this, of course. He might have decided just to play good clean baseball, for instance. But Dock saw his team backing down, not for lack of physical talent but for lack of a psychological edge. It was for this reason that he met the threat head-on in his own creative rendition of aggressive playmaking. Years later, his strategy is thought to have worked. The Pirates snapped out of their funk to win a division title in 1974.*

TABLE C. CALLING AND RUNNING A CRAZY IVAN	
Call and run this play because . . .	■ You want to dictate the terms of the engagement. You are otherwise waiting to be attacked at a time and place of your opponent's choosing. ■ You want to create options where none exist, perhaps even an escape route. ■ You want to get past a negative more quickly. ■ You want to force a mistake by your opposition, to catch them off-guard. ■ A competitor is expected to inflict damage on you in some predictable or inevitable way. ■ No means are available to eliminate or slow the opponent's progress or divert its attention from you, the target. ■ The competition is distracted or overconfident. This ensures an element of surprise. ■ You're out of options, but you can't let your opponent get away with what they're doing. ■ You want to go out with a bang.

* Ellis is also known for his claim that he pitched a no-hitter on LSD, which is no small accomplishment, but has nothing to do with playmaking. For the record, the Pirates never really got on top of the Reds. Even in 1974 when they returned to win their division, they went four and eight against Cincinnati.

No Kidding

Far outside the fun and games of baseball and over a decade later, another Crazy Ivan was run with far weightier significance, in early June 1989 when student-led demonstrations shook the People's Republic of China.

Over three spring months, a million young protesters marched in Beijing's Tiananmen Square, decrying economic instability and denouncing political corruption. The demonstrations ended when martial law was imposed and students were gunned down, jailed, or executed in a withering display of power by the PRC government and its military. The students' overarching strategy—their *alpha* play—was a Call Out to expose civil injustices. It was carried out by way of a variety of supporting or *beta* plays, one of them being a well-remembered Crazy Ivan. (For more information see "Alpha and Beta Plays," p. 291.)

On June 5, a lone man stood before a column of seventeen tanks, daring to be crushed and martyred. Many minutes passed as he faced the lead tank, at one point even jumping on to shout at its driver and afterward repeatedly sidestepping into its path when it tried to drive around him. The protester survived the incident, though he is thought to have been executed or driven into hiding. His act, however, stands as an enduring symbol of China's underground prodemocracy movement and its will to invite its rival's wrath.

From a Cold War game of tag to a student-led uprising, this takes us to a battle within a battle, fought in the Pennsylvania countryside in June of 1863 during the American Civil War. The Battle of Gettysburg, which marks the turning point of the war, involved 150,000 soldiers of the Union and Confederate armies, one third of whom were killed, wounded, or went missing in three days of fighting. It still ranks as the bloodiest battle ever fought on American soil.

As much as the Battle of Gettysburg is known for its great frontal assaults, like the fateful Pickett's Charge, one lesser-known clash of North and South took place at the left end of the Union army's line, a long fishhook formation, commanded by a Union army colonel, Joshua Lawrence Chamberlain, and his Twentieth Maine Regiment. Chamberlain, with his men spread across a small hill called Little Round Top, had been ordered to defend the formation's flank at all costs. His opponent came in the form of the Fifteenth Alabama Infantry Regiment, under the command of Colonel William C. Oates, sent to overwhelm the Union's left flank.

Oates came to the bottom of Little Round Top and began a ninety-minute assault on Chamberlain, inflicting heavy casualties upon the Twentieth Maine with each wave.

Despite clever maneuvers that extended his line, Chamberlain soon saw that the Confederates would prevail. His men were calling for ammunition and he knew he could not repulse another attack. So he issued what can only be described as a rather insane order, and what easily qualifies as a Crazy Ivan and some elements of a deceptive Red Herring. Against all odds, and perhaps against his better judgment, he directed the far left end of his depleted regiment to attach their bayonets and charge downhill onto the advancing Fifteenth Alabama. This, in coordination with a frontal assault of his remaining soldiers, caught the Confederates off-guard, who, fearing they were outnumbered, turned tail. *"We ran like a herd of wild cattle,"* Oates later wrote.

It *should* have been Chamberlain who ran. He had no way to avoid another attack or divert it. The question of his defeat was only *when*. But what did remain was the final option to *speed up* the time of the impending slaughter. This is key to the Crazy Ivan. The acceleration of a conflict offers the possibility—sometimes only a slim one—that an opponent might not be ready to deliver its final blow. A giant, with his foot on a struggling dwarf, is often prone to yawn and admire himself. In the case of Joshua Chamberlain, his sense of strategy and timing were perfect and for his cunning he later received the Medal of Honor.

TABLE D. DECODING AND COUNTERING A CRAZY IVAN	
How do I decode this play? *(i.e., How do I know it's being run against me?)*	■ Crazy Ivans rely on the element of surprise. You might not know it until the play is under way. ■ It will seem illogical that you're being attacked. After all, you've got superior resources and rhetorical ammo. *"Who are these guys to be coming at us?"* you might ask.
How do I counter this play?	■ If a Crazy Ivan is coming at you, commence your attack with Call Outs, Challenges, or Fiats. Your rival is merely trying to catch you off-guard. ■ If you suspect a Crazy Ivan, curb your public confidence and don't forecast your intentions. These are the actions that encourage a Crazy Ivan. Most important, move to battle stations and scenario-plan. ■ Deflect it. Give the attack no credence. ■ Jam them. Try to freeze their action. ■ Screen behind a "high road" issue. Remember, you likely have the upper hand. Act like it. A surrogate such as a Proxy might help here. ■ Run a Red Herring. Feign that their attack has hurt more than it actually has. Continue on course. ■ Label your opponent as crazy, aggressive, or both.

Surrogates

In basketball, smart players know that the ball is not always theirs to dribble or shoot because there are other players, and often better players, who can be relied upon to get the job done, perhaps by virtue of their experience and skill or because of their position and circumstance. Likewise, in playmaking, most good playmakers know that playing alone in a marketplace is risky business; it limits one's options and increases the predictability of one's plans. So the trick, of course, is to create a following, a loyal constituency of people and organizations that will support you and want more of what you have to say or do. Finding third parties who will collaborate, evangelize, or even secretly push your cause is an essential skill of every successful playmaker.

> def. **Surrogate:** *A representative of a player or a player's agenda, from the independent co-equal to the bought-and-paid-for.*

These third parties are called *surrogates*—the Partner, Proxy, and Plant—shown above and located at the lower left-hand corner of The Playmaker's Table. Detailed in Chapters 26–28, they are the means by which a player expands its brand, reputation, access, channels, and expertise by *borrowing* some combination of *someone else's* brand, reputation, access, channels, and expertise. Aided by surrogates, players have a better shot at strengthening the perception that the issues, ideas, events, or developments of their marketplace are bigger than they are—truer, more organic, and authentic. Working together, they can create memes, media viruses, bandwagon effects, network effects, groundswell, word-of-mouth—all of the much-studied phenomena that are constructed from play types and which ultimately put players in charge of the sentiments, discussions, and decisions of marketplaces.

For marketers launching a brand, sales executives rolling out a promotion, CEOs championing a new initiative, bloggers exposing a scandal, or activists planning a campaign, surrogates are crucial additives to forming the perceptions and opinions of the player and its programs. They are key to establishing thought leadership, starting a discussion, and creating a category because they are, as the word *surrogate* suggests, virtual representatives of the player and as such they are proof positive that others beyond the single player buy into what that player is saying, doing, or planning to do. Because they *facilitate* play action, it's important to remember this:

> *Surrogates are not plays, they're players.*
>
> They are the vehicles by which plays are carried out. They are extensions of a player that, under its own power, can also run plays, either on behalf of a host player, for the mutual benefit of the host and the surrogate, or by itself and even on its own terms.

CYRANO DE BERGERAC

If there's a poster child for surrogacy, I'd nominate an enduring figure made famous in the French theater, the 1600s-era French duelist and satirist Cyrano de Bergerac. Portrayed by playwright Edmond Rostand as a legendary master of the Plant, Cyrano had a notable love, a maiden named Roxane, and two notable skills, his silver sword and his silver tongue. With these assets you'd think he'd win over his beloved, but no. The incurable but principled romantic needed someone else to do his bidding, to run his plays, because despite his formidable talents with sabers and verse he was cursed with an equally formidable and terrifically large nose that, well, took some getting used to.

When it came to wooing his precious Roxane, Cyrano could only attempt the long-shot gamble, a Crazy Ivan. Going against conventional wisdom, he befriended Roxane's current crush, and willingly armed the more handsome suitor with soaring prose and ghostwritten letters to arouse the lady's interest. *Someday, somehow, she'll know these words are mine,* Cyrano desperately hoped. In the end—the dying end—that is how it worked out. Cyrano's quiet quest was finally revealed, and briefly, before his death, the patient playmaker prevailed in his competitive marketplace of love.

THE TRADEOFFS

Whether you're an expert in relationship management (like Cyrano, maybe), brand management, reputation management, direct marketing, one-to-one marketing, relationship selling, negotiation, grassroots campaigning, coalition development, word-of-mouth generation, buzz building, undercover marketing, viral marketing, or guerrilla marketing, you have as a playmaker a variety of options for choosing what surrogates should run your plays and under what conditions.

To be sure, there are many. Any third party operates with varying degrees of positional advantage, organizational ability, experiential bias, availability, interest, motivation, competence, and popularity. But however a surrogate does function and by whatever means it may be motivated, the player who brings a surrogate into or near its tent must choose carefully, because the character and tendencies of a surrogate should be well matched with the conditions and settings of a marketplace. In this regard, there are three overarching trade-offs that any surrogate-using player must keep in mind:

■ **Control** When a surrogate possesses high credibility in a marketplace, it's certainly a credit to the team but typically tougher to control. The fact that it embodies some level of believability or trust is a reflection of some level of marketplace accomplishment and so, naturally, such a surrogate has its own ideas of what to say and how to get things done.

Consider, for instance, the typical partnership between a motion picture studio (the player) and a successful film director (the surrogate). For all the director's credentials, he'll be given a wide berth to make a great movie. But if the film runs long, you can also bet he'll resist any efforts to cut it. Likewise, when surrogates lack credibility they are generally more easily controlled. Think of the obscure politician (the surrogate) whose party backers (the player) have helped him win his local election. As the newly minted lawmaker begins his term he'll not just be coming to work with the people's interests in mind, he'll be coming with his party's interests too. He knows well enough who's buttered his bread.

Partners, because they are more self-determined and less reliant on the player, are credible, collaborative, and open advocates, but they have a mind of their own and can often go off-script. Proxies, as defenders and evangelists for their player, are credible, too, but less so because they are perceived to lack objectivity. And Plants, of course, are dedicated operatives; they're on the dole. While they're typically the most easily controlled kind of surrogate, they manufacture their credibility through deception and that, of course, is a slippery slope for any player and third party in the playmaking game.

■ **Commitment** The commitment of a surrogate to its player can range widely. Partners can be solidly linked collaborators. Take the partnership between carmakers Renault and Nissan. But they can be dangerously casual or fickle too. Think of Microsoft and Apple, whose occasional alliances are born of a wary and uneasy trust.

Some Proxies will charge any hill for their player. Think of the zealous political campaigner, of the right or left, either way. *I hope you'll vote on Tuesday. This ballot measure will save our schools!* Or . . . *I hope you'll vote on Tuesday. This ballot measure will keep Sacramento out of our classrooms!* Winning seems to be everything to these Proxies. But others might just eke out a cheer, like for instance the alumni section of a Harvard football game (sorry, Harvard).

Finally, Plants, hidden in their marketplace camouflage, can take things to an extreme. A player's instructions to dig up some dirt might be taken as an order to steal a file or a fax. But equally, they might just go through the motions and miss the nugget they were tasked to legally unearth.

■ **Scale** Insofar as surrogates come with varying degrees of control and commitment, their use can also range widely and wildly in scale. At the simplest end of the surrogacy spectrum, a player might recruit a single scholar or expert to lend her credentials and speak or write in the host player's defense, perhaps of an endangered wetland.

At the other extreme, the more ambitious or better-funded player might involve *many* eminent scholars to build the sense of a grassroots movement. And it might enlist the support of like-minded associations, membership organizations, community leaders, lawmakers, and even schoolkids to jump into the fray of its wetlands protection initiative, to organize blogging campaigns, mass mailings, fund raisers, and even protests to drive a broader campaign.

Finally, if a player is savvy, it will also serve as a surrogate itself, folding its own coalition and resources into other like-minded organizations with complementary but bigger aspirations and challenges.

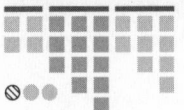

Chapter 26

Partner : PN

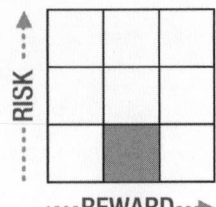

RISK

REWARD

To defend or develop a position or to advance a common agenda, players can team with other coequal third parties. Perhaps, obviously, this surrogate is called a Partner because it requires mutual levels of respect and support from the host player.

Think of the way in which Democrats have historically partnered with African-Americans to promote equal rights and policies of economic and social parity. Together, they've run Screens to associate their common cause with strong symbols of fair play, invoking passages of the U.S. Constitution, the Bill of Rights, and the Thirteenth and Fifteenth Amendments, as examples. Think of how Apple has partnered with the band U2 to ensure the success of the iTunes music downloading business model. The innovator in technology and the innovator in pop music have paired their prestigious products and song tracks to run Peacocks, splashy, dominating campaigns that have further entrenched their respective levels of influence and marketplace leadership.

As Partners, players can lean on one another to broaden their collective base and ensure the success of a mutual interest. Their positions and agendas can be expanded across multiple stakeholders, markets, and regions. As a solo act, a player's participation in a marketplace tends to be niched, localized, and underpowered.

TABLE A. BASICS OF A PARTNER

Class	N/A
Subclass	N/A
Type	*Partner*
Definition	A third party aligned with the player but who operates as a coequal. Partners typically receive reciprocal levels of support in pursuit of a common agenda or business purpose.
Upsides	■ Increases a player's marketplace momentum. ■ Helps build coalitions and grassroots support of the player's platform. ■ Generates an implied or pointed endorsement of the player's agenda or objectives. ■ Suggests to the marketplace that the player's agenda or position is expansive and not exclusively self-serving. ■ Creates efficiencies for both player and partner, such as economies of scale, operational expertise, product differentiation, and expanded channels of distribution. ■ Places you in a marketplace that you may have trouble cracking on your own.
Downsides	■ Partners don't come cheap. They require significant levels of planning, negotiation, integration, and support. ■ Partners can defect. They are by nature independent and may find better alternatives. ■ Partners can go off-script and may need to be jettisoned, causing fallout and hard feelings. ■ Meshing values or processes can be difficult. ■ You can lose your autonomy. Where you once made decisions swiftly and by yourself, you now have to involve others.
Related Terms	■ Affiliate ■ A third party
Related Play Types	■ Plant ■ Proxy

TABLE B. EXAMPLES OF A PARTNER

Partners to remember...	
	■ **Auto Alliance** When carmakers Renault and Nissan hooked up in 1999 it was an alliance born of strategy and necessity. It put the French/Japanese partnership among the six largest car manufacturers in the world, tossed Nissan a financial lifeline, and gave Renault a channel for its own recovery and growth.
	■ **Apple and U2** Though Apple and the rock band U2 exchanged no money, they combined forces in 2005 to support each other's cause—Apple's iPod/iTunes combo and the band's new track "Vertigo." The marriage also helped fuel the mutually advantageous music downloading business model.
	■ **Tsunami Relief** In the aftermath of the 2004 Indian Ocean tsunami, former presidents Bush and Clinton combined forces in a bipartisan call for Americans to donate relief funds to the devastated and displaced.

TABLE C. CALLING AND RUNNING A PARTNER

Use this surrogate because...	
	■ It can create a bandwagon effect.
	■ It can expand marketplace perception that your ideas and offerings enjoy genuine support and commitment.
	■ It gives you access to new data, customers, clients, constituents, channels, prospects, and media.
	■ You want to build your circle of friends and your war chest of resources and options.
	■ You want to hitch your sagging offering to a strong brand or a stronger reputation.
	■ You want to gain operational efficiencies that you don't have. Growing organically will take time; utilizing a partner's expertise will get you to market quicker.
	■ Your position or platform has "hooks" (e.g., relationships, technology, access) that others can attach to, extend, enhance, and energize.
	■ Customers, clients, constituents, prospects, or media seem tired of you but like your products, services, or ideas.
	■ You're getting outnumbered. Your opponent is racking up wins using Proxies and Partners. It's time to fight fire with fire.

TABLE D. DECODING AND COUNTERING A PARTNER

How do I decode this play? *(i.e., How do I know it's being run against me?)*	■ You'll feel like you're fighting two wars if the player and partner are well coordinated. One will hit you high, the other will hit you low. ■ A Partner will spread your opponents' gospel and carry their water. They're now best friends and business partners. ■ The partner you wanted has been taken.
How do I counter this play?	■ Run a Mirror on the credentials or background of your rival's Partner. ■ Determine through opposition research and market intelligence where the player and its Partner part company. Then drive a wedge with taunting plays (e.g., Bait, Call Out, Challenge, Label). ■ Pick up the seconds. In many cases, your rival will have had to choose, leaving one or more prospective Partners on the outs. ■ Fake it with Proxies. Drop down to the pool of surrogates whose time and attention can be bought but who will speak with their own voice.

Chapter 27

Proxy : PX

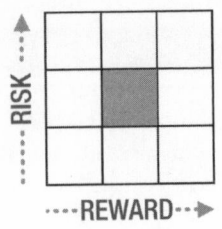

I n lieu of the coequal Partner, players can also recruit third parties to represent their interests directly, to either beef up their position with existing stakeholders or expand their base. These surrogates are called Proxies, a term borrowed from law. They represent and support the player's wishes or purpose and, generally, do not receive a reciprocal level of support from the recruiting player. Proxies, in other words, don't drive a two-way street.

They come in the form of attorneys, making a filing perhaps on their client's behalf or painting an alternative picture of their client's actions or motives by way of a Recast. (Remember, surrogates are not plays, they're players.) *Ladies and gentlemen of the jury, this is a case of mistaken identity, not wanton corruption!* They are spokespeople for an organization who, as an example, might be attempting a Deflect. *I'm sorry, the company does not comment on rumors and, oh, would you look at that . . . we've run out of time.* They are campaigners for a politician or ballot initiative, counted on to echo the party line and sanctioned Labels. *Kerry's a flip-flopper.* They are celebrities or athletes whose endorsements help players associate their products or services with the excellence or aura that encircles the surrogate—all by way of a Screen. *Whoo, Tiger Woods is amazing. Nice threads too. I'll pick some up at the pro shop.*

In any case, Proxies are surrogates that willingly and publicly support the position or agenda of a player and yet are not so close to the host player that they sacrifice their own position in a marketplace.

TABLE A. BASICS OF A PROXY

Class	N/A
Subclass	N/A
Type	*Proxy*
Definition	An associate who advocates for and supports the agenda of a player, usually for a fee or some form of consideration. A Proxy is allied with the player but credible to others—even competitors—and conveys a sense of free will and independence.
Upsides	■ Enhances the perception that a player's platform enjoys independent support, is authentic and grassroots-driven. ■ Creates a bandwagon effect. Fuels support for the player or dissent against an opponent. ■ Borrows from the strong brand of your Proxy. Their goodwill is now yours. ■ Allows you to step back. The market may be tired of you and your message: Let someone else drive.
Downsides	■ Proxies can backfire . . . or they can fire back. ■ Closely allied Proxies, prone to parrot a player, naturally suffer from low credibility. If a rival sees through the veneer, the damage to both player and third party can be significant. ■ Loosely affiliated Proxies enjoy strong credibility but are prone to go off-strategy or off-message. They may be at an arm's length from the player, but their own self-interest can be defocusing and destructive. ■ Proxies are easy to counter. Your opponent can just as easily enlist the right person to further their agenda. ■ The right Proxy can be costly.
Related Terms	■ Parrot ■ Puppet
Related Play Types	■ Partner ■ Plant

TABLE B. EXAMPLES OF A PROXY

Proxies to remember . . .	
	■ **Swift Boats** During the 2004 presidential campaign, John Kerry enlisted the help of his former Swift Boat crewmen, who testified to the senator's wartime bravery. Not to be outdone, the GOP found its own Proxies, so-called "Swift Boat Veterans for Truth," who countered with a different story.
	■ **Tiger Woods** In 2001, Nike signed golfing superstar Tiger Woods to a huge endorsement contract, rumored at $100 million over five years—just enough to get Tiger's support of Nike and to pump sales of Nike sports gear.
	■ **Gay Marriage** When in 2004 San Francisco Mayor Gavin Newsom ordered City Hall to open its doors to gay and lesbian couples seeking marriage licenses, the young politician was acting in the interests of his constituents and their cries for same-sex marriage.

TABLE C. CALLING AND RUNNING A PROXY

Use this surrogate because . . .	
	■ The Proxy has expertise and credibility that you don't.
	■ Your brand isn't sexy, but the Proxy is.
	■ The market is tired of you. Let someone else take your position or adopt your agenda.
	■ Your competitors will if you won't. Proxies are essential to expanding a marketplace's interest in and acceptance of a player's position.
	■ The appeal of your organization—its leaders, products, services, or policies—is limited by geography, background, personality, perceived bias, etc.
	■ Your brand or profile isn't big enough to drive the program on its own.
	■ Your interests are seen as self-serving and somehow distracting to the primary mission.
	■ Someone else can say it or do it better than you can.

TABLE D. DECODING AND COUNTERING A PROXY

How do I decode this play? *(i.e., How do I know it's being run against me?)*	▪ With your gut or good data, you sense a bandwagon effect developing in favor of your rival. ▪ Key leaders—executives, public officials, prominent citizens, etc.—seem out of step with you and in step with your opponent. ▪ Your competition's activity hasn't increased, but support for its products, services, or policies has. ▪ You suddenly see prominent third parties speaking or acting on your opponent's behalf.
How do I counter this play?	▪ Run a Pause. Conduct opposition research on the suspected Proxies. ▪ Run a Mirror. Expose the Proxy's loyalties and interests to the sponsoring player. ▪ Run a Call Out to position the Proxy as a bought-and-paid-for Plant. ▪ Run a Jam. Look for wedge issues to drive the Proxy off-message. ▪ Run a Bait. See if you can pull the Proxy off-message. It may not be well-informed about the player it's representing. ▪ Run a Crazy Ivan/Preempt combination to recruit the Proxy onto your team. ▪ Fight fire with fire. Recruit your own Proxies . . . quickly.

Chapter 28

Plant : PT

RISK

REWARD

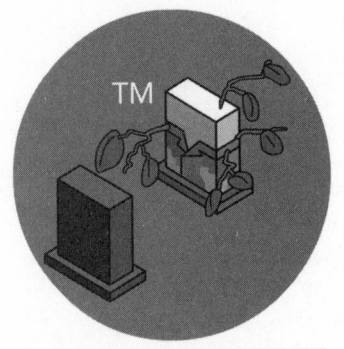

When Partners and Proxies can't or shouldn't be enlisted to do a player's bidding, the Plant emerges as the next, and usually last, surrogate option. This is because Plants are recruited to do things that players can't do directly, *planted* in positions that are usually well away from the player, leaving no trace of attribution or influence. They are, as they say in matters of finance, perceived to be an arm's length transaction away from the host player, though in fact they are bought-and-paid-for operatives of the host player, their connection and inherent conflict of interest being deliberately concealed. This, of course, takes surrogacy to a shady extreme, and it often confronts both surrogate and host player with regulatory and ethical quandaries or, at a minimum, simple questions of propriety.

A Plant makes possible an undercover marketing play: A supermodel glides into a hot-spot bar and orders a new brand of vodka . . . precisely as her concealed client, a liquor distributor, has quietly instructed her to do. Everyone watches. *I'll have what she's having,* they gape, and the word spreads, like a virus, of the model's simple play, a Fiat, in this case. A Plant can be a sharky competitor, cruising your trade-show booth, his badge hidden from view, asking questions and allowing the presumption that he's a customer. His play, perhaps a probing Ping, is made possible through his anonymity. A Plant is the marketing manager who slips into her competitor's press conference to see what's new. She's running a Pause to see what the competition is doing and, perhaps, to see if her own plays are having their intended effects. And a Plant is the operative who's been placed in a press conference to run a Bear Hug and ask safety-valve questions of a beleaguered official or spokesperson. *This ordeal has been hard for you, sir. How are you and your family holding up? Maybe, too, it's the surrogate who's been coached to run a Challenge by asking the radioactive question. This ordeal has been hard for you, sir. Is there truth to the rumor that your health is failing?*

TABLE A. BASICS OF A PLANT	
Class	N/A
Subclass	N/A
Type	*Plant*
Definition	A trusted and confidential ally—usually disguised or undisclosed to the opponent—who is placed by a player to seed or sense information and movements in a marketplace.
Upsides	■ Helps a player control its position or agenda by controlling the discussion and the decision makers around it. ■ Enables a player to anonymously set (or reset) a premise in a marketplace discussion. ■ Allows a player to react to information, perhaps a rhetorical question, rather than having to initiate discussion. ■ Gives the player access and information that's normally off-limits.
Downsides	■ Tacitly endorses techniques of secrecy and deception—a dangerous message to your team and a disaster if you're found out. ■ If a Plant is neither subtle nor legitimate, it can be exposed—sometimes forcing a player to fend off accusations of tampering and bad ethics. ■ Even Plants can go off-message or off-task. You don't have total control over their actions.
Related Terms	■ A ringer ■ A shill ■ A stooge
Related Play Types	■ Partner ■ Proxy

TABLE B. EXAMPLES OF A PLANT

Plants to remember . . .	
	■ **PETA** From 2002 to 2003, an activist for PETA (People for the Ethical Treatment of Animals), worked inside the testing labs for Procter & Gamble's Iams pet food division and chronicled the lab's work on animals. Armed with their insider's accounts, PETA officials later charged violations of animal rights through twenty-seven destroyed "research associates" and other inhumane practices such as debarking.
	■ **Rumsfeld** In December 2004, during a "Town Hall Meeting" with U.S. troops in Iraq, U.S. defense secretary Donald Rumsfeld was put to the test when a national guardsman asked a question about subpar vehicle armor. Later, an embedded reporter from the *Chattanooga Times Free Press* admitted to coaxing the unwitting soldier to fire the rehearsed question.
	■ **Evel Knievel** In 1967, when daredevil Evel Knievel was getting his motorcycle-jumping career off the ground, he placed calls to the Las Vegas casino Caesars Palace CEO Jay Sarno, posing each time as a reporter. *So tell me about this Evel Knievel's plan to jump your fountains?* he probed. Sarno knew nothing but, soon enough, wanted to meet Evel and get the show on the road.

TABLE C. CALLING AND RUNNING A PLANT

Use this surrogate because . . .	
	■ You can't come right out and say it or do it, but someone else can.
	■ A Plant is sometimes one of your only options for creating on-strategy discussions or forcing on-strategy actions.
	■ It may be the best way to initiate a play series (e.g., enlisting a Plant to run a Call Out).
	■ If you don't seed the marketplace with what you want to talk about, who else will?
	■ The Plant can bring credibility, expertise, or access that you don't have.
	■ Your competitor is spinning a story that no one but a Plant would dare expose.
	■ You want to comment on something the marketplace regards as taboo.
	■ It cloaks your moves and motives.

TABLE D. DECODING AND COUNTERING A PLANT

How do I decode this play? *(i.e., How do I know it's being run against me?)*	▪ You might not know. A well-placed Plant is hard to detect. ▪ Questions are raised that seem out of context, loaded, or rhetorical. ▪ The source of a question or statement is not known, not offered, or is difficult to determine (e.g., a conference attendee who's not wearing a badge).
How do I counter this play?	▪ Expose the play. Run a Bait on any suspicious source. Make them repeat or clarify their point. Make them identify themselves—Who are they? Whom do they represent? Why are they here? ▪ Run a Label. Slap a tag of dishonesty onto your opponent. ▪ Run a Pause. If the marketplace wasn't listening to the player, who's to say they'll listen to the Plant? ▪ Run a Red Herring. See if you can draw the Plant off-message or off-task. ▪ Counter with a whisper campaign, a form of a Leak, suggesting that your rival is avoiding tough questions or even planting favorable ones.

Turning the Table

What I've done to this point is illustrate, describe, sort, classify, and name the twenty-five discrete stratagems of playmaking. To my way of thinking, this is the best and most thorough taxonomy for managing competition, reputation, brand, and buzz.

But there are, in fact, other ways to organize plays. Here are two approaches, called Clusters and Pairs, that slice the data a little differently. They don't map to the class/subclass/play type convention I've advanced to this point, and some plays appear in more than one grouping. But they *do* help creative playmakers consider from other angles their best possible moves and countermoves for a busy marketplace.

Do these different takes undermine the underlying assumptions of The Playmaker's Table? That's for you to decide. Playmaking is a young discipline, and invariably there will be other ways to explain how plays get called, run, decoded, and countered in competitive marketplaces. But in the interest of serving the playmaker and advancing the discipline, here are a couple of things to think about:

Play Type Clusters

While the subclasses cover a good deal of instinctive territory—from detaching to attacking, for instance—playmakers exert themselves in ways that are not specifically identified in The Playmaker's Table. As the preceding chapters make quite clear, they are also prone to (1) defy convention, (2) create distractions, (3) associate with other things, and (4) tease other players. But what plays help them do that? This is where clusters come in. Clusters are imperfect, overlapping bunches of play types that are arranged around these four propensities, again, irrespective of their assigned classes and subclasses.* For the player who's bent on going against the grain, throwing up a smoke screen, slipping into new settings, or just making fun of everyone, the clusters make it more clear what plays can or might suit these tendencies. With a bit of poetic license, I have taken to naming and describing these groups in the following ways:

- **Contra Plays** Whether on a battlefield, baseball diamond, poker table, or in a marketplace, it's an essential skill of every successful playmaker to go against the grain of conventional wisdom every now and then, to buck a trend, to do what's not expected, even to go against its better judgment. Without this occasional misdirection, a player can bypass opportunities to both surprise or confuse a rival and reduce the predictability of its own detectable playmaking habits. There are five plays that do this—the Bear Hug, Crazy Ivan, Disco, Lantern, and Pause—and accordingly, they are nicknamed *Contra* plays for their abilities to *contra*dict or adopt a *contra*ry position.

Contras

- **Decoy Plays** While The Playmaker's Table distinguishes between plays that pull a player *into* play action (i.e., Lure) and drive a player *from* it (i.e., Divert), there is in playmaking, just as there is in hunting, the basic motivation to set decoys. Whether to narrow the distance between a player and its target or expand it, competitive strategy often thrives on a player's ability to draw its quarry toward or away from some intended position. Three plays serve this purpose—the Bait, Red Herring, and Screen.

Decoys

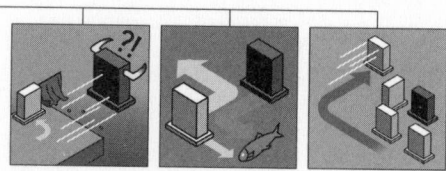

* The Bait, Bear Hug, Label, and Screen each reside in multiple clusters.

■ **Linker Plays** Just as playmakers employ surrogates to increase a program's reach and representation, there is a five-play cluster that helps playmakers expand their campaigns, promotions, and initiatives. It includes the Bear Hug, Crowd, Draft, Label, and Screen. Whether a player's purpose is to position itself or de-position a competitor, any of these five plays allows a player to *link* a position or agenda to things that will support its central playmaking strategy—to symbols, for instance, like flags, monuments, or logos; other players such as like-minded CEOs, politicians, or celebrities; or issues like customer privacy or border protection.

Linkers

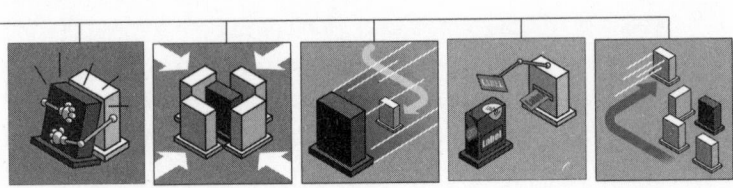

■ **Taunter Plays** Finally, there are occasions in playmaking when a player has reason to toy with or taunt a competitor, usually as a prelude to other planned plays and play action. These *taunting* plays, which include the Bait, Call Out, Challenge, and Label, may be provocative and can put pressure on a player's codes of conduct or ethics, but playmaking is not always a gentle or collaborative process, so these things must be considered in the total mix of the playmaking arsenal.

Taunters

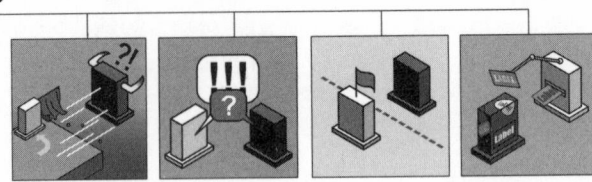

Play Type Pairs

Beyond Clusters, plays also have a tendency to buddy-up, in what I simply term *Pairs*. Like twins separated at birth, some plays seem to have a common motivation. The Mirror and Call Out, for example, are exceptionally similar insofar as they're designed to expose a rival's shortcomings. Because the Mirror seeks to stop an opponent and the Call Out seeks to provoke it, each resides under a different class of The Playmaker's Table. While one approaches with facts and the other with attitude, they share the common urge to turn what is private into something that is quite public.

Another pair, the Lantern and Disco, are similar, too, though for different taxonomic reasons. They're both members of the Freezing subclass because each endeavors to stop a developing threat by coming clean in the face of mounting odds. What separates them, however, has all to do with timing. The Lantern brings revealing information forward because someone else might do it *first*. The Disco acknowledges the revelation because someone else already *has*.

The incidence of paired plays makes for a surprisingly long list and it creates the impression that some plays were somehow hatched from the same egg or born of the same base instinct, only later to evolve into more specialized and unique play forms.

Below are the play pairs that share a common motivation or behavior in the game of playmaking:

FIFTEEN PLAY TYPE PAIRS	
Motivation	*Play Pair*
To join	Bear Hug and Crowd
To reveal	Call Out and Mirror
To one-up	Challenge and Call Out
To fight	Challenge and Crazy Ivan
To keep up	Crowd and Draft
To duck	Deflect and Pass
To come clean	Disco and Lantern
To borrow	Draft and Screen
To tell	Fiat and Peacock
To minimize	Fiat and Pass
To declare	Fiat and Ping
To spin, rationalize	Filter and Recast
To reverse	Jam and Preempt
To expose	Label and Mirror
To suggest	Ping and Screen

Methods and Variables of Playmaking

The Playmaker's Process

So how have they done it?

How have executives from Richard Branson to Oprah Winfrey and organizations from Apple Computer to the Republican Party bonded so well with their customers and constituents? How have Kraft, Pepsi, Cirque du Soleil, Oracle, and rapper 50 Cent kept competitors off balance? How have McDonald's, Nike, Johnson & Johnson, and even O.J. Simpson gotten themselves *out of* trouble? How have the likes of Senator Lloyd Bentsen, Morgan Spurlock, PETA, and Chinese dissidents gotten their competitors *into* trouble? How have Boeing, John Kerry, and Napster won their battles but lost their wars? And how have Enron, Dan Rather, General Motors, Bill Clinton, and Mark McGwire dug themselves into such inescapably deep holes?

The blueprints for these famous (or infamous) players are complex and I won't claim that their successes or failures hinge exclusively on their mastery of playmaking. But it's fair to say that in this age of intangible assets, where brand, reputation, credibility, and trust dominate, their abilities (or lack thereof) to call, run, decode, and counter plays have figured heavily in their respective fates. So you have to wonder, as playmakers, how have they done it?

That is where The Playmaker's Process comes in.

Compared to The Playmaker's Table, its counterpart subsystem, The Playmaker's Process is structurally quite simple. It reduces the work and wonder of playmaking to a five-step methodology to explain the methods by which plays are enlisted, introduced, and managed for competitive advantage. Just as twenty-five plays can be distilled from strategy, the processes of playmaking can be gleaned from the activities and best practices of the strategist playmaker. In the same way that plays can be illustrated, described, sorted, classified, and named, so can the manner in which plays are applied and practiced in the marketplace—presented, in this case, in the form of The Playmaker's Process (see graphic below).

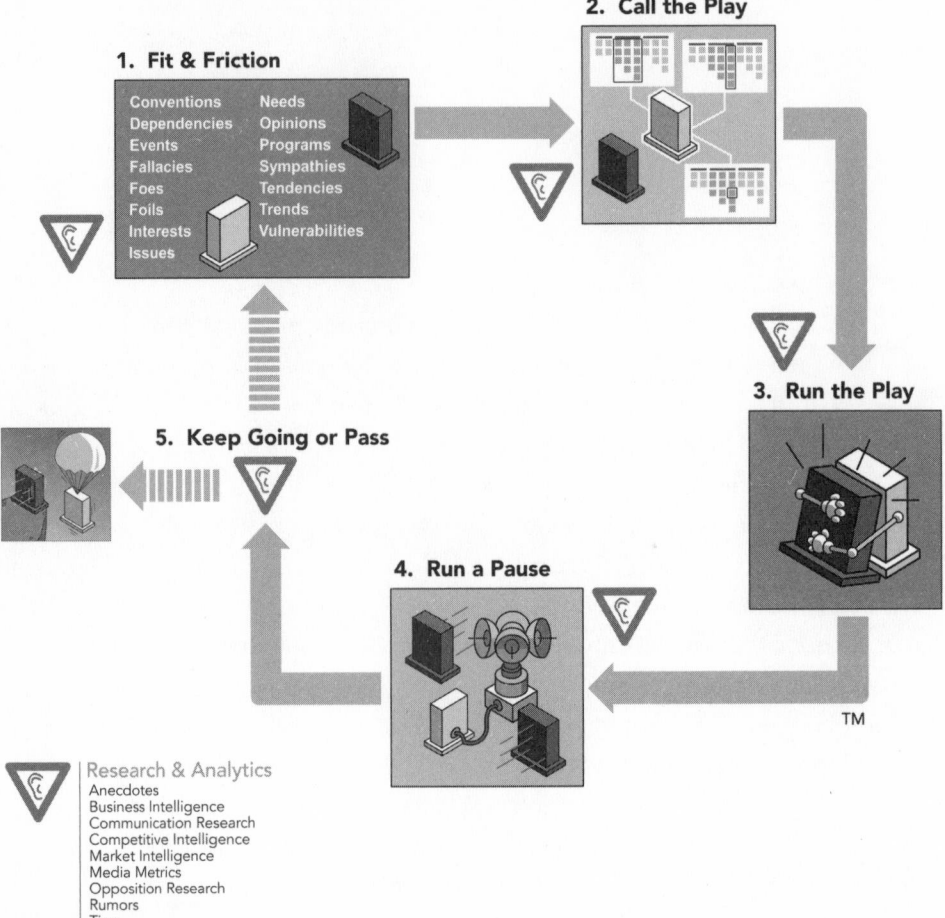

The Playmaker's Process yields more insights into the techniques and tricks of playmakers than I can feasibly present in this book. After all, the principal purpose of this book is to introduce you to the existence of playmaking and to provide full and exhaustive details of the twenty-five play strategies that are elemental to the discipline. Nonetheless, this section provides a basic summary of the process by which playmakers enter and, ultimately, prevail or fail in the playmaking game, followed by expanded explanations of some of the finer aspects of this playmaking methodology, notably of Fit & Friction, Alpha and Beta Plays, and Harmonics.

The Five Steps of Playmaking

In a real-world setting, you might only blink and realize that a play has been run. It *can* be a deliberate and sequenced process, from start to end, but playmaking is as instinctive a process as it is ordered, so it sometimes happens in an instant, or seems to. It's like the split second you might wait for a file to download: You hit a button, you watch the hourglass, and, pop, up comes your song, movie, document, etc. Though it seems simple enough, the task is the result of a series of complex instructions and processes that are largely invisible to you. In the same way, when plays are run a lot happens in a very short period of time, creating the appearance of one simple act. But just like the downloading of a song track or video clip, there is a method to the miracle it produces.

What might also be unapparent to the casual observer is the extent to which playmakers rely on research. Whether by way of sophisticated business intelligence systems, competitive intelligence, market intelligence, opposition research, communication research, media metrics, anecdotes, tips, and even rumors, playmakers are naturally habituated to data and findings because these are their ammunition; research improves their defenses and it points to their probabilities for winning, losing, or holding even. Whether they've been scrupulously combed or instinctively logged, information and insight are the lifeblood of playmakers. Data are collected and scrutinized at every step of The Playmaker's Process—even if unconsciously—from the sharpening of a strategy to the running of a play to the monitoring of a reaction to an ensuing countermove or an exit. For this reason, you'll see in the schematic of The Playmaker's Process the yield sign of the research process, embedded in each of the five steps, placed there to emphasize the critical role of research, both formal and informal, in playmaking.

You might think of The Playmaker's Process as a model for the efficient and effective practice of playmaking, something akin to the Japanese *kaizen*, a term that speaks to the continuous improvement of a process, its outputs and outcomes. Successful playmaking, perhaps like Japanese manufacturing, amounts to a spiraling chain of connected plays, each circle representing the completion of the five-step process of a single play. Here is where the playmaker begins in its climb to the top:

STEP 1. FIT & FRICTION

Since the goal of playmaking is to achieve relative competitive advantage, then no play can be usefully run without attaching itself to a feature, benefit, idea, issue, or analogy that is distinctly embraceable or debatable, or both. Competitive advantage, after all, is the by-product of distinction, so shrewd playmakers look for things that *fit* with the sensibilities of other players, things that resonate, like an alternative fuel technology or a steroid testing program, things that are arguably good. They also look for ideas that have *friction*, that are dissonant with prevailing values, policies, events, or other trends, like a bigger, heavier SUV or public school prayer, things that rub against the grain of someone or some organization, things that are arguably *not* good.

Take the earlier featured cases of two ambitious Brits of the bygone and modern eras, respectively: When Winston Churchill was called to consider his candidacy for prime minister his principal play relied on the taut silence of his nervous adversary. It was friction that fueled Churchill's infamous and uncharacteristic Pause (see Chapter 2, p. 63). Richard Branson's more recent Full Monty over Times Square was little more than a Peacock (see Chapter 21, p. 218) to seed his new Virgin mobile phone service. But to do this, he relied on a simple and time-honored source of fit *and* friction— public indecency. His nude suit–donning stunt was eye-catching and intriguing to some and eye-catching and detestable to others. But it propelled his play. (For more information, see "Fit & Friction," p. 287.)

STEP 2. CALL THE PLAY

Again, plays can be called and run in the blink of an eye, so to suggest that play-makers choose their plays with forethought might seem far-fetched. Do you think, for example, that when Senator Lloyd Bentsen famously called out VP-hopeful Dan Quayle he stopped and thought to himself, *Okay, this punk's comparing himself to JFK. Let's see . . . I think I'll run an Engage-class play. Yeah, that's it; I'll move into the Attack subclass and run a Call Out . . .?* Not quite. Perhaps he did leaf through his mental notes, but with more instinct than reason the veteran lawmaker simply gathered himself, summoned his collective experience and wit, and spat out the fabled and fatal putdown, *"Senator, you're no Jack Kennedy."* (See Chapter 22, p. 222.)

This is not to say that the moves of Lloyd Bentsen or any other fast-thinking playmaker can't be broken down or, when time allows, rationally and even meticulously planned out. To that end, the simple task of identifying or *calling* a play can be done through a series of quick deductions within The Playmaker's Table.

■ **Select a Class** Without exception, all plays reside in one of three classes of playmaking: (1) Assess, (2) Condition, or (3) Engage. Nothing more, nothing less, because if you're not in one of these three modes, you're simply not playing in your marketplace. So when it's time to run a play, or if you're attempting to dissect the moves of other players, the simplest place to begin is to determine which of the three fundamental classes you're working in. If, for example, your opponent seems to consistently edge its way around an issue, never commenting directly, never committing, there's a high likelihood that its plays are anchored in the most subtle class, Assess. If, as another example, you're persuaded—through orders, instincts, or research—to take a competitor to task, you're probably operating at the opposite end of the playmaking spectrum, in the most confrontational class, Engage. The graphic below depicts the selection of the second and middle playmaking class, Condition.

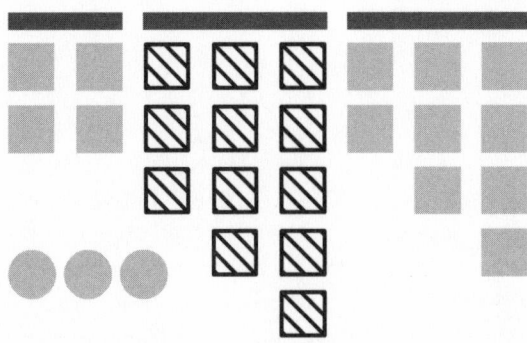

▪ **Select a Subclass** To many players, the exercise of picking just one of three play-making modes is child's play and not too revealing. They know well enough that what they're seeing or plan to do is to the left, center, or right on The Playmaker's Table, so they jump automatically to the next level below—the eight subclasses that overarch all twenty-five plays. If a player knows, for example, that a rival is attempting to condition a marketplace, then it's only a question of determining which of the three Condition subclasses—Divert, Frame, or Freeze—is housing the culprit's play. The graphic below depicts the selection of the Frame subclass.

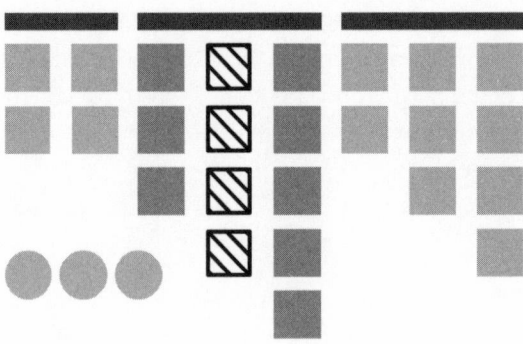

▪ **Select a Play** Once the subclass is chosen, a player can review its specific play op-tions. Some subclasses are more limited than others, of course. If you're operating in the Test subclass, there are only two selectable plays, the Ping and Trial Balloon. Conversely, if you're running a Freeze play, there are as many as five. Advanced playmakers, like chess masters, will plot multiple moves in sequences, patterns, and even harmonic "chords" of blended plays, depending on the makeup and mo-tivations of their marketplace. (For more information, see Harmonics, p. 292.) And, as in chess, they'll also think a few moves ahead, maybe many moves, depending on their playmaking acumen. The graphic below depicts the selection of the Label play type, a member of the Frame subclass and Condition class.

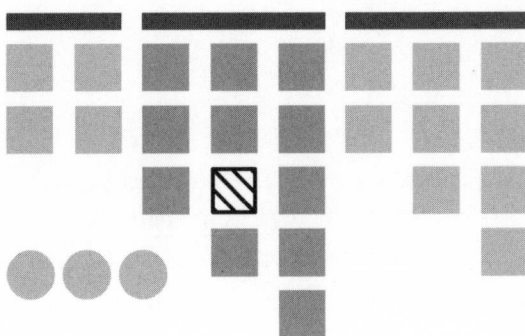

You might ask, *Why can't I just go to the plays directly? Why do I have to go through the classes and subclasses to get to my play?*

You can. In my experience, The Playmaker's Table and its twenty-five play types are quickly learned, so this is often where players begin and end their stop, at Step 2. Even so, when experts of The Playmaker's Standard choose their play they often find it helpful to reflect, even briefly, on the class or subclass their play supports. If, for instance, a player has opted instinctively to run a Crowd, it's useful to know that the strategy of crowding falls under the Press subclass and that such a move is part of the very right-sided Engage class. It's not necessarily earth-shattering information but it's easily gathered and it helps a player understand more precisely the row and seat number, per se, of the play it's chosen to call. In this case, it reminds the playmaker that its chosen play is right-sided and, as such, may invite right-sided responses or paint the player as more aggressive than subtle.

STEP 3. RUN THE PLAY

Here is where the player commences play action, acting on its best judgment or re-acting as circumstances dictate. Having presumably found sources of fit and/or friction, having identified what it believes are appropriate and powerful plays, the player faces what might seem like the relatively routine task of running that play. But, remember, the discipline of playmaking is tuned to the management of intangibles (e.g., brands, reputations, credibility, trust) so the complexities and importance of Step 3 should never be underestimated. At a minimum, the running of any play requires of the playmaker this knowledge:

- *Where* to run the play, i.e., in what market(s) or segment(s) thereof.
- *Whom* to run the play on or with, i.e., what customers, clients, constituents, prospects, or media to target, what surrogates to enlist.
- *When* to run the play, e.g., after the market closes, before a contractual clause expires, simultaneously with a rival's product launch.

Below is a posting from The Playmaker's Forum (http://blog.plays2run.com) that describes a simple Screen run by Wal-Mart and its CEO in late 2005. The play was fashioned around a distinct source of fit, and called and run with varying degrees of success and distinction—you decide.

Wage Mart

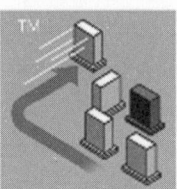 On Monday Oct 24, Lee Scott, CEO of Wal-Mart <u>urged Congress to raise the minimum wage</u>. This may be seen as altruistic, showing that the retail giant cares for its employees and for low-wage workers throughout the country. It is a way for Wal-Mart to burnish its anti-competitive reputation by <u>attaching itself</u> to a social issue.

But critics of Wal-Mart argue that the call for a higher minimum wage will actually benefit Wal-Mart, a company that pays almost $10 per hour, well above the current $5.15 minimum wage. An editorial in the Oct. 26 Wall Street Journal states that "... calling for an increase in the minimum wage amounts to Wal-Mart calling for a hike in the labor costs of its smaller rivals..." A raise in the minimum wage could hurt Wal-Mart's competitors with crippling pay hikes, all the while putting more disposable income in the hands of Wal-Mart's lower-income shoppers. This well-run <u>Screen</u> advances Wal-Mart's agenda while restricting their opponents' ability to compete.

November 9, 2005

Here, below, is a simple analysis of Wal-Mart's Screen, using the minimum play-running criteria described above:

WAL-MART RUNS A SCREEN	
The Player	Wal-Mart
The Fit	Higher minimum wage
The Friction	N/A
Principal Class/Subclass/Play	Condition/Frame/Screen
Tactic employed?	Speech
Where was the play run?	On Capitol Hill, Washington, D.C.
Who was the play run with or run on?	Members of Congress
When was the play run?	In the midst of Wal-Mart's well-publicized PR offensive

STEP 4. RUN A PAUSE

In the ten-frame game of bowling every player gets two chances per frame to knock down ten heavy pins standing at the end of a sixty-foot-long alley of well-finished maple and pine planks. If, on the first attempt, a bowler knocks every pin down—a *strike*—he'll get extra points and a break from rolling the second ball. If some are left standing, he'll study the pattern, choose a strategy for his second roll, and let it fly. Now, I suppose that two balls *could* be thrown at once or, perhaps, one right after another before the blocking barrier falls—just mow 'em down and sit down—but it might waste resources (and points) and there'd be no way for the bowler to know which of the two balls had a better effect. Rolls and strategy would both be wasted . . . and of course the bowling alley manager would be ticked.

The point here is that a well-run play, like a well-rolled bowling ball, impacts its marketplace uniquely, so playmakers are well-advised to run plays *one at a time*, to see what effects they have and to be assured that the next-called play is the best-run play.

Unlike Steps 1–3, Step 4 prescribes that a player run a Pause—a deliberate but temporary withdrawal from the playing field to see what's changing and to make sure that the certain noise of a player's own play action hasn't deafened it to new developing threats and opportunities. If, leading up to this step, a player is already running a Pause, then, of course, the necessity for Step 4 is erased. Nonetheless, when the Pause is run, these are some questions a player will want to ask of itself and its team before proceeding:

- Is our play working? Is it accomplishing its desired results?

- Is the play creating—directly or indirectly—any unforeseen consequences?

- How are our stakeholders responding, and particularly our opponents and allies?

- Does the play need more time to ripen before we call and run another?

This is not to say that plays *can't* be run together. As I describe on page 292, plays can be usefully blended as so-called *harmonics*. Playmakers can run parallel plays, each at separate and distinct targets, like betting two hands in poker. They can also deploy one-two combinations, like the setting and spiking of a volleyball. Savvy playmakers, in other words, multitask; they play many games at once, presiding over the subplots of a complicated marketplace, running plays at and on various targets in one interwoven tapestry of master strategy.

STEP 5. KEEP GOING OR PASS

At this point, the player should know if the play it's run is working. If it is, then it's back to Step 1, not to start over, but to build upon the foundation that the original play has forged. If it isn't working, then it's simply time to run a Pass and *really* start over, perhaps with a different set of new findings and revised assumptions or in a different area of the marketplace altogether. Below is a quick reference for when to keep flying the plane and when to bail out.

KEEP GOING IF . . .	RUN A PASS IF . . .
Your position is on-strategy.	Your position is off-strategy.
The research says, *Keep going what you're doing.*	The research says, *Bad Move.*
This first go-around is part of a multimove play action strategy.	This first go-around is your only planned move.
The marketplace needs prodding.	The marketplace is too sensitive to your prodding.
The marketplace needs prodding,	The marketplace is too sensitive to your prodding.
The marketplace, like the wind, has changed on you. It's time to adjust the sails.	The marketplace reacted just as you thought it would. You're done. Move on.
Your opponent thinks you bailed. It's time for the knockout punch.	Your opponent thinks you will fight back. Maybe it's time to hibernate.

The Playmaker's Process is a special-purpose methodology, designed to shed light on the ways in which playmakers hone a strategy, fashion it into set plays, apply those plays to a setting or circumstance, listen and gauge reaction, make another move, leave the scene, or keep managing it. To my knowledge, there is no better model for explaining and prompting the moves and countermoves of the influencer strategist.

Consider these cases and how far their featured plays proceeded in the playmaking cycle. Did they run the circle many times with many plays? Or did they even get past Step 5?

■ **Perfect Spiral: Rathergate** In the wake of a *60 Minutes* exposé on the president's murky military service record, conservative bloggers saw that CBS was scrambling to respond to their howling posts. They knew their first volley of Call Outs had worked. So they moved again to Step 1, looking for the fit and friction that would fuel another set of confrontational plays. In this case, they ran more Call Outs, this time casting doubt not only on the veracity of the reports but on the motives of the reporters and their sources. They connected one completed circle of smart playmaking to another and, like a rising spiral, drove their campaign to a kangaroo-court-style reprimand of *60 Minutes* and the stunning resignation of veteran anchor Dan Rather. (See Chapter 13, p. 155.)

■ **Nonstarter: Chernobyl** When Soviet leaders saw that they couldn't hide the disaster of the exploded Chernobyl nuclear reactor, they aborted their first attempt to stonewall the crisis, running instead a Filter. When that failed, they resorted to equally ineffective attempts at Call Outs, Bear Hugs, Recasts, and Screens. In no case did any one play ever get past Step 5. They didn't go around the wheel again, running the same play to build momentum. They simply stopped and started over, again and again. . . . (See Chapter 2, p. 67.)

■ **Lesson Learned: Nike** When Nike incurred the wrath of human rights activists over the treatment of its underpaid and abused Southeast Asian contract workers, it first ran a series of Conditioning plays, each designed to Divert, Frame, or Freeze the embarrassing public attacks. Around and around the process circle it went. Only years later did its calling and running of a full and thorough Disco get it out of the hurt locker and back onto the playing field. (See Chapter 16, p. 181.)

But because The Playmaker's Process focuses solely on playmaking, you should be aware of some important voids in the methodology. Conspicuously absent, for example, are separate steps for synchronizing play action with the stated objectives of a playmaker's organization. As important as this is to the success of any campaign, promotion, issue, activity, or initiative, it is a base that playmakers are presumed to have covered and absorbed into each of the five prescribed steps, particularly at Step 1, the front end of the methodology. Also missing is the practice of playmakers to aim their efforts at stratified targets, from broad coalitions to individuals, in parallel, sequences, or both. Again, to preserve a focus on the playmaking process, I have omitted the targeting function, believing that The Playmaker's Process is compatible with the many available techniques and technologies for getting at and grabbing the eyeballs, wallets, and votes of even the most obscure demographic.

Finer Points of Playmaking

FIT & FRICTION

If there's an object lesson for playmakers, it's this: You can't move a marketplace if you don't stand for something, and what most of the many cases in this book have in common is that they have all succeeded or failed to do just that—to stand for or stand against something. In playmaking, this is achieved through the principle of *Fit & Friction.*

Steve Jobs, even in his earliest days as a technology evangelist, would rail against IBM as an incompetent steward of early personal computing. Toward IBM, his position and agenda was pure *high-friction* poison. He grated on the computing establishment. But toward his customers, employees, and investors, his mission was *high-fit* excitement. He enabled the common computer user by mocking the big business alternative. (See Chapter 24, p. 238.) The same can be said of Martin Luther King Jr. His sermons touched both ends of the fit-and-friction spectrum, being both quite agreeable and quite loathed. To his followers and supporters of civil rights his words resonated deeply; they fit. And to his bigoted detractors, they scorched and scraped with frictional social heat. (See Chapter 11, p. 137.)

Jobs and King moved their marketplaces because they stood for something. They used not only the energy and momentum of their backers to fuel their purpose, but perhaps more important, they deliberately and even bravely sought the resistance and criticism of those standing in their way—all to accentuate the merits of their positions and agendas.

This is why Larry Ellison was so consistently successful in his campaigns against Bill Gates and Microsoft. While his message of network computing had merit, it was the foil he found in Bill Gates and Company that made for such interesting commentary and counterpoint. (See Introduction, p. 17.) This is why Morgan Spurlock, the independent filmmaker of the hit documentary *Super Size Me*, was so roundly celebrated. Sure, it was intriguing to watch the producer/director feast on a diet of fatty American fast food. But that his gluttony came at the hands of the sacred all-American brand McDonald's was surely the secret sauce of his success. (See Chapter 14, p. 163.)

While these players fed off the friction of their playmaking ways, others succeeded more through fit. Take again the example of Oprah Winfrey and her gimmick of a massive new-car giveaway. It was high-fit in the extreme when every unwitting member of her 276-person studio audience was handed the keys to a fresh-off-the-line GM car, no questions asked. (See Chapter 21, p. 216.) Consider, too, the strategy of Cirque du Soleil, the Canada-based reinventor of the modern circus. Its success is underpinned by its contrast to the old-time three-ring act; there's a useful friction in that inherent comparison. But what has ultimately driven Cirque du Soleil's popularity is the curious and comfortable chord it strikes with its mesmerized audiences. It is a cozy fit that brings them back for more. (See Chapter 24, p. 240.)

Correspondingly, players who mine the middle have a far lower chance of increasing, much less holding, a competitive advantage. The player who takes the homogenous road—whether because it's averse to risk or committed to finesse—is destined to fail as a playmaker.

Consider the losing effort of U.S. presidential hopeful John Kerry, who by most accounts never really stood for much. He failed to energize his base, the supporters with whom he should have enjoyed a high-fit relationship, and he failed to engage his high-friction opponents, those with whom he was bound to disagree and create a provocative dialog. Was it courage he lacked? Or was it strategy? Was he short on the guts, command, or control he needed to rally his voting troops and to take his detractors to task? Or did he mistake his party's objective of a political middle-ground for a strategy of political agreeability? In either case, Kerry's commitment to moderation surely earned him his loss in the marketplace of American voters. He never played the ends.

The same can be said of Nike in its multiyear and multilayered attempt to navigate the scandal of its Southeast Asia subcontractor sweatshops. It couldn't really develop a fit strategy; there were no practical allies to defend it from the harsh image of an underaged Vietnamese worker gluing together Nike-branded high tops. There was no debate to create, per se. There was, of course, a powerful fit strategy to adopt—a position of concern and a commitment to change—that could return Nike to the ranks of the most admired companies. But for years Nike ignored this option. Until its founder and leader, Phil Knight, categorically acknowledged the problem, until Nike moved in concert with the marketplace, it incurred enormous erosions of public goodwill and market share. Like John Kerry, it suffered the fate of a flip-flopper because it refused to play at the extremes. (See Chapter 16, p. 181.)

This is all to say that the enemy of good playmaking is *indecision*, to edge and hedge one's way around the issues, ideas, policies, events, and developments of a marketplace. Avoiding critics and neglecting supporters is an MO that advances a position or agenda inch by inch, customer by customer. It doesn't create the fawning success of an Oprah Winfrey and Richard Branson. It doesn't assure the commanding competitive edge of a Karl Rove strategy or a James Carville campaign. It doesn't produce the resounding victories of the iPod media player or Cirque du Soleil. It amounts to vaguely interesting things that vaguely enhance a player's competitive position.

In my twenty-five years in business, I have been consistently amazed at the number of companies that are utterly fear-struck to compete in their markets, who have no confidence that they can join in the discourse of their industry, much less influence or even lead it. More than a few CEOs and other executives have told me during strategy sessions, *We want to rise above. We want to take the high road.* Others have wagged their fingers, *We don't bash our competitors.* Strangely, I don't ever recall recommending that a client take the low road or talk trash, but this is sometimes how old-school leaders respond to a call to action.

In playmaking, a reticence to engage, condition, or even assess a marketplace is suicidal because it is precisely the willingness to run plays that creates the potential for competitive advantage. *Rising above* is like walking *over* the playing field, staying irrelevant, and watching the marketplace go by. At best, it relies on a fit-only philosophy, and that translates into an entirely disingenuous, inauthentic profile. *Taking the high road* is like never driving on it at all.

If you think there are riches in the middle ground, that's well and good. But that is not where you'll find the companies who are now great and were once good. That is not where you will see campaigns, promotions, issues, activities, or initiatives reaching their proverbial tipping points. That is not where you will find the chasm-crossing companies of excellence and the practitioners of flawless execution. You will find these players in the thick of rich discussions and lively debates that create not just awareness but understanding and loyalty to their cause.

This is not to say that you have to be a Richard Branson–class marketing animal to be a good playmaker. Alan Greenspan, as the chapter on Pinging points out, was hardly an extrovert. This is not to say that you have to be a business bad boy, like Oracle, to make other players move over. Again, Cirque du Soleil shows us that carrots can be just as useful as sticks. What you *do* need is a commitment to play at the ends of a kind of sympathetic-to-antagonistic continuum, extolling the virtues of what you can strongly support or enhance and confronting the players and issues that will resist you. Without this kind of range, you are sure to confuse or underwhelm your marketplace and dehydrate your good brand and reputation.

Here, for the fit-and-friction-minded player, are fifteen touch points (listed alphabetically) that a playmaker can tap to comfort or contort its marketplace.

- **Conventions** Established techniques, practices, or traditions that can be called into question; systems that can be bucked or bypassed, e.g., mainstream journalists, personal stockbrokers, travel agencies, and full-service gas attendants.

- **Dependencies** Habituating things that can be taken away, e.g., caffeine, fatty foods, fax machines, paper tickets, and televisions.

- **Events** Moments and meetings that serve as a backdrop to run your plays, e.g., a product launch, faux pas, protest, hacker attack, and lawsuit.

- **Fallacies** False statements or erroneous arguments that you can rail against, e.g., baseball is a clean sport, the sound barrier can never be broken, Al Gore invented the Internet, Moore's law has its limits, Iraq has weapons of mass destruction, and al Qaeda = Islam.

- **Foes** Adversaries that can be taken to task, e.g., Bill Gates if you're Larry Ellison, pro-lifers if you're pro-choice, an LCD display if you're a plasma screen, and an SUV if you're a hybrid.

- **Foils** People, organizations, or ideas that contrast with or magnify your agenda, e.g., just as Steve Ballmer uses Bill Gates to validate his business initiatives, just as Spain uses France to validate its foreign policy, and just as activists use Cindy Sheehan to validate their antiwar crusade.

- **Interests** Topics that draw attention, e.g., gossip items, family values, national security, job security, and sustainability.

- **Issues** Debates you can solve or enflame, e.g., sliding K–12 test scores, offshoring, school prayer, gay marriage, and reporter shield laws.

- **Needs** Demands for products or services you can satisfy, e.g., lighter sneakers, hair replacements, lower-mileage cars, cheaper air fares, and easier tax filings.

- **Opinions** Positions you can support or question, e.g., Pepsi tastes better than Coke, immigrants steal jobs, you should diversity your portfolio, video games are addictive, O'Hare is a nightmare, and the Red Sox got lucky.

- **Programs** Initiatives you can support or decry, e.g., No Child Left Behind, Six Sigma, Alternative Minimum Tax, and Voluntary Movie Rating System.

- **Sympathies** Heartstrings you can pull on . . . or pull out, e.g., a bad day, a good meal, bad cold, call center runaround, drunk driving death, famine, and a genocide.

- **Tendencies** Characteristics you can massage or mangle, e.g., Fox News is conservative/*The New York Times* is liberal, Japanese are honor-bound/French are contrary, and Dell is quick/HP is slow.

- **Trends** Repeating patterns or inclinations that you can dovetail or derail, e.g., soaring gas pump prices, less legroom in coach, jobs moving offshore, and crowded classrooms.

- **Vulnerabilities** Susceptibilities to injury or attack, e.g., as Windows is to hackers, as United is to low-fare carriers, as IBM is to start-ups, as Democrats are to family values, as McDonald's is to health foods, and as Virginia is to smoking laws.

ALPHA AND BETA PLAYS

As I wrote in Section I (see "What's a Play?" p. 23), and as the chapters on Crazy Ivan, Fiat, Jam, Lantern, Pass, Peacock, and Screen demonstrated, there is an enormous gap between an organization's objectives and its specific tactical methods of execution. Strategy lies in that gap, and correspondingly, it is open to many different interpretations of its purpose and role. However *you* might define strategy, it is surely clear that individual stratagems (what I call plays) can expand and contract to suit the strategist's needs. In one setting, a play can be subordinate, or a *beta*, to another play. But in a different circumstance, it can be dominant, or an *alpha*. Here are some examples from preceding chapters:

- The Pass run by IBM in 2004 to exit the PC industry was an alpha play. This was IBM's overarching strategy—to withdraw from the commoditized desktop and laptop markets. But in a case where my own firm once ran a Pass, where we resigned an important client relationship, we employed the Pass as a beta play, a strategy that undergirded our larger plan to get the client back by way of a Preempt (see Chapter 1).

- Sun Microsystems CEO Scott McNealy, when he quipped that Windows was a "hair ball," was running a Call Out as an alpha play. His beta play was a Label. But in the Rathergate controversy of 2004, conservative bloggers ran beta-level Call Outs to cast doubt on the credibility of a CBS producer's sources (see Chapter 22).

- Finally, the Lantern was used by Ronald Reagan in his second debate with Walter Mondale as an alpha. But Richard Nixon used the Lantern in his famous Checkers speech as a beta (see Chapter 15).

HARMONIC PLAYS

Plays are run not only in patterns and sequences but they can also be run simultaneously by the playmaker within those patterns and sequences to achieve a nuanced and more powerful effect. I call these combination plays *harmonics* because, as with musical notes that can be formed into chords, plays can also be combined to mix the special character of one stratagem with that of another, all for a fuller and more resonant effect. Like a conductor who blends the instruments of an orchestra against a musical score, playmaking incorporates experience, instinct, and instruction to merge the single instruments of plays into a powerful harmonic performance—all to achieve an improved level of relative competitive advantage.

For a harmonic in action, take the case in July 2004 when the giant European aircraft manufacturer Airbus ran a tidy three-play package at the renowned Farnborough Air Show. Its goal: to set its industry straight on a few things and to put archrival Boeing in its place.

Leading up to the show, Boeing had already fired a series of hard shots, claiming that Airbus was receiving illegal subsidies, that its new design 787 was selling oh-so-well, and perhaps making sure that everyone had seen independent reports that Airbus's prized new design, the double-decker A380, was four to five tons heavier than planned. Airbus responded with a volley of three simultaneous plays:

- A weak Call Out, saying mysteriously that the touted 787 orders were *"misleading."*

■ A cute Label, likening Boeing's unproven 787 to its proven design—*an A330 with a sexy paint job*, they said.

■ A thought-provoking Recast of Boeing's sales boast: Said a facetious Airbus executive, *"We are pleasantly surprised by the yawns [the 787] is getting in the marketplace."*

Aviation insiders might note that Airbus didn't dignify the subsidy issue (see Chapter 12, p. 148) so you could say that Airbus ran a fourth simultaneous play, a Pause, by holding its tongue on a burning issue. Pauses, as we already know, are plays that are notable for their *absence* of action, so this void was conspicuous only for the fact that Airbus *wasn't* commenting on the subsidies matter, at least on that day.

Factors at Play

What remains to be shown of The Playmaker's Standard is a final, but by no means insignificant, piece of the playmaking puzzle. It is a simple reference table of marketplace variables that enables playmakers to separate the plays they run from the game they play and all its attendant rules, quirks, conditions, and hazards. What you must know is this:

Factors are not plays, they influence plays.

They are like dials on a sound engineer's board. They aren't the vocals or instruments; they are the effects that enhance the song. They are to plays what a crystal

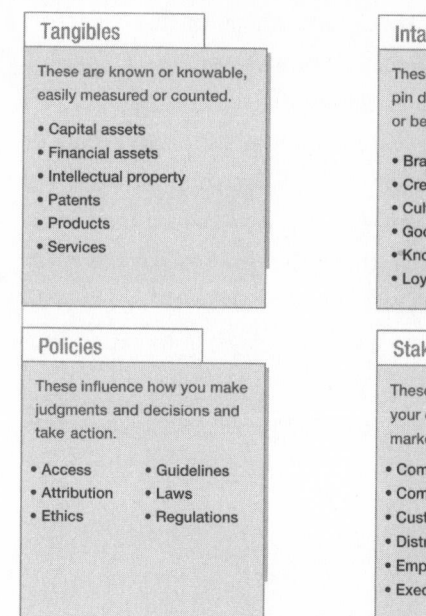

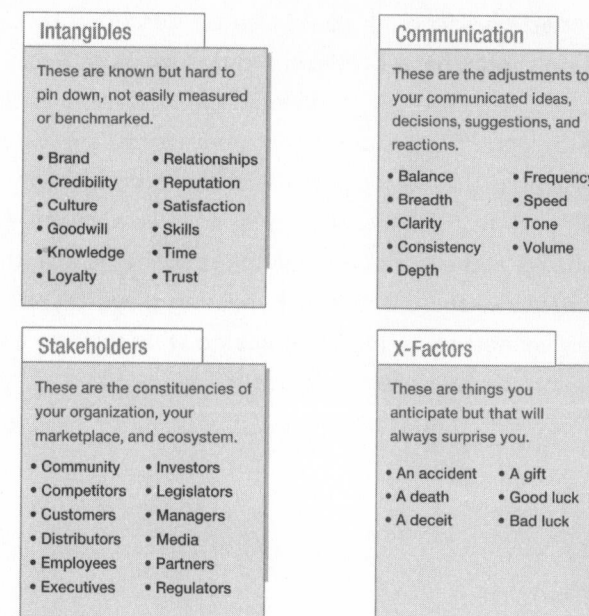

Tangibles

These are known or knowable, easily measured or counted.

- Capital assets
- Financial assets
- Intellectual property
- Patents
- Products
- Services

Intangibles

These are known but hard to pin down, not easily measured or benchmarked.

- Brand
- Credibility
- Culture
- Goodwill
- Knowledge
- Loyalty
- Relationships
- Reputation
- Satisfaction
- Skills
- Time
- Trust

Communication

These are the adjustments to your communicated ideas, decisions, suggestions, and reactions.

- Balance
- Breadth
- Clarity
- Consistency
- Depth
- Frequency
- Speed
- Tone
- Volume

Policies

These influence how you make judgments and decisions and take action.

- Access
- Attribution
- Ethics
- Guidelines
- Laws
- Regulations

Stakeholders

These are the constituencies of your organization, your marketplace, and ecosystem.

- Community
- Competitors
- Customers
- Distributors
- Employees
- Executives
- Investors
- Legislators
- Managers
- Media
- Partners
- Regulators

X-Factors

These are things you anticipate but that will always surprise you.

- An accident
- A death
- A deceit
- A gift
- Good luck
- Bad luck

goblet is to a fine wine, what spices are to a meal, what wind is to a sailboat. The graphic below lists six categories of these critical marketplace variables:

To understand Factors at Play, take the simple example of a business-to-business ad campaign, perhaps the introduction of a new chemical or the launch of a microprocessor. Its success would be influenced by many of the concepts in the *Intangible* category (center box, upper row), such as the *Brand* of the given business-to-business product, the *Reputation* of the manufacturer, and the *Loyalty* of the targeted customer base. Its message would be explained by the terms of the *Communication* category (right-hand box, upper row) like *Frequency* of the ads and their certain *Tone*. And its targets would be described by constituents of the *Stakeholders* category (center box, lower row), such as *Employees, Partners, Distributors, Customers, Community,* and *Media.*

Take, as another example, a looming corporate or political crisis, maybe a toxic spill or a criminal indictment. The setting would be dominated by Factors in the *Policies* category (left-hand box, lower row), including the prevailing *Laws* and *Regulations* of a player's industry, and its self-imposed guidelines for *Access* or *Ethics*. The situation could involve elements of the *Tangibles* category (left-hand box, upper row), perhaps the *Capital Assets* of a manufacturing plant or the *Financial Assets* of an unreported transaction. It could also be described by circumstances of the *X-Factors* category (right-hand box, lower row), such as an *Accident* or a *Deceit*.

Without these things, it would be impossible to differentiate a strategy from its environment. Factors at Play, in other words, are the things that surround a play or play action. They reside partially in the hands of playmakers, but also in the hands of rivals and neutral playmakers and, of course, in the ambient environments of ever-changing and ever-fickle marketplaces. They are all these things—except the plays themselves—and are crucial to helping playmakers better understand how, in infinitely variable ways, marketplaces do what they do and how plays, in infinitely variable forms, also do what they do.

Section IV.

The Making of The Playmaker's Standard

To call this strategy system a standard is presumptuous but appropriate. But for lack of any alternative and given what is obviously a sprawling network of strategists in business, politics, and popular culture, it is clear that a framework—a standard of sorts—of organized terms, definitions, and best uses is needed to propel and perfect the influence industries. You and the marketplace will decide, of course, if *any* standard in playmaking should or shall exist, but this first generation of twenty-five plays and playmaking processes is a base on which to build our understanding of playmaking, and something that smart researchers can use to confirm the existence of these proposed new play types, their relationships to one another, and their effects in marketplaces.

The Playmaker's Standard was, in fact, conceived in a single moment, the product of a fleeting hunch (see "Where Playmaking Got Its Start," p. 17). Could plays be described, like a named chess move, *castling*, a species, *Homo sapiens*, or a color, *turquoise?* I wondered. Could there be a periodic table or a kind of color wheel of applied strategies, a system that laid bare the building blocks of influence? Over time, the stratagems of this unique system came into view, along with other structures and groupings, and thus we come to this point of the discovery process.

All of this was developed through inductive reasoning, not a deductive experimental process where, for example, variables are removed to isolate a single effect. That would have been premature, because I didn't yet have the subjects on which I might experiment. As my father, a retired cell biologist, explains, *good science starts with good observation.* So The Playmaker's Standard, at least this first iteration of it, was derived through an accrual of experiences and, specifically, by way of a five-part research and development process over a thirteen-year period:

Field Observation

I had to go looking for plays because they hadn't come looking for me; they don't just jump in your lap, it seems. I'd had the sense that they existed, as I described in the Introduction, but without direct observation I was hard-pressed to say what it was I was after. So, I turned to my own backyard and walked into the marketplace jungle of the high technology industry to observe plays directly and the playmakers that ran them. Along the way, I was fortunate to have access to and the support of a variety of distinguished global companies and local start-ups of the high technology community, including Adobe, BEA Systems, Cisco, Genentech, Hewlett-Packard, Informatica, Motorola, Oracle, PayPal, SeeBeyond, SeeCommerce, Sequent, StorageTek, Sun Microsystems, TechNet, VeriSign, Veritas Software, Vitria, and Wind River Systems. With a bright staff of partners and consultants, I was thrust into the exceedingly competitive niches of database software, display technology, e-business services, enterprise applications software, middleware, network computing, printer technology, semiconductors, and storage media among others.

It's primarily these companies and markets from which I drew my initial observations about plays, playmakers, and playmaking.

Marketplace Experience

But I didn't just watch. I partook. As a consultant, primarily in the capacity of a communications and research firm CEO, I advised my clients on playmaking strategies, and with my coworkers, I implemented them too. We called what were then only embryonic plays but we ran them nonetheless, gaining over time incrementally better understanding of a play's effects, its best uses, and consequences. And when our clients were on the wrong end of the spear, as it were, we learned the means by which a play could be decoded and countered.

In mixing observation with intervention, one might worry that I tainted the very environment I set out to observe because I introduced into it my own biases and their presumed effects. While this might be true, the experience gave me direct contact with the discipline I'd begin to call playmaking and a sense of how, initially, I could go about illustrating, describing, sorting, classifying, and naming the plays. Even more, it provided me the insights I needed to organize plays into the subclasses and classes presented in this book.

Literature Review

From these experiences, I realized that each emerging play had a common orientation to the other: to compete. Each, in its own way, had a unique ability to influence a marketplace by pushing and prodding or positioning and de-positioning, all in the interest of holding or improving some measure of relative competitive advantage. I also saw that plays were based on not only words but deeds—that they could be carried out as easily through a deft action, a subtle mention, or even represented in symbols. So I next looked to the literature to understand what pastimes, practices, disciplines, fields, and sciences were common to this jelling general theory of applied strategy. I was met with a rush of findings from two broad sources:

- **Professional Practices and Disciplines,** namely management, strategy, marketing, sales, advertising, public relations, public affairs, law, and the younger pursuits of word-of-mouth and buzz. These, quite obviously, all share the common objective of influencing marketplace stakeholders.

- **Fields and Sciences,** from the ageless and even ancient studies of communication, rhetoric, debate, maneuver warfare, and politics to the cutting-edge pursuits of artificial intelligence, negotiation, game theory, and research and planning, to the less reputable practices of military psychological operations and propaganda.

They all had something to say about the subjects of competition and influence, and so I took the better part of two years to do the necessary reading, refreshing myself on such classics as *The Art of War,* Porter's writings on competitive strategy, dense game theory texts, and other respected writings on various famous—and infamous—campaigns, especially in business and politics but also in popular culture. After all that, I can't say I'm an expert interpreter of the great warrior Sun Tzu, a worthy student of game theory, or even a qualified pundit of politics, but I do know from this literature that plays, playmakers, and playmaking inhabit them all.

Prototype Previews

Coinciding roughly with the literature review, I worked with a gifted group of consultants and advisors to develop prototypes of The Playmaker's Standard. I then sought reactions from accomplished professionals and scholars in biology, business management, communication, corporate marketing, direct marketing, forensic de-bate, game theory, integrated marketing, political science, psychiatry, rhetoric, and, of course, strategy. I also presented the developing framework to graduate students at prominent schools of business and communication and to professionals at market-ing, research, and communication conferences, and other forums. In all cases, whether through one-on-one meetings, lectures, Webinars, seminars, or speeches, I asked my subjects, *"What have you seen that resembles this?"* With the exception of a single political strategist who sniffed, *"Oh, well, sure. We do that stuff,"* the uniform reac-tion was one of instant curiosity and a kind of upwelling recognition. Some correlated the plays to politics: *So was it a Screen that Bush ran last week?* Some saw them through a business lens: *This company plays way to the left on The Playmaker's Table; the other one plays way to the right . . . right?* Others recognized them in everyday life and popular culture: *Hey, isn't that what Bluto and his frat brothers did in* Animal House*?!*

Pilot-Testing

Finally, I conducted a pilot program of a Web-based beta version of The Playmaker's Standard with four global Fortune 500 companies in the technology, chemical, and pharmaceutical industries. This put the system into the hands of a variety of profes-sionals, typically in competitive strategy, marketing, and corporate communication. In most cases, two training and education workshops were delivered to the pilot us-ers as well as on-call support to answer spot questions or advise on developing com-petitive threats and opportunities. All told, the program involved nearly a hundred professionals over approximately eighteen months and it produced a windfall of in-sights for refining and enriching the playmaking framework. And best of all, The Stan-dard and its lexicon of twenty-five plays were absorbed into the organizations of two global teams and have, to date, produced substantially improved levels of competi-tive acumen, analysis, strategy development, and tactical execution.

Conclusion

t's 1:00 A.M. on a spring morning—my mother's birthday, as it happens—and, yes, of course, I sent flowers. I'm already thinking about my morning cup of coffee and *The Washington Post,* a dividend of my recent move from Silicon Valley, mecca for innovation and marketing, to the nation's capital, mecca for strategy and spin. The book is done except for this conclusion, but I know what I want to leave you with—some simple reminders that plays are everywhere. Now that you know what they are, you'll never see things in quite the same way. You run plays. Plays are run on you. And they all have a name, a purpose, and consequences for being run; this is finally clear.

If you're wondering, the flowers were a Peacock. These were Dutch Iris, no less, and to my mom that's a big deal. But I worry about my siblings. Has one of those skunks run a Preempt, beating my floral outpouring with their own spring spray? They're allies now, sure, but can you ever *really* trust a reformed rival? I should do some opposition research.

I check some news sites before I hit the hay. Sure enough, the Republican strategist Karl Rove is at it again. *Hillary's got the primaries wrapped up,* he's braying sarcastically. He did this to Howard Dean in 2003, an alpha Jam and beta Bait that reflect his mastery of the Factors at Play. Mr. Bush is still defending his wiretapping ways, acting in the interest of national security, he says, a not-so-dumb Deflect/Screen harmonic. He's a friction-first, fit-second kind of guy, I now know, and he'd no sooner resign than run a Disco. But Democrats are dancing, breathlessly running a Call Out. *This President has overstepped his authority and, this time, the law,* they trumpet and grouse. Sports superstar Shaquille O'Neal's grousing too—wants to be unleashed to play his bruising *A game* under the hoop. *To hell with fouling out,* he huffs. Probably a Ping aimed at his coach.

You send flowers, you read the news, you go about your daily life, and sure enough, plays are everywhere. Some are in jest, more carefree than cutthroat. Some are in passing, an instinct of the moment. Some are indelicate, a blood sport played for keeps. But they're all plays, conceptually pushed by players around the looping Playmaker's Process to move the marketplace, if even imperceptibly, and to kick-start another round of playmaking genius.

Fashion industry marketers are prone to Pings and Trial Balloons—testing strategies to palpate and pulse trend-setting buyers. *This year's line isn't about color, it's about comfort.* Political campaigners are given to Screens—framing plays with bandwagon-building surrogates to bend discussions and condition voters. *This candidate understands what trade unions ensure—the American way of life!* And tech entrepreneurs are geared to engage, often by way of Crowds and Drafts. For their quick-buck VC backers they might copy ideas and co-opt new markets—*If we launch next month we'll stay with the first-movers.* Or, perhaps, they'll reinvent an old idea and blow past its stodgy leaders—*You know, we could change the game if we could just change the distribution model.*

My wife shuffles into my office. *"You should come to bed,"* she says in a familiar dusty yawn. I'm suddenly alert. Was she saying, *You should get your tired ass to bed,* in which case it's a compassionate Fiat? Or was she saying, *Let's cuddle,* which is, I suppose, a veiled Challenge? This calls for a counterplay.

Good night, and thanks for reading.

If The Elements of Influence *has changed the way you look at the world and the work you're doing in it, let me know at alan.kelly@plays2run.com or join us online at The Playmaker's Forum at http://blog.plays2run.com.*

Acknowledgments

This book is the product of so many things—my upbringing, the love of my family, support and enthusiasm of dear friends, my mentors and colleagues with whom I've shared many early ideas and many late hours, my clients who've benefited from—and sometimes endured—my passion for playmaking, professional associations I've tried to support and whose members have surely supported me, universities and corporations whose executives and scholars have taken time to listen to what's new and have helped me to learn what's not, and to a host of sure-footed craftsmen who've sanded this rough idea and polished it for publication. I am in their debt and delighted, finally, to share this long-promised work.

A hundred thanks and kisses to my incredible wife, Kim, who advised me in her waking hours and listened to me in her sleep; to my dad, Doug Kelly, a retired cell biologist who long ago took me to see *Inherit the Wind* and made sure I know a thing or two about the scientific method; to my brother, Brian, an avionics and human factors expert who made sure I know a thing or two about usability; to Alison, who combed and cleaned the supporting citations and references; to Bob Vaughan, who always has a new idea and words of encouragement; to Denver Watkins, for sharing his writing and war stories; to Katie, for her delightful interest in the book and willing attempts not to stomp around in her bedroom, just over my head; and to Leo, who eagerly drew up a few plays of his own—the *Triangle* and *Drag-and-Drop*, in particular.

This book reflects the fine touch of my collaborator, researcher, critic, and cheerleader, Dan Keating. It is a far better work in no small way due to his unique intelligence and steady counsel. Likewise, The Playmaker's Standard would be a mere cudgel of a strategy tool without the curiosity of Cathy Babington, Melissa Brotz, Jennifer Smoter, and their tremendous colleagues at Abbott. It owes many more refinements to the bright-eyed enthusiasm of Jan Botz, Laura Asiala, Bill Gagliardi,

Karen Heenan-Davies, Su-yeon Lee, Mary Lou Benecke, Jarrod Erpelding, and their many wonderful colleagues at Dow Corning. Alan McNab, Tim Heffernan, Jim "Zugzwang" Doherty, and others at Symbol Technologies were the first to try it and reassure me of its potential. An old friend, Jack Browne at MIPS Technologies, and new friends, Mary Henige of General Motors and Jennifer Brown of Limited Brands, also helped test the early foundations of The Standard.

Two others stand out for their bitter-end loyalty and interest in this work, Peter Buchanan and John Hurley. Cups of coffee and Tastee Diner waffles seemed always enough to have their company and expert advice, though I owe them more.

The Playmaker's Standard is a natural outgrowth of Applied Communications, founded in 1992 on the northern edge of Silicon Valley. No one knows this better than Tim Marklein and Burghardt Tenderich and the two hundred brilliant professionals who brought Applied to distinction and helped incubate and evangelize the philosophy of playmaking. I will always be in your debt for giving me precious slices of your professional lives, for pushing the boundaries in public relations and communication research, and working so hard as participants, not spectators, in technology history. It was a dirty trick, I know now, to have preached playmaking without a text, but you answered the call anyway.

Of course we shared in the success of many of high technology's best companies. Most notable among them was software giant Oracle. Special thanks to playmakers Zach Nelson, Margaret Lasecke Jacobs, Mark Jarvis, Gary Bloom, Kevin McGuirk, and many others for the high adventure and satisfaction of beating Microsoft and others over and over and over again.

If Oracle was the power user of playmaking, the driven and incurably clever Joe Jennings was its father. He seeded the provocative ideas of running and calling *plays,* and for a time, I resisted. But his were among the best lessons I've ever been taught.

As The Standard evolved, I was encouraged and critiqued by distinguished professors of academia, particularly the irrepressible Don Stacks of the University of Miami's School of Communication, Jim Grunig of the University of Maryland's Department of Communication, Jim O'Rourke of the University of Notre Dame's Eugene D. Fanning Center for Business Communication, Michael Goodman of Fairleigh Dickinson University and the Corporate Communication Institute, Maria Russell and Sue Alessandri of Syracuse University's S. I. Newhouse School of Public Communications, Clarke Caywood of Northwestern University's Department of Integrated Marketing Communications, Nick Kanas of the University of California at San Francisco, Todd

Allesandri of Syracuse University's Whitman School of Management, Larry Matteson of the University of Rochester's Simon School, James Rubin and Elizabeth Powell of the University of Virginia's Darden Graduate School, Priscilla Murphy of Temple University, Krishnamurthy Sriramesh of Nanyang Technological University in Singapore, Michael Cornfield of George Washington University, Robert "Pritch" Pritchard and Melvin Sharpe of Ball State University, and Jerry Swerling of USC's Annenberg School. Four graduate students were particularly helpful for their timely insights and offerings: Alex Ranson of the University of Virginia's Darden School, Guodong "Aaron" Wang and Mark Craven of the University of Rochester's Simon School, and Dana Lucas of Syracuse University's S. I. Newhouse School of Public Communications.

Some saw the playmaking baby in its infancy and thought to help it along. I'm indebted to this care and feeding by the commission members, fellow trustees, and executives of the Institute for Public Relations, notably Jack Felton, Frank Ovaitt, Ward White, Peter Debreceny, Lou Williams, Don Wright, Fraser Likely, Katie Paine, Brad Rawlins, and Michelle Hinson. I'm also thankful to the Arthur W. Page Society and its members for giving me a sensitive sounding board on which to test and tune new ideas.

Whether others were dragged in through my door or whether they knocked on it unexpectedly, I was delighted and lucky to have the help of a variety of special people and former coworkers, among them Bud Michael, Ed Callahan, Brent Hanson, Jennifer Jones, Frank Wylie, Steve Hoechster, John Brodeur, Jack Bergen, Andy Lark, Sabrina Horn, John Berard, Kirk Stewart, Paul Bergevin, Amy Jackson Rind, Colonel Michael Daily, Chuck Rieger, Burt Lee, Peter Goldmacher, Ben Wightman, David Eichberg, Jill Waymire Paine, Michael Lewis, Jonathan Spira, Mark Bowman, Meredith McClintock, Jessie Keating, Susan Whyte-Simon, David Domeshek, John Renner, Richard Simpson, Michael Lennon, Maria Jordan, and David DeRamus.

I was also fortunate to have the advice and interest of many distinguished professionals and pundits, among them Paul Albright, Dan Schnur, Geoffrey Moore, Paul Holmes, Julia Hood, Ron Ricci, Craig Albright, Brian Lloyd, Mike Mansbach, Seok Lin Hong, Andrew Bernstein, David Phillips, Kevin Burns, John Hlinko, Bill Lenoir, Jeff Peck, Jim Hanson, and scary-smart members of the George Washington University Parliamentary Debate Society.

What you're holding is the product of a stellar team of business partners. Most prized among them are my literary agent, the talented and inexhaustible Jeremy Katz and his team at Sanford J. Greenburger Associates, my uncompromising editor Mitch Hoffman, publisher Brian Tart, Erika Kahn, Lisa Johnson, and Ashwini Ramaswamy of

Dutton Books, attorneys Andrew Sherman and Jeremy Cubert of Dickstein Shapiro Morin & Oshinsky and Jaime Wolf of Pelosi Wolf Effron & Spates, Stuart Weinstein of RINA Accountancy, and graphics illustrators Tim Saguinsin and Brian Kaas. Not forgotten are the talented developers Matthew Stevens, Greg Vassallo, the clever cats at 2nd Nature, and, finally, my alpha friend in publishing, Paul "10s & 20s" Brown.

Finally, a special thanks to Jennifer Chisholm Martella, who was the first to utter those infectious words, *"You should write a book!"*

Play Action Maps

Below are analyses of three cases, their players, and individual plays plotted on a timeline. We call these Play Action Maps, simple representations of play-making activity (i.e., play action) that yield powerful insights on the patterns, sequences, trends, and tendencies that influence a player's moves in its marketplace. Each can be viewed online at www.plays2run.com, and similar maps can be created online using the subscription-based web tool, The Play Action Whiteboard.

Nike's Sweatbox

The first map, called "Nike's Sweatbox," drawn from the Harvard Business School case study, *Hitting the Wall: Nike and International Labor* (September 6, 2002), details representative moves and counter-moves of the giant sports-gear maker Nike and activist nongovernmental organizations (NGOs). As the play action illustrates, NGOs ran not one but a series of plays, largely Call Outs, to expose worker abuses and the sports-gear maker's ostensible negligence of the brutal conditions in its Asian subcontractor manufacturing sites. Nike responded with Deflects to minimize the damage and, when that didn't work, recruited Proxies to again tamp down the fiery attacks. In the end, Nike ran a Disco to make the NGOs go away and get back into the public's good graces. And as you'll note in Table D of Chapter 22, that is one good way to counter and quell a well-placed attacking Call Out.

I Have a Dream

The second map showcases the playmaker prowess of a different kind of playmaker: Dr. Martin Luther King Jr. The alpha play of King's famous 1963 speech to Washington, D.C., marchers is a Challenge, meant to rouse his followers and critics alike and rally the nation toward a proper standard of racial equality. As you can see, he throws the playmaking book at his audience, running a series of beta-level plays, from Bear Hugs to Call Outs to Discos to Labels to Mirrors to Recasts and, especially, Screens. It is one of the great masterpieces of playmaking and a testament to the fact that plays can be run for a common good and with historic lasting effect.

Rathergate

The third play action map unfolds the drama that surrounded the veteran CBS news anchor Dan Rather and his lusty, probably hasty, reporting of President George W. Bush's shifty service in the Texas Air National Guard. Take note in the illustration that bloggers immediately went on the attack. There were no Pauses to collect their thoughts or hone their strategies. There were no mild Mirrors or spinning Recasts. They immediately went to one of the most confrontational, right-sided plays in the playmaker's arsenal, the Call Out. CBS, on the other hand, played on the left side of The Playmaker's Table with weak and ultimately ineffective Deflects, dismissing bloggers' arguments as technically inaccurate. Perhaps CBS and Rather should have fought the rhetorical punches with Call Outs of their own or exposed the biased bloggers through Mirrors. But they didn't, and this story, like the two that precede it, ends with historic meaning and serves to remind us of the sometimes brutal application of playmaking.

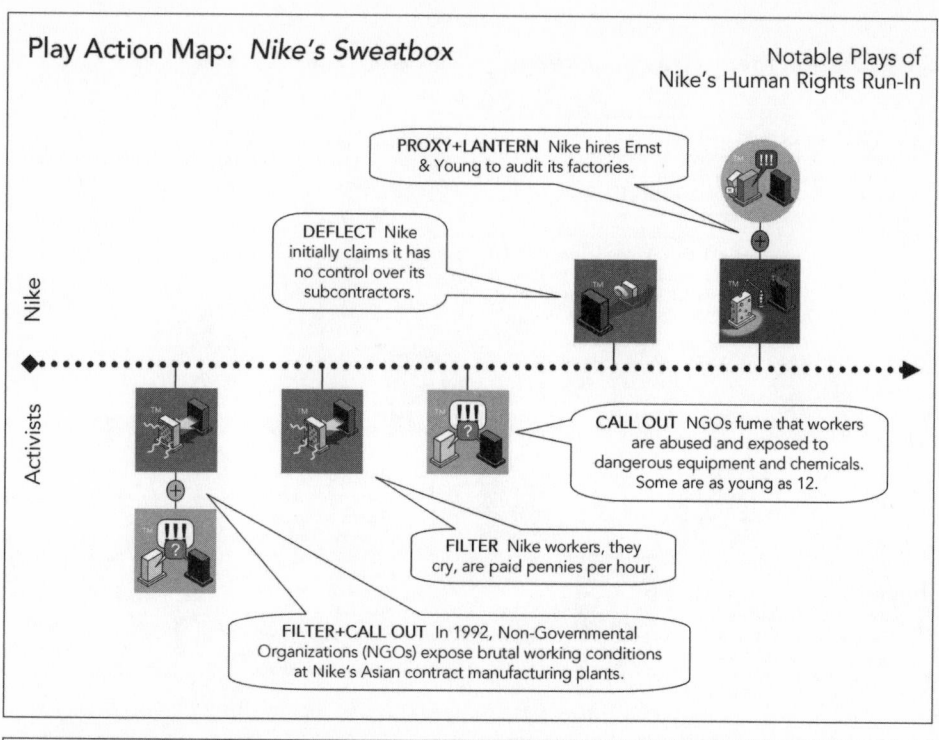

Play Action Map: *Nike's Sweatbox*

Notable Plays of
Nike's Human Rights Run-In

PROXY+LANTERN Nike hires Ernst & Young to audit its factories.

DEFLECT Nike initially claims it has no control over its subcontractors.

Nike

Activists

CALL OUT NGOs fume that workers are abused and exposed to dangerous equipment and chemicals. Some are as young as 12.

FILTER Nike workers, they cry, are paid pennies per hour.

FILTER+CALL OUT In 1992, Non-Governmental Organizations (NGOs) expose brutal working conditions at Nike's Asian contract manufacturing plants.

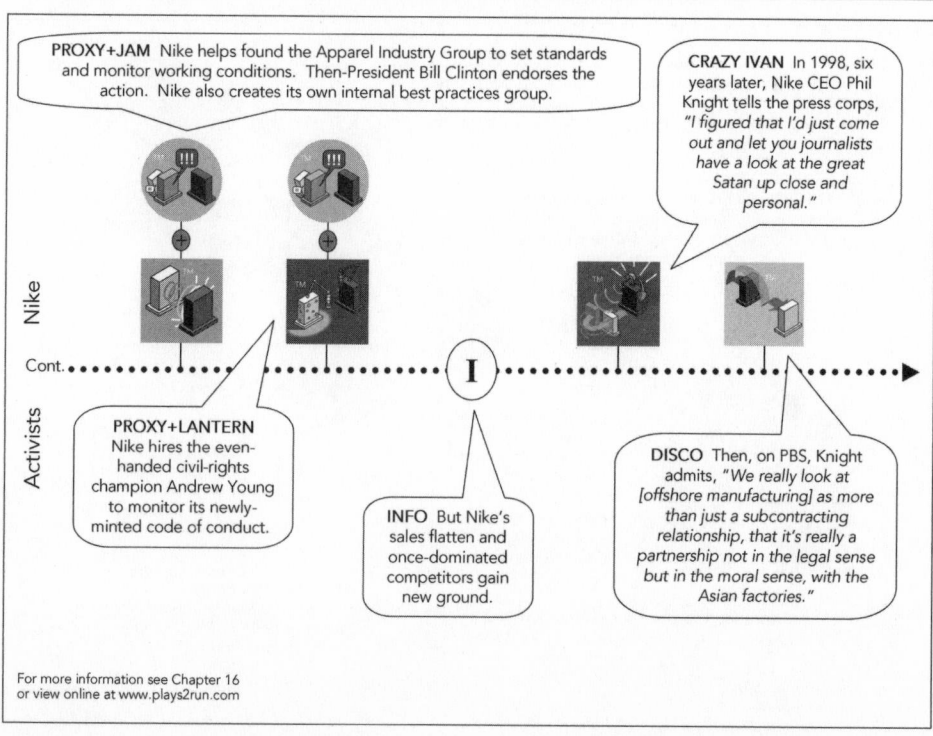

PROXY+JAM Nike helps found the Apparel Industry Group to set standards and monitor working conditions. Then-President Bill Clinton endorses the action. Nike also creates its own internal best practices group.

CRAZY IVAN In 1998, six years later, Nike CEO Phil Knight tells the press corps, *"I figured that I'd just come out and let you journalists have a look at the great Satan up close and personal."*

Nike

Cont.

Activists

PROXY+LANTERN Nike hires the even-handed civil-rights champion Andrew Young to monitor its newly-minted code of conduct.

INFO But Nike's sales flatten and once-dominated competitors gain new ground.

DISCO Then, on PBS, Knight admits, *"We really look at [offshore manufacturing] as more than just a subcontracting relationship, that it's really a partnership not in the legal sense but in the moral sense, with the Asian factories."*

For more information see Chapter 16
or view online at www.plays2run.com

Play Action Map: *I Have A Dream*

Notable Plays of Dr. Martin Luther King Jr.
1963 Speech to D.C. Marchers

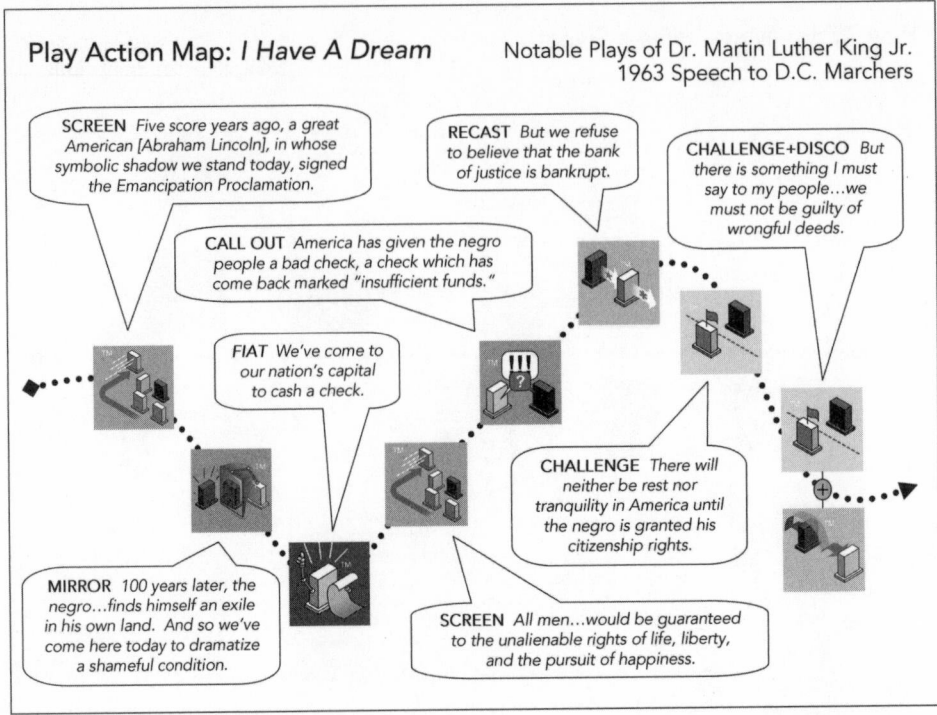

SCREEN *Five score years ago, a great American [Abraham Lincoln], in whose symbolic shadow we stand today, signed the Emancipation Proclamation.*

RECAST *But we refuse to believe that the bank of justice is bankrupt.*

CHALLENGE+DISCO *But there is something I must say to my people…we must not be guilty of wrongful deeds.*

CALL OUT *America has given the negro people a bad check, a check which has come back marked "insufficient funds."*

FIAT *We've come to our nation's capital to cash a check.*

CHALLENGE *There will neither be rest nor tranquility in America until the negro is granted his citizenship rights.*

MIRROR *100 years later, the negro…finds himself an exile in his own land. And so we've come here today to dramatize a shameful condition.*

SCREEN *All men…would be guaranteed to the unalienable rights of life, liberty, and the pursuit of happiness.*

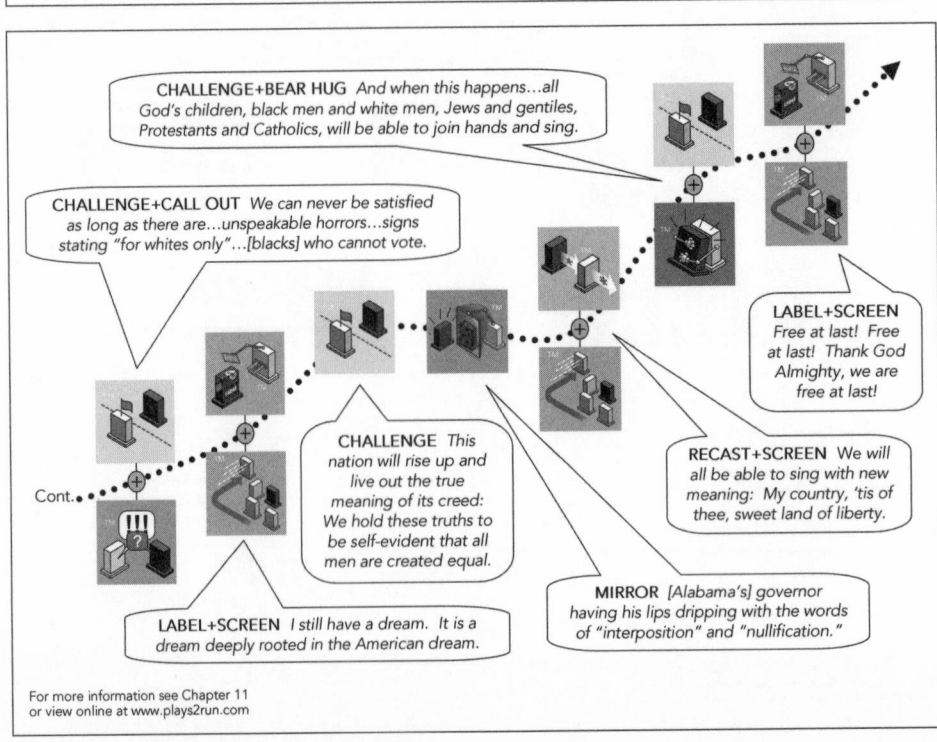

CHALLENGE+BEAR HUG *And when this happens…all God's children, black men and white men, Jews and gentiles, Protestants and Catholics, will be able to join hands and sing.*

CHALLENGE+CALL OUT *We can never be satisfied as long as there are…unspeakable horrors…signs stating "for whites only"…[blacks] who cannot vote.*

LABEL+SCREEN *Free at last! Free at last! Thank God Almighty, we are free at last!*

Cont.

CHALLENGE *This nation will rise up and live out the true meaning of its creed: We hold these truths to be self-evident that all men are created equal.*

RECAST+SCREEN *We will all be able to sing with new meaning: My country, 'tis of thee, sweet land of liberty.*

MIRROR *[Alabama's] governor having his lips dripping with the words of "interposition" and "nullification."*

LABEL+SCREEN *I still have a dream. It is a dream deeply rooted in the American dream.*

For more information see Chapter 11
or view online at www.plays2run.com

Play Action Map: *Rathergate*

Notable Plays of CBS in Its 2004 Face-Off with Conservative Bloggers

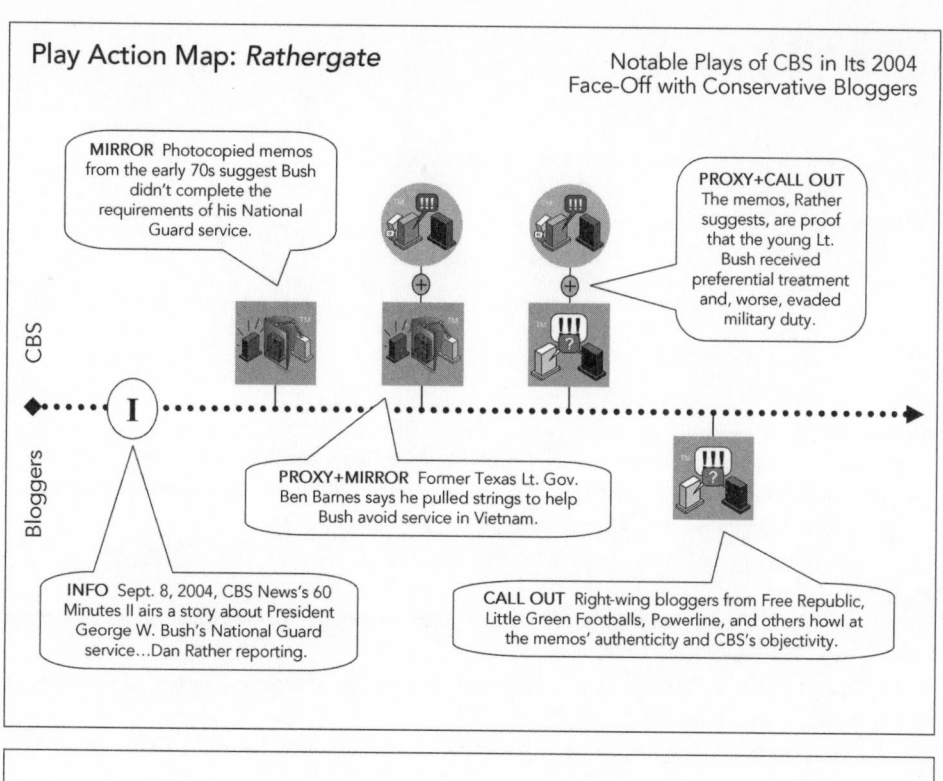

MIRROR Photocopied memos from the early 70s suggest Bush didn't complete the requirements of his National Guard service.

PROXY+CALL OUT The memos, Rather suggests, are proof that the young Lt. Bush received preferential treatment and, worse, evaded military duty.

CBS

Bloggers

PROXY+MIRROR Former Texas Lt. Gov. Ben Barnes says he pulled strings to help Bush avoid service in Vietnam.

INFO Sept. 8, 2004, CBS News's 60 Minutes II airs a story about President George W. Bush's National Guard service…Dan Rather reporting.

CALL OUT Right-wing bloggers from Free Republic, Little Green Footballs, Powerline, and others howl at the memos' authenticity and CBS's objectivity.

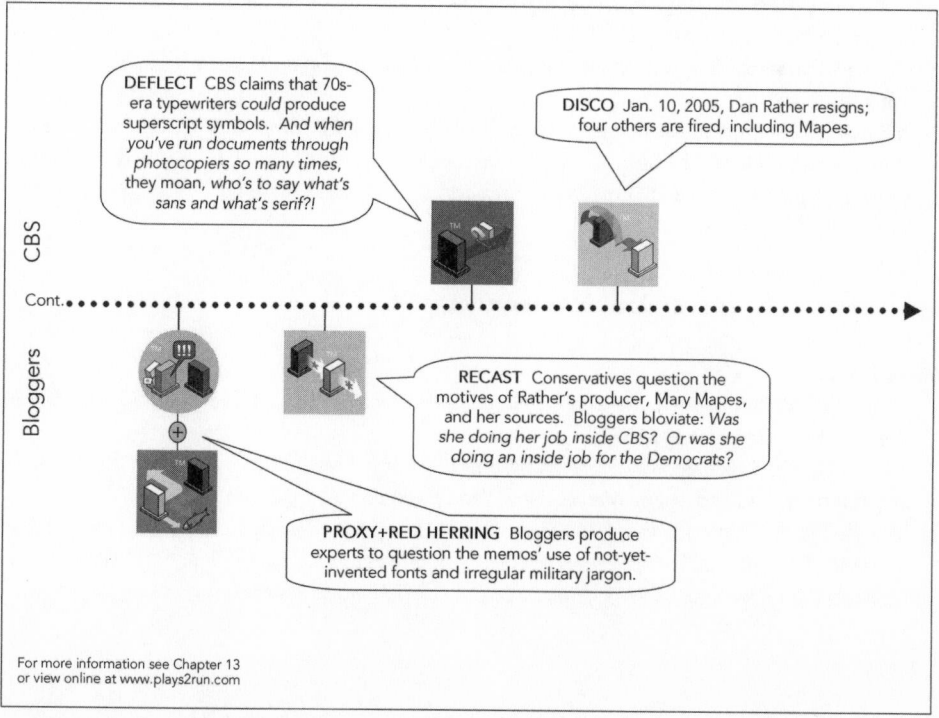

DEFLECT CBS claims that 70s-era typewriters *could* produce superscript symbols. *And when you've run documents through photocopiers so many times, they moan, who's to say what's sans and what's serif?!*

DISCO Jan. 10, 2005, Dan Rather resigns; four others are fired, including Mapes.

CBS

Cont.

Bloggers

RECAST Conservatives question the motives of Rather's producer, Mary Mapes, and her sources. Bloggers bloviate: *Was she doing her job inside CBS? Or was she doing an inside job for the Democrats?*

PROXY+RED HERRING Bloggers produce experts to question the memos' use of not-yet-invented fonts and irregular military jargon.

For more information see Chapter 13 or view online at www.plays2run.com

Notes

Preface

1. James A. Grunig and Larissa A. Grunig, "Implications of Symmetry for a Theory of Ethics and Social Responsibility in Public Relations." Paper presented to the Public Relations Interest Group, International Communication Association, Chicago, Ill., May 23–27, 1996.

Introduction

1. Michael Porter, *Competitive Strategy: Techniques for Analyzing Industries and Competitors* (New York: The Free Press, 1998), ix–xvi.
2. Sun Tzu, *The Art of War: Complete Text and Commentaries,* trans. Thomas Cleary (Boston: Shambhala Publications, 2000).
3. Kaihan Krippendorff, *The Art of the Advantage: 36 Strategies to Seize the Competitive Edge* (London: Thompson/Texere, 2003).
4. Matthew Symonds, *Softwar: An Intimate Portrait of Larry Ellison and Oracle* (New York: Simon & Schuster, 2003).
5. Jeffrey M. O'Brien, "Shock Troops of Mind Share," *Marketing Computers* (November 1996).
6. Marc Ferranti, "News: IT Forum: Ellison, Gates Jockey for Position on Info Highway," IDG News Service, September 4, 1995, http://www.javaworld.com/javaworld/jw-03-1996/idgns.java.1995/idgns.java.1995.028.html.

SECTION I. THE BASICS OF PLAYMAKING

What's a Play?

1. Larry Bossidy, Ram Charan, and Charles Burck, *Execution: The Discipline of Getting Things Done* (New York: Crown Business, 2002).
2. John Zagula and Richard Tong, *The Marketing Playbook: Five Battle-Tested Plays for Capturing and Keeping the Lead in Any Market* (New York: Penguin Group, 2004).
3. Michele Norris, "Sifting Through the Friday News Dump," *All Things Considered,* National Public Radio, June 30, 2005, http://www.npr.org/templates/story/story.php?storyId=4725120.
4. "Eskimo Words for Snow," Wikipedia, http://en.wikipedia.org/wiki/Eskimo_words_for_snow.

What's a Playmaker?

1. In a December 1991 telephone interview with the author, Edward L. Bernays, then one hundred years old, said, *"According to the U.S. Census, there are one hundred thousand people who call themselves public relations practitioners, but only fifteen thousand of them are members of PRSA (Public Relations Society of America). [Even then] PRSA doesn't demand of these any special qualifications. [If you want to] generalize about public relations, you have to survey a hundred thousand people. Without professional licensing, any generalization [about public relations] is simply an opinion because no one has found what all these people do. Any nut, weirdo, kook, or dope can call themselves a public relations practitioner."*

2. R. Helderman, "Maryland Moms Say No to Coverup at Starbucks," *The Washington Post*, August 9, 2004, B3.

3. Jim Lovel, "UPS, FedEx in Air War with DHL," *Atlanta Business Chronicle*, August 30, 2002, http://atlanta.bizjournals.com/atlanta/stories/2002/09/02/story2.html.

The Discipline of Playmaking

1. Aristotle, *The Art of Rhetoric* (London: Penguin Books, 1991).

2. "Propaganda," *Webster's Third New International Dictionary*: (1) A group or movement organized for spreading a particular doctrine or system of principles. (2) Dissemination of ideas, information, or rumor for the purpose of helping or injuring an institution, a cause, or a person.

3. "Psychological Operations," Department of Defense Dictionary of Military Terms, Defense Technical Information Center: Planned operations to convey selected information and indicators to foreign audiences to influence their emotions, motives, objective reasoning, and ultimately the behavior of foreign governments, organizations, groups, and individuals. The purpose of psychological operations is to induce or reinforce foreign attitudes and behavior favorable to the originator's objectives. Also called PSYOP. See also overt peacetime psychological operations programs; perception management, http://www.dtic.mil/doctrine/jel/doddict/data/p/04292.html.

4. Avinash Dixit and Susan Skeath, *Games of Strategy*, 2nd ed. (New York: W. W. Norton & Co., 1999).

5. "Propaganda," Department of Defense Dictionary of Military Terms, Defense Technical Information Center: Any form of communication in support of national objectives designed to influence the opinions, emotions, attitudes, or behavior of any group in order to benefit the sponsor, either directly or indirectly. See also black propaganda; grey propaganda; white propaganda, http://www.dtic.mil/doctrine/jel/doddict/data/p/04270.html.

6. "White Propaganda," Department of Defense Dictionary of Military Terms, Defense Technical Information Center: Propaganda disseminated and acknowledged by the sponsor or by an accredited agency thereof. See also propaganda, http://www.dtic.mil/doctrine/jel/doddict/data/w/05784.html.

7. "Grey Propaganda," Department of Defense Dictionary of Military Terms, Defense Technical Information Center: Propaganda that does not specifically identify any source. See also propaganda, http://www.dtic.mil/doctrine/jel/doddict/data/g/02319.html.

8. "Black Propaganda," Department of Defense Dictionary of Military Terms, Defense Technical Information Center: Propaganda that purports to emanate from a source other than the true one. See also propaganda, http://www.dtic.mil/doctrine/jel/doddict/data/b/00748.html.

SECTION II. THE PLAYMAKER'S TABLE

1. David Yoffie and Mary Kwak, *Judo Strategy: Turning Your Competitors' Strength to Your Advantage* (Boston: Harvard Business School Press, 2001), 119–146.
2. George Lakoff, *Don't Think of an Elephant: Know Your Values and Frame the Debate* (White River Junction, Vt.: Chelsea Green Publishing Company, 2004), 3–34.

Chapter 1. Pass

1. John G. Spooner and Michael Kanellos, "IBM sells PC group to Lenovo," CNET News.com, December 8, 2004, http://news.com/IBM+sells+PC+group+to+Lenovo/2100-1042_3-5482284.html?tag=st.prev.
2. Sun Tzu, *The Art of War: Complete Text and Commentaries*, trans. Thomas Cleary (Boston: Shambhala Publications, 2000).
3. Kaihan Krippendorff, *The Art of the Advantage: 36 Strategies to Seize the Competitive Edge* (London: Thompson/Texere, 2003).

Chapter 2. Pause

1. Martin Gilbert, *Churchill: A Life* (New York: Owl Books, 1991), 640.
2. Winston S. Churchill, *Memoirs of the Second World War: An Abridgement of the Six Volumes of "The Second World War"* (London: Houghton Mifflin Co., 1959), 223–224.
3. Alex Ranson, "Euronext N.V.: The Fight for LIFFE" (Charlottesville, Va.: University of Virginia Darden School Foundation, 2005).
4. Vincent Borland, "Bid for LIFFE Would Be Icing on the Cake for LSE: A Takeover of the Futures Exchange Would Complete a Stunning Turnaround for London's Stock Market," *Financial Times*, August 15, 2001, Companies & Finance UK.
5. Patience Wheatcroft, "Sir Brian Williamson," *The Times*, September 29, 2001.
6. John Greenwald, "Deadly Meltdown," *Time*, May 12, 1986, http://www.time.com/time/daily/chernobyl/860512.cover.html.
7. John Greenwald, "Gorbachev Goes on the Offensive," *Time*, May 26, 1986, http://www.time.com/time/daily/chernobyl/860526.gorbachev.html.
8. Priscilla Murphy, "Game Theory Models for Organizational/Public Conflict," *Canadian Journal of Communications*, vol. 16, no. 2 (1991).

Chapter 3. Ping

1. Albert E. Theberge, "Sounding Pole to Sea Beam," National Oceanic and Atmospheric Association, http://www.history.noaa.gov/stories_tales/poletobeam2.html.
2. "Everything You Ever Wanted to Know About Sonar but Were Afraid to Ask," Simrad USA, http://www.simradusa.com/docs/faq_history_sonar.html.
3. "Single-Ping Echo-Ranging," Submarine Sonar Operator's Manual, Maritime Park Association, http://www.maritime.org/fleetsub/sonar/chap6.htm.
4. "Ping," Urban Dictionary.com, http://www.urbandictionary.com/define.php?term=ping.
5. "The Story of the PING Program," U.S. Army Research Laboratory, http://ftp.arl.mil/~mike/ping.html.
6. "Preparing for West Point's Third Century," United States Military Academy, June 1991, 45, http://www.west-point.org/publications/PWPTC2.html.

7. "Marketplace: News Archives," American Public Media, http://marketplace.publicradio.org/shows/1997/05/09_mpp.html.

8. Capt. Charles I. Plosser, "A New Year and New Leadership at the Federal Reserve," William E. Simon School of Business Administration, University of Rochester, December 6, 2005, http://www.simon.rochester.edu/pdf/economic_outlook2006.pdf.

9. "Remarks by Chairman Alan Greenspan," The Federal Reserve Board, December 5, 1996, http://www.federalreserve.gov/boarddocs/speeches/1996/19961205.htm.

Chapter 4. Trial Balloon

1. Ward Churchill, *On the Justice of Roosting Chickens: Reflections on the Consequences of U.S. Imperial Arrogance and Criminality* (Oakland, Calif.: AK Press, 2003).

2. Pamela White, "The Man in the Maelstrom," *Boulder Weekly,* February 10, 2005, http://www.kersplebedeb.com/mystuff/s11/churchill_interview_pw.html.

3. "Ward Churchill," Wikipedia, http://en.wikipedia.org/wiki/Ward_Churchill.

4. Dave Curtin and Arthur Kane, "CU Weighs Buyout for Firebrand Prof: The University Is Worried About the Long-Term Impact of the Ward Churchill Controversy and Wants to End the Nonstop Allegations in the Media, According to Sources," *The Denver Post,* February 27, 2005, A1.

5. Merissa Marr, "Redirecting Disney: CEO Iger's Push for Change Goes Far Beyond iPod Deal; Fewer Films, Evolving Parks," *The Wall Street Journal,* December 5, 2005.

6. Ylan Q. Mui, "Schools Turn to Comics as Trial Balloon," *The Washington Post,* December 13, 2004, B01, http://www.washingtonpost.com/wp-dyn/articles/A59964-2004Dec12.html.

Chapter 5. Deflect

1. "Planets block press access," USATODAY.com, November 21, 2005, http://www.usatoday.com/news/offbeat/2005-11-21-planets-thailand_x.htm.

2. "McGwire mum on steroids in hearing," CNN.com, March 17, 2005, http://www.cnn.com/2005/ALLPOLITICS/03/17/steroids.baseball/.

3. "McGwire admits nothing; Sosa and Palmeiro deny use," ESPN.com, March 18, 2005, http://sports.espn.go.com/mlb/news/story?id=2015420.

4. Mike Allen and Dan Balz, "Bush Aide Deflects Questions on Rove," *The Washington Post,* July 12, 2005, A01, http://www.washingtonpost.com/wp-dyn/content/article/2005/07/11/AR2005071101568.html.

5. Dana Milbank, "Spokesman Holds Tongue During Intense Grilling," *The Washington Post,* July 12, 2005, A04, http://www.washingtonpost.com/wp-dyn/content/article/2005/07/11/AR2005071101284_2.html.

Chapter 6. Leak

1. "The Watergate Story," Washingtonpost.com, http://www.washingtonpost.com/wp-dyn/content/linkset/2005/05/31/LI2005053100696.html.

2. Michael R. Beschloss, *The Crisis Years: Kennedy and Krushchev, 1960–1963* (New York: Harper Collins, 1991), 329–332.

3. "Conversation with Daniel Ellsberg," Conversations with History, Institute of International Studies, UC Berkeley, http://globetrotter.berkeley.edu/people/Ellsberg/ellsberg98-0.html.

4. "America & The Holocaust Primary References," Public Broadcasting Service, http://www.pbs.org/wgbh/amex/holocaust/filmmore/reference/primary/.

5. "Silverman Forwards Riegner Cable to Wise," Jewish Virtual Library, The American-Israeli Cooperative Enterprise, http://www.jewishvirtuallibrary.org/jsource/Holocaust/riegner2.html.

6. "Linda Tripp," Wikipedia, http://en.wikipedia.org/wiki/Linda_Tripp.

7. Luke Timmerman and David Heath, "Drug Researchers Leak Secrets to Wall St.," Seattletimes.com, August 7, 2005, http://seattletimes.nwsource.com/html/businesstechnology/drugsecrets1.html.

Chapter 7. Red Herring

1. "Red Herring," *Webster's New Universal Unabridged Dictionary*: "Something intended to divert attention from the real problem or matter at hand, a misleading clue" (New York: Barnes & Noble, 2003).

2. "Debate Transcript: The Second Reagan-Mondale Debate," Commission on Presidential Debates, http://www.debates.org/pages/trans84c.html.

3. Scott Rosenberg, "Microsoft's .Net: Visionary or vaporware?" Salon.com, June 30, 2002, http://www.salon.com/tech/col/rose/2000/06/30/microsoft_dotnet/.

4. Joel Spolsky, "Microsoft Goes Bonkers," Joel on Software, July 22, 2000, http://www.joelonsoftware.com/articles/fog0000000049.html.

5. "Steve Ballmer Speech Transcript—Forum 2000," Microsoft, http://www.microsoft.com/presspass/exec/steve/06-22f2k.mspx.

6. Arthur T. Hadley, "Maneuver Warfare and the Art of Deception," *An Anthology: Maneuver Warfare* (Novato, Calif.: Presidio Press, 1993), 364–365.

7. "MacGuffin," Wikipedia, http://en.wikipedia.org/wiki/MacGuffin.

Chapter 8. Filter

1. Steve Coll, "Army Spun Tale Around Ill-Fated Mission," *The Washington Post,* December 6, 2004, A1, http://www.washingtonpost.com/wp-dyn/articles/A37679-2004Dec5.html.

2. Josh White, "Army Withheld Details About Tillman's Death," *The Washington Post,* May 4, 2005, A3.

Chapter 9. Recast

1. Dr. Seuss, *The Sneetches and Other Stories* (New York: Random House, 1989).

2. Frank Gillett, "Commentary: Get with Utility Computing," CNET News.com, September 9, 2003, http://news.com.com/2030-1069-5073591.html.

3. Jill Dougherty and Catherine Berger, "Cheney Blasts Kerry Over 'Sensitive War' Remark," CNN.com, August 12, 2004, http://www.cnn.com/2004/ALLPOLITICS/08/12/cheney.kerry/.

Chapter 10. Label

1. "Neutron Jack," *BusinessWeek* Online, http://www.businessweek.com/2000/00_50/b3711014.htm.

2. Rachael Bell, "Leona Helmsley: 'The Queen of Mean,'" CourtTV.com, http://www.crimelibrary.com/criminal_mind/scams/leona_helmsley/.

3. Phil Jones, "McNealy, the Internet Toothbrush, & 'The Big C++ Hairball,'" Computergram International, October 18, 1999, http://findarticles.com/p/articles/mi_m0CGN/is_1999_Oct_18/ai_56473968.

4. Doug Linder, "The Trial of Orenthal James Simpson," 2000, http://www.law.umkc.edu/faculty/projects/ftrials/Simpson/Simpsonaccount.htm.

5. "John F. Kennedy Moon Speech—Rice Stadium," Space Movies Cinema, http://vesuvius.jsc .nasa.gov/er/seh/ricetalk.htm.

6. "I Have a Dream," Douglass Archives of American Public Address, http://douglassarchives.org/ king_b12.htm.

7. "Tear Down This Wall: Remarks at the Brandenburg Gate West Berlin, Germany, June 12, 1987," The Reagan Foundation, http://www.reaganfoundation.org/reagan/speeches/wall.asp.

8. "Richard M. Nixon Denies Involvement in the Watergate Affair," The History Channel: Speeches & Videos, November 17, 1973, http://www.historychannel.com/broadband/clipview/index .jsp?id=v4t11.

9. George Lakoff, *Don't Think of an Elephant: Know Your Values and Frame the Debate* (White River Junction, Vt.: Chelsea Green Publishing Company, 2004), 3.

Chapter 11. Screen

1. "I Have a Dream," Douglass Archives of American Public Address, http://douglassarchives.org/ king_b12.htm.

2. Keven Fagan, "Race Tragedy Tale: Oracle CEO Tells All to St. Francis Yacht Club," *San Francisco Chronicle*, January 20, 1999, A14, http://www.sfgate.com/cgi-bin/article.cgi?f=/c/a/1999/01/20/ MN74465.DTL&hw=ellison+st+francis+hobart&sn=004&sc=676.

3. Rob Walker, "Ad Report Card: Financial Responsibility for Sale," *Slate*, January 22, 2001, http:// www.slate.com/id/1006921/#ContinueArticle.

4. Carol Devine-Molin, "Candidate Wesley Clark," *Enter Stage Right*, September 22, 2003, http:// www.enterstageright.com/archive/articles/0903/0903clark.htm.

Chapter 12. Mirror

1. "Michael Dukakis, 1988—Another Landmark Image," *Life*, http://www.digitaljournalist.org/ issue0309/lm10.html.

2. "Cheney Calls Kerry's Goose Hunt an 'October Disguise,'" *USA Today*, October 22, 2004, http:// www.usatoday.com/news/politicselections/nation/president/2004-10-21-goose-cheney_x .htm?POE=NEWISVA.

3. Al Franken, *Lies and the Lying Liars Who Tell Them* (New York: Dutton, 2003), 65–67.

4. Richard Lacayo and Amanda Ripley, "*Time* Magazine's Persons of the Year 2002: Cynthia Cooper, Coleen Rowley & Sherron Watkins," *Time*, December 22, 2002, http://foi.missouri.edu/ whistleblowing/whistle2002/persons.html.

5. Dan Ackman, "Boeing, Airbus Showdown at 40,000 Feet," Forbes.com, May 31, 2005, http:// www.forbes.com/manufacturing/2005/05/31/cx_da_0531topnews.html.

6. "Speeches and Articles by Peter Mandelson: Statement on Boeing, Airbus, and the WTO," The Information Centre, http://europa.eu.int/comm/commission_barroso/mandelson/speeches_ articles/temp_icentre.cfm?temp=sppm032_en.

7. "Boeing Statement on Launch Aid for Airbus A350," Boeing, October 6, 2005, http://www .boeing.com/news/releases/2005/q4/nr_051006b.html.

8. "A NewsHour with Jim Lehrer Transcript: Air War," Online NewsHour, May 31, 2005, http://www .pbs.org/newshour/bb/europe/jan-june05/airwar_5-31.html.

9. Hans Christian Andersen, "The Emperor's New Clothes," http://hjem.get2net.dk/chenero/hca/ hcaev009_en2.html.

Chapter 13. Jam

1. Richard H. Cole, "Operation Just Cause: The Planning and Execution of Joint Operations in Panama" (Washington, D.C.: Joint History Office, 1995), 57–63, http://www.globalsecurity.org/military/library/report/1995/justcaus.pdf.

2. Marc S. Malkin, "PETA Protesters Smell Blood," *New York* magazine, June 2, 2003, http://newyorkmetro.com/nymetro/news/people/columns/intelligencer/n_8749/.

3. Anna Sophie Loewenberg, "The Anti-Ad Campaign of the Month: PETA's Members Target Vogue, Using Blood and Intestines as Ammunition," The New York Review of Magazines, 2001, Columbia University, http://www.jrn.columbia.edu/studentwork/nyrm/2001/features/peta.html.

4. "PETA Vs. Vogue: It Ain't a Pretty Picture," FurIsDead.com, http://www.furisdead.com/feat-wintour.asp.

5. Transcript by the Office of the Independent Counsel, "Videotaped Testimony of William Jefferson Clinton President of the United States Before the Grand Jury Empanelled for Independent Counsel Kenneth Starr," Jurist: The Law Professors' Network, August 17, 1998, http://jurist.law.pitt.edu/transcr.htm.

6. Timothy Noah, "Bill Clinton and the Meaning of 'Is,'" Slate.com Chatterbox, September 13, 1998, http://www.slate.com/id/1000162/.

7. "Acoustic Jamming," Department of Defense Dictionary of Military Terms, Defense Technical Information Center: The deliberate radiation or reradiation of mechanical or electroacoustic signals with the objectives of obliterating or obscuring signals that the enemy is attempting to receive and of disrupting enemy weapons systems. See also barrage jamming; electronic warfare; jamming; spot jamming, http://www.dtic.mil/doctrine/jel/doddict/data/a/00020.html.

8. "New Scrutiny of Bush's Service," CBS News, September 9, 2004, http://www.cbsnews.com/stories/2004/09/10/politics/main642489.shtml.

9. Corey Pein, "Blog-Gate," *Columbia Journalism Review*, Columbia University's Graduate School of Journalism, http://www.cjr.org/issues/2005/1/pein-blog.asp.

10. Margot Hornblower and Hannah Beech, "The Battle in Seattle," *Time* Asia, December 13, 1999, http://www.time.com/time/asia/magazine/99/1213/business.madashell.html.

11. "WTO Boss: Protesters Harm the Poor," BBC News, December 1, 1999, http://news.bbc.co.uk/1/hi/business/544543.stm.

12. Tom LeCompte, "The Notorious Flight of Mathias Rust," *Air & Space Smithsonian* (July 2005), 20.

Chapter 14. Bear Hug

1. "Sun Tzu," Wikipedia, http://en.wikiquote.org/wiki/Sun_Tzu.

2. *"Super Size Me: A Film of Epic Portions,"* http://www.supersizeme.com/home.aspx?page=bythelb.

3. "McSupersizes to be Phased Out," CNN.com, March 3, 2004, http://www.cnn.com/2004/US/03/02/mcdonalds.supersize.ap/.

4. "The Bush/McCain Love!," FreeRepublic.com, August 10, 2004, http://www.freerepublic.com/focus/f-news/1188858/posts.

5. Elliott J. Gorn, "Gouge and Bite, Pull Hair and Scratch: The Social Significance of Fighting in the Southern Backcountry," *The American Historical Review*, volume 90, February to December 1985, 18–43.

6. "The Betamax vs VHS Format War," MediaCollege.com, http://www.mediacollege.com/video/format/compare/betamax-vhs.html.

7. Matt Berger, "Whatever Happened to OS2? Chased Years Ago from Desktops by Windows, OS2 May Now Disappear from Its Remaining Server Market as Well." IDG News Service, October 1, 2001, http://www.pcworld.com/news/article/0,aid,64184,00.asp.

8. "Bear Hug," InvestorWords.com, http://www.investorwords.com/441/bear_hug.html.

9. *"The Godfather, Part II,"* http://www.angelfire.com/oh/quotations/movies/g/thegodfatherII.html.

Chapter 15. Lantern

1. Chris Matthews, *Hardball: How Politics Is Played, Told by One Who Knows the Game* (New York: Touchstone, 1988), 155–167.

2. "1984 Debate Transcript: The Second Reagan-Mondale Presidential Debate," Commission on Presidential Debates, http://www.debates.org/pages/trans84c.html.

3. Steve Booth-Butterworth, "Inoculation Theory," West Virginia University, 1988, http://www.as.wvu.edu/~sbb/comm221/chapters/inocul.htm.

4. W. McGuire, "Resistance to Persuasion Conferred by Active and Passive Prior Refutation of the Same and Alternative Counterarguments," *Journal of Abnormal and Social Psychology* (1961), 63, 326–332.

5. W. McGuire and L. Berkowitz, ed., "Inducing resistance to persuasion: Some Contemporary Approaches," *Advances in Experimental Social Psychology,* Vol. 1 (New York: Academic Press, 1964).

6. "Senator Nixon's Checkers Speech: September 23, 1952," Watergate.info, http://www.watergate.info/nixon/checkers-speech.shtml.

7. "Checkers Speech," Wikipedia, http://en.wikipedia.org/wiki/Checkers_speech.

8. John Ince, "Where Is the Money?" *Upside,* May 29, 2002, http://www.altassets.net/casefor/countries/2002/nz2428.php.

9. John Ince, "Venture Capital at the Crossroads," *Upside,* July 2001, 60–65, http://www.bowne.com/newsletters/friendly.asp?storyID=279.

Chapter 16. Disco

1. "A Boy Named Sue," Maninblack.net, http://maninblack.net/Songs_Boy_Named_Sue.html.

2. Jim Hanson, *NTC's Dictionary of Debate* (Lincolnwood: National Textbook Co., 1990), 53.

3. Per the preceding reference, in an August 2004 e-mail to the author, Jim Hanson clarified the origin of the Disco. "*Disco* got coined because 1) it was like someone was dancing their way into a victory—maneuvering their way cleverly; 2) it resurrected a previous era's way of dancing—like resurrecting a previous argument and making it good again; 3) it was flashy—you took notice of someone doing a disco during a debate."

4. John Meany and Kate Shuster, *On That Point! An Introduction to Parliamentary Debate* (New York: The International Debate Education Association, 2003), 322.

5. Lawrence G. Foster, "The Johnson & Johnson Credo and the Tylenol Crisis," *New Jersey Bell Journal* (1983).

6. Tamara Kaplan, "The Tylenol Crisis: How Effective Public Relations Saved Johnson & Johnson," The Pennsylvania State University, http://www.personal.psu.edu/users/w/x/wxk116/tylenol/crisis.html.

7. Debora L. Spar, "Hitting the Wall: Nike and International Labor," *Harvard Business Review* (September 6, 2002).

8. Simon Zadek, "The Path to Corporate Responsibility," *Harvard Business Review* (December 2004).

9. Greg Rushford, "Nike Lets Critics Kick It Around," *The Wall Street Journal,* May 12, 1997, A14.

10. "Newsmaker Phil Knight: The 'NewsHour with Jim Lehrer,'" Transcript, Public Broadcasting Service, May 13, 1998, http://www.pbs.org/newshour/bb/business/jan-june98/nike_5-13.html.

Chapter 17. Challenge

1. Wylie Wong, "'Who Wants to Be a Millionaire?' Oracle's Ellison Asks," CNET News.com, October 3, 2000, http://news.com/2100-1001-246553.html?legacy=cnet.

2. Wylie Wong, "Oracle Offers $1 million challenge—again," CNET News.com, December 20, 2000, http://news.com/2100-1001-250144.html?legacy=cnet.

3. Melanie Austria Farmer, "Ellison: Oracle Will Save Additional Billion," CNET News.com, February 13, 2001, http://news.com/2100-1001-252495.html?legacy=cnet.

4. "John F. Kennedy Moon Speech—Rice Stadium," Space Movies Cinema, http://vesuvius.jsc.nasa.gov/er/seh/ricetalk.htm.

Chapter 18. Bait

1. "Bully for Bugs Story Detail," The Big Cartoon Database, http://www.bcdb.com/cartoon_synopsis/3762-Bully_For_Bugs.html.

2. C. T. Evans, "Muhammad Ali," http://novaonline.nvcc.edu/eli/evans/his135/events/ali98.htm.

3. Tim Dirks, "*Sudden Impact,* 1983," Greatest Films, http://www.filmsite.org/suddi.html.

4. Juliet Eilperin, "Rove Spends the Fourth Rousing Support for Dean," *The Washington Post,* July 5, 2003, A5, http://www.washingtonpost.com/ac2/wp-dyn?pagename=article&node=&contentId=A10541-2003Jul4&notFound=true.

5. Following his talk at the Arthur Page Society fall 2005 conference in Napa Valley, California, I asked Joe Trippi, campaign manager for Dean for America, about Rove's ploy and if it hurt the campaign. He nodded and said, *"Oh, yeah . . . he [Rove] knew what he was doing."*

Chapter 19. Fiat

1. "Google Inc. Files Registration Statement with the SEC for an Initial Public Offering," The Google Press Center, April 29, 2004, http://www.google.com/press/pressrel/reg_statement.html.

2. "Clinton Denies Sexual Relationship," Washingtonpost.com, January 26, 1998, http://www.washingtonpost.com/wp-srv/politics/special/clinton/stories/whatclintonsaid.htm#Edu.

3. "Nikita Khrushchev, Historical Document, November 1956," U.S. Department of Energy Office of Environmental Management, http://web.em.doe.gov/timeline/nov1956.html.

4. Yahoo! Terms of Service Agreement, http://docs.yahoo.com/info/terms/.

5. Craig Whitlock and Walter Pincus, "Bin Laden: Attacks on U.S. Being Prepared: Tape Also Offers Truce For Troop Withdrawal," *The Washington Post,* January 20, 2006, p. A1.

6. "The Declaration of Independence," UShistory.org, http://www.ushistory.org/declaration/document/index.htm.

7. "Ten Commandments," Wikipedia, http://en.wikipedia.org/wiki/Ten_Commandments.

8. Charles Darwin, "The Origin of Species: Introduction," Talk Origins Archive, http://www
.talkorigins.org/faqs/origin.html.

9. "Dolly the Sheep," Wikipedia, http://en.wikipedia.org/wiki/Dolly_the_sheep.

10. Ben & Jerry's Product Mission, http://www.benjerry.com/our_company/our_mission/.

11. "New Orleans Mayor, Louisiana Governor Hold Press Conference," CNN.com, August 28, 2005, http://transcripts.cnn.com/TRANSCRIPTS/0508/28/bn.04.html.

Chapter 20. Crowd

1. "GM Gives Employee Discount to 'Anyone,'" ConsumerAffairs.Com Inc., May 24, 2005, http://www.consumeraffairs.com/news04/2005/gm_discounts.html.

2. "Ford, Chrysler Join GM in Offering Employee Discounts to Everyone," ConsumerAffairs.Com Inc., July 5, 2005, http://www.consumeraffairs.com/news04/2005/gm_discounts2.html.

3. "GM Extends Employee Discount Program," ConsumerAffairs.Com Inc., August 2, 2005, http://www.consumeraffairs.com/news04/2005/gm_discounts_extended.html.

4. "General Motors Ends Employee Discount Program; Ford, DaimlerChrysler to End Theirs Monday," The Auto Channel, September 30, 2005, http://www.theautochannel.com/news/2005/09/30/144524.html.

5. Lorl Reese, "'Happy Days' Again," *Entertainment Weekly*'s EW.com, May 26, 2000, http://www.ew.com/ew/report/0,6115,85244_3_0_,00.html.

6. Ken Tucker, "Quiz Flow," *Entertainment Weekly*'s EW.com, January 11, 2000, http://www.ew.com/ew/article/commentary/0,6115,82937_3_0_,00.html.

7. Lynette Rice, "Let's Get Quizzical," *Entertainment Weekly*'s EW.com, October 27, 2005, http://www.ew.com/ew/report/0,6115,278200_7_0_,00.html.

Chapter 21. Peacock

1. "The Publicity Stunts Hall of Fame," *Business 2.0* (July 2005), 61.

2. "Go.com 'Hamster,'" Sterling Storm, http://www.sterlingstorm.com/reel.html.

3. Mark Hughes, *Buzzmarketing: Get People to Talk About Your Stuff* (New York: Portfolio, 2005), 9–23.

4. Ann Grimes, "Webheads bid high for Ally McBeal," *The Wall Street Journal* Online, December 9, 1999, http://news.zdnet.com/2100-9595_22-517192.html?legacy=zdnn.

5. Ann Oldenburg, "$7M Car Giveaway Stuns TV Audience," USAToday.com, September 13, 2004, http://www.usatoday.com/life/people/2004-09-13-oprah-cars_x.htm.

6. "Oprah Car Winners Hit with Hefty Tax," CNN Money, September 2, 2004, http://money.cnn.com/2004/09/22/news/newsmakers/oprah_car_tax/?cnn=yes.

7. Tara Burghart, "Oprah's Car Giveaway Hailed as Marketing Coup," *The Cincinnati Enquirer,* September 15, 2004, http://www.enquirer.com/editions/2004/09/15/biz_biz1yoprah.html.

8. G. Chambers Williams III, "Pontiac G6 quietly succeeding," MySanAntonio.com, July 24, 2005, http://www.mysanantonio.com/business/stories/MYSA072405.1F.Pontiac.110547.html.

9. Karl Greenberg, "Ford to Fete Dr. Phil's 500th," *Mediaweek*, May 5, 2005, http://www.mediaweek.com/mw/search/article_display.jsp?schema=&vnu_content_id=1000911059.

10. Alan Deutschman, "The Gonzo Way of Branding," *Fast Company* (October 2004), 91.

Chapter 22. Call Out

1. "Hip hop rivalries," Wikipedia, http://en.wikipedia.org/wiki/Hip_hop_rivalries#Ja_Rule_.28_The_Inc..29_vs_50_Cent_.28Aftermath.29.
2. 50 Cent, "Back Down," A–Z Lyrics Universe, http://www.azlyrics.com/lyrics/50cent/backdown.html.
3. Ja Rule, "Thing's Gon' Change," A–Z Lyrics Universe, http://www.azlyrics.com/lyrics/jarule/thingsgonchange.html.
4. Fournier, Susan, "Introducing New Coke" (Boston: Harvard Business School Publishing, 1999).

Chapter 23. Preempt

1. "Sputnik Program," Wikipedia, http://en.wikipedia.org/wiki/Sputnik.
2. Asif A. Siddiqi, "Korolev, Sputnik, and The International Geophysical Year," NASA History Office, http://www.hq.nasa.gov/office/pao/History/sputnik/siddiqi.html.
3. "Vanguard Rocket," http://www.robsv.com/cape/c18lv.html.
4. "Why Kraft Decided to Ban Some Food Ads to Children," *The Wall Street Journal,* October 31, 2005, A1.

Chapter 24. Draft

1. Michael Hiltzik, *Dealers of Lightning: Xerox PARC and the Dawn of the Computer Age* (New York: Harper Collins, 1999), 332–333, 337, 343.
2. Douglas K. Smith and Robert C. Alexander, *Fumbling the Future* (New York: William Morrow & Company, Inc., 1988), 235.
3. "About Cirque du Soleil," First Look Studios, Inc., http://www.flp.com/films/Alegria/about_cirque_du_soleil.htm.

Chapter 25. Crazy Ivan

1. Isakovic, "The Kursk Crisis," DeepSpace4, http://www.deepspace4.com/pages/military/kursk/kursk.htm.
2. "Definition of Crazy Ivan," WordIQ.com, http://www.wordiq.com/definition/Crazy_Ivan.
3. "Bertelsmann 'Steps Up' Napster Bid," BBC News, April 5, 2002, http://news.bbc.co.uk/1/hi/business/1913519.stm.
4. Julius Lester, *Uncle Remus: The Complete Tales* (New York: Phyllis Fogelman Books, 1999).
5. Martin Shubik, *Game Theory in the Social Sciences: Concepts and Solution* (Cambridge, Mass.: The MIT Press, 1982), 254.
6. "Tiananmen Revisited," http://edition.cnn.com/SPECIALS/2001/tiananmen/.
7. The Baseball Reliquary, The Shrine of the Eternals, 1999 Electees, Dock Phillip Ellis, Jr., http://www.baseballreliquary.org/ellis.htm.
8. "Gettysburg National Military Park: Little Round Top," National Park Service, http://www.nps.gov/gett/getttour/tstops/tstd2-10.htm.
9. "Little Round Top," Wikipedia, http://en.wikipedia.org/wiki/Battle_of_Little_Round_Top.

Surrogates

1. "Undercover Marketing Uncovered," *60 Minutes,* CBS News, July 25, 2004, http://www.cbsnews.com/stories/2003/10/23/60minutes/main579657.shtml.
2. Edmond Rostand, *Cyrano de Bergerac,* trans. Lowell Blair (New York: Signet Classic, 1972).

The Playmaker's Process

1. Ann Zimmerman, "Wal-Mart Urges Congress to Raise Minimum Wage," *The Wall Street Journal,* October 25, 2005, A2.

Other References

1. John F. Antal, "Thoughts About Maneuver Warfare," *An Anthology: Maneuver Warfare* (Novato, Calif.: Presidio Press, 1993), 64–65.

2. Ken Auletta, *Backstory: Inside the Business of News* (New York: Penguin Press, 2003).

3. Otto F. Bauer, *Fundamentals of Debate* (Omaha: Rockbrook Press, 1999).

4. Eric Berne, *Games People Play: The Basic Handbook of Transactional Analysis* (New York: Ballantine Books, 1992).

5. Carl von Clausewitz, *On War,* trans. Michael Howard, ed. Peter Paret (Princeton: Princeton University Press, 1976).

6. William A. Covina, *The Elements of Persuasion* (Needham Heights, Mass.: Allyn & Bacon, 1998).

7. Morton D. Davis, *Game Theory: A Nontechnical Introduction* (Mineola, N.Y.: Dover Publications, Inc., 1983).

8. Avinash K. Dixit and Barry J. Nalebuff, *Thinking Strategically: The Competitive Edge in Business, Politics, and Everyday Life* (New York: W. W. Norton & Co., 1991).

9. Al Golin, *Trust or Consequences: Build Trust Today or Lose Your Market Tomorrow* (New York: AMACOM, 2004).

10. Capt. B. H. Liddell Hart, "The 'Man-in-the-Dark' Theory of Infantry Tactics and the 'Expanding Torrent' System of Attack," *Journal of the R.U.S.I.* (1921).

11. Robert S. Kaplan and David P. Norton, *Strategy Maps: Converting Intangible Assets into Tangible Outcomes* (Boston: Harvard Business School Press, 2004).

12. William S. Lind, *Maneuver Warfare Handbook* (Boulder, Colo.: Westview Press, 1985).

13. John McDonald, *The Game of Business: Modern Game Theory and the Interactions of People in Economic Life* (New York: Doubleday & Co., 1975).

14. John Meany and Kate Shuster, *On that Point!: An Introduction to Parliamentary Debate* (New York: International Debate Association, 2003).

15. Harry Mills, *Artful Persuasion: How to Command Attention, Change Minds, and Influence People* (New York: AMACOM/American Management Association, 2000).

16. Stephen Potter, *The Theory and Practice of Gamesmanship: Or, the Art of Winning Games Without Actually Cheating* (London: Moyer Bell, 1998).

17. Sun Tzu, *The Art of War,* trans. Samuel B. Griffith (New York: Oxford University Press, 1963).

Glossary

Alpha Play A stratagem that broadly defines a player's given position or its intended plans. Alpha plays typically serve to guide or inform one or more lower-order beta plays. For example, a player's alpha play—a Draft—was designed to stalk and overtake the incumbent. Its beta plays—a Bear Hug and Jam—were designed to freeze the opponent from moving ahead un-checked.

Assess Class One of the three foundation classes of The Playmaker's Table. Assessing plays are characteristically subtle, typically passive, and are often used to monitor and profile other players and marketplaces. The Assess class encompasses four of the twenty-five plays in the two subclasses Detach and Test.

Attack Subclass One of three supporting subclasses of the Engage class of The Playmaker's Table. Attacking plays, which include Call Out, Preempt, Draft, and Crazy Ivan, describe a player's attempt to compete directly for its desired position.

Bait : BT The overt provocation of an opponent through action or information, usually intended to draw an emotional, rather than rational, response. This play typically compels an opponent to move in the direction of the player—like a bull charging a cape—against its better judgment (see Chapter 18).

Bear Hug : BG The conspicuously public support or embrace of an opponent's position or message (see Chapter 14).

Beta Play A stratagem that supports a high-order alpha play. For example, a player's beta plays—a Preempt and Call Out—were designed to nip damaging speculation in the bud. Its alpha play—a Pass—was to exit the market.

Call Out : CT An overt public expression of doubt or concern, usually aimed at a competing person or organization, intended to call into question a flaw in the opponent's position or message set. Call Outs often have a tone of moral authority; they're judgmental and direct (see Chapter 22).

Challenge : CH A public appeal, suggestion, or demand by a player, designed to mobilize and/or inspire a person, organization, or broader constituency to consent or take action. While Challenges may range from timid to caustic, they convey a benefit to the targeted player (see Chapter 17).

Cluster Plays Loosely organized and overlapping groups of plays that share various common abilities to contradict, decoy, link, or taunt other players in a marketplace. Such plays cut across the traditional boundaries of The Playmaker's Table and sometimes exist in multiple clusters (see Turning the Table, Play Type Clusters, p. 268).

Compound Strategies Plays that embody a multiplicity of strategic principles (e.g., Fan the Fire, Smoke Out a Competitor, Drive a Wedge, Flood a Market, Corner a Market, Create a Market, Re-brand a Product, or Enhance an Offering).

Condition Class One of the three foundation classes of The Playmaker's Table. Conditioning plays are characteristically moderate, often indirect, and are frequently used to encourage or suppress actions or to influence or reform the sentiments of other players and marketplaces. The Condition class encompasses twelve of the twenty-five plays in the three subclasses Divert, Frame, and Freeze.

Contra Plays A cross-table "cluster" of five plays—Bear Hug, Crazy Ivan, Disco, Lantern, and Pause—that are innately contrary and go against a player's instincts or a set of marketplace conventions (see Turning the Tables, Play Type Clusters, p. 268).

Crazy Ivan : CZ Alters the course or circumstances of an impending attack by inviting or initiating the attack. It is most commonly employed as a last option (see Chapter 25).

Crowd : CW The attempt by a player to match or adopt an opponent's position in a marketplace or to affiliate with a trend, idea, or issue (see Chapter 20).

Decoy Plays A cross-table "cluster" of three plays—Bait, Red Herring, and Screen—that pull a player *into* play action or drive a player *from* it but, in either case, with the intention of moving a player off its preferred position or intended course of action (see Turning the Table, Play Type Clusters, p. 268).

Deflect : DF An attempt by a player to divert a rival's attack, either to avoid or minimize its impact. Deflects typically bend—they do not break or significantly alter—an opponent's play action. They are usually run under duress and on-the-fly by a player with inferior resources against a superior threat (see Chapter 5).

Detach Subclass One of two supporting subclasses of the Assess class of The Playmaker's Table. Detaching plays, which include Pass and Pause, involve the exit by a player from a marketplace, briefly or even permanently.

Disco : DX Requires a player to concede or sacrifice an element of its platform in order to preserve or advance its overall agenda or argument. The central tenet of a Disco is that forward progress cannot be achieved by the player unless or until the player first moves backward (i.e., one step back, two steps forward). Disco is a technique of argumentation, coined by debate teams in the 1980s (see Chapter 16).

Divert Subclass One of three supporting subclasses of the Condition class of The Playmaker's Standard. Diverting plays, which include Deflect, Leak, and Red Herring, are generally designed to distract other players or reroute their intended course of action.

Draft : DR An attempt by a player to feed off the energy of a developing marketplace, innovation, or best practice with the intent of overtaking incumbent leaders (see Chapter 24).

Engage Class One of the three foundation classes of The Playmaker's Table. Engaging plays are characteristically active, usually overt strategies whose purposes are to destabilize players and marketplaces, assert a player's leadership, or invite competitive responses. The Engage class encompasses nine of the twenty-five plays in the three subclasses Lure, Press, and Attack.

Factors at Play A reference table of more than fifty marketplace variables in six categories—tangibles, intangibles, communication, policies, stakeholders, and X-factors—that help playmakers better understand how, in infinitely variable ways, marketplaces do what they do, and how plays, in infinitely variable sequences and combinations, drive relative competitive advantage. Factors are not plays, they influence plays (see p. 294).

Fiat : FT The declaration of information or demonstration of capability to a marketplace. Fiats are characteristically run without fanfare and rely on the position of the player or the merits of the declaration to shift a competitive dynamic (see Chapter 19).

Filter : FL The selective retransmission of information, where a player promotes and/or withholds information to build or defend its position. A Filter is typically employed to reshape characterizations so that their impact or relevance is minimized or, better, put to work for the player (see Chapter 8).

Fit Plays Resonating issues, ideas, policies, events, and developments that a playmaker deliberately invokes or promotes as a means of praising, appealing, condoning, or otherwise endorsing the characteristics and conventions of a marketplace and its players. Fit-based plays create a kind of rhetorical and ambient marketplace appeal that typically supports other players and embraces their preferred positions and agendas (for more information, see Finer Points of Playmaking, p. 287).

Frame Subclass One of three supporting subclasses of the Condition class of The Playmaker's Table. Framing plays, which include Filter, Recast, Label, and Screen, are typically used to adjust the criteria and context of discussions and actions in a marketplace.

Freeze Subclass One of three supporting subclasses of the Condition class of The Playmaker's Table. Freezing plays, which include Mirror, Jam, Bear Hug, Lantern, and Disco, inhibit the movement and motives of a competitor, or prevent further erosion to the player's position and agenda.

Friction Plays Discordant issues, ideas, policies, events, and developments that a playmaker deliberately invokes or promotes as a means of upsetting, provoking, intriguing, or otherwise contradicting the characteristics and conventions of a marketplace and its players. Friction plays create a kind of rhetorical and ambient marketplace heat that typically goes against the grain of competitive players and which questions or displaces their preferred positions and agendas (for more information see Finer Points of Playmaking, p. 287).

Harmonic Play A pair or trio of plays and surrogates that are run together to achieve a nuanced and more powerful effect. Like musical notes, plays can be combined into "chords" to blend the special character of one stratagem with another, all for a fuller and more competitively potent potential.

Jam : JM An attempt to disable or disorganize a rival's activities or communications. A Jam is typically intended to obscure, slow, or stop the delivery or acquisition of ideas or information of a rival (see Chapter 13).

Label : LB A word or phrase—self-given by a player or attributed to an opponent—that reshapes or deepens the meaning of the recipient's position, brand, or reputation. A Label, typically rooted in symbols and metaphors, is characterized by simplification, alliteration, and other semantic tricks (see Chapter 10).

Lantern : LN The deliberate and preemptive disclosure by a player of its own flaw, mistake, or some source of potential embarrassment or controversy (see Chapter 15).

Leak : LK The selective disclosure by a player of normally privileged or confidential information to a specified target (e.g., reporter, customer, prospect, colleague). A Leak is typically covert and employed to divert or accentuate a developing idea in the marketplace (see Chapter 6).

Linker Plays A cross-table "cluster" of five plays—Bear Hug, Crowd, Draft, Label, and Screen—that help playmakers associate their campaigns, promotions, and initiatives with meaningful symbols, public figures, issues, trends, and inanimate marketplace features (see Turning the Table, Play Type Clusters, p. 268).

Lure Subclass One of three supporting subclasses of the Engage class of The Playmaker's Table. Luring plays, which include Challenge and Bait, dare a rival player or players to take action.

Mirror : MI A specialized form of a Call Out, a Mirror introduces into a marketplace new facts or information that contradicts a rival's position or point of view. Like forcing someone to look at their own reflection, a Mirror typically prevents a rival from credibly pursuing its agenda (see Chapter 12).

Partner : PN One of three surrogates on The Playmaker's Table. A Partner is a third party whose interests are aligned with a host player but which operates as a co-equal. Partners typically receive reciprocal levels of support in pursuit of a common agenda or business purpose (see Chapter 26).

Pass : PS The strategic withdrawal from a marketplace or play action. Typically a player will exit or "bail out" of a marketplace to preserve its resources and/or focus them elsewhere for competitive advantage (see Chapter 1).

Pause : PZ The strategic suspension of activity by a player, intended to allow the player to assess the opposition and marketplace and let playing conditions ripen (see Chapter 2).

Peacock : PK The unsolicited parading by a player of a novelty to generate attention in a marketplace. Peacocks typically hinge on an unusual action, innovation, or precedent-setting development—to spur market talk (see Chapter 21).

Ping : PG An oblique reference or suggestion, enabled either by a player's mere presence in a marketplace or its implied interest in topics, ideas, events, and developments (see Chapter 3).

Plant : PT One of three surrogates on The Playmaker's Table. A Plant is a trusted and confidential third party—usually disguised or undisclosed to opponent(s)—that is placed by a host player to seed or sense information and movements in a marketplace (see Chapter 28).

Play A stratagem, one of a finite set of discrete strategic maneuvers a person or organization employs to improve its relative competitive advantage in a marketplace.

Play Action The presence and movement of plays as they are called and run by players in a bounded marketplace.

Play Action Map Illustrated representations of playmaking activity (i.e., play action) that yield insights on the patterns, sequences, trends, and tendencies of player's moves in a marketplace.

Playmaker A strategist whose stock in trade is to call, run, decode, and counter competitive moves in a marketplace. Playmakers have influence over a player's policy, position, and agenda and are stewards of its intangible assets.

Playmaker's Process, The A five-step methodology that illustrates the fundamental steps of playmaking, from the conception of a differentiated idea to the identification of a play sequence to the commencement of play action to countermeasures and back. This proprietary circular process helps playmakers better understand how to apply so-called *fit* and *friction* to playmaking plans, when to call and run plays, how to react to the prevailing play action, and, finally, whether to exit a marketplace or accelerate within it for competitive advantage (see Section III, p. 273).

Playmaker's Standard, The The first classification system of moves and countermoves that people and organizations employ in business, politics, and popular culture to develop a position or advance their agendas in competitive marketplaces.

Playmaker's Table, The A landmark taxonomy of twenty-five irreducible influence strategies. The table features an easily interpreted and detailed classification of plays and their respective examples, risk-reward assessments, definitions, best users, and methods by which plays may be decoded and countered.

Playmaking A discipline for deploying and systematically managing plays—in combinations, sequences, and patterns—to continually influence, control, and sustain the sentiments, discussions, and decisions of a marketplace.

Preempt : PE Reverses competitive position, giving the player a superior advantage, limiting a rival's ability to exploit a player's weakness, or both. Preempts are usually decisive and swift so as to surprise and disable the competition (see Chapter 23).

Press Subclass One of three supporting subclasses of the Engage class of The Playmaker's Table. Pressing plays, which include Fiat, Crowd, and Peacock, employ authority, ability, or audacity to establish or assert a player's position in a marketplace.

Proxy : PX One of three surrogates on The Playmaker's Table. A Proxy is a third party who advocates for and supports the agenda of a host player, usually for a fee or some form of consideration. It is allied with the player but credible to others—even competitors—and conveys a sense of free will and independence (see Chapter 27).

Recast : RC The reinterpretation of an action, event, information, message, or symbol by a player so as to lend support to that player's position or agenda or to neutralize or weaken that of its rival (see Chapter 9).

Red Herring : RD The Red Herring is an action or communiqué that draws an opponent—usually a competitor—away from its preferred position or intended course of action (see Chapter 7).

Screen : SN An attempt by a player to borrow issues, ideas, events, or other symbolic references to advance its agenda or thwart a competitor's movements (see Chapter 11).

Surrogate A person or organization that runs plays, either on behalf or in support of a host player and its position or agenda. Surrogates are not plays; they're recruited Partners, Proxies, or Plants that expand the reach and influence of a player's normal scope and capability.

Taunter Plays A cross-table "cluster" of four plays—Bait, Call Out, Challenge, and Label—that help a player tease or provoke other players in a marketplace (see Turning the Table, Play Type Clusters, p. 268).

Test Subclass One of two supporting subclasses of the Assess class of The Playmaker's Table. Testing plays, which include Ping and Trial Balloon, size up the issues, ideas, events, or developments of a marketplace and forecast a player's needs or wishes.

Trial Balloon : TB The preview and testing of preliminary ideas or tentative plans. To reduce a player's exposure, Trial Balloons are often run without attribution to the player or are positioned as temporary (see Chapter 4).

Index of Figures and Tables

Index

Alan Kelly, CEO and founder of The Playmaker's Standard, LLC, is a foremost expert in competitive strategy and a leading innovator in the fields of communication, research, and technology marketing. He approaches his work with a simple but provocative charter—that the moves and counter-moves of business, politics, and pop culture can be mapped and managed for competitive advantage. His development of a breakthrough taxonomy of strategy types, which shares the company's name, is a testament to Kelly's vision for a comprehensive standard in the industries of influence—of management, strategy, marketing, sales, advertising, public relations, public affairs, and even law. It is a system that names, describes and prescribes the work of playmakers everywhere and which exhaustively catalogues, as his book describes, *The Elements of Influence.*

Kelly, 48, has made his mark on the business landscape, notably through his formation and leadership of Applied Communications, a public relations and research firm that earned distinction for its unique philosophy of competitive communications and quantitative grounding. From its founding in 1992 to the sale of its consulting assets in 2003, the firm garnered numerous best-in-class recognitions for its work with Oracle, Hewlett-Packard, Cisco, Sun Microsystems, Genentech, VeriSign, Veritas Software, TechNet, BEA Systems, and Informatica, among others.

Kelly is a member of the Arthur W. Page Society and serves on the board of trustees of The Institute for Public Relations. He holds a master's degree in communication research from Stanford University and a bachelor's degree in public relations from the University of Southern California. He lives with his wife and two children in Maryland, and is an enthusiastic sailboat racer.

About The Playmaker's Standard, LLC

The Playmaker's Standard, LLC, is a consulting and software services firm that specializes in competitive strategy. Based in Maryland, the company's charter is to advance for professionals in the industries of influence—in management, strategy, marketing, sales, advertising, public relations, public affairs, and even law—the practice and development of the discipline of playmaking.

Through industry leadership and world-class products and services, including *The Elements of Influence* and the breakthrough Play Action Whiteboard web tool, The Playmaker's Standard delivers for its clients and online users a unique accelerated path toward competitive advantage.

CEO and founder Alan Kelly and his team of Standard-certified playmakers offer a variety of services for companies and organizations in competitive and fast-paced markets. These include introductory and advanced workshops, webinars, class lectures and conference speakers, and custom consulting and research.

For more information or to contact The Playmaker's Standard, please visit www.plays2run.com, read and participate in The Playmaker's Forum, a blog at http://blog.plays2run.com, or e-mail info@plays2run.com.